The Basic English Handbook

The Basic English Handbook

Margaret W. Taylor
Cuyahoga Community College

HarperCollinsCollegePublishers

Acquisitions Editor: Ellen Schatz
Developmental Editor: Shellie Taggart
Project Coordination: York Production Services
Cover Design: York Production Services
Production: Christine Pearson
Compositor: Alphabet Graphics
Printer and Binder: R.R. Donnelley & Sons
Cover Printer: Coral Graphic Services, Inc.

The Basic English Handbook

Library of Congress Cataloging-in-Publication Data
Taylor, Margaret W. (Margaret Wischmeyer), 1920-
      The basic English handbook / Margaret W. Taylor.
             p.   cm.
      Includes index.
      ISBN 0-673-46907-7
      1. English language—Rhetoric—Handbooks, manuals, etc.
2. English language—Grammar—Handbooks, manuals, etc.   I. Title.
PE1408.T35   1995
808'.042—dc20   94-6579
                                          CIP

94 95 96 97 9 8 7 6 5 4 3 2 1

To My Students

deep affection and great respect

To Callers on the Grammar Hot Line

appreciation for what we learned

To Chester

very much love

Contents

Chapter 4
....

Sentences   241

Chapter 7
Usage 397

More than 100 puzzlers that most bother students and the general public calling on the college Grammar Hot Line, arranged alphabetically from *a, an* to *your, you're* 397

Foreword

St. Peter hears a knocking at the Gates of Heaven and calls out, "Who's there?"

"It is I," a voice responds.

"Oh no," sighs St. Peter, "not another English teacher."

That's pretty much the picture that society has of English teachers—bearded patriarchs (of either gender) who devote their lives to protecting nominative pronouns ("It is I"), relocating terminal prepositions, unsplitting infinitives, and undangling participles. In the minds of many, the teacher of English is a schoolmarm (of either gender) who may not be able to show students how to write well but certainly can teach them "correct English," whatever that is.

Margaret Taylor is not such a teacher. She subscribes to Alexander Pope's time-honored dictum that "true ease in writing comes from art, not chance." She recognizes that learning to write is a serious business, but it need not be a solemn one. The voice of this book is that of a cheerful and spirited guide who knows the landscape and is delighted to show us around personally, providing maps, blueprints, and even sprightly cartoons. The premise of *The Basic English Handbook* is that everyone can enjoy the process of learning to write better.

In the jargon of computers, equipment that does what it is supposed to do without baffling the user is called user-friendly. This book is reader-friendly. Rather than building castles of writing theory on midair, the author puts foundations under them. Among these foundations are actual drafts of actual essays by actual students. Throughout *The Basic English Handbook* appears genuine, authentic language rather than contrived textbook explanations and models. This is an expert teacher and writer sending her notes from the trenches.

Margaret Taylor helps writers to write so that their prose is a pleasure that carries knowledge and insight with it. She helps writers to discover what they did not know they knew—about writing and about themselves.

So, St. Peter, when the time comes, please let Margaret in. The one with a bunch of papers and a red pen in one hand and a copy of *The Basic English Handbook* in the other . . . the one wearing the broadest grin, excited at the prospect of meeting new students . . . that will be she.

Richard Lederer, Ph.D.
Language Author and Grammar Columnist
Concord, N.H.

To the Instructor

When I die, I want my ashes scattered down the steep bluff between the Michigan lake that I love and the woods beyond, where jack-in-the-pulpits preach breezy summer sermons and forget-me-nots are grave markers for the eternal cycle of life. But *if* I were going to have a tombstone, I would want it to announce to all passersby, "She tried." All my life, I've tried.

I tried to make this book the most usable writing text in existence.

I felt it was important to get students writing as soon as possible, so I postponed the chapters on the mechanics of writing—parts of speech and participles and punctuation—until after the chapters on writing paragraphs and compositions. I thought perhaps I could first interest my students in the process of writing, and they could then apply the necessary rules to what they were actually producing. It seemed to work in my classes.

Before an English textbook is published, it is sent out several times to English instructors all over the country for review. With the HarperCollins-commissioned reviews and the opinions I solicited informally, this book has been critiqued by more than three dozen college instructors of freshman English and, very important, by a few hundred of my students.

There was general agreement that the content was more than complete, the reading was easy, and the tone was nonthreatening; but there was no consensus on the order of presentation. I had put "Paragraphs" first to get students started writing immediately. The earliest reviewers, however, thought that "Words," being the smallest element usually studied in writing, should come first. I could see orderly progression from small part to complete whole as the advantage to this arrangement. I could live with that (I would just have *my* students begin with the chapter on paragraphs). It sounded so simple to move the chapter on words to Chapter 1, but it wasn't. Interrelated subjects were then all out of order; in the exercises, Mozart died before he had composed his first sonata.

The instructors participating in later reviews felt that students should start writing before delving into the intricacies of transitional phrases and transitive verbs. Back to Square One; I moved the chapter on paragraphs back to the start. I had always felt more comfortable with writing first, then grammar plugged in to the writing; and Mozart didn't seem to care one way or the other. With the present organization, instructors who want to consider "Words" before "Paragraphs" have merely to start with Chapter 3. "Sentences" first?—begin with Chapter 4.

Each chapter in *The Basic English Handbook* is arranged in steps (of usefulness to the student). Step One considers the most basic principles, the most frequent problems, the mistakes that probably need to be corrected first. I collected these not only from my students but also from members of the community who called the Grammar Hot Line, which I started at Cuyahoga Community College. Step Two contains somewhat less basic rules, and Step Three deals with concepts that are perhaps more difficult but less frequently needed. With this arrangement, you can at any time pause in one chapter to have the whole class, or individual students, work on an appropriate step in another chapter—whatever works best for you and your students.

In the "To the Student" section which follows, the importance of learning standard American English is emphasized even though other varieties of speech and writing are not necessarily wrong. This section can provide your students with a writing sample and relevant information from each student.

The following is a list of features that distinguish *The Basic English Handbook*:

- FLEXIBILITY OF INSTRUCTION: Chapters have been written as self-contained units and may be taught in any order, except that Chapter 1 should precede Chapter 2.

- FLEXIBILITY OF LEARNING: Arrangement of material in steps of difficulty and usefulness makes it possible for the individual student or the whole class to learn at the most appropriate skill level.

- COMPLETENESS OF SUBJECT MATTER: This book is not only an exceptionally effective learning tool in the college classroom, providing for detailed work on all problem areas of grammar, usage, and writing; but it is also, because of its comprehensive coverage, a valuable reference book for all levels of learning, both in and out of school.

- REALISTIC COVERAGE OF USAGE NEEDS: Topics were gathered not only from the classroom but also from a college's grammar hot line serving the general public, making this book a bridge from the classroom to the "real world."

- CLARITY: Principles and practices are explained clearly in everyday language. Organization is logical, with one subject treated (in steps) in one place rather than scattered throughout the book; therefore, a minimum of cross-referencing (which students often disregard anyway) is required.

- USEFUL INDEX: An exceptionally detailed index makes finding subjects easy.

- BLENDING OF THEORY AND PRACTICALITY: Many issues of grammatical correctness and creative style are blended into sections on the practice of writing skills instead of being covered in seemingly unrelated separate chapters.

- HANDBOOK/WORKBOOK FORMAT: Abundant exercises follow each discussion, allowing the student as much or as little practice as needed, with answers given for do-it-yourself instant feedback or for class discussion. After a chapter and its exercises (with answers) have been assigned, an instructor can photocopy, without answers, any exercise or "quiz yourself" and use it for testing.

- EXTENSIVE USE OF STUDENT WRITING: Examples written by former students provide encouragement for present students and, with lines or paragraphs numbered, a convenient base for instructor comments.

- EMPHASIS ON THE IMPORTANCE OF STANDARD ENGLISH: The benefits of learning standard English are pointed out, but the language that a student brings to the classroom is not rejected. Frequently mentioned is the fact that language is constantly changing to accommodate usage.

- A USER-FRIENDLY TONE: The student is helped to cope with, possibly even to enjoy, the study of English by the easy, unintimidating tone of the book, the cartoon illustrations, and the friendly, encouraging attitude of the writer, who remembers being a student herself.

Margaret Taylor
Cleveland, OH

To the Student

"How many of you don't like English?" I always ask my students at the start of the first class.

Usually one hardy soul holds up his or her hand, then another student and another, until perhaps a quarter of the class have their hands in the air.

Then I ask, "How many of you *do* like English?" Another fourth of the class may hold up hands this time. Of course, that leaves half the class undecided or afraid to make known an opinion.

My theory is it's not your fault if you don't like English. At some time in your life, you probably were in an environment where English was spoken with little regard for seeing that the subjective case followed a being verb, or for using *lie* to mean *recline* and *lay* to mean *put;* so certain violations of standard English sound and look right to you. Or perhaps your previous English classes didn't emphasize grammar and writing skills. It's understandable that you don't appreciate parentheses and predicates and paragraphs; and it is natural for all of us to dislike things we're not comfortable with, not particularly good at.

The way you spoke English the day you started kindergarten was a gift from your family, friends, and neighbors. You received this gift, like the color of your eyes, without being asked whether you wanted it or not. Anyone who lives on a street heavily populated by a particular ethnic, foreign-born, racial, occupational, religious, or socioeconomic group learns to talk as the majority talk; and it may not be so-called standard American English, the language of education and business. Speaking and writing nonstandard English does not make you a less worthwhile person; you are a less worthwhile person only if you fail to take advantage of the opportunity to learn something that will be useful to you.

As you shape the gift of language that you bring to this class, remember that nonstandard English is not bad. What you learn here will be an extension of the useful language you already know. But learning to speak and write standard American English better will give you a much greater opportunity to achieve the goals that bring students to college in the first place.

Your knowledge of the language shows every time you speak or write. The fine points of English, which may sometimes seem trivial, even useless, could possibly keep you from passing a college course, from getting the job you want or the raise you deserve, or from earning the respect of your associates— perhaps deprive you of a relationship with a person you admire.

While speaking and writing correctly may not make you a better person, it makes you—fairly or unfairly—*seem* like a better person in the eyes of the people who can help you accomplish what you want from life. And it does a great deal toward improving your opinion of yourself.

It is also important to the company or institution you may work for. If the way you talk is full of errors or if you send out reports and letters with mistakes in them, the whole organization looks bad. Be assured, **learning to speak and write standard English is very important to you.**

Whether you like English or not, I'll make you a promise, the same promise I make my students the first day. I'll do my best to make taking this course, oh, maybe not the *most* fun thing you've ever done in your life, but at least easier and more worthwhile than you thought it would be.

English, particularly grammar, need not be the dreaded subject it is for too many students today. True, some of the rules may seem strict or illogical. But so, sometimes, are other aspects of life.

If rules of writing seem tedious, don't think for a minute you have to memorize them all. They will become more familiar with practice. And as you go through college, and life, you may want to keep this book as a reference to answer all sorts of questions. Just look in the index, and choose what you can use at the time.

You can certainly learn to cope with English and make it understandable and useful to you. You can probably even learn to like it. I have had many students who brought to college a poor high school record and an even poorer incentive to make friends with the English language. But those who convinced themselves they were in control and could master the basics overcame their English phobia. Most have done well in advanced composition courses. Some even confessed, "Gee, I like to write now." Several graduates are enjoying jobs that require a great deal of writing.

This book will do more than any other book I know to help you, for two reasons: it is written in an easy-to-read style by a very sympathetic English teacher (me, Margaret Taylor), and it is arranged in steps for logical learning, with the most basic material considered first.

It is full of exercises, with answers given to all of them except those you alone can answer in your own way. The following exercise is one of those.

FIRST EXERCISE Write a paragraph about *one* of the following subjects: your home, a member of your family, a good friend, a pet, what you like or dislike about your job, a pet peeve, what you most like to do in your spare time, or what you would do or be if all your dreams could come true. You will not be graded on this. Do not get help on it, but write it the best way you can.

Remember, though, you are just starting. You are not expected to do everything perfectly. Otherwise, you would not need to take this course–you could teach it and teach your instructor, too.

Use a piece of scratch paper to jot down your ideas before you begin to write. After you have written the paragraph, answer the following questions:

1. What do you consider your strong points in writing?
2. What are your biggest problems in writing?
3. What do you dread most about taking this course?
4. What benefits do you expect to get from this course?
5. What English courses have you taken before this one?

It was fun writing this book and anticipating your using it. Students and instructors, please send corrections, suggestions, additions, criticisms (if you must) and plaudits (if you please) to me, c/o Basic Skills Editor, HarperCollins College Publishers, 10 East 53rd St., New York NY 10022.

Acknowledgments

Thanks to *The World Book Encyclopedia, Encyclopaedia Britannica,* Dr. Richard Lederer, and Wyrick & Co. for background information and for material included in the text, and thanks to Mark Paluch of HarperCollins for making this book possible.

Credits

Chapter 3: p. 191—CALVIN AND HOBBES © 1986 Universal Press Syndicate. Reprinted with permission. All rights reserved; p. 193—MOTHER GOOSE AND GRIMM reprinted by permission: Tribune Media Services; p. 198—SHOE reprinted by permission: Tribune Media Services; p. 213—FRANK AND ERNEST reprinted by permission of NEA, Inc; p. 222—Cartoon by Henry R. Martin: "We admired the content..." © 1987 Henry R. Martin; p. 228—CALVIN AND HOBBES © 1990 Universal Press Syndicate. Reprinted with permission. All rights reserved. **Chapter 4:** p. 269—SHOE reprinted by permission: Tribune Media Services; p. 270—BORN LOSER reprinted by permission of NEA, Inc; p. 278—SUBURBAN COWGIRLS Reprinted by permission: Tribune Media Services; p. 283—B.C. reprinted by permission of Johnny Hart and Creators Syndicate. **Chapter 5:** p. 304—FAMILY CIRCUS reprinted with special permission of King Features Syndicate; p. 306—PEANUTS

1 Paragraphs

Step One: From Idea to Final Draft

Since satisfactory communication is the best hope for humankind's well-being, from happy personal relations to world peace, it pays to learn the basics of both speaking and writing well. Writing is harder than speaking for a couple of reasons. When we speak, we can make use of facial expressions, gestures, and tone of voice to help tell a story; the mistaken use of a comma instead of a period at the end of a sentence is not obvious in speaking. But writing must do the whole job. And writing is more permanent than speaking—spoken words are usually quickly gone; written mistakes remain visible for many years.

Almost all of the writing we do in our lives involves writing paragraphs, both the expository writing (writing to explain, inform, or instruct) that we do in college and in the business world, and the entertaining or sometimes personal material that we may write for the pleasure of others or ourselves.

Definition of a Paragraph

A **paragraph** is a group of sentences all developing a single controlling idea about the subject. The **controlling idea** is nothing more than the message about the subject that you want to get across to the reader, what you think about your subject, the point you want to make, what you want the reader to believe when you are through; it is also called the **topic sentence** of the paragraph.

When there is a shift in the thought of what you are writing, you should start a new paragraph. The first line of a paragraph is indented. Indention helps readers because, while going through a several-paragraph composition, they can visually anticipate shifts in ideas.

A paragraph may, once in a while, be as short as one word, but usually it is several sentences. Every paragraph does not, however, have to have five to seven sentences, as many of my students learned somewhere in previous classes. That may be a fine length for a paragraph, but content should determine length.

Short paragraphs are easier on the eye and the brain of the reader. But just as too many short sentences become choppy and monotonous, too many short paragraphs may spoil the flow of the whole composition.

On the other hand, if a paragraph focused on a single idea becomes too long, it is usually possible to divide it into shorter, easier-to-read paragraphs with the use of appropriate transitional phrases.

Be aware that a class assignment to write a paragraph may result in a longer-than-normal paragraph because it is an exercise in relating many sentences to a topic sentence.

The Half Dozen Steps for Writing a Good Paragraph

The process for writing a good paragraph (in fact, for all writing) includes six steps:

1. Choosing a subject and a controlling idea (controlling idea = topic sentence = a complete sentence stating the point you want to make to your reader about your subject).

2. Strengthening the controlling idea—considering the tone (your attitude toward your subject), your purpose, and the audience for whom you are writing, to get your point across in the best way.

3. Outlining to organize your ideas, with emphasis on **unity.**

4. Writing a rough draft.

5. Revising and correcting (rewriting and editing) the rough draft, with emphasis on **clarity, coherence,** and **creativity.**

6. Writing the final draft, incorporating the Step 5 improvements, and double-checking for full development of the four guide words for good writing: unity, clarity, coherence, and creativity.

We'll go over the process step by step, showing how a couple of students handled the write-a-paragraph assignment.

1. Choosing a Subject and a Controlling Idea. This first step is the foundation, and it must be laid carefully. You should choose a subject you are interested in and can handle effectively in the allotted time and space. Even if your subject is selected by your instructor, you will have to state clearly the point about the subject that you want to get across to the reader: this will be the topic sentence, the controlling idea, of the paragraph.

But I've heard more times than I care to remember, "I can't think of *anything* to write about." Here are some ways to get ideas.

Observing. The first suggestion should surely be observing. Stop, look at, and listen to things within yourself, as well as things, people, and conditions around your school, workplace, home, or town, or in the outdoor world. One of my students wrote a clever piece about how the lowly dandelion has been given a highly bum rap. Other papers I remember concerned how the writer had to learn to walk again after a terrible auto accident, how fall is like a beautifully dressed woman waiting for her lover to come cover her with a blanket of white, how parking gates at the college should be abolished and the cost of maintaining the parking lot added to tuition.

Recalling. Recalling what past experience and memories have to tell you often turns up a good subject. One student wrote a description of her aunt's kitchen, painting such a vivid picture that I can still remember how the sunlight hit the spice jars on the windowsill. Another paper described how the writer and his son agreed to light a candle in church for a beloved dog who had died. Accounts of older people who have influenced the writer's life can be beautiful. I remember a paper about a young man's grandmother, her hardships when she came to this country, and his heritage from her.

Having a baby, discovering your wife has multiple sclerosis and will be an invalid the rest of her life, the trauma of taking English again after many years out of school, your opinion of what should be done about the environment, or homeless people, or abortion—any embarrassing, inspiring, frightening, frustrating, or otherwise highly emotional experience that you remember may prove to be an interesting subject. Be confident that you have plenty of good ideas—you are an authority on your own thoughts and experiences.

Reading. Reading is one of the best sources of subjects—newspapers, magazines, books, plays, pamphlets, advertisements, letters, and clippings. The library can help you not only with the printed word but also with cassettes and videotapes on a wide variety of subjects. More facts (and fun) than you can imagine are available, free, at your school or local library.

Watching Television. After the normal quota of squabbles when our children were young, I never thought I'd be suggesting watching television, but there are excellent programs to be found by the discriminating viewer. Sometimes something you see on TV may steer you toward a subject.

Fictionalizing. Although most of your writing in life as well as in class will be expository writing, fictionalizing may spark your interest. Ask your instructor if what you write has to be factual. He or she may be willing to evaluate your writing ability on the fictional subject of how you befriended the little people from space who landed in your backyard as well as on the expository subject of what it's like to be the office "gofer" or how American education compares to Japanese education.

Keeping a Journal. Many writers and aspiring writers find that keeping a journal (writing daily or at specified intervals on happenings, hopes, needs, satisfactions, dissatisfactions, or interesting thoughts) suggests topics to investigate further as subjects for writing. An orderly file of clippings and a list of ideas jotted down while you're waiting on hold or standing in the checkout line or trying to fall asleep can also become a fertile subject source. I keep a notepad beside my bed.

EXERCISE 1.1 Keep a journal for a week. At a regular time daily (night is often a good time), enter your thoughts of the day, your high spots, your low spots, things you liked, things you disliked, things that interested you, things you learned, things you became curious about, etc. After a week, list five subjects from your journal that you think would make interesting paragraphs. You may become so enthusiastic about keeping a journal that you will continue.

1. _____
2. _____
3. _____
4. _____
5. _____

Possible answers on page 63.

Brainstorming. Still nothing appeals to you? You still can't think of a *thing* to write about? Then try brainstorming. Talk over your dilemma informally with a friend or a family member. Ask upperclass students what they wrote about; it's okay to use someone else's subject, but it's plagiarism, stealing, to use the development of someone else's subject without giving credit to that person, even if you don't quote directly.

Get together with some of your classmates over a cup of coffee and see if, since half a dozen heads have more ideas than yours alone, the group can't come up with enough possibilities for all. Usually a teacher doesn't mind if several students write on the same subject—the treatment will be different in each case. If your teacher doesn't suggest it, ask him or her to let the class have a few minutes in small groups to toss ideas around.

Free Writing. If you still can't come up with a subject, sometimes the best way to get started is just to start. Try free writing. This is a process of simply starting to write whatever comes to your mind without being inhibited by attempts to correct errors or even being coherent. Let your thoughts fall where they may. This process often works to start your thinking going in a direction that will result in finding a subject of interest.

The following is a bit (a big bit) of free writing done by Gail Gist, one of my students, in an attempt to come up with a subject for an assignment to write a paragraph. She didn't worry about mistakes; she just wrote.

```
                     Free Writing

    I'll never get a decent paragraph started tonight. I
should have started sooner. Why can't I plan my time
better. I know why. I'm a single parent, and there are
never enough hours in the day. I wonder who created the
time clock and decided the day should contain only 24
hours. I'm sure it was a man who went home expecting
dinner on the table b6 6 p.m. and spent the remainder of
his evening sitting in his recliner, cmoking a pipe and
watching television. I should have gotten my education
sooner. Why did I act so crazy at college the first time,
but why dwell on the past? I've got to keep focused. I can
do this. Maybe I should title this Starting Over. As
always on New Year's Eve I prayed the New Year in for as
long as I can remember, but this year was different. For
as long as I can remember, I have celebrated the New Year.
No. This is the way it should start. I spent New Year's
Eve with my church family. As the old year turns into the
metaphoric term "next year," suddenly I realized this year
```

was different, because as I looked at my little infant. No that's not it. Than's too dull. Maybe I'll just take some things off the top of my head. I'll number them. (1) My education means finding a job. (2) Priorities. I qualify. I have essential skills. (3) I am learning the right way, a chance to express hidden talents. (4) I am unlocking parts of my brain I have never explored. (5) A chance to network with other individuals who are in the same or similar situations. (6) realization that some people aren't ready for college at 18, maybe even 28. You've got to want to learn. (7) Realization that I can do it, I can be successful. (8) Game plan/strategy (challenges, maturity, self-esteem). (9) Opportunities.

Maybe I can write about procrastination. I've made an art out of procrastinating. I wait till the last minute for everything, including starting this paragraph for English class. They no longer expect me to be on time for family dinners, weddings, or funerals. Today I mhave decided that pro. must exit my life. I am going to study every minute I am awake meaning I will forsake all for studying. Family says they'll velieve I've changed when they see it. They're still mad because i was late with the ham for Christmas dinner. I'm even late when I'm asked to bring dessert. But who wants to write about Pro. I live it every day.

Maybe my first college experience would make a story. I took a year off after high school to "grow up", I tole people, but the real reason was that in the midst of my senior year fun, I put off filling out college applications until it was too late. If I'd done college

right after high school, I wouldn't be sitting here
tonight trying to write this paragraph with a sick baby
upstairs, bloodshot eyes, and yawning profusely.

I would really like to be a nurse. I wish I had known
what I wanted to do 17 years ago. Maybe I'll write about
how I wasted my first year of college and what it's like
returning to college as an adult, wanting very much to be
a nurse. I really want to be a nurse (I'm tired of
temporary, no-future jobs), and I think I will be a good
one.

It took a lot of writing, but now Gail had some ideas. Although she thought procrastination, the difficulties of being a single parent, going back to college long after high school, and deciding on a career in nursing would be interesting, she put these ideas on hold, filing them in a "Future Writing Ideas" folder, and turned her attention to the subject of her wasted years since high school.

EXERCISE 1.2 You, like Gail, have been assigned to write a paragraph on a topic of interest to you. Pretend (and you may not have to pretend) that you can't think of anything to write about. Start free writing, and see what ideas you come up with. List three ideas from your free writing that might be appropriate subjects for a paragraph.

1. _____
2. _____
3. _____

Sometimes you know the instant you select your subject exactly what point about it you want to get across to your reader (your controlling idea). Other times you may have decided what you want to write about, the subject; but you may not be quite clear on the point you want to make, the controlling idea.

Finally, Gail had decided on her subject: the years she wasted after high school. But what *about* those years? What point does she want to make about her subject? What will be her controlling idea?

The controlling idea of a paragraph, called the **topic sentence,** must be a complete sentence. It usually comes at the beginning of the paragraph so that the reader knows what to expect. It is sometimes restated at the end of the paragraph as a summary, to emphasize its importance so that the reader will remember it. But it may, rather rarely, appear somewhere in the middle of the paragraph; or once in a while it is never actually stated but the reader learns without a doubt from the writer's words what the writer's point is about his or her subject.

The topic sentence not only indicates what the writer's point is, but it also begins to provide **unity** by limiting what the paragraph can contain: only sentences that are relevant to the topic sentence. In a paragraph that has unity, every sentence helps develop the topic sentence.

You must be sure that your topic sentence is focused, that it is not too general: not "Education is beneficial," but rather "A college degree in computer studies will help land you a job." You could hardly cover all the benefits of education in a paragraph!

Focused Free Writing. Gail now knew what she wanted to write about, but she still couldn't seem to come up with a clear idea of the point she wanted to make; so she tried focused free writing, which is nothing more than free writing about the subject you've already chosen. Again, don't interrupt your flow of thoughts to correct mistakes now; save that for later. Here is Gail's focused free writing, her attempt to write whatever came to her mind on her now-chosen subject, her wasted years.

```
                      Starting Over

     590 Buchtel, Apt. 15—I remember it well because we

made our address into a party chant that we would sing

during our spur-of-the-moment parties. Our apartment was

known as the University Hotel to visiting college

students. My roommate and I were quite a pair. We came

from similar backgrounds. Her mother had been my third-

grade teacher. Both families were from the south. We girls

both liked to party. We had common goals—Marijuana and

Kanai wine and $3 gin and vodka. If we wanted to splurge,

we got the good stuff, $5 a fifth, just for certain

guests. When I did attend attend class, my head went

immediately to the desk. Pretending to listen to the

lecture, I slept off many a hangover. I never saw the

inside of the college library. But if you wanted

directions to the student center, shopping malls, bars, or
```

24-hour eateries, I was the one to ask. Returning to
college as an adult is part good, part bad, and part ugly.
Good is you're finally proving to family and friends,
after 17 wasted years, that you're not the nincompoop they
thought you were. Also you are able to broaden your
horizons and build self-confidence. The bad is I feel
guilty leaving my darling daughter at a day care center
while I'm in school, or weekends with her grandparents
while I catch up on sleep or put in some extra study time.
The ugly is that I look like a disaster because I haven't
taken time for months to style my hair or have a manicure
and the long days and nights have made my eyes bug out and
turn red.

Jotting and Clustering. Another method of focusing your controlling idea is
jotting and clustering. Start by simply writing down words related to your subject that come to your mind. When you have jotted all you can think of, see if
you can pick out a few major ideas and circle them. Then see which minor
ideas are related to which major ideas, and make clusters of ideas by connecting the many minor ideas by lines to the fewer major ideas.

Gail still needed a clearer controlling idea, so she jotted and clustered her
ideas.

Incidentally, free writing, focused free writing, and jotting and clustering are good for purposes other than college assignments, such as getting yourself going on a speech you have to give or writing a difficult letter or just about any other problem you're stuck on.

Through the techniques of focused free writing and jotting and clustering, a topic sentence had begun to take shape in Gail's mind: "I was stupid to play around and not take college seriously."

Now for a bit of practice in arriving at topic sentences.

EXERCISE 1.3 If you were given the following five subjects to write a paragraph about, what would your topic sentence for each be?

1. The length of public school summer vacations. _____

_____

2. The right for a woman to have an abortion. _____

_____

3. Putting Elvis on a U.S. postage stamp. _____

_____

4. Crowning a coed queen for homecoming weekend. _____

_____

5. Financial aid for college students. _____

_____

Possible answers on page 63.

EXERCISE 1.4 From subjects that you are interested in and know about, write five good topic sentences, stating clearly in a complete sentence the point you would want to make in a paragraph about each of these subjects.

1. Subject: _____

Topic sentence: _____

_____

2. Subject: _____

Topic sentence: _____

_____

3. Subject: _____

Topic sentence: _____

_____

4. Subject: _____

Topic sentence: _____

_____

5. Subject: _____

Topic sentence: _____

_____

_____

EXERCISE 1.5 Your answers to this exercise will be used, as we proceed, in outlining and writing *your* paragraph.

1. Now go back to Exercise 1.2 on page 7 or Exercise 1.4 on page 10. Select one of these subjects to write a paragraph about.

   My subject is _____

2. By jotting and clustering, organize your thoughts into major and minor ideas, and see how they relate to each other. Practice **jotting and clustering** for the subject you have chosen.

3. Then come up with your controlling idea, a topic sentence for a paragraph on the subject you selected.

   My topic sentence is _____

   _____

2. Strengthening the Controlling Idea. So far, we have taken only the first step in the process of writing, choosing the subject and determining the controlling idea, the topic sentence; but it's a giant step. Now it's time to check the topic sentence to be sure it will clearly get your point across.

Tone. Take a moment to consider tone, the writer's attitude toward the subject. It may be lighthearted, serious, critical, cynical, outraged, bemused, humorous, sympathetic, dismayed, or any other of a wide latitude of attitudes. You need to be sure how you feel about your subject so you can choose the words that best convey your point to your reader.

Gail's tone, one of complete disgust with herself, was an attitude she felt she could easily convey to her reader.

Purpose. Deciding whether the purpose of your material is to entertain, to inform, or to persuade will help you clearly state your topic sentence. Entertainment will probably best be served by nonintellectual, perhaps even humorous, wording. Information should be conveyed in a serious vein, with terms defined if the audience may not be familiar with them. Persuasion must be done in terms relevant to the reader and must be logical and convincing.

Gail's purpose was both to inform and to persuade, to show others what had happened to her and to persuade them not to do the same thing, so her controlling idea would be serious and persuasive.

Audience. Whether your audience consists of readers of a children's magazine or of a scientific journal will help you determine how to phrase your controlling idea. Gail's audience, although primarily her instructor this time, could well have been high school students or college freshmen. She needed to tell them how badly she had handled her life. Her topic sentence was becoming clearer, more emphatic: What a waste it is not to do anything constructive after high school.

EXERCISE 1.6 Go back to the subject and the topic sentence you selected in Exercise 1.5 on page 11.

Subject: _____

Topic sentence: _____

_____

1. What is your tone, your attitude toward your subject? Are you dead serious about your subject? Are you poking fun at your subject? Is your subject something you can hardly believe? Is your subject something you are extremely sympathetic with? Is your subject something you want to convince others to believe?

   Tone: _____

   _____

2. Exactly what is your purpose? What are you trying to accomplish?

   Purpose: _____

---

3. For what type audience are you writing?

Audience: _____

4. Can you make your topic sentence any stronger now?

Stronger topic sentence, if possible: _____

_____

Everything checked; Gail now knew clearly the point she wanted to make, her topic sentence: "It's a crime to throw away 17 years of one's life that could have been devoted to a career of service." Your topic sentence, too, is ready. You are both ready for outlining.

3. Outlining. Outlining is necessary for unity, for well-organized writing. A paragraph has unity when every sentence helps develop the controlling idea, the topic sentence. Every sentence helps move the paragraph in the direction that brings the topic sentence to complete development.

In writing a paragraph or a short paper, I usually recommend a very informal outline. I ask my students just to list words, topics, or whole sentences, whatever they want, with smaller items arranged under the appropriate bigger items, and all of them heading toward a unified end. But writers must **have a plan** in order to ensure unity.

In making the outline, you may find that you can't get there from here; you certainly can **change your plan if necessary.** If you still have too broad a topic to cover in the time and space allotted—and this is a common problem— it's not too late to narrow the subject or focus even more your controlling idea.

The main thing is, have a plan. **Control your writing.** Don't let your writing control you, taking you with it wherever it aimlessly wanders.

Very few writers can count on doing the outlining in their head and coming out with a unified piece of work. Write the outline down. If you are doing a more formal outline, there is a standard format that should be followed. (See Chapter 2, pages 77-78, for more complete information on formal outlining.)

Gail's informal outline (sometimes called a scratch outline) follows. She moved things around a bit until it seemed that each small part was relevant to a larger part, and each larger part helped, in logical order, to develop the topic sentence. Following this outline should result in a paragraph with unity.

1. Deliberately wasted 17 years, a crime—will be topic sentence
2. First year of college completely wasted. Did just about everything wrong picked major haphazardly
   partied all the time
   didn't go to class

didn't appreciate education

3. Second year deceitful
   flunked out, told parents I was in school
   really working as waitress, more partying

4. After 17 years, have come to senses
   want in the worst way to be a nurse, to serve people
   need and want education
   willing to study now
   kicking myself for wasting so much time

5. Know I'll be a good nurse; having got myself back on track will probably even make me better nurse

---

EXERCISE 1.7   Follow Gail's example, and make an informal outline of your
paragraph. Be sure that your selection and arrangement of topics and subtopics
make for unity. Eliminate topics that don't directly relate to the topic sentence
and don't help move it toward its complete development.

---

4. Writing the Rough Draft.   Gail is now ready to write her rough draft. The
idea of the rough draft is to put the ideas from the outline into sentences and
the sentences into a paragraph. Gail will just let her ideas flow in the direction
the outline dictates. She will not worry about complete sentences or subject-
verb agreement or proper case of pronouns or any other points of correct grammar at this point. She will not check her punctuation or spelling. She will just
write.

When the assignment is to write a paragraph, the instructor usually wants a
title. Gail has selected a title, although it is not really necessary at the rough-
draft stage and is certainly subject to change.

Starting Over

1   Boy, did I mess up my life—for 17 years! It all started
2   when I graduated from high school. I fiddled around and it
3   was to late to apply for college. So there was one year
4   wasted, waiting tables. Then I did go to college. But
5   picked my major in 5 minutes, with no thought, from a
6   brochure lying in the counsellor's office. I was equally
7   thoughtless about the way I acted. Another girl and I
8   shared an apartment. Partyville, U.S.A. I hardly ever went

9   to class. no idea what an education was, let alone how it

10 might help me. Incredable, but my second year was even

11 worse. I still partied all the time, but I had flunked out

12 and not told my parents. In the 15 years since, my best

13 job has been waiting tables. But absolutly don't want the

14 rest of my life to be like these last years. Now I know I

15 want an education. I want to be a nurse. I want to make up

16 for the years I wasted that could have been devoted to a

17 career of service.

EXERCISE 1.8 Now write a rough draft of *your* paragraph. Follow your outline, but let your ideas flow freely. Just write. Don't worry about correct grammar or punctuation or spelling, but do be sure your writing maintains the unity of your outline, with every sentence related to the topic sentence and helping develop it.

---

5. Revising and Correcting the Rough Draft. Since in the rough draft you were eager to get your ideas down on paper without worrying about correctness, the revision and correction stage is an exceedingly important checkpoint.

Revision. Do the revising first. The main purpose of revision is to **double-check and improve unity,** and to be sure your writing follows your plan, your outline. Be sure each sentence in the paragraph is related to and helps develop the topic sentence. Move sentences if they don't seem to follow your plan. Add or subtract sentences if necessary. You can still change arrangement or content, even your outline—yes, even your topic sentence—if such changes make the paragraph more unified and fulfill your purpose better.

Correction. Correction of the rough draft, vital to the improvement of your writing, comes next; **double-check and improve clarity, coherence, and creativity.** Now is the time to locate and eliminate any lack of clarity, so the reader can understand the writing; to strengthen coherence, so the writing can be read easily; and to enhance creativity, so the writing will be exciting and fun for the reader.

Your meaning may not be clear to the reader if your grammar and mechanics of writing are sloppy. **Clarity** includes accuracy of facts, complete sentences, and correct punctuation, capitalization, and spelling. Clarity also involves proper choice of words for your purpose and your audience, and understandable sentences to get your ideas across.

Coherence is the art of arranging sentences so that each idea seems to evolve from the preceding one, with the sentences "stuck together" so that one sentence flows smoothly into the next and is part of an integrated whole. Certain words and expressions can help the content flow smoothly from one sentence into the next. They are called **transitions.** (See pages 101-102 for a detailed listing.)

When you get to Gail's final draft, which follows, you will see that the smooth flow of her sentences is aided by a number of transitional expressions. Transitions that introduce sentences include *As it was, It all began, The truth was, Of course,* and *I know.* She uses conjunctions and adverbs to good advantage in making her writing flow: *if, and, but, when, so, after, because, once in a while, then, until, again, despite, already.* It was in the correction stage that she strengthened her transitions and improved the flow of the paragraph.

But you should be careful not to use unnecessary transitions. Children, in telling a story, often begin every sentence with *then.* When content or form (for example, a chronological sequence) carries the reader along smoothly, transitions may not be needed.

Creativity is finding unusual topics and subtopics to develop in your paragraph, saying things in a way that is out of the ordinary, using imagination and inventiveness in order to appeal to and stimulate your reader. Creativity is the development of *your* style.

Now put the rough draft aside for as long as your deadline allows; then go back to it. Don't hesitate to do a second, improved rough draft and another and another. Rewriting is the name of the game.

Gail went through the checklists and revised and corrected her rough draft. She decided her paragraph had unity, all the sentences helping develop her topic sentence; but the topic sentence was in two parts, in both the first and the last sentence So she put the two parts together and made the topic sentence more interesting in the final draft. After two sentences to attract the reader's attention, she expressed the topic sentence clearly in the third sentence: "It's a crime to throw away such a big chunk of one's life that could have been devoted to a career of service."

As she improved the rough draft, she went into more detail on how she picked her major (line 13 of the final draft) and told more about her present plans (after she "wised up," line 22 of the final draft), which makes the whole development more convincing.

She decided that "Boy, did I mess up my life" (line 1 in the rough draft) and "fiddled around" (line 2) were too informal at the beginning of the paragraph and detracted from the importance of her message. She eliminated fragments: line 4 "But picked my major in 5 (she should have written *five,* see page 380) minutes," line 8 "Partyville U.S.A.," line 9 "no idea what an education was," and line 13 "But absolutely don't want. . . "

Her transitions were good in the rough draft, but she refined them in the final draft, adding even more coherence, by using more effective words, such as "As it was" and "The truth was." She corrected the spelling of *too* (line 3); she used the preferred spelling *counselors* (line 6), and corrected *incredible* (line

10) and *absolutely* (line 13) but then didn't use these words. She made sure that the first word of every sentence was capitalized. She used *messed-up* in the next-to-last sentence, feeling it was effective there.

Checklist for Revision

Unity

1. What is the topic sentence? Is it clearly expressed?

2. Does each sentence of the paragraph relate in some way to (and help develop) the topic sentence?

3. Do sentences proceed in logical, understandable order from the start of the paragraph to the end?

4. Are the sentences in the best order to help the reader grasp the ideas presented?

5. By the end of the paragraph, is the topic sentence completely developed?

Checklist for Correction

Clarity

1. Have you checked your facts for accuracy? When in doubt, check it out or leave it out. If your readers can catch you in even the slightest inaccuracy, it destroys their confidence in your whole paper.

2. Have you eliminated fragments, comma splices, and fused sentences? See pages 243-246 and 250-252.

3. Are sentences clear in meaning?

4. Do subjects and verbs, pronouns and their antecedents agree? See pages 159-164 and 201-202.

5. Is verb tense appropriate and consistent? See pages 177-178 and 267.

6. Are pronouns in proper case? See pages 196-199.

7. Are equal sentence elements treated in parallel fashion? See page 265.

8. Are words capitalized correctly? See pages 371-374.

9. Did you check the dictionary for the spelling of words you were in doubt about?

10. Did you relocate misplaced modifiers? See pages 281-284.

11. Are unnecessary and unnecessarily complex words eliminated? See pages 268-271.

12. Is the language appropriate for your purpose and understandable for your audience? Is your tone consistent?

Coherence

1. Are sentences linked together smoothly for ease of reading and understanding?

2. Does each sentence seem to evolve from the sentence before it?

3. Does each idea flow smoothly into the next with no sidetracking of thought?

4. Are transitions used as bridges to connect sentences smoothly? See pages 101-102. If sentences lead into following sentences because of content or form, are unnecessary transitions eliminated?

5. When you read the paragraph aloud (often mistakes are obvious to the ear), do you move through it effortlessly with nothing to interrupt the flow?

Creativity

1. Have you tried to present your ideas in a fresh, interesting way?

2. Is sentence structure (simple, compound, complex, and compound-complex, see pages 257-259) mixed to prevent monotony?

3. Are sentence length and emphasis within sentences (see pages 262-263 and 274) varied for more interesting reading?

4. Is the language free of clichés and euphemisms? Have you used words in a new way instead of using old, tired expressions? See pages 277-278.

5. Do strong verbs and verbs in active voice predominate? See pages 275-276.

6. Are nouns, adjectives, and adverbs specific? Are concrete and connotative words used? See pages 276-277.

7. Have you painted vivid pictures for your reader, done more showing than just telling, with your creative use of words?

8. Is your total approach original, yet appropriate and interesting to your audience?

Perhaps the biggest improvement as she worked over the rough draft was in her creativity. The first sentence of the final draft, with its *summa cum laude,* is a real attention-grabber. The last sentence is excellent, repeating the first sentence and tying beginning to end, completing the development of the topic sentence with great coherence. She is more specific about her partying, mentioning marijuana and booze, showing instead of telling. Her humor about "finding herself" (line 8) is good.

6. Writing the Final Draft. Some students, like Gail, arrive at the final draft only after following every step possible, from choosing an idea to the final polishing. Gail worked the final draft over several times, which is easy to do on a computer, adding zip to her writing through her creative changes, almost right up until time to hand in her paragraph. A clever title finished the job. Here is the final draft.

Summa Cum Party

1   If I had majored in Party, Party, Party and minored

2 in Marijuana and Cheap Booze, I would have graduated summa

3 cum laude. As it was, I flunked out and wasted not only my

4 freshman year but all the years since, a total of 17. It's

5 a crime to throw away such a big chunk of one's life that

6 could have been devoted to a career of service. It all

7 began when I postponed entering college for a year after

8 high school, telling friends and family I needed to find

9 out who I was, to get in touch with myself. The truth was

10 I had procrastinated so long in filling out college

11 applications that I was too late. So the next fall, after

12 I had "found myself," I entered college to study sales and

13 merchandising, a major I selected because I liked the

14 picture on the brochure advertising that program. My

15 roommate and I shared an apartment that soon came to be

16 known as the University Party Center. I made it to classes

17 once in a while, but my head went immediately to the desk

18 top as I slept off my hangover. Of course, I flunked out

19 and then spent the whole next year living in the

20 apartment, working as a waitress, neglecting to tell my

21 parents I wasn't in college. After "college" came to an

22 end, the parties kept going, until I finally wised up. Now

23 I am a first-year (again) student at a different college.

24 I am determined, despite the obligations of being a single

25 parent, to get a B.S. degree in nursing. I'm hooked on

26 education. I study every chance I get. I know I'll make a

27 good nurse because already I've cured one sick, messed-up

28 life, my own. Summa cum laude, here I come.

It had been a long, hard labor for Gail, but a beautiful paragraph was born.

EXERCISE 1.9 Write your own final draft of the paragraph you have been working on, using the suggestions in the sections on revision and correction. Use the checklists to remind you of some of the possible weaknesses in your paragraph that may need to be strengthened. Read your paragraph aloud before "finalizing" the final draft.

Many students do not have to go through all the steps of choosing a subject and a controlling idea. Bill Stein, another of my students, arrived at his final draft in a much shorter sequence. This time the assignment was to write a paragraph about a family member, telling the reader what he or she is or was really like. Students had to decide "My mom is a truly loving, understanding mother," or "My mother was always too busy being a supermom to be a good mother," or "My dad never had time for us kids," or "My dad always listened to my troubles better than Mom did," or "My sister taught me my values," or whatever was the case.

1. Choosing Subject, Controlling Idea. Choosing the subject was done for Bill by the assignment—he knew immediately that he wanted to write about his father. The controlling idea was clear to him—his father was a great guy.

2. Strengthening the Controlling Idea. His **tone** would be one of admiration tinged with reality. His **purpose** was to fulfill the assignment and to inform his classmates and his family of how much he admired his father; the paragraph would also be a tribute to his dad, who had died seven years before. For an **audience** of classmates and family, he could use ordinary conversational language. His controlling idea, "Dad was a great guy," seemed okay.

3. Outlining. He got ready to make his outline by writing down ideas as they occurred to him:

> Like a best friend, there when I needed him, listened, had time for me.
>
> Taught me right from wrong and always had lessons in conduct to share.
>
> Was stickler for good behavior, strict disciplinarian, but put love first.
>
> Liked sports, taught my brother and me, coached my Little League team.
>
> Always encouraged me to do my best (school, sports).
>
> Had bad temper, outspoken, straightforward, swore something awful.
>
> Was breadwinner, successful in his profession, well-liked by everyone.
>
> Was drill sergeant in the army, then in reserves after he took another job.
>
> Often under stress, took a nap when he got home.
>
> Married Mom when he was 20, she was 19.
>
> Smoked and drank too much, stayed up late watching TV.
>
> Always remembered his humble beginnings, believed in unity of family.
>
> Active in church.

By now, the controlling idea should be either reinforced or changed to fit Bill's latest thoughts: My dad had his faults, tried to act tough but was tender at heart, was a wonderful father. Certain major points will stand out, with minor points that may be placed under them. Next Bill organized these points in an informal outline so that he would know exactly where his paragraph was going.

  I. Had his faults
    A. Smoked
    B. Drank
    C. Swore, bad temper
    D. Too strict
    E. Stayed up late
    F. Was under stress because of job

 II. One strong point: was family man, believed strongly in love
    A. Never forgot his parents; visited them frequently
    B. Put family first
    C. Strict disciplinarian but kind underneath
    D. Worked and played with his kids
    E. Encouraged kids to do well, to work hard

III. Great father for me
    A. Best friend
    B. Always had time for me: give examples, show rather than tell
    C. Taught values and lessons
    D. Coached sports for my brother and me

E. Encouraged me to succeed
F. Showed his love for me

4. Rough Draft. Here is Bill's rough draft, Step 4 out of six on his way to a finished paragraph.

Dad

1   My dad had many faults; he acted tough but was tender
2 underneath, a great father. He was a drill sergeant in the
3 Army. He chose that profession because at the time he
4 graduated from high school, jobs were scarce. He had to
5 make a living for himself somehow. Besides, he was in love
6 with my mom and they wanted to get married. She was 19; he
7 was 20. They married; he managed to support her—and later
8 they had three kids, me, my younger brother, and my younger
9 sister. The trouble was, being a drill sergeant rubbed off
10 on his family relationships. He liked to boss us around and
11 maintain Army-like discipline at home. But if you could
12 overlook the fact that he lost his temper and swore like a
13 drill sergeant, drank a bit too much, and smoked enough to
14 give us all lung cancer, he was the best, most loving dad
15 that ever was. Always there for the whole family. Taught us
16 kids what was right; he punished us if we did wrong; he
17 made us hard-working and responsible. He encouraged us in
18 school and at sports. He listened to me and gave me good
19 advice. Couldn't have asked for a better dad.

5. Revision and Correction. The rough draft was now ready for revision and correction. Often in my classes, students in groups of three read each other's work and criticize it. Bill's critics felt that he had departed from his outline, which did have unity, enough that his paragraph had lost its unity. They could see no reason for his going into how his dad got into his profession or for even mentioning his mother, how old she was when they married, how many children they had, etc.

Even though the topic sentence was clear in the rough draft, the best statement of it was now buried in the middle of the paragraph, starting on line 11,

"But if you could overlook. . ." Bill was persuaded to put an improved topic sentence first. In fact, the first sentence is so much improved (over the rough draft's "My dad had many faults. . .") that it really grabs your attention and makes you want to read on. It makes a very creative beginning.

A jury of his peers also persuaded Bill to mention the important fact that his dad had died seven years ago, which makes the paragraph even more meaningful.

Bill put his subtopics in logical order for better coherence, using mainly co-ordinating conjunctions (*and, but, so*) for transitions. Instead of eight short, choppy sentences and main clauses at the start, he used a mixture of short and long sentences for more interest. He eliminated three fragments: "Always there for the whole family." "Taught us kids what was right." "Couldn't have asked for a better dad."

Best of all, he added specific examples, like the game of H-O-R-S-E, his father's sneaking money back into his bank, and the home run. He found that re-wording is rewarding. And finally, he came up with a tantalizing title (more interesting than "Dad") to convey his now-unified, clear, coherent, and creative paragraph.

6. Final Draft. Here is Bill's final draft.

Hut, Two, Three, Four

1   He smoked enough to give the whole family some

2   dreaded disease secondhand, drank so much that he was

3   forever sleeping off a hangover, swore like a whole

4   regiment, and took a belt to my bottom when I misbehaved;

5   but in spite of his bad habits and his attempts to be

6   stern, he was the greatest, most loving dad in the world.

7   He died seven years ago, but the lessons he lived are

8   still very much alive. He was a drill sergeant in the

9   United States Army, so I learned discipline. He would

10   never have admitted it, but love kept showing through. He

11   taught me to value hard work, good health, and

12   responsibility; he used his belt on me if I raised any

13   doubts. He'd let me bet a hard-earned quarter on our

14   basketball game of Horse (each time you missed a shot, you

15   got another letter until you were a full-fledged H-O-R-S-E),

16 and he'd make me pay up. I didn't know until later that he
17 sneaked the money back into my coin bank. He was never too
18 busy to listen or help me build a birdhouse or coach my
19 Little League team. . . . It was the season's last game; my
20 bat had yet to make contact with the ball. Finally, on my
21 last at-bat, with the bases loaded and Dad still rooting
22 me on, I crushed the ball and made it all the way around.
23 As I got near home plate, there stood Dad. Instead of
24 touching home, I jumped into his arms and gave him a big
25 hug. The ump didn't have the heart to call me out. Some
26 things are more important than the formality of touching
27 home plate. I learned that from my dad.

EXERCISE 1.10 Fill in the blanks.

1. Do you get a good picture of what Bill's dad was like? How would you describe him in just a few words? _____

_____

2. What is the topic sentence for this paragraph? _____

_____

3. Where is the topic sentence located in the paragraph? _____

_____

4. What precedes the topic sentence? _____

5. Do the sentences all help develop the topic sentence? _____

Explain _____

Answers on page 64.

EXERCISE 1.11 Go through the six steps to produce a good paragraph from a
subject and topic sentence of your choice. Be prepared to show your outline,
your rough draft, and your final draft. Circle your topic sentence.

QUIZ YOURSELF ON STEP ONE Fill in the blanks.

1. What is the definition of a paragraph? _____

_____

2. What is another name for the topic sentence? _____

_____

Where is it usually found? _____

_____ **3.** Free writing is   (a) writing for which you don't get paid.   (b) writing on the subject of independence.   (c) writing whatever comes to your mind.

_____ **4.** Tone is   (a) a signal to start writing.   (b) the writer's attitude toward his or her subject.   (c) a classy way of writing.

5. List the six steps for good writing.

_____

_____

_____

_____

_____

_____

Answers on page 64.

Step Two: From Good Paragraph to Better

Paragraphs: By Beginning Writers

It sometimes helps, in learning how to write paragraphs, to see bad paragraphs and decide how you would improve them. I have two beautiful examples of first-week-of-class writing samples, written by students who had had little or no previous help in writing. Read them, and get your criticisms and suggestions ready.

The first was by a student who had come back to school 12 years after high school graduation.

Back to School

1   English shouldn't be required of people coming back
2 to school after being out of high school 12 years. I'm
3 scared about college. I'm sure high school was more fun. I
4 was a cheerleader, made fairly good grades, and even met
5 my husband there during our senior year. He was on the
6 football team. I never did like English much, and I've
7 gotten along for 12 years with the English I know. My high
8 school teachers weren't all that good either. We did a lot
9 more reading than writing. I'm not sure I'll make it in
10 college because I have so many other things on my mind. My
11 littlest one has chickenpox, and it's driving me up a wall
12 finding someone to stay with her. It seems funny that
13 there are vaccines for everything but chickenpox. I may
14 have made a mistake coming back to school at my advanced
15 age. I don't think as fast as I used to. I was in an auto
16 accident. I didn't react fast enough. My husband paid for
17 the repair of my car.

EXERCISE 1.12 Fill in the blanks.

1. What is your reaction to this paragraph? _____

_____

2. What is the topic sentence? _____

_____

3. Are the words suitable for the writer's purpose and audience? Is creativity in choice of words evident? _____

_____

4. Are the sentences varied in structure so as to make interesting reading?

_____

_____

5. What needs to be corrected grammatically? Look for sentence errors, non-agreement of subject-verb, tense faults. _____

_____

Answers on page 64.

The paragraph above is living proof that writing can have clarity (the sentences are grammatically correct, and the meaning of each sentence is clear) but be totally lacking in unity, coherence, and creativity, the other characteristics of good writing.

The second don't-write-like-this paragraph was also a writing sample from the first week of school. The assignment was to write a well-organized, grammatically correct paragraph on one, only one, of the following: Cats Make Better Pets Than Dogs, or Dogs Make Better Pets Than Cats. Here it is.

I Like Cats

1   I have both a cat and a dog, and I feel that cats are
2   much better friends than dogs. When I was a child, I lived
3   on a farm in the country, and the cats took their job of
4   catching mice very seriously. Cats are always bothering
5   you. I know because I am the owner of a cat, in fact, two
6   cats, to be precise. To me, I feel safe in a home with a
7   dog. In my opinion, I feel cats are really nice clean pets
8   to have. But they may claw your furniture and shred your
9   couch to bits all the time. Dogs on the other hand are a
10   better investment for your money. Although cats are mostly
11   loners who like to be by themself. Dogs are loyal through
12   thick and thin. Whenever you need them. Although both pets
13   have lovingly persuasions on the security of the home, the
14   dog has a more direct affect on the atmosphere in the home

15 while the cat has been known for its softness. So finally

16 in conclusion, when animals prefer each other better to us

17 humans, in my own case I believe you should find a human

18 to make friends with and leave the animals to themselves.

I did not make that up. Honest. I was going to apologize somewhere for the fact that the student writings yet to come in this book are so well done that they might discourage the beginning writer. But having included the two examples above, I no longer feel the need to. You must realize that the excellent paragraphs and compositions that you will read in this chapter and the next are end-of-the-course products of students who worked hard and had a great deal of advice from fellow students and from the instructor. And the two anonymous students just featured improved their writing tremendously before the end of the course.

EXERCISE 1.13 Fill in the blanks.

1. What is your reaction to this paragraph? _____

_____

2. What is the topic sentence? _____

_____

3. Are the words suitable for the writer's purpose and audience? Is creativity in

choice of words evident? _____

_____

4. Are the sentences varied in structure so as to make interesting reading?

_____

_____

5. What needs to be corrected grammatically? _____

_____

Answers on page 65.

Better Paragraphs: All Sentences Developing the Topic Sentence

As you know, for unity, every sentence of the paragraph must support and help in some way to develop the topic sentence.

EXERCISE 1.14 As you read the following paragraph, circle the topic sentence, and underline two sentences that do not support the topic sentence.

Shake, Partner

1   Persons who claim to be experts on shaking hands say
2 there are right ways and wrong ways to shake. The gesture
3 is made up of four parts: eye contact, pressure, pumps,
4 and verbal accompaniment. The shaker should hold eye
5 contact long enough to determine the color of the shakee's
6 irises. The pressure should be considerably firmer than a
7 limp fish but not bone-breaking. Early politicians dipped
8 their right hand in pickle juice to toughen the skin. We
9 are warned against over or under pumping: too little is
10 insincere, and too much is desperate. Two pumps for
11 business shakes and seven for friendship are recommended,
12 with political pumping in between. The verbal
13 accompaniment should be friendly, businesslike, aloof, or
14 overjoyed, whatever fits the occasion. Happy hand shaking;
15 do it right. If you want to avoid the stupid air kiss that
16 is threatening to replace the good old handshake, place
17 your left hand on the forearm of the would-be kisser to
18 keep him or her at a distance, and shake away.

Answers on page 65.

EXERCISE 1.15 Circle the topic sentence and underline the two sentences that are unrelated to it. When you're through, you'll know more about handshaking than, perhaps, you cared to know.

How-De-Do, Mr. President

1   Presidents of the United States and presidential
2 hopefuls through the years have shown quite different
3 styles of handshaking. Stephen Douglas, who ran against
4 Abraham Lincoln in 1860, is thought to be the first
5 candidate to offer a friendly hand to voters. President
6 Lyndon B. Johnson's exuberant style of shaking brought
7 back into popularity the phrase from a generation before,
8 "pressing the flesh," and made him a candidate not only
9 for office but for the title of handshake king. Candidate
10 Hubert Humphrey learned to shake protectively, by offering
11 both hands and sandwiching the voter's hand in between to
12 control the pressure. Vice President Nelson Rockefeller
13 was a gold-medal handshaker who could hardly wait to wade
14 into the crowds and give them a hand. Baby kissing has
15 always been another method of demonstrating political good
16 will. Ronald Reagan was a strong and durable handshaker
17 because he worked out with a hand-strengthening device.
18 President George Bush has been described as more of a
19 waver whereas Bill Clinton is a down-to-earth shaker. Just
20 as high officials govern in different ways, so they shake
21 hands in varying styles. Women, who have been frequent
22 handshakers only since the 1960s, should take the
23 initiative by offering their hand first.

Answers on page 65.

EXERCISE 1.16 Which of the following statements would help develop the topic sentence "Caves are among the most interesting tourist attractions throughout the world." Write *Yes* in the blank if the statement supports the topic sentence, *No* if it does not. In the blanks at the end of the exercise, write the numbers of the five Yes sentences in what you think would be the best order to develop the topic sentence.

_____ **1.** People lived in caves 500,000 years ago.

_____ **2.** Thousands of tourists visit these well-known caves every year.

_____ **3.** Interesting caves in other countries include the Blue Grotto on the Isle of Capri, Italy, filled with sapphire-blue light; the Waitomo Cave on North Island, New Zealand, with thousands of tiny glowworms clinging to the ceiling; and the Gouffre (pit or chasm) de la Pierre St. Martin on the border between France and Spain, noted for its depth of about one mile.

_____ **4.** Carlsbad Caverns in Southeastern New Mexico contain some of the world's largest and most beautiful stalactites, icicle-like formations hanging from the ceiling, and stalagmites, pillar-like formations rising from the floor.

_____ **5.** Each cave has its own unique characteristics, from sheer size to majestic formations.

_____ **6.** I once had a friend whose hobby was spelunking, exploring caves.

_____ **7.** The longest cave system ever explored is the Mammoth-Flint Ridge System in Central Kentucky, with more than 190 miles of connected passages and chambers, including underground lakes and rivers.

_____ **8.** Bats spend their days in caves, flying out at night to hunt for food.

_____ _____ _____ _____ _____

Answers on page 66.

EXERCISE 1.17 (1) What would be a good topic sentence for a paragraph containing the following sentences? (2) Do all the sentences support one controlling idea?

1. In college we don't have to stay on campus all day as we did in high school.

2. There are no required study halls.

3. We are free to wander anywhere in the building when we aren't in class—without passes.

4. In some college classes, attendance is not even compulsory.

5. Some instructors don't check to see whether or not we've done our homework.

6. Most instructors let us bring a cup of coffee into class, which helps a lot on sleepy mornings.

Good topic sentence: _____

_____

All these sentences do/do not support one controlling idea. _____

Answers on page 66.

In Exercises 1.14, 1.15, 1.16, and 1.17, the writers seem to have started with topic sentences they wanted to develop and then written sentences to develop them. Sometimes a topic sentence may be supported by quoting someone else's words on the subject. This is particularly true in a longer research paper, where the controlling idea is documented by quotations from authorities on the subject.

But sometimes an event happens first, and then a topic sentence naturally arises from it. That is the case in the following two exercises.

EXERCISE 1.18 (1) What would be a good topic sentence for a paragraph containing the following sentences? Make up a topic sentence from what is there and/or from what you add. (2) Do all the sentences support one controlling idea? This is a paragraph that I might write if my assignment were to tell of an unpleasant personal experience.

1. Stamp collecting has been called "the hobby of kings and the king of hobbies."

2. Of course, I'm not a king; but I was a philatelist, a stamp collector, for a while, and it almost cost me my reputation.

3. I was doing fine until I ordered some special stamps from a company whose name I shall not mention because they would not hesitate to try to sue me—again.

4. The company sent me the stamps I ordered plus about $15 worth of stamps I hadn't ordered and didn't want.

5. I was darned if I was going to pay for postage to return the unwanted stamps, so I sent them back in an envelope with no stamp and no return address.

6. When I began getting threatening letters from the stamp company, I sacrificed a stamp and sent them a letter telling them what I had done; but this was not good enough.

7. Next I started receiving letters from a collection agency, then letters from a local lawyer, all vowing to ruin my credit rating.

8. It didn't matter that I had never been late with payments for credit card charges or cars, even houses—this company was investing a lot of money to ruin me for $15 worth of stamps that I didn't even have any more.

9. But I knew what to do; I called the Better Business Bureau, and I never heard from the (bleep) Stamp Co. again.

10. It didn't take much to convince me to give up philately and take up philosophy.

Good topic sentence: _____

_____

All sentences do/do not support one controlling idea. _____

Answers on page 66.

EXERCISE 1.19 (1) Add a good topic sentence for a paragraph containing the following sentences. (2) Do all the sentences support one controlling idea? This is a paragraph that I might write if my assignment were to tell of a pleasant personal experience.

1. This was proved to me by a four-year-old I used to know.

2. She and I were coming out of the grocery store when we saw a one-legged man on crutches slowly making his way across the parking lot.

3. My daughter had never seen a person with only one leg, and she stared open-mouthed at him.

4. When we were out of his hearing, I told her that it wasn't nice to stare at him, that he undoubtedly felt bad enough for having lost a leg without having people stare at him.

5. I also told her that if she ever happened to be talking to such a person, she shouldn't mention the fact that he had lost a leg.

6. I could almost hear the four-year-old wheels turning, and then she came out with the wisdom of one still unschooled in the unkind ways of the world.

7. "You're right, Mommie," she said solemnly. "If I were talking to him, I wouldn't mention the missing leg. I'd look up at him and smile and say, 'My, that's a nice leg you have.'"

Good topic sentence: _____

_____

All sentences do/do not support one controlling idea. _____

Answers on page 66.

Better Paragraphs: Locating the Topic Sentence

The topic sentence of a paragraph usually comes at the beginning to serve as a signpost telling readers where they are going. Often it is the first sentence, but it may be preceded by an attention-grabber to make sure the reader looks into the paragraph.

However, there are times when the topic sentence is at the end, particularly in paragraphs developed by narration, or storytelling, in which the writer tells the story and only at the end tells the reader the purpose, the moral, the controlling idea. There are also times when the topic sentence appears at the beginning and again at the end in modified form to sum up the paragraph, a good technique; and there are times when the topic sentence is not expressed at all but is clearly understood from the message in the paragraph, particularly in descriptive and sometimes in narrative paragraphs. It may even be spread over a couple of sentences waiting for the reader to put it in his own words. Just be sure there is a controlling idea that the reader can easily recognize.

EXERCISE 1.20 Put sentences (a) through (g) in order as they should appear in a well-organized paragraph, with the topic sentence first in blank 1 and the concluding sentence last in blank 7. If sentence (c) should be the first sentence, put **(c)** in blank 1; if sentence (d) should be the second sentence, put **(d)** in blank 2. Ready?

a. In 1974 religious fundamentalists in Kanawha County, W. Va., forced from the county's schools *The Three Little Pigs* (too much violence) and *Pinocchio* (parental disobedience; Pinocchio disobeys his creator, the woodcarver Geppetto); but these children's classics refused to go out of style.

b. Censorship has never worked and probably never will.

c. As far back as the eighth century B.C., attempts were made to clean up the *Odyssey* for immature readers.

d. The good news is that, despite wine-guzzling grannies and huffing-puffing-house-blowing-down wolves, libraries and school systems manage to keep on their shelves, available to the public, 90 percent of the material challenged by would-be censors.

e. You may recall that since the early part of this century, books banned in Boston have immediately hit the bestseller list.

f. Most recently under fire has been an illustration in which Little Red Riding Hood's basket appears to contain a bottle of wine.

g. And attempts to ban racy books in other cities have not succeeded in putting the publications out of circulation.

1. _____   5. _____

2. _____   6. _____

3. _____   7. _____

4. _____

Answers on page 66.

EXERCISE 1.21 Put sentences (a) through (g) in order as they should appear in a well-organized paragraph. If sentence (c) should be the first sentence, put **(c)** in blank 1; if sentence (d) should be the second sentence, put **(d)** in blank 2. Tell what the topic sentence is and where it is located. Freshman John Novak wrote this paragraph, which he called "Splitting Up."

  a. While we are on the subject of messes, her idea of cleaning house is moving the magazines she reads the rest of the afternoon from one pile on the floor to another.

  b. The sun is straight up as are both hands of the clock when she finally ambles to the bathroom, fills the tub to the top with scalding water, and then reads the morning paper while the water cools, wasting all kinds of energy except, of course, her own.

  c. And when dinnertime comes, she's a whiz at thawing something in the microwave.

  d. If ever I am in the vicinity of Hyatt Legal Services, I'd have every reason to stop in and start divorce proceedings.

  e. All of this may be grounds for divorce; but to tell the truth, I'd never consider leaving her—we love each other too much.

  f. Why? My wife begins her day by refusing to get out of bed.

  g. After she is dressed, she drives to the nearby mall by way of a fast-food drive-in, whose cups and wrappers provide more debris to adorn her already-messy car.

  Topic sentence _____

  Where located _____

  1. _____   **5.** _____

  2. _____   **6.** _____

  3. _____   **7.** _____

  4. _____

Answers on page 67.

EXERCISE 1.22 As you read the following paragraph, by Jennifer May Beach, look for the topic sentence. Answer the questions at the end.

In Out of the Cold

1   "Even if they slam the door in your face," our
2 minister had told us, "be polite, and be sure to say
3 thank-you." He was briefing those of us who had
4 volunteered to collect canned goods for the Hunger Crisis
5 Center. We were to go door-to-door, bring the cans back to
6 be stamped by our church, then drive them to the Hunger
7 Crisis Center downtown. But Dan and I had canvassed 12
8 blocks, he on one side of the street and I on the other,
9 and had collected less than 50 cans each. It was a
10 horrible day to be outside, the temperature around
11 freezing and enough wind to blow the chill factor clear
12 through our bones. We decided to finish the block we were
13 on and postpone the remaining five blocks till the next
14 day—or maybe never. I rang the bell at the last house on
15 my side of the street. I could see a man sitting by the
16 window, so I knew this at least wouldn't be another Nobody
17 Home. He finally opened the door and stared vacantly
18 somewhere above my head as I told him my mission. He asked
19 me to come in out of the cold and explained that he was
20 blind and had been out of work seven months. Realizing
21 that I shouldn't be asking *him* for a contribution, I
22 started to leave, but he said that I should wait, that
23 he'd find something. He returned with a can of peas. I
24 thanked him and crossed the street to add my cans to
25 Dan's, complaining to Dan that all I'd got from the last
26 four houses was one lousy can of peas, and that from a
27 poor blind man I had no business taking it from. I handed
28 it to Dan. "Look, Jen," he shouted, "it's stamped UMC! He
29 must have got it from our church's contribution to the

30 last food drive!" Suddenly we were feeling warm all over.

31 The generosity of a person who so badly needed help

32 himself had set our values straight—we decided to finish

33 the remaining five blocks before we quit.

1. What is the topic sentence? _____

_____

2. Where is it located? _____

3. What is the effect of locating it there? _____

_____

4. Is the tone appropriate for this paragraph? _____

_____

5. What can you say about the sentence structure? _____

_____

Answers on page 67.

Mrs. Murphy, an English teacher at our college, may sometimes envy teachers of other subjects because they never have the hard job of making up sentences to demonstrate grammar rights and wrongs and they don't have long papers to evaluate. Mrs. Murphy would have to admit, however, that teachers of basic English writing have the very interesting task of grading homework in which students bare their souls. Students often ask if it's all right to write in first person. I feel that it is quite all right when practicing writing skills because it ensures that students are writing about something they are familiar with.

Sometimes, as we've said, the topic sentence is never stated, but the paragraph makes clear what the writer thinks about the subject. In descriptive paragraphs, the writer may never come out and say, "This was the most beautiful winter night I'd ever seen," but that is the unexpressed topic sentence.

Sometimes in paragraphs developed by narration, the topic sentence is unstated but becomes clear in the storytelling, as in the following student first-person, soul-baring paragraph, anonymous for obvious reasons. An exercise about this paragraph will follow; so, as you read, be on the lookout for the topic sentence that is never expressed.

Imagine My Surprise . . .

1 I had cheated my way through Sociology 101 clear to

2 the midterm. I admit it. The class was large; the seats

3 were close together; the tests were always multiple-

4 choice. I sat next to this smart guy who surely knew but

5 didn't seem to mind that I copied all the answers to

6 quizzes from his paper. It's no trick, you know, if you

7 lean on your elbow just right, with your hand sort of half

8 over your eyes, to sneak as many glances as you need. Of

9 course, I knew I'd be sunk if he were ever absent on a

10 test day, but he had never missed a class. Came the

11 midterm. As usual, I hadn't even bothered to look things

12 over the night before. Fortunately, as usual, he was in

13 class bright (I hoped) and early. I copied his answers

14 without even reading the questions. When the teacher

15 handed back the midterms at the end of the next class, I

16 saw an A at the top of his paper; I smiled to myself. But

17 when I got mine back, there was nothing at the top of the

18 first page. On the last page was a large zero with the

19 note, "Zero for the midterm; F for the course. This time I

20 gave look-alike but *different* tests to every other

21 student. Yours and John's were not the same test, but your

22 answers were the same. I had been watching you for several

23 weeks. You can take the course over next semester if the

24 Ethics Committee allows you to stay in school." I left the

25 room in a daze. What would I tell my parents? Why had I

26 been so stupid?

EXERCISE 1.23

1. What is the topic sentence (the controlling idea) of the paragraph called

"Imagine My Surprise . . . "?_____

_____

2. What is the effect of not stating the topic sentence at the start? _____

_____

3. What is the effect of not stating the topic sentence at all? _____

_____

Answers on page 67.

Better Paragraphs: Developing Them by 10 Different Methods

Instructors often assign a paragraph or a composition to be written using one of the following 10 methods of development. That is good practice even though it should be the other way around: the subject, controlling idea, tone, purpose, and audience should dictate the method of development. Here are the common methods for developing a paragraph. You are almost sure to use one or another of these methods even if you don't know you are doing it, but your writing will be better if you consciously select the method best suited to your subject, controlling idea, tone, purpose, and audience.

As you will see in the next chapter, these same 10 methods are used for developing a composition. As you will also see, in both paragraphs and compositions the methods overlap. Almost all methods will contain some description. A cause-and-effect paragraph may well be told in story (narrative) form. Argumentation often makes use of examples; process is sometimes part description. Rarely is a piece of writing developed by one method alone.

1. Examples. The use of examples is a common method of development. If you tell the reader that there are many rare animals to be seen at the zoo and then list them and tell about them, you are using examples to develop your paragraph. If you want to discuss the kinds of vegetables that can be grown in a 10-by-10-foot garden, you will need to list examples—or if you write about tests (essay, multiple-choice, etc.) or cars or dogs or books. If you state as your topic sentence, "Three teams in the American Football League are among the best ever to play the game," and then list the three, telling something about them, you have used three examples to prove the truth of your topic sentence.

2. Definition. Definition is used to explain what the subject is. Suppose you want to write about existentialism, or democracy in school government, or being a chocoholic, or having a bad neighbor, or developing procrastination to an art form (Gail's particular talent, as she admitted when she was trying to find a topic for her paragraph, pages 5 to 10): you would probably use the strategy of developing your paragraph by definition.

3. Process. Process is the technique of telling "how to," how something is done or made. One student wrote a great paper on how to make a D in English (he got an A). You might want to write on how to build a better mousetrap, how to throw a fabulous party, how to look helpless so someone will stop and change your tire for you, how to win the lottery (let me know; I suppose it might help if I bought a ticket), how bosses decide who gets promoted, how Thanksgiving turkeys are raised, how macaroni is made, or how to be a great quarterback.

4. Classification and Analysis. The method commonly called classification and analysis is really two methods of developing a paragraph. Usually only one at a time is used. Classification is writing about a group of people or things by breaking the group into subgroups or categories that the writer has created. I have had good papers on customers written by students working as waiters or waitresses (excuse me, as food service technicians). Their subgroups of customers might include the impatient customer, the demanding one, the complaining one, the cheap tipper, the generous tipper, the thoughtful person, etc. Or, gadgets ordered by mail could be categorized as those that work, those that don't work, those that are useful, those that get shoved to the back of the closet, and those that self-destruct within 24 hours after delivery.

Analysis is writing about one item or idea by breaking it into its component parts. If you categorize different types of home heating systems, you are using classification. If you take the heat pump and break it down into its parts, you are using analysis. The "demo" student composition on friendship in the next chapter is a good example of analysis.

5. Comparison and Contrast. Comparison and contrast would be a suitable method for developing a paragraph about your hometown as you remember it from childhood and your hometown now, or about two of your instructors, or about pro and college basketball, or about instant potatoes and real mashed potatoes. Comparison points out likenesses; contrast emphasizes differences. A paragraph may incorporate only likenesses, only differences, or both.

There are two methods of accomplishing comparison and contrast: alternating and block. Assume we are comparing San Francisco and New York City. In the alternating (or point-by-point) method, the writer would proceed in this order: location of SF, location of NY; size of SF, size of NY; climate of SF, climate of NY; educational and cultural opportunities of SF, educational and cultural opportunities of NY; summary of SF as a place to live, summary of NY as a place to live. In the block (or whole-by-whole) method, the writer would proceed in this order: location of SF, size of SF, climate of SF, educational and cultural opportunities of SF, summary of SF as a place to live—then the same things about NY. In other words, everything about SF, then everything about NY. The point-by-point method is better for longer papers because the reader is likely to forget what the climate in SF is by the time he gets to the climate in NY if everything else about SF has intervened.

6. Cause and Effect. Cause and effect is a type of development that may concentrate more on causes, may concentrate more on effects, or may treat the two more or less equally. If the subject of your paragraph is "Why I Flunked Sociology," you are probably going to have many causes (didn't go to class, didn't study, didn't do the term paper, etc.) and only one effect (I flunked). If your topic is "Flunking Sociology Is Killing Me," you are probably going to have one cause (flunking sociology) and many effects (parents grounded me, have to take sociology over, won't graduate on time, etc.). Good paragraphs could be written on the causes of absence from classes, the effects of censorship of the campus newspaper, the causes of tennis elbow, or the effects of recycling pop cans.

In addition to many-causes-one-effect and one-cause-many-effects, you may develop a causal chain, in which a cause leads to an effect, which in turn becomes a cause leading to another effect, etc. Perhaps at a resort town near a beautiful lake, septic tanks have been permitted too close to the lake; this causes the lake to become polluted; this causes the fish to die and the water to become unattractive to swimmers; this causes tourists not to want to come to this lake; this causes the town to go bankrupt.

7. Narration. Narration, or telling a story, is one of the most-used methods of paragraph development. Almost every other pattern of development is likely to include a bit of narration. And, as we have noted, sometimes the topic sentence becomes obvious without being stated in narration. You may want to tell the story of your most embarrassing moment (the unstated topic sentence might be, Don't speak before you think). Or you might write of your visit to a nursing home or of your first experience at scuba diving.

8. Description Description is almost certain to overlap other types of development. It's hard to use examples or comparison or process or any other form of development without using some description. But if you are asked to write a paragraph developed mainly by description, you might want to consider the hospital where you lost your appendix, your little sister when she is particularly obnoxious, the inside of your garage (in need of a garage sale), or the silhouette of a sailboat in the moonlight. The topic sentence of a descriptive paragraph, often not expressed, might be simply "This is an elegant room" or "This is an interesting-looking piece of machinery."

9. Analogy. Analogy is a form of comparison that explains something hard-to-understand by likening it to something well-known. The body's circulatory system is often likened to a water pump; the geological layers of the earth may be compared to the layers of an onion.

10. Argumentation. Argumentation takes us full circle because a good argument is almost certain to require the use of examples, the first method of development we considered. Argumentation is one of the most satisfactory methods for most of us because we enjoy presenting our views on controversial matters. Every letter to the editor, every editorial, every plea asking for money, every request for a promotion, and every politician's bid for election employs the method of argumentation. You might want to write an argumentative paragraph suggesting that more speakers on environmental issues be brought to campus, or that the quarter system be dropped in favor of semesters, or that teachers return graded papers more quickly, or that the board of trustees have a student representative with a vote, or that men share the housework, or that the 40-hour job week be divided into four instead of five days, or that a traffic light be installed at the corner.

EXERCISE 1.24 Look back at the paragraphs we have already studied. Fill in the blanks with the method (or methods) of development used in each.

1. Gail's paragraph on wasting 17 years of her life, page 19? _____

2. The paragraph on Bill's father, page 23? _____

3. The paragraph on the right way to shake hands, page 29? _____

4. The paragraph on presidential handshakes, page 30? _____

5. The paragraph on censorship, page 35? _____

6. The paragraph on not splitting up, page 36? _____

7. The paragraph on collecting canned goods, page 37? _____

8. The paragraph on cheating, page 38? _____

Answers on page 67.

EXERCISE 1.25 Write a paragraph about a subject of your choice, developing your topic sentence mainly by one of the 10 methods of development, stating which method. Don't forget to observe the guidelines for unity, clarity, coherence, and creativity.

Better Paragraphs: Organizing Them in Three Different Patterns

Three patterns of organization are commonly used to develop a paragraph:

   1. Chronological, arrangement of the sentences in the order that events happened.

   2. In order of importance or of complexity or size, from most to least or from least to most, with the latter being the more common.

3. Spatial, in order of location, from left to right, from top to bottom or down to up, from in to out, from north to south, or from nose to tail.

Descriptive paragraphs are frequently spatial, and narrative paragraphs chronological. Often the patterns overlap, and a paragraph will, for example, be both chronological and in order of importance. If there seems to be no pattern but several things are being described in no particular order, call it spatial, going from one item to another to the next.

As with methods of development, you are almost bound to use one of these patterns of organization whether you plan to or not, but your writing will be better if you consciously incorporate one pattern or another into your paragraph to best develop your subject, controlling idea, tone, and purpose for your audience.

EXERCISE 1.26 Look back at the paragraphs we have already studied. Fill in the blanks with the pattern of organization that was used in each.

1. Gail's paragraph on wasting 17 years of her life, page 19? _____

2. The paragraph on Bill's father, page 23? _____

3. The paragraph on the right way to shake hands, page 29? _____

4. The paragraph on presidential handshakes, page 30? _____

5. The paragraph on censorship, page 35? _____

6. The paragraph on not splitting up, 36? _____

7. The paragraph on collecting canned goods, page 37? _____

8. The paragraph on cheating, page 38? _____

Answers on page 68.

Although in the eight paragraphs just mentioned, the chronological pattern is by far the most common, many of my students have written good paragraphs using the other patterns of organization. Order of importance was used in paragraphs on living with a mentally retarded child, packing for a camping trip, enjoying football as a spectator sport, and getting a date with a person of the opposite sex whom you have admired from afar. I remember a paragraph developed spatially describing the writer's bedroom, from the door clockwise back to the door, with emphasis on the luxury of the bed in the center, surrounded by stereo equipment. Other spatial patterns told of the wonderful selections available in a discount store, walking along a leaf-strewn country road in the fall, paddling a canoe around a lake, and visiting a flea market.

EXERCISE 1.27 Write a paragraph about a subject of your choice developing your topic sentence by one of the 10 methods of development and consciously using one of the three patterns of development, chosen to best suit your subject, controlling idea, tone, purpose, and audience. Don't forget to observe the guidelines for unity, clarity, coherence, and creativity. At the top write which method of development and which pattern of organization you have used.

Better Paragraphs: Making Beginning and End Effective

How many times have you glanced at an article, read the first sentence, and then decided on the basis of that sentence alone whether or not you wanted to read the article? Never underestimate the power of the first sentence of a paragraph. If the topic sentence itself can't be worded in such an interesting way as to attract the reader, an attention-grabber should precede the topic sentence.

Which paragraph would you be more likely to read?—one beginning "Dogs can be difficult," or one beginning "After sending me to the emergency room twice, incurring the wrath of most of my neighbors, and then costing me a week's salary for obedience school, Mutt and I have finally come to a meeting of the minds: he admits, reluctantly, that I am the boss; and I admit, readily, that taming a pup with size 13 paws is no picnic by the fireplug." (The controlling idea is the same in both: dogs can be difficult. And while the second sentence is far more interesting, don't be misled into believing that long is better. It's more often the other way around.)

The conclusion of a paragraph is almost as important as the beginning. It should let the reader know he or she is finished, that the writer has made his point and is finished too. Don't let a paragraph on mastering basic English wind down to nothing. Beef it up with a summary of the controlling idea. For example, if you are writing a paragraph on the benefits of learning standard English, don't conclude with your last-mentioned benefit, that you will do better in your personal relations. Conclude with a bang. "You can see that if you master the basics of standard English, you will be well on your way to success in college, on the job, and in your personal relations. This is one language you can't afford not to learn." (Note the interest injected by the double negative = a positive.)

Usually **selecting the title** comes after you have written the conclusion, but sometimes you have in mind a good title even before you start writing. Try to make it something that will grab the prospective reader's attention (just like the first sentence) because it is natural for readers to pick up the reading matter that has the most interesting title. They may not even get as far as the attention-grabbing first sentence if the title doesn't turn them on. A good title should either tell what the paragraph is about in an interesting way or should be provocative enough to make the reader want to find out what the paragraph is about.

One error that students sometimes make is to put the topic sentence in the title and then neglect to put it in the paragraph—for example, title the paragraph "Censorship Is Wrong" and then launch into examples without ever stating the topic sentence in the paragraph. The topic sentence must be in the paragraph too.

QUIZ YOURSELF ON STEP TWO   Fill in the blanks.

_____ **1.** The single most important thing in writing a unified paragraph is (a) having seven sentences in the paragraph. (b) using short sentences. (c) having all the sentences helping develop the topic sentence.

_____ **2.** T or F. The topic sentence of a paragraph should always come first to give the reader a clue as to what is coming.

_____ **3.** Descriptive paragraphs and some narrative paragraphs are likely to have (a) no stated topic sentence. (b) a topic sentence in the middle. (c) a topic sentence that is an incomplete sentence.

_____ **4.** Name as many as you can of the 10 common methods of developing paragraphs.

_____   _____

_____   _____

_____   _____

_____   _____

In 5, 6, and 7, explain the three patterns of organization for paragraphs.

5. _____

_____

6. _____

_____

7. _____

_____

8. Why is the beginning of a paragraph so important? _____

_____

9. Why must the writer conclude the paragraph with care? _____

_____

10. Why is a good title important? _____

Answers on page 68.

Step Three: From Better Paragraph to Best

Every paragraph has a subject; every paragraph has a controlling idea or topic sentence, expressed or understood, which provides unity for the paragraph. Every paragraph should reflect the tone of the writer (the writer's attitude toward the subject) and be appropriate to the purpose the writer hopes to achieve with the audience at which the writing is aimed.

Every paragraph should be clear (easily understandable) and coherent (each part supporting the controlling idea and each part flowing easily into the next part, to achieve a whole that is both logically and smoothly put together). And every paragraph should be creative (with original ideas written in an innovative manner).

There are 10 common methods of development for paragraphs (and compositions), and within each method of development, sentences may be arranged according to three patterns of organization. Very often the methods of development and the patterns of organization overlap. You can see that the combinations are limitless. You have many choices to make. That is the fun of writing.

Ten Student Paragraphs, the Best

Next we will consider student-written paragraphs developed by the 10 common methods. There is one of each method here. Don't forget, these paragraphs are the best these students could produce at the end of the course after having had a great deal of help from their fellow students and instructor.

1. #32952-060

by Daniel Rode

1   The steel door slammed shut with a hollow thunk, and
2 a chill ran down my spine. One dim light bulb swung slowly
3 from the stained ceiling. At first I was numb, but as the

4   echo of the clanking keys faded, a sinking feeling crept
5   over me. I was trapped, and there was nothing I could do
6   to get out. I stared blankly at the filthy cement walls.
7   The rubbery tan paint had peeled in spots, exposing
8   patches of dirty green. Profane graffiti covered the rest
9   of this windowless pit like sickening wallpaper. I lay
10 down on the dank gray floor. The concrete was hard against
11 my cheek. I could feel my joints stiffen and begin to ache
12 as the chilling dampness seeped into my body. As I lay
13 there, mesmerized by isolation, a part of me faded away;
14 something in me died. . . . No apology can ever repair this
15 damage. No amount of money can ever buy back what I lost
16 in that dungeon of cement and steel. There is no such
17 thing as "a simple case of mistaken identity."

EXERCISE 1.28   Fill in the blanks.

1. What is the controlling idea, the topic sentence? _____

_____

2. Is the topic sentence at the beginning or at the end of the paragraph?

_____

3. Which of the 10 methods of development is/are predominant?

_____

4. What pattern/patterns of organization (chronological, by importance,
spatial) predominate? _____

5. What can you say about the writer's use of words or effectiveness of
sentences? _____

_____

6. What are the strong or weak points of this paragraph? _____

_____

Answers on page 68.

2. Don't Change That Channel!
by Azeb Taffere

1   The bed isn't made, breakfast dishes clutter the
2 kitchen sink, last week's laundry is stacked on the
3 washing machine, newspapers litter the floor, the vacuum
4 stands lonesome in the middle of the dining room—but it's
5 time for Alem's favorite soap opera. She *has* to find out
6 who is going to end up with Laura's husband; she also *has*
7 to finish her homework before the end of the next show.
8 She got a job working nights and signed up for one early-
9 morning course so that nothing would interfere with her
10 soaps, but the homework *would* interfere if she'd let it.
11 She wonders idly, after Laura's encounter with Jeff's
12 wife, why she isn't getting better grades. . . . If the
13 "show" fits, put it on. If you are anything like Alem, you
14 are a television addict.

EXERCISE 1.29 Fill in the blanks.

1. What is the controlling idea, the topic sentence? _____

_____

2. Is the topic sentence at the beginning or at the end of the paragraph?

_____

3. Which of the 10 methods of development is/are predominant? _____

_____

4. What pattern/patterns of organization (chronological, by importance,

spatial) predominate? _____

5. What can you say about the writer's use of words or effectiveness of sentences? _____

_____

6. What are the strong or weak points of this paragraph? _____

_____

Answers on page 69.

---

3. Road Signs to Reading
by Daniel Brennan

1   Just as it would be pretty rough-riding to drive
2 without road signs, it would also be pretty rough-reading
3 to understand written material without punctuation and
4 paragraphs. Periods are like stop signs; you must come to
5 a complete stop, look both ways, and, if necessary, let
6 cross traffic through. A semicolon brings you to a
7 somewhat shorter stop; after only a brief pause, you may
8 be on your way. A traffic light is like the end of a
9 paragraph; you must stop for longer than at a period or
10 semicolon, and the road ahead may take a different turn.
11 Commas are slippery-when-wet signs; you must slow down to
12 navigate safely. Exclamation points are like signs showing
13 the road reversing its direction or winding like a snake—
14 danger! Question marks are the construction-next-five-
15 miles signs; you're never sure what may be in store.
16 Dashes indicate a detour in thought. Without the reader's
17 even realizing it, punctuation makes the trip easier. Can
18 you imagine driving without road signs?

EXERCISE 1.30 Fill in the blanks.

1. What is the controlling idea, the topic sentence? _____

_____

2. Is the topic sentence at the beginning or at the end of the paragraph?

_____

3. Which of the 10 methods of development is/are predominant?

_____

4. What pattern/patterns of organization (chronological, by importance, spatial) predominate? _____

5. What can you say about the writer's use of words or effectiveness of sentences? _____

_____

6. What are the strong or weak points of this paragraph? _____

_____

Answers on page 69.

4. Weighing the Odds

by Tracy Rubin

1   The definition of overweight is "More weight than is
2 desired, needed or allowed; surplus weight." Over the
3 years, society has distorted this definition to mean lazy,
4 unintelligent, and undesirable. This discrimination occurs
5 in every facet of an overweight person's life. Job
6 interviews are rough enough for a thin person but are a
7 no-win situation for the fat applicant, who is often
8 viewed as lazy and unintelligent. All other things being
9 equal, guess who gets the job. And relationships are as
10 hard to come by as jobs. The overweight person is thought

11 to be jolly and not in need of friends. A romantic

12 attachment with a fat person is viewed as degrading. Just

13 as degrading is trying to find clothes. Large-size clothes

14 are not only hard to find, but they are very expensive and

15 usually outdated and ugly. All this discrimination against

16 the fat person makes it hard for us to fit not only into

17 clothes but also into the whole scene of today's thin-

18 oriented society.

EXERCISE 1.31 Fill in the blanks.

1. What is the controlling idea, the topic sentence? _____

_____

2. Is the topic sentence at the beginning or at the end of the paragraph?

_____

3. Which of the 10 methods of development is/are predominant?

_____

4. What pattern/patterns of organization (chronological, by importance, spatial) predominate? _____

5. What can you say about the writer's use of words or effectiveness of sentences? _____

_____

6. What are the strong or weak points of this paragraph? _____

_____

Answers on page 69.

---

5. All the World Needs One

by Karen Hamsho

1   I think I'd always wanted to be a clown, but it was

2 only a couple of months ago that I learned my best friend
3 Colleen had the same secret desire. After all, you don't
4 go greeting even your good friends with, "You wanta be a
5 clown?" Colleen and I created costumes and worked with
6 makeup, and before very long Snickers and Doodles were
7 born. On our way to our first adventure, entertaining the
8 patients at Sunny Acres, an extended-care hospital, I had
9 to stop by school to pick up a book, and we were invited
10 to visit the Child Care Center. We were so successful that
11 by the time we were ready to leave, most of the kids would
12 have followed us home. As we walked through the building
13 and out to our car, we tried to clown with some of the
14 senior citizens who had had a program that day on campus.
15 Some looked the other way and tried to pretend we didn't
16 exist; others asked suspiciously what we wanted but turned
17 to avoid any answer. We left, disappointed that we were
18 such a flop with the older crowd. But as we walked into
19 the hospital, someone shouted, "Here come the clowns."
20 Enthusiasm skyrocketed. The patients, many of whom were
21 senior citizens, reached toward us to be touched. We
22 clowned, they giggled, they laughed, they clung to us. We
23 could only conclude that these adults, like the children,
24 could relate to our clumsiness and our imperfection,
25 whereas we made the unimpaired adults feel uneasy as we
26 invaded their more sophisticated territory. Perhaps all
27 the world needs a clown and just doesn't know it.

EXERCISE 1.32 Fill in the blanks.

1. What is the controlling idea, the topic sentence? _____

_____

2. Is the topic sentence at the beginning or at the end of the paragraph?

_____

3. Which of the 10 methods of development is/are predominant?

_____

4. What pattern/patterns of organization (chronological, by importance, spatial) predominate? _____

5. What can you say about the writer's use of words or effectiveness of sentences? _____

_____

6. What are the strong or weak points of this paragraph? _____

_____

Answers on page 70.

6. There Is Life After Divorce
by Maria A. Casarona

1   How could I ever get along without Tom after 10 years
2 of marriage and now a divorce? It's been two years, and it
3 still isn't easy, but it can be done. You have to be both
4 mother and father to Daddy's little girl and to Mama's
5 darling boy. You have to learn how to talk earned-run
6 averages and TDs scored. You have to be stern when the
7 budding nurse has the kid next door undressed on the
8 "operating table." You have to hug with the left arm and
9 spank with the right hand. You make the time spent with
10 your children more productive than you ever thought it
11 could be. You do the laundry, grocery shop, and go to the
12 park with hot chocolate and marshmallows all in one
13 afternoon. If you want any semblance of an adult social

14   life, you must first provide a caretaker for the two most
15   important beings in your life. You get used to juggling
16   because one job plus child support doesn't stretch very
17   far. But when the child with the hole in his shoe and the
18   other in the outgrown blouse put their arms around you and
19   say, "I love you, Mommy," you know you must have done
20   something right.

EXERCISE 1.33 Fill in the blanks.

1. What is the controlling idea, the topic sentence? _____

_____

2. Is the topic sentence at the beginning or at the end of the paragraph?

_____

3. Which of the 10 methods of development is/are predominant?

_____

4. What pattern/patterns of organization (chronological, by importance, spatial) predominate? _____

5. What can you say about the writer's use of words or effectiveness of sentences? _____

_____

6. What are the strong or weak points of this paragraph? _____

_____

Answers on page 70.

---

7. The Power to Heal

by Stephanie Smith (a pseudonym)

1   As I looked in the mirror and realized it was made of
2   stainless steel instead of glass, I knew that this was not

3 the Waldorf or the Ritz but rather Section Two of the
4 psychiatric hospital, and glass was not permitted here. At
5 first, I was reluctant to leave the sanctuary of my room
6 even to eat, let alone to play volleyball or join in the
7 sing-along. Acceptance gradually lured me out of my fear.
8 One day Rob gave me the small plastic vase he had won in
9 bingo because I hadn't won any prize. Jane and Sue, about
10 my age, shared talk about family, school, jobs, and
11 clinical depression. Tom, large and burly, with a temper
12 it was said sometimes had to be restrained by the guards,
13 gently helped me fit together the parts of the bird feeder
14 I was clumsily building in occupational therapy. As the
15 days passed, trust and patience deepened. We dispensed
16 support and optimism to each other. We were heartened by
17 each other's little successes and commiserated with each
18 other's difficulties. The morning of my discharge, my
19 friends gathered in the hall to see me off, with hugs,
20 tears, and expressions of encouragement. The heavy metal
21 door clanged shut behind me. Already I missed them. I
22 tried to analyze what had united us so beautifully. On the
23 inside, we no longer needed to keep our guard up, to
24 conceal our pain or mask our fears. And with this freedom,
25 we found the capacity to reach out and heal each other as
26 no one from the "normal" world could.

EXERCISE 1.34 Fill in the blanks.

1. What is the controlling idea, the topic sentence? _____

_____

2. Is the topic sentence at the beginning or at the end of the paragraph?

_____

3. Which of the 10 methods of development is/are predominant?

_____

4. What pattern/patterns of organization (chronological, by importance, spatial) predominate? _____

5. What can you say about the writer's use of words or effectiveness of sentences? _____

_____

6. What are the strong or weak points of this paragraph? _____

_____

Answers on page 71.

Answers on page 71.

8. The Lesson

by Wendy Carbone

1   Large droplets of rain poured from the dark gray sky,
2 and an eerie heaviness hung in the air. Last night's
3 dishes, a pile of dirty clothes, an ironing board heaped
4 with wrinkled clothes, and a floor badly needing scrubbing
5 waited for me. It all seemed so menial, so unimportant, so
6 petty. My mood matched the weather. The doorbell rang, and
7 I opened the door to a man in a blue uniform. We exchanged
8 hellos, and I got ready to sign for the package he was
9 holding. Suddenly he dropped the package, shoved the door
10 wide open, and pushed past me, nearly knocking me to the
11 floor. His hand hovered over his pocket, as if ready to
12 pull out a gun. I froze while he made his way to the
13 dining room and packed my silver in a bag. As he was on
14 his way to the bedroom, and to my jewelry, I screamed. I
15 felt someone shaking me. I was in bed. "You've had a

16 nightmare," said my husband. I just lay there, too
17 relieved to speak. I looked out the window. The sun was
18 coming up. It was going to be a beautiful day. I couldn't
19 wait to get started with my chores.

EXERCISE 1.35 Fill in the blanks.

1. What is the controlling idea, the topic sentence? _____

_____

2. Is the topic sentence at the beginning or at the end of the paragraph?

_____

3. Which of the 10 methods of development is/are predominant?

_____

4. What pattern/patterns of organization (chronological, by importance, spatial) predominate? _____

5. What can you say about the writer's use of words or effectiveness of sentences? _____

_____

6. What are the strong or weak points of this paragraph? _____

_____

Answers on page 71.

---

9. I've Been There

by Toby Taylor

1   I want to be a social worker, and I think I can
2 convince you I'll be a good one. I'd like to work with
3 addicts or in some preventive program that would help
4 youths learn to cope before they end up in gangs or in the
5 court system for drug offenses. Or I would like to help

6   convicts, while they are incarcerated, deal not just with

7   their "time" but rather with real preparation for

8   reentering the community, not just with their drug or

9   alcohol problem but with housing, job, community reaction,

10 family, parole, and probation. What are my qualifications?

11 My family was loving and caring, and I was taught to

12 practice the Golden Rule but also to stand up for my

13 beliefs. We were somewhere between middle- and upper-

14 middle-class (my father was an engineer and my mother a

15 teacher), and though I wanted for nothing, I was taught

16 not be extravagant. If you are thinking that doesn't sound

17 like such a great background for a social worker, who will

18 have to find help for those who are down-and-out, you

19 might be right except for the fact that there's more to my

20 story. I am a recovering addict (four years clean), an ex-

21 convict (for drug-related offenses), and a former homeless

22 person who has lived in complete poverty. With the values

23 my family instilled in me, I managed to pull myself back

24 to a useful life, including college at age 40. True, I'm

25 off to a late start, but I'll make up for it. As a social

26 worker, I know I'll be one of the best. I've been there.

EXERCISE 1.36 Fill in the blanks.

1. What is the controlling idea, the topic sentence? _____

_____

2. Is the topic sentence at the beginning or at the end of the paragraph?

_____

3. Which of the 10 methods of development is/are predominant?

_____

4. What pattern/patterns of organization (chronological, by importance, spatial) predominate? _____

5. What can you say about the writer's use of words or effectiveness of sentences? _____

_____

6. What are the strong or weak points of this paragraph? _____

_____

Answers on page 71.

---

10. A Bargain in Entertainment

by Anne P. Andrews

1 My skinny purse is stretched until it squeaks with
2 pain, but it's worth it. Keeping four brown squirrels in
3 peanuts and sunflower seeds is an expense no college
4 student should have to bear, but the result is a show
5 worthy of an Oscar or an Emmy. Every morning and every
6 afternoon late, I make four piles of squirrel food in the
7 front yard. First comes Lady, a gentle little girl who
8 sits on her haunches with front paws folded as if she is
9 saying grace before eating. Daintily she picks up a nut or
10 a sunflower seed and deliberately eats it before she takes
11 another. Then comes Hobo, a real bum who shows up one day
12 and then maybe not for two or three days. He obviously has
13 others to mooch from. His tail looks as if a dog had dined
14 on it at some time or other. He stuffs himself
15 gluttonously, then zips on down the street like a commuter
16 about to miss his bus. Third is Snatch, who crouches over
17 his food, eyeing the others from side to side as he

18 nibbles. When the others aren't looking, he scoots over
19 and steals their food, after which he demolishes his own,
20 bent protectively over it so no one can pull a snatch on
21 him. Scamp is the fourth, the fattest, and the naughtiest.
22 When he finishes his pile of food, he takes his plump
23 belly up the blue spruce to the chickadee feeding platform
24 to scrounge anything he can find there. Then he jumps to
25 the awning, where two tube bird feeders hang and, like a
26 bushy-tailed Tarzan, swings on one and peers in the
27 kitchen window, saying very plainly that he wants an
28 encore. Where else could you get a show like this for mere
29 peanuts?

EXERCISE 1.37 Fill in the blanks.

1. What is the controlling idea, the topic sentence? _____

_____

2. Is the topic sentence at the beginning or at the end of the paragraph?

_____

3. Which of the 10 methods of development is/are predominant?

_____

4. What pattern/patterns of organization (chronological, by importance,
   spatial) predominate? _____

5. What can you say about the writer's use of words or effectiveness of
   sentences? _____

_____

6. What are the strong or weak points of this paragraph? _____

_____

Answers on page 72.

In Chapter 2 on writing compositions, you will find that all your practice in putting paragraphs together will make building compositions out of paragraphs quite easy for you. It's just a matter of doing the same thing you've been doing but on a bigger scale. Paragraphs are minicompositions. You are ready to write unified, clear, coherent, creative compositions.

QUIZ YOURSELF ON STEP THREE Fill in the blanks.

_____ **1.** T or F. Almost every paragraph contains only one method of development.

2. What is process (as a method of paragraph development)?

_____

3. What is classification (as a method of paragraph development)?

_____

4. What is analysis (as a method of paragraph development)?

_____

5. Which of the 10 common methods of development would be appropriate

for a paragraph on your friend's antique jalopy? _____

_____

6. Which of the 10 common methods of development would be appropriate

for a paragraph on life as a beachcomber versus life as a businessman or

businesswoman? _____

7. Teaching the reader the fine art of flying a kite would utilize which method

of development? _____

8. A paragraph on foods that commonly are responsible for allergic reactions

in young children might make use of which two methods of development?

_____

9. What is the pattern of organization (chronological, by importance, or

spatial) most commonly used with the narrative method of development?

_____

_____**10.** T or F. It has been strongly hinted several times in this chapter that paragraphs and compositions are very much alike in their construction. This should make Chapter 2 on compositions easy for you to get along with.

Answers on page 72.

Answers to Exercises

Possible Answers to Exercise 1.1, page 4

Of course, no one can answer this exercise for you; but if I had kept a journal this past week, five of my topics would certainly be **(1)** the telephone frustration of being kept on hold for an eternity, then hearing a "click" of disconnection; **(2)** the excitement of finding an occasional Indian arrowhead, recalled upon receiving a letter from a childhood friend whose family, like mine, vacationed in Northern Michigan; **(3)** reasons for letting students withdraw or be withdrawn by the instructor even though the fifth week of the term has passed; **(4)** the hope that all establishments where people must line up to be waited on may some day have one line, the way banks do, from which customers can be taken, fairly, in order of their arrival; **(5)** the satisfaction of doing a favor, something you would never be expected to do, for a person you hardly know.

Possible Answers to Exercise 1.3, page 10

1. Public school summer vacations of three months allow time for older students to get jobs and valuable working experience. OR Public school summer vacations are wasteful of the students' time and of the school's faculties and facilities.

2. Every woman should have the right to decide for herself whether or not to have an abortion. OR Abortion is murder and should not be permitted except in cases of rape or incest, or if it is necessary to save the mother's life.

3. It's about time the U.S. Postal Service began to recognize well-known popular heroes on its stamps. OR It's disrespectful to put Elvis on stamps in the same company with United States presidents and great scientists and other men and women who have made significant contributions to society.

4. Crowning a queen adds considerably to the glamor and excitement of homecoming weekend. OR The crowning of a queen at homecoming should be discontinued because on almost every campus her (or in a few cases his) selection is just a matter of politics.

5. The federal government should provide more financial aid for college students because many worthy students are being deprived of higher education, with grants and loans so hard to come by. OR Students should work their way through college instead of getting in the habit of relying on the government for a handout.

Answers to Exercise 1.10, page 24

1. Yes, I think we get a realistic picture of what Bill's dad was like, his good and his bad characteristics. Words to describe him might be *tough but tender, family oriented, loving, rigid but flexible, role model with high standards,* etc.

2. The topic sentence is "In spite of his bad habits and his attempts to be stern, he was the greatest, most loving dad in the world."

3. The topic sentence is located at the beginning of the paragraph, in the last part of the first sentence.

4. Preceding the topic sentence, in the first part of the first sentence, is an attention grabber, a main clause with four verbs that startle the reader into wanting to read the paragraph.

5. Yes, the sentences all help develop the topic sentence and lead into the hug at home base, which shows that this man was a great dad.

Answers to Quiz Yourself on Step One, page 25

1. A paragraph is a group of sentences all developing a single controlling idea about the subject. 2. The controlling idea. At the beginning of the paragraph. 3. c. 4. b. 5. Choosing a subject and a controlling idea, strengthening the controlling idea, outlining, writing the rough draft, revising and correcting the rough draft, and writing the final draft.

Answers to Exercise 1.12, page 26

1. The reaction of most readers would be, What is she trying to tell me?

2. I defy you to find a topic sentence, one controlling idea for the whole paragraph. The meaning of each sentence is clear, but the thoughts lead nowhere. You can't make an outline from this even *after* the fact, which, by the way, is not recommended procedure for outlining. It flips from "English is unnecessary" to "I'm scared" to "High school was fun" to "I have a lot on my mind" to "I don't react quickly any more." If you want to write about cheerleading or chickenpox, go ahead, but don't mix them up with coming back to school. It's 11 o'clock; do you know where your topic sentence is?

3. The words are clear for almost any audience. The only clue we have as to the author's purpose is her complaining, worried tone; the language is appropriate enough for that. There is little creativity in choice of words and some positive noncreativity: *driving me up a wall, advanced age.*

4. The sentences are somewhat varied in structure, but there are far too many short sentences, which makes for a bit of choppiness in reading. The last five sentences are short simple sentences.

5. Grammatically, it's okay, which proves that good grammar doth not necessarily a good paragraph make. However, let me emphasize, bad grammar *doth* a bad paragraph make.

Answers to Exercise 1.13, page 28

1. You can undoubtedly describe your reaction better than I can.

2. Like the paragraph preceding this one, there is no topic sentence. The writer first prefers cats as friends, then dogs for safety, then cats for cleanliness, then dogs as nonclawers and a better investment and more loyal, then both as security guards, then dogs for improving the atmosphere, then cats for softness, then a person rather than either a cat or a dog.

3. Since we don't know what the writer's purpose is, this is hard to answer. I guess the best answer is that writing like this is not suitable for any purpose or any audience. As for creativity in choice of words, or lack thereof, *through thick and thin* is a cliché; there are many unnecessary words in the redundant expressions mentioned in No. 5; there is lack of consistency throughout the paragraph, including the number of cats owned, first one, then two. But let's end on a positive note: the third sentence about cats taking their job of catching mice very seriously is interesting and effective.

4. The sentence structure is varied and might be all right if all the sentences were complete and otherwise correct.

5. There are two fragments: *Although cats are mostly loners* and *Whenever you need them.* There are several redundancies: *a farm in the country, In fact . . . to be precise, To me I feel. . . , In my opinion I feel. . . , a better investment for your money, loners who like to be by themself, finally in conclusion, In my own case I believe.* There is no such word as *themself* (see page 415). *Affect* is used for *effect* (see page 398).

Answers to Exercise 1.14, page 29

1. The (circled) topic sentence is "There are right ways and wrong ways to shake [hands]."

2. The two (underlined) sentences that are unrelated to the topic sentence are the following: "Early politicians dipped their right hand in pickle juice to toughen the skin" and "If you want to avoid the stupid air kiss that is threatening to replace the good old handshake, place your left hand on the forearm of the would-be kisser to keep him or her at a distance, and shake away."

Answers to Exercise 1.15, page 30

1. The (circled) topic sentence, located in the first sentence and repeated in another form in the next-to-last sentence (which should have been the last sentence), is "Presidents of the United States and presidential hopefuls through the years have shown quite different styles of handshaking."

2. The (underlined) last sentence about women is irrelevant to the topic sentence. Many beginning writers have the bad habit of tacking on at the end of a paragraph a statement that is only distantly related to the topic sentence. The other (underlined) irrelevant sentence deals with kissing babies.

Answers to Exercise 1.16, page 31

The *No* sentences are **1, 6,** and **8.** The best order for the *Yes* sentences is **5, 7, 4, 3, 2.**

Answers to Exercise 1.17, page 31

(1) The topic sentence might be, "As college students, we have considerably more freedom than we did in high school." **(2)** Do.

Answers to Exercise 1.18, page 32

(1) The topic sentence might be, "Although stamp collecting has been called 'the hobby of kings and the king of hobbies,' it is not for everyone." **(2)** Do.

Answers to Exercise 1.19, page 33

(1) The topic sentence might be, "There is nothing more beautiful than the innocence of a small child." **(2)** Do.

Answers to Exercise 1.20, page 35

b. Censorship has never worked and probably never will. **c.** As far back as the eighth century B.C., attempts were made to clean up the *Odyssey* for immature readers. **e.** You may recall that since the early part of this century, books banned in Boston have immediately hit the bestseller list. **g.** And attempts to ban racy books in other cities have not succeeded in putting the publications out of circulation. **a.** In 1974 religious fundamentalists in Kanawha County, W. Va., forced from the county's schools *The Three Little Pigs* (too much violence) and *Pinocchio* (parental disobedience; Pinocchio disobeys his creator, the woodcarver Geppetto); but these children's classics refused to go out of style. **f.** Most recently under fire has been an illustration in which Little Red Riding Hood's basket appears to contain a bottle of wine. **d.** The good news is, despite wine-guzzling grannies and huffing-puffing-house-blowing-down wolves, libraries and school systems manage to keep on their shelves, available to the public, 90 percent of the material challenged by would-be censors.

1. __b__   5. __a__
2. __c__   6. __f__
3. __e__   7. __d__
4. __g__

The topic sentence, Censorship has never worked and probably never will, is reinforced (restated in a different form) by the last sentence.

Answers to Exercise 1.21, page 36

d. If ever I am in the vicinity of Hyatt Legal Services, I'd have every reason to stop in and start divorce proceedings. **f.** Why? My wife begins her day by refusing to get out of bed. **b.** The sun is straight up as are both hands of the clock when she finally ambles to the bathroom, fills the tub to the top with scalding water, and then reads the morning paper while the water cools, wasting all kinds of energy except, of course, her own. **g.** After she is dressed, she drives to the nearby mall by way of a fast-food drive-in, whose cups and wrappers provide more debris to adorn her already-messy car. **a.** While we are on the subject of messes, her idea of cleaning house is moving the magazines she reads the rest of the afternoon from one pile on the floor to another. **c.** And when dinnertime comes, she's a whiz at thawing something in the microwave. **e.** All of this may be grounds for divorce; but to tell the truth, I'd never consider leaving her—we love each other too much.

1. __d__   5. __a__
2. __f__   6. __c__
3. __b__   7. __e__
4. __g__

   The topic sentence (paraphrased) is split: "I'd have every reason to get a divorce" is the first sentence; "but I love her too much ever to leave her" is the last sentence, making a clever surprise ending.

Answers to Exercise 1.22, page 36

1. The generosity of a person who so badly needed help himself had set our values straight.
2. At the end.
3. Having the topic sentence at the end makes for suspense throughout the paragraph and makes the reader want to keep going.
4. The tone, at first cold and complaining and then upbeat and warm, is very appropriate. The title, plucked from the story, is good.
5. The sentence structure is varied, interesting, and easy to read.

Answers to Exercise 1.23, page 39

1. Honesty is the best policy.
2. Suspense is created to keep the reader reading to the end.
3. Unnecessary words are saved; the topic sentence is quite clear without being stated.

Answers to Exercise 1.24, page 43

1. Narration, with a bit of comparison and contrast. 2. Description. 3. Process. 4. Examples. 5. Examples. 6. Narration. 7. Narration. 8. Narration.

Answers to Exercise 1.26, page 44

1. Chronological + in order of importance, from least to most.

2. In order of importance, from least to most.

3. Certainly not chronological or in order of importance. Spatial, inasmuch as consideration of handshakes almost goes from left to right. Not the best example of spatial.

4. Chronological.

5. Chronological.

6. Chronological in a 24-hour period.

7. Chronological + in order of importance, from least to most, + a bit spatial since walking up and down streets is involved.

8. Chronological + in order of importance, from least to most.

Answers to Quiz Yourself on Step Two, page 46

1. c.

2. F.

3. a.

4. Examples, definition, process, classification and analysis, comparison and contrast, cause and effect, narration, description, analogy, argumentation.

5. Chronological organization is arranging sentences in a paragraph by time, in the order in which events happen.

6. Organizing by order of importance or complexity is arranging sentences in a paragraph from most to least or from least to most important or complex.

7. Organizing spatially is arranging sentences in a paragraph so that the subject is seen from left to right, from up to down or down to up, from north to south, or from head to tail.

8. The beginning of a paragraph makes the reader either want to read on or not.

9. The reader must feel that the writer's ideas on the subject have been clearly and completely conveyed.

10. An interesting title makes the reader want to read the paragraph.

Answers to Exercise 1.28, page 48

1. A miscarriage of justice causes irreparable psychological damage to the victim.

2. At the end.

3. Description.

4. Spatial.

5. Dan's use of words is excellent. Concrete language makes us hear the hollow thunk and the clanking keys, makes us see the dim light bulb and the peeling paint, and makes us feel the hard concrete (concrete language *usually* doesn't have anything

to do with concrete; it is language that appeals to the senses) and the chilling damp-ness. With the exception of the word *mesmerized*, the language is fairly simple and straightforward, as it should be in telling a stark story. Sentence length is varied and interesting.

6. The strongest point is its description, especially of the surroundings but also of his feelings. Dan paints a vivid picture in very few words.

Answers to Exercise 1.29, page 49

1. This is what a television addict is like.

2. At the end.

3. Definition, description.

4. Spatial in the description of the room, chronological in Alem's activities.

5. The vocabulary seems right for the purpose of this paragraph. The use of sentences is good. By the way, the first sentence is not a collection of comma splices; it is all right to connect short sentences in a series like that with commas.

6. The strong point is a good description of a television addict that most readers can identify with. A TV addict is defined.

Answers to Exercise 1.30, page 51

1. Punctuation and paragraphs make reading easier just as road signs make driving easier.

2. At the beginning, repeated in a different form at the end.

3. Analogy, with the analogy developed by examples.

4. Spatial.

5. The repetition (of marks of punctuation) could have been deadly, but Dan has han-dled it rather well, with only slight monotony.

6. The strong point is the use of analogy to compare punctuation, the proper use of which is probably something of a mystery to many people, with road signs, which we are all familiar with.

Answers to Exercise 1.31, page 52

1. Overweight people are discriminated against.

2. In the third sentence, after two interesting, if not attention-grabbing, sentences. It is restated in an interesting way at the end.

3. It appears to start as definition, is also cause and effect, but is really much more ex-amples: jobs, relationships, clothes.

4. More spatial than anything else, as if Tracy were looking around and seeing places where she finds discrimination. It isn't chronological; and it can't be by importance, or the most important area of discrimination in my opinion (relationships) would not be in the middle.

5. The sentences could be more varied. Of the 12 sentences, nine are simple (a bit choppy in spots), two are complex, and one is compound.

6. I think the paragraph would be better organized if it were by importance, with relationships first, then jobs, then clothes, in descending importance. However, the examples are good, and the reader feels the writer's plight. This writer, incidentally, is now working on her master's degree in career counseling.

Answers to Exercise 1.32, page 53

1. The world needs more clowning, more uninhibited happiness.

2. At the end.

3. Comparison and *contrast* mainly, some cause and effect, with narration used throughout as a vehicle for the contrast.

4. Chronological, but spatial too, with three different settings.

5. The wording is appropriate; most sentences are well done.

6. The first sentence is hardly exciting. Wouldn't one of these be more likely to make you want to read on? "'You wanta be a clown?' It's hardly a question you'd routinely ask your friends and acquaintances." OR "Snickers and Doodles were born after Colleen and I found we had the same secret desire: to be a clown." The end is good—concise and thought-provoking.

Answers to Exercise 1.33, page 55

1. It's hard, but a single mother can make a new life after divorce.

2. At the beginning, but emphasized at the end with the statement that she must have done something right.

3. Process, with some cause and effect.

4. It isn't chronological, and the arrangement doesn't seem to be by importance. That leaves spatial, with all the how-to accomplishments arranged in the space surrounding this single mother (a weak diagnosis on my part, I'm afraid). I believe the paragraph would be improved by putting the sentences in order of importance from least to most, from talking earned-run averages to being both mother and father. What do you think?

5. There are probably too many simple sentences—certainly too many *You have to*s and not enough *You make the time*s. The wording in the last sentence is very effective.

6. The weak points are the pattern of organization, described in 4, and the monotony of the language, described in 5. The strong point is the writer's success in getting her point across despite these weaknesses because of her interesting *how to*s. Obviously, it's a subject close to her heart.

Answers to Exercise 1.34, page 56

1. Deeply satisfying, healing relationships are possible when people can relax and be sincere with each other, no longer feeling they need to be on guard.

2. At the end.

3. It is cause and effect, told as a narrative, with examples.

4. Chronological.

5. Sentence structure is interesting and appropriate. The examples "Stephanie" gives as a means of showing instead of telling (Rob giving her his prize, the girls sharing their personal lives, Tom tenderly helping her put her bird feeder together), are good examples of how much more effective specific language is than generality (i.e., Rob was generous, the girls were compassionate, Tom was gentle).

6. The strengths of this paragraph are the subject, with which we all identify in a reverse way, hoping we won't need to spend time in a mental hospital, and the specific examples given to show the characteristics of the people who taught "Stephanie" about healing relationships.

Answers to Exercise 1.35, page 58

1. We don't appreciate what we have until someone or something threatens to take it away from us.

2. It is never expressed but is clearly understood from the narration.

3. Narration, plus cause and effect.

4. Chronological.

5. The words in the first four sentences about weather and mood and accumulated chores are extremely descriptive. When the action begins, the verbs become strong: *dropped, shoved, pushed, hovered, froze, screamed.* The sentences are varied, and the last eight short sentences give the reader a feeling of breathless relief.

6. There is good description in the first few sentences. The topic sentence is made very clear, though unstated, through the events. Words fit mood and action well.

Answers to Exercise 1.36, page 59

1. Toby argues he will make a good social worker.

2. Both at the beginning and at the end.

3. Argumentation.

4. Order of importance, from least to most.

5. Nothing spectacular, but okay. First sentence could be more exciting.

6. The strong point is his saying the reader may think his background is not sufficient, but immediately counteracting that by saying he has been in the situation of the people he wants to help. Then he says he knows he's getting a late start, but he'll make up for it. His seeing the possible flaws in his argument and refuting them lends strength to his position.

Answers to Exercise 1.37, page 61

1. Feeding squirrels produces a show that is well worth the money.
2. The topic sentence is the second sentence and is repeated in a different way in the last sentence.
3. Classification.
4. Spatial, looking at the squirrels, essentially, from left to right.
5. Sentences are varied in length and structure to maintain interesting reading. Use of descriptive words is excellent: *purse stretched until it squeaks, front paws folded as if she is saying grace, like a commuter about to miss his bus, bushy-tailed Tarzan.*
6. A good classification of four types of squirrels, determined by their eating habits, cleverly fitted into a pseudo complaint about the cost of feeding them.

Answers to Quiz Yourself on Step Three, page 62

1. F.
2. Process is the technique of telling "how to," how something is done or made.
3. Classification is writing about a group of people and things by breaking the group into subgroups or categories.
4. Analysis is writing about one item or idea by breaking it into its component parts.
5. Description.
6. Comparison and contrast, possibly a bit of cause and effect.
7. Process.
8. Examples and cause and effect.
9. Chronological.
10. T, very true.

2 The Composition

Step One: From Paragraph to Composition

Definition of a Composition

Just as a paragraph is a group of sentences all developing a single controlling idea about the subject, a **composition** is a group of paragraphs all developing a single controlling idea about the subject. The controlling idea in a paragraph is called the topic sentence. In a composition, the controlling idea is called the **thesis** or **thesis statement.** Just as the topic sentence of a paragraph must be a complete sentence, so the thesis of a composition must be a complete sentence. And like the topic sentence in a paragraph, the thesis in a composition is the point about the subject that the writer wants to get across to the reader. Also like the topic sentence of the paragraph, it usually comes at the beginning to let the reader know where he or she is going; but it may not come until the end, or it may not be expressed at all.

The steps for writing a composition are the same as the six steps for writing a paragraph (or any writing). The composition, of course, will be longer, consisting of more than one paragraph.

The Half Dozen Steps for Writing a Good Composition

1. Choosing the Subject and the Controlling Idea. The process of choosing a subject and a controlling idea for a composition is identical to that for a paragraph. If you can't think of anything to write about, look back at Step One in Chapter 1, and go through some of the steps recommended there: perhaps reading, or recalling, or observing, or keeping a journal, or free writing.

Even though a composition is longer than a paragraph, you still have to be careful to limit your subject to one that you can handle in the time and space you have. If you are interested in ecology, don't try to handle the whole field; perhaps you could write an argumentation paper saying we should do more about preserving the ozone layer, or a comparison and contrast paper on the problem of rubbish disposal 50 years ago versus the much more serious problem now.

Usually, the deeper the feelings you have about your subject, the more interesting your thesis will be. Be sure your thesis is not some indisputable fact that your reader, and everyone else, already believes: for example, "Weather predicting is not always 100 percent accurate" or "Birds have trouble finding food when the ground is covered with snow." Instead, you will want to develop a more specific thesis: "The weatherman's inaccurate prediction almost cost me my life," or "The chickadees are practically knocking on my window—that's how hard this winter has been on birds."

EXERCISE 2.1 In the blank write **S** if what follows would make a suitable thesis statement, **U** if it would be unsuitable. Remember that a thesis must be a complete sentence, but not every complete sentence is suitable for a thesis.

_____ **1.** My summer vacation.

_____ **2.** My summer vacation was a complete waste because I hadn't done my homework on resorts.

_____ **3.** I found a way to make my spring break pay double dividends—I not only slept late every morning, but I spent my afternoons learning to use my brother's computer.

_____ **4.** School vacations give students a break from their studies.

_____ **5.** Training a puppy.

_____ **6.** Training my dog was almost as much a matter of training me as of training him.

_____ **7.** Learning to type.

_____ **8.** Learning the keyboard should be compulsory by fourth grade.

_____ **9.** School psychologists can help students.

_____**10.** When I finally got up courage to visit the school psychologist, I learned why I am so paranoid about making telephone calls.

Answers on page 140.

EXERCISE 2.2 Create a good thesis from each of the following topics. If using two sentences makes the thesis clearer, that's all right.

1. Evaluation of instructors by students. _____

_____

2. Getting more education by enlisting in the armed services. _____

_____

3. Parents who make their children feel worthless. _____

_____

4. Children's TV shows filled with violence. _____

_____

5. A more user-friendly library. _____

_____

Possible answers on page 140.

EXERCISE 2.3 You have been assigned to write a composition on a topic of interest to you. Pretend (and you may not have to pretend) that you can't think of anything to write about. Start free writing, and see what ideas you come up with. List three ideas from your free writing that might be appropriate subjects for a composition:

1. _____

2. _____

3. _____

Now make up a thesis statement about each subject, what you think about the subject, what you want your reader to believe when he or she has finished your composition. Circle the number of the one thesis you want to develop into a composition.

1. _____

_____

2. _____

_____

3. _____

_____

Here is the way my student Ruthie Tanner handled the free writing and the selection of a subject and thesis. She let her mind wander wherever it would, paying no attention to grammar or spelling or *who*s and *whom*s.

Free Writing

How do I know what I want to write about? Maybe my job in the division Office at school. Nice job. Get to know faculty better. Most are super, a few a bit on the demanding side. Or the people at church. Could say almost the same thing about them—most are super, a few on the too holy, look down their nose side. Then there are classmates who you can't help but assiciate with, and friends who seem to be in the friendship for what they can get out of it, and friends who seem to be in the friendship for what they can give you—really want to do you favors. There are social friends and business friends and neighbors and intimate friends and acquaintances and lovers and relationships. Funny how many kinds of friends there are. But we all really need friends. How could we live without friends? Of course, we'd still have relatives, but the friendship of relatives is not exactly voluntary—it is forced upon you, and them, because of the fact they are family. It would be terrible to go through life with just family and no friends. That seems like a good thing to write about: we all need friends, many kinds of friends.

Ruthie is truly a "people" person, so it was natural that she should decide to write about friends.

2. Strengthening the Controlling Idea. Follow the same procedure as in writing paragraphs: double-check to be sure the subject and the thesis will convey your desired tone (your attitude toward your subject) and to be sure they fit your purpose and the audience for whom you are writing. The thesis must be a complete sentence. Sometimes it is clearly expressed in one sentence; sometimes the reader arrives at one thesis sentence by combining ideas from a couple of sentences in the composition.

Decide upon your method of development (the same 10 methods as for paragraphs, pages 40-43) and your pattern of organization (the same three patterns as for paragraphs, pages 43-44). Like paragraphs, hardly any compositions are developed by just one method; usually they use a couple of methods mixed together, like examples but with some description, or cause and effect held together by narration. The pattern of organization may also be a mixture.

Even if you had never heard of these methods of development or these patterns of organization, you would undoubtedly use them in writing—there's hardly any other way. But consciously developing your thesis according to a method and a pattern helps you end up with a better composition.

Ruthie decided her tone would be loving and sincere as she told about good friends, critical as she told about the types of "friends" that nobody needs or wants. Her purpose was to prove that friends are not a luxury but a necessity. Her audience? Who else? Her friends.

Classification seemed the appropriate method of development, and her pattern of organization would be order of importance, from the least valuable kinds of friendships to the most. She was ready to outline.

3. Outlining. If your instructor asks for a **formal outline** (on longer papers he or she probably will), there are three possibilities: a sentence outline, a topic outline, or a mixed outline.

A **sentence outline** uses complete sentences for the outline divisions. A **topic outline** uses words, phrases, or incomplete sentences for the outline divisions. A **mixed outline** uses complete sentences for major divisions, and uses words, phrases, or incomplete sentences for subdivisions. The following box illustrates outlining form.

I. Major topics are marked by Roman numerals.
  A. Then uppercase letters.
    1. Then Arabic numerals.
    2. Always at least two subtopics, can be more.
      a. Then lowercase letters.
      b. A second subtopic here, or any number of subtopics.
        (1) Arabic numeral in parentheses.
        (2) No period after number in parentheses.
          (a) Lowercase letter in parentheses.
          (b) About as detailed as outlines usually go.
            1) Arabic numeral with right parenthesis only.
            2) Again, no period with parenthesis.
              a) Lowercase letter with right parenthesis.
              b) Usually no more subdivisions needed.
  B. Must have B if there is an A.
II. Must have II if there is a I.
  A. Subtopics are successively indented, as shown.
  B. Need B if there is A; otherwise A combined with II.

The procedure for outlining compositions is the same as for paragraphs, minor ideas under major headings, all leading toward a unified development of the controlling idea. Compositions, being bigger than paragraphs, are usually divided into three sections: introduction, body, and conclusion. The outline below will show you how similar the organization of a paragraph is to the organization of a composition.

Paragraph	Composition
I. Introduction.	**I.** Introduction.
A. Attention-grabber.	**A.** Attention-grabber.
B. Strong, clear topic sentence.	**B.** Strong, clear thesis.
II. Body.	**II.** Body.
A. Sentence developing topic sentence (smooth flow to next sentence).	**A.** Paragraph developing thesis (smooth flow to next paragraph).
B. Sentence developing topic sentence (smooth flow to next sentence).	**B.** Paragraph developing thesis (smooth flow to next paragraph).
C. Sentence developing topic sentence (smooth flow to next sentence).	**C.** Paragraph developing thesis (smooth flow to next paragraph).
D. Sentence developing topic sentence (smooth flow to next sentence).	**D.** Paragraph developing thesis (smooth flow to next paragraph).
E. Fewer or more sentences as needed.	**E.** Fewer or more paragraphs as needed.
III. Conclusion, emphasizing topic sentence (or smooth flow to next paragraph, if this paragraph is part of a composition).	**III.** Conclusion, emphasizing thesis, restating it in different way.

Please note statement E in the outline above, "Fewer or more paragraphs as needed." Just as some students come to college English with the idea that paragraphs have to have five to seven sentences, so also some come believing that compositions come in no size other than five paragraphs. And just as five to seven sentences may be a fine length for a paragraph, so five paragraphs may be a fine length for a composition; but then again, it may not be. Content should determine length. You need at least three paragraphs if you are to separate introduction, body, and conclusion. A few students seem to believe that the longer the composition, the better the grade they will get. Not so. Tight writing (concise writing, no words wasted) is better—and harder to do.

EXERCISE 2.4 Using one of the thesis statements from Exercise 2.2 on page 75, develop an outline that could be the basis for a good paragraph.

Possible answer on page 140.

Here is **Ruthie's outline** for her composition about friendships. She seems to be trying to put all her friends and associates into orderly categories.

I. Introduction. Friendships are needed to provide us with entertainment and recreation companionship, community and religious support, business dealings, professional contacts, and intimate relationships. Friends are absolutely necessary to our well-being.

II. Body.
    A. Entertainment and recreation companionship.
    B. Community and religious support.
    C. Business dealings.
        1. People who can help financially.
        2. People who sell us what we need.
    D. Professional contacts.
        1. People who work or study where we do.
        2. People who are in the same line of work elsewhere.
        3. People who can serve as references for us.
    E. Intimate relationships.
        1. Sexual.
        2. Best friends.
III. Conclusion.

Ruthie got only that far with her outline—she hadn't started filling in A or B—when she realized she had bitten off much more than she could digest into a two- or three-page composition. She decided that instead of dividing friends into many categories (classification), she would write in depth on only one category, "best friends." Her paper would be developed by analysis rather than classification, with order of importance as her pattern of organization. She made a **new outline.**

I. Introduction. We need all kinds of friends, but "best" friends are, as you might expect from the name, best. Best friends are both givers and receivers.

II. Body.
    A. What best friends give.
        1. Understanding.
        2. Support.
        3. Material things.
        4. Time.
        5. Energy.
    B. What best friends receive.
        1. Us (as is).
        2. Our problems.
        3. Our beliefs.

C. Receiving sometimes more difficult than giving.

III. Conclusion. Best friends receive as well as give.

EXERCISE 2.5 Make an outline, formal or informal, of your composition. Be sure that your thesis is strengthened by attention to tone, purpose, and audience. Decide on a method of development and a pattern of organization. Then select and arrange your topics and subtopics for the most unity. Eliminate topics that don't directly relate to your thesis and don't help move it toward its complete development.

---

4. Writing the Rough Draft. Although one purpose of this book is to point out the importance of good English in the writing process, the rough draft of a composition, like the rough draft of a paragraph, should be done quickly from the outline without worry about correct grammar and mechanics. Just get your ideas down; corrections and revisions can come later.

I have had students tell me that they refuse ever to pay attention to the rules of grammar because to do so might stifle their creativity. I reply, "What good is creativity if the end product is so improper grammatically that the reader can't appreciate it?" Ah, but the rough draft—this is the place to let your creativity loose, knowing you will take care of semicolons and subordinate clauses later. But even in the final draft, creativity, as we learned in writing paragraphs, need not be stifled by writing correctly. Following is **Ruthie's rough draft.**

```
                            Friends


¶1       There are lots of kinds of friends, but we are lucky

    if we have a best friend. A best friend is a giver of

    time, loyalty, love, and support to enhance the life of

    another. But a best friend knows how to receive too.

¶2       A best friend expects nothing in return. One time a

    friend gave me a bag of bread, fresh home-baked,

    smelling-good bread!!! As I removed the bread from the

    bag, I noticed something different at the bottom of the

    bag. Thirty dollars tightly rolled up, waiting for me. My

    friend knew I was having a hard time making ends meet.

¶3       I have another friend who would call me every day,
```

any time of the day or night, just to talk about her life and her problems, but when I wanted to talk about anything, she was too busy and she always promised to call me back later which she never did. Which friend do you think was my best friend?

¶4   Best friends should receive as well as give. The friend who never listened to me was no good at receiving. Someone said that their best friend was their psychiatrist. Others have called their friend a sounding board because they could talk to that person and he or she would just listen for however long it took, and they did not have to pay one cent! That's how a best friend is a receiver. A best friend also doesn't try to change you or make you change your beliefs.

¶5   Best friends receive as well as give.

EXERCISE 2.6 Now write a rough draft of your composition. Follow your outline, but let your ideas flow freely. Just write. Don't worry about correct grammar or punctuation or spelling, but do be sure your writing maintains the unity of your outline, with every well-organized paragraph relating to the thesis and helping develop it.

---

5. Revising and Correcting the Rough Draft. Suggestions for revising and correcting the rough draft of the paragraph are valid for revising and correcting the rough draft of the composition too.

Do the revising first. Move paragraphs if they don't seem to follow your plan. Add or subtract paragraphs if necessary. You can still change arrangement or content, even your outline, if such changes make the composition more understandable or more interesting, keeping in mind your attitude toward your subject, your purpose, and your audience.

Be sure each paragraph in the composition is related to and helps develop the controlling idea, the thesis. If any paragraph fails to meet this test, "deep-six" it. If you need to add information to prove a point, find it (remember the library) and add it. If some of your material proves to be not completely relevant to your thesis but is *so* interesting you can't bear to part with it, perhaps your thesis

...ing so that the fascinating material then becomes relevant. Be sure ...h flows smoothly into the next.

...uction. Never underestimate the importance of the introduction. The ...ce is exceedingly important. With so many written works competing for ...you have only a sentence or two to make a reader decide to read what ...written. Sure, your instructor, a captive audience of one, is going to read ...he first sentence, no matter what. But instructors, too, look warmly on a ...us start.

...e thesis itself is not a real attention-grabber, start with a sentence that is, ...d by the thesis. A relevant quotation may make an interesting begin- ...or a surprise bit of information or a brief anecdote or a bit of humor— ...d to the thesis, of course. But beware of questions for starters; they must ...ly provocative, not foolish like, "Would you like to win a million dollars?" ...ttention-grabbing sentence preceding the thesis serves as an appetizer, teas- ...and easing the reader smoothly into the composition.

Suppose one composition began this way: "I lost all my keys the other day." ...ppose another began this way: "A key ring is a fiendish device that causes you ...lose, not just the key to your locker, not just the key to your car, not just the ...ey to your house, but all your keys at once." Which is more likely to make you ...vant to read on? The second one, I believe.

Suppose one composition began this way: "'We believe we have your ...daughter for you.' It's a voice on the phone. This is it. This is the call you've been ...waiting for. A year? Two years? A lifetime." Suppose another began this way: "We ...had to wait a long time to adopt our daughter." I think you'd be more likely to ...want to read the first one.

The Conclusion. With all the other things to remember about writing good com- positions, don't neglect the conclusion. The conclusion may be a summary of the main points or a restatement, in a different way, of the thesis. In argumentation, the conclusion is usually a call to action or a plea for a change of belief, in conformity with the thesis.

The conclusion of a composition is important because it wraps up the whole work and leaves the reader satisfied that no more need be said about the subject just now. For that reason, do not bring up a new subject at the end of a compo- sition. If you have been developing the thesis, "No one over 50 should be allowed to drive a car on any public road," don't sign off with a tale of how your 55-year old Aunt Minnie not only shouldn't be allowed to drive but also shouldn't be allowed to smoke for fear she will burn the house down.

Don't spare the revising. Revise and re-revise. Your writing will be better for it.

Now correct errors. Use the revision and correction checklists on pages 17- 18 in the chapter on paragraphs. If you have questions about the mechanics or the skills of writing, use the index and read about the solution to your problem in other chapters of this book.

Put the rough draft aside for as long as your deadline allows; then go back to it. Read it aloud. If you are in class or in the library, pretending you are reading it out loud may help you "hear" a mistake. Don't hesitate to do a second, improved rough draft and another and another.

Ruthie decided her rough draft had lost some of the unity of her outline, so she was careful to revise, including all the topics and subtopics of the outline and no irrelevant ones (the psychiatrist, for example). She corrected her grammatical mistakes. And then she came up with what she thought was a creative way to begin and end the composition.

Now see where your rough draft can be improved. Use the revision and correction checklists in preparation for writing the final draft. Once in a while, even at this late stage, you may find your ideas just aren't working. It may be better to start all over. That's okay—it's not a complete loss. You have learned what won't work for you.

6. Writing the Final Draft. Don't hesitate to write your final draft two or three times, as long as you can find anything to revise or correct. Improve words, improve sentences, improve paragraphs, improve arrangement, improve creativity—discover new and interesting ways of getting your message across.

And don't forget to attach a snappy title, either something fascinating that will tell what the composition is about, or something provocative enough to make the reader want to dip into the composition to see what it is about. Here is **Ruthie's final draft.**

```
        Far Be It From Me to Dispute the Bible, But . . .
```

¶1   It is not always more blessed to give than to receive, popular opinion notwithstanding. Best friends, participants in that most cherished of relationships, are often best when they are receiving.

¶2   True, best friends are those on whom we can count to give us understanding, give us support, give us material things we need and want, and give us time and energy by doing needed favors for us.

¶3   There is nothing more beautiful than a friend who gives freely of understanding. When we have a tragic death in the family, a best friend understands our need to grieve, our need to have someone to talk to and to cry with, our need later to be alone with our sorrow.

¶4   Or when we feel strongly that by winning a certain position, we could considerably improve the procedures for the whole organization, a best friend gives support in every way possible: designing campaign fliers, giving speeches in our behalf, promoting our candidacy with every possible means. Or the friend supports our heart-felt cause, helping rescue the environment, by starting a recycling program at our church.

¶5   When we need to pay the overdue gas bill but don't have the money, a best friend gives (gives, not loans) us the money. If we have admired a piece of jewelry while passing through a shopping mall, the friend buys it and tucks it away to give on our next birthday.

¶6   If we are running out of time for completing an English composition and finishing other homework due tomorrow, a best friend makes a gift of time by offering to type the final draft of the composition into the computer. If we are exhausted, too tired to fix dinner, the gift may be dinner out or dinner brought in.

¶7   But best friends are also good receivers. They receive us as we are and don't insist on changing us. They are willing to receive our troubles and our complaints and, just by being uncritical, they help us accept our situation. They receive our beliefs and respect them without trying to improve upon them.

¶8   Often receiving is more difficult, and perhaps therefore more blessed, than giving. It is not too difficult, for example, to give time that we have plenty of or material items that we have too many of or that we are easily able to buy. It is not too difficult to give with the expectation of receiving something better in return.

¶9   But best friends give only because they love and they care, and they receive for the same reasons. And best friends teach us that it is sometimes more blessed to receive than to give.

EXERCISE 2.7 Write the final draft of the composition you have been working on. Use the revision and correction checklists on pages 17-18 to remind you of some of the possible weaknesses in your composition that may need to be strengthened. Don't hesitate to do more than one "final" draft.

QUIZ YOURSELF ON STEP ONE Fill in the blanks.

1. How are a paragraph and a composition alike? How is a composition different from a paragraph? _____

_____

2. What is the controlling idea of a composition called? _____

_____ **3.** A composition has unity and coherence when   (a) each paragraph supports the controlling idea, each sentence flows smoothly into the next sentence, and each paragraph flows smoothly into the next paragraph.   (b) the language in each paragraph is connotative.   (c) the sentences are compound and complex and not simple.

_____ **4.** The thesis of a composition must always be   (a) at the beginning of a composition.   (b) a complete sentence.   (c) stated in clear words somewhere in the composition.

_____ **5.** The first sentence of a composition is   (a) a paraphrase of the title.   (b) exceedingly important.   (c) always shorter than the following sentences.

_____ **6.** One of the most important requirements of successful writing is   (a) a word processor.   (b) a college education.   (c) rewriting.

_____ **7.** As you write using one of the 10 common methods of development, you must remember that these methods   (a) are very difficult to master.   (b) should be announced at the start of your composition.   (c) often overlap.

_____ **8.** T or F. You should never write more than one final draft because you might spoil the spontaneity and the creativity of your writing.

_____ **9.** T or F. A question like "Have you ever wondered what life is all about?" would be a good first sentence for a composition on your philosophy of life.

_____ **10.** T or F. In the conclusion of your composition, it is a good idea to bring up a new subject so that the reader will know you're not limited to writing about one thing.

Answers on page 141.

Step Two: From Good Composition to Better

Quality Control

Students almost always ask me how many pages an assigned composition has to be. I reply that I am looking for quality, not quantity. Quality in compositions is ensured by paying heed to those four guide words that assured us of quality in the writing of paragraphs: **unity, clarity, coherence,** and **creativity.**

Assigned to write a short composition on a subject of their choice, four students came up with the following choices. As you read their compositions, evaluate them for U, C, C, C (sounds like the name of a college).

1. The Case of Debby Levine-Herman. She picked a title almost before she had a thesis: The Miracles of Electronics. Here is her **scratch outline.**

```
A. I am an electronics freak: two phone lines, call
   waiting, three-way calling, conference calling,
   instant redial, answering machine, five VCRs (in
   case I want to tape two shows off the air and copy
   a tape and watch a program at the same time), CD
   player, computer with built-in FAX, laser printer,
   intercom connected to front door so I can screen
   visitors, security system connected to the police
   department, beeper, pager, probably some other
   stuff I can't think of just now.
```

B. I'm empathetic to all things electronic, but one thing makes me mad: the computerized voice mail that commands you to press a number on the phone and sends you from one message to another to another. Heaven forbid you should reach a real live person.

C. I would like to get revenge on the college Bursar's Office. My conversation with them went like this:

A. If you want to find out what our current fees are, press 1.

B. If you want to find out when fees are due, press 2.

C. If you want information about applying for financial aid, press 3.

D. If you have a problem with a current student loan, press 4.

E. If you need information about canceled classes, press 5.

F. If you think you are entitled to a refund of tuition because of canceled classes, press 6.

G. If you want to discuss a refund of tuition because you changed your mind, press 7.

H. If you want information about increased dorm fees, press 8.

I. If you want to reserve a 19-meal or a 15-meal plan, press 9.

J. If you want to return to the original menu, press 10.

D. Press 10??? There ain't no 10! Reminds me of the

kid whose parents told him to dial "Nine-eleven" in
an emergency. He couldn't find the "11" on the
dial.

E. And all I wanted to know was whether the Bursar's
Office accepted credit cards.

F. Heaven help you if you hit the wrong button or get
disconnected and have to start all over again.

G. I'd like to program my phone. First I'd have
callers punch in their name, address, telephone
number, Social Security number, driver's license
number, car make and model, car license number, and
number of home appliances in need of repair.

H. Plus 52 other irrelevant things they have to enter
and press.

I. When they finally get me, I won't be home and
they'll get my answering machine.

What is your opinion of Debby's outline? When it was submitted to the
scrutiny of a couple of classmates, here were the comments.

- No unity.
- Controlling idea not clear. Is it that you are an electronics freak or
  that being served by a recording is not satisfactory to you or that you
  want revenge. I think it is that you want revenge.
- This has great possibilities as a satiric piece on a system that we all
  put up with, that is becoming increasingly common and annoying.
- It would be more effective to show, not tell. Write yourself a humorous program that would give you revenge by taking the caller 10
  places before getting to you.
- Stick to what you would have *your* recordings say. That will make it
  clear, without taking up the space to say so, that you have been highly annoyed by programs like that of the Bursar's Office. Unity is sacrificed when you try to cover both their program and your program.
- If you achieve unity by sticking to your program, it will be irrelevant
  that you are an electronics freak.

- The humor is delightful, and the topic is one that every reader can identify with.
- Limit the subject, and make the controlling idea clear. It doesn't need to be stated in so many words, but I believe the point is clear: "I would like to get even with all those phone systems that never let me speak to a real live person."
- Irrelevant that kid couldn't find 11 on the dial.
- Don't forget the Press 1 *now* and the quick, clipped *Thank you*s.

I think her revised outline and rough draft will show through her final draft without making you read them. Here is **Debby's final draft.**

Voice Blackmail

¶1   When I win the lottery, I'm going to spend whatever it takes to program my phone so that it does unto others what they have been doing unto me.

¶2   "Hello. You have reached Debby Levine-Herman.

¶3   "Please press the Centigrade temperature wherever you are and the last four digits of your Social Security number, *now*. Than'Q.

¶4   "If you are a bill collector, please press Zero *now* for an immediate disconnect. Than'Q.

¶5   "If you are a salesman with a great buy on an oceanfront lot in Las Vegas, admit it up front, and press One *now* to be put on hold until Tuesday of next week. Than'Q.

¶6   "If you are calling for the balance in your checking account and your last five transactions, please hang up *now* and call your bank. Than'Q.

¶7   "If you are calling for a weather report, please press Two and look out your window *now*. Than'Q.

¶8   "If you are calling specifically to catch me at dinnertime, you will be happy to know you caught me just as I was about to sit down to steak and French fries, hot, and that's just what I still intend to do. Than'Q.

¶9   "If your call did not go through, please press Three *now*, and dial again. Than'Q.

¶10   "If you have died and left me money, please press Four *now*, and please stay on the line, please. Than'Q.

¶11   "If you don't know the extension of the person you are calling, please press Five *now*, and the next available customer service representative will be with you in seven minutes. FCC regulations require us to inform you there is a charge of $10 for each minute of this call. Than'Q.

¶12   "If you have good news or something nice to say to Debby, please press Six *now*, and I will answer immediately. Than'Q.

¶13   "Hello, this is Debby. . . . Oh? Wrong number? Sorry." Click. "Than'Q."

The consensus of the student critiquers was that the controlling idea (I'd like to put those people with programmed voice mail through what they put me through) now comes through loud and clear without being expressed, that unity is achieved by omitting material on the electronics freak and the call to the Bursar's Office. Transitions for coherence are not a concern because the format, pressing one number after another, makes each sentence lead into the next smoothly. The end is fun and effective.

2. The Case of Kevin Crawford and His Furry Ferret Friend. Kevin's **rough draft** follows. What is your reaction to it?

Ferrets: Technical and Household Uses

¶1   Today, boys and girls, I'm going to talk about a useful household tool that is often overlooked by the busy homemaker the ferret. The ferret, along with their relatives the mink, martin, weasel, skunk, and marmoset, make excellent cleaning tools. Their thick, soft fur and sphericity make for an enormous cleaning surface, and if a firm grip is kept on it's head injury is *so* limited.

¶2   Before I go any farther, friends, I'm going to need to explain the proper care and feeding of your ferret. Make certain you feed your ferret a lot of nice, shiny entrails and animal organs. Ferrets just *love* animal organs. Your ferret cage should also be nice and tight. Some ferrets can squeeze through a hole the size of a gold doubloon, so if you wake up one night. Don't say you weren't warned if Freddie Ferret is gnawing out your eyes and eating them like grapes.

¶3   One job for which ferrets are exceptionally useful is a drain cleaner. In this case, grasp it firmly by the end and throw it down the drain head first. Note that if you fail to turn off the garbage disposal before inserting the ferret, you may damage it severely. Also, expect a fountain of ferret chunks to come blowing up out of the drain. Ferret nuggets will never replace chicken nuggets.

¶4   Sometimes, as we all know, small children need to be disciplined for their own good. A ferret is excellent for training a child. In many cases, the simple threat of being lashed with a live ferret is enough to quiet it down.

¶5   Ferrets can be easily tamed but they may harm infants. They hunt and kill animals—they were trained to drive wild animals from their subterranean haunts. They are cannibals, but they seldom eat the animals they kill—

they just suck their blood.

¶6   You can't hardly afford to be without a ferret.

I think the reaction of most readers would be that clarity is lacking, that Kevin couldn't possibly have made an outline first, and that, after he gets his organization straightened out, he needs to clear up some problems with vocabulary and grammar.

Paragraph 1: What boys and girls? Is the busy homemaker a ferret? A martin is a bird; a marten is a relative of the ferret. A marmoset is a monkey and not related to the ferret. *Sphericity* is an unnecessarily complex way of saying spherical shape, but the ferret is not spherical anyway. The ferret . . . *their* relatives, *Their* thick, soft fur? *It's* should be *its*. It sounds as if the ferret has a head injury— a comma after *head* is needed.

Paragraph 2: *Farther* should be *further*. The diversion into ferret care and feeding destroys unity. How big is a gold doubloon? *If you wake up one night* is a fragment.

Paragraph 3: Is *drain cleaner* a person or a product? You may damage *it*— the disposal or the ferret?

Paragraph 4: Enough to quiet *it* down—the child or the ferret?

Paragraph 5: From their *subterranean haunts?* Possibly from their *holes* or *burrows?* A contradiction: a cannibal is a human who eats human flesh or an animal that eats its own kind, but the ferret seldom eats the animals it kills.

Paragraph 6: You *can* hardly afford to be without a ferret. (Want to bet?)

I probably missed a few, but as Kevin hastened to point out, that was only a rough draft. He jotted an extremely informal outline, revised and corrected, added a couple more far-fetched ideas, and came out with a delightful spoof of the advertising hype sometimes inflicted upon us consumers. What do you think of his **final draft?**

The Far-Fetched Ferret

¶1   If you don't have a ferret at your house to help you with your chores, you are definitely underequipped. Ferrets have many uses. They may be dusting tools, drain cleaners, baby sitters, chicken guarders, health enhancers, and/or a golfer's best friend. It's hard to imagine life before ferrets.

¶2   Ferrets, you see, were fetched from faraway Africa. They can be easily tamed and were originally trained by hunters to drive wild animals out of their burrows. They are about 14 inches long, have slender bodies, and view the world through pink eyes. I realize the color of their eyes is irrelevant to this composition and I am risking a red "Unity" in the margin, but I happen to think the fact is interesting.

¶3   The ferret's thick, soft fur makes it an ideal tool for dusting. Just grab it by its fairly long tail, not included in the aforementioned 14 inches, and swing away. As a drain cleaner, the ferret is thrust down the sink head first and maneuvered up and down a few times. If you accidentally hit the garbage disposal button, you can have ferretburgers for a delicious supper, serendipity at its best.

¶4   A ferret left in charge of an infant will protect him or her from attack by carnivorous animals, the only problem being that the ferret may eat him or her itself. If you leave your ferret guarding your chicken house, the ferret will help you get ready for Sunday dinner by killing a few chickens and just sucking their blood rather than eating them. The chickens will be neater in your refrigerator that way. But ferrets will devour red meat, helping your family avoid high cholesterol. And if you have a putting green in your back yard, you can train your ferret to retrieve the golf ball from the hole and drop it at your feet.

¶5   If you will excuse me now, I must return to the library to ferret out more information about this indispensable animal. I'll bet you can't wait to get one. . . . Oh, you can?

3. The Case of Camper Jerie Ireland Green. Here is **Jerie's rough draft.**

Camping

¶1   Last year a friend and I went camping. We drove to a camp in Pennsylvania. This camp had a "carry-in, carry-out" policy. No water, no toilet facilities, no trash cans. Nature in her pristine beauty. That meant no facilities were provided. You had to bring in everything you needed, and when you left you were supposed to take it *all* back home with you.

¶2   It has advantages. You don't have to go to a particular camp area where you may find close neighbors. There's nothing wrong with the idea. You can camp anywhere. You can really get back to nature.

¶3   We carried tons of stuff in. It wasn't easy. There was a stream with a log most of the way across it.

¶4   It was beautiful though. Guess who fell in!

¶5   So much for carry in, carry out. We went back to the same spot earlier this year. Instead of natural woods and stream, the stream was littered with pop and beer cans. The woods now were filled with rubbish, even a tire. It was hard to tell. At least we thought it was the same spot. We won't go back. We can see trash and old tires in the city. It's hard to believe people are such slobs.

Jerie's biggest lack, her critics agreed, was coherence. Sentences were not always in the best order, and there was a lack of smooth flow from one sentence into the next. Transitions were almost nonexistent, resulting in short, choppy sentences. Here is her much-improved **final draft.**

Who Killed Mother Nature?

¶1   I'd gone to drive-ins for lunch, shopped for bargains at cash-and-carry stores, and taken carryouts home to eat; but I had never visited a "carry-in, carry-out" camp until last summer. It was brand new.

¶2   Carry in, carry out means no facilities—no water, no toilets, no trash cans. You have to bring in everything you need; and when you leave, you are supposed to take it *all* back home with you. Nature in all her pristine beauty, before you come, while you are there, and after you go.

¶3   There's nothing wrong with the idea. In fact, it has certain advantages. You don't have to go to a particular camp area where you may find close neighbors. You can camp anywhere. You can really get back to nature.

¶4   We carried in tons of stuff, blazing a trail through deep woods, crossing a creek balanced on a log, finally arriving at a small clearing, and then repeating the process again and again. I fell into the creek only once. We were so tired by the time we set up camp that we didn't enjoy nature for a full 24 hours. But after that, we had a truly beautiful experience.

¶5   In five days, we religiously carried out all our gear and every potato peel and gum wrapper. The natural beauty we left behind made us want to go back.

¶6   We did earlier this year. So much for carry in, carry out. We went back to the same spot; at least we thought it was the same spot, but it was hard to tell. Instead of woods as God created them, the land was lit-

tered with pop and beer cans, plastic cups, and every
other type of rubbish, even a tire. We had trouble catching a glimpse of Mother Nature. I slipped on some kind
of garbage that had lodged on the log and fell in the
creek again.

¶7   We won't go back. We can see trash and old tires in
the city. And we don't have to drive miles and miles and
carry loads and loads of stuff and fall into a creek to do
it.

Jerie's composition now reads smoothly because sentences in the right order
are held together with appropriate transitions. Jerie must have mastered coherence because she is now editor and publisher ("and chief cook and bottle washer," she says) of the monthly *Lake County* (Ohio) *Business Journal* and a frequently published freelance writer.

4. The Case of Bill Fishburn. Of course, rough drafts aren't supposed to be perfect grammatically. Although Bill's rough draft suffered rather severely from all
four of the ailments we are trying to cure, the most glaring trouble was lack of
creativity. His **rough draft** was b-o-r-i-n-g. See whether you agree.

The Tuba

1   To start off, a look at the tuba's history and
2   functions are a necessity to understanding how to perform
3   on this instrument. First, let's see what the dictionary
4   says about the tuba: in ancient Rome, a straight trumpet;
5   any of a family of brass instruments of semi-conical bore,
6   having a cup mouthpiece and three to five valves. The
7   ancient Roman "trumpet" would most likely be an almost
8   exact length to todays tuba. If a tuba's pipes were
9   stretched out, they would reach about 10 yards, I think.
10   This instrument got it's actual start in the 1700's.
11   It was used as a brass substitute to the wooden stand-up
12   bass in the operatic orchestras. The tuba that was first

13 used is what we now call the "F" tuba. Since it's tuning
14 note is the F key. Due to the instruments size, it takes a
15 particular type of person to play this instrument; tuba is
16 misunderstood, to be discussed later.

17   However, in todays music world there are three
18 different types of tubas, and two categories of valves.
19 The three different types of tubas are the F, the C, and
20 the BB-flat. Each different tubas name is that of its
21 tuning note. The f tunes at a f, the C to a c, and the BB-
22 flat to a B-flat.

23   The two different categories of valves are, the
24 Piston valve, and the Rotary valve. The two both have
25 there advantages and their disadvantages. The Piston valve
26 is the simpler of the two, because it acts like a piston
27 would in a car. When pressed down the piston goes straight
28 down, letting the air go through a longer pipe that it
29 would if it was not pressed down.

30   The Rotary valve is a bit more complicated than the
31 Piston but is looked on as the better of the two because
32 it has a smoother transition from one position to the
33 other.

34   Due to the size of the tuba it is not an easy
35 instrument for all to play. Since it is the biggest
36 instrument it takes a lot of air to get out a little
37 sound. So a good player must be able to use their air
38 well, and learn how to get the most out of their breaths.
39 But the tuba plays an important role in a band or
40 orchestra, since it is the lowest sounding instrument even
41 though you are the butt of many jokes because of its size
42 and its overpowering, rumpus-like voice.

43 Now that you've read this, and understand a little

44 bit of the tubas history, you are now ready to go and

45 start playing, but if you don't think you'll make a good

46 tuba player don't worry because there are many other

47 instruments that are just as interesting.

For starters, Bill could not possibly have been working from an outline. Even his thesis is far from clear. He seems to be wanting to make the point that the tuba is a very special instrument requiring a very special person to play it; but he veers off course into the history of the instrument, its anatomy, and the implication that you can walk right up to a tuba and play it but not to worry if you should prefer some other instrument.

Between rough draft and final draft, Bill focused on his special relationship with his special instrument, corrected the errors (the line numbering will help in a class discussion of the needed corrections), and, best of all, added lots of notes of creativity. Here is his **final draft.**

Big Bertha

¶1 Don't tell me—I know. I'm too young to form a

strong, permanent attachment to a member of the opposite

sex, but I can't help it. My relationship with Bertha is

the loving liaison of my life.

¶2 I've been with Bertha going on five years. As far as

I'm concerned, happiness is having Bertha sit on my lap

and, well, just sort of wrap herself around me. She has

a deep, friendly, almost comic voice. For that reason,

lots of people laugh at her and don't take her seriously.

But she has done so much for me that I am giving up my

first-choice career for her.

¶3 Bertha is my tuba. I had always wanted to be a vet-

erinarian. But I couldn't see how going to vet-med school

and then running a hospital for animals would be compati-

ble with being a serious tuba player. So I'm happy to

say I'm going to major in theater and minor in music.

That way Bertha and I can be together longer.

¶4   The tuba is a very special instrument. It came into being as a substitute for the wooden stand-up string bass in opera orchestras. Tubas weigh 30 to 40 pounds, their case adding another 10 to 15 pounds, and they take up as much room as an overstuffed person whenever they travel. As the lowest-sounding voices in an orchestra or band, they are very important to balance the more numerous higher-sounding instruments.

¶5   Just as the tuba is a special instrument, so tuba players are a special breed. Unlike players of the brassier trumpets, who love to toot their own horns, tuba players seem to be humbled by their instruments. And literally they rarely blow their own horns because a good tuba costs between $10,000 and $12,000. Many schools own one or two (Bertha belongs to my school), but it is hard to persuade anyone to take up tuba. So the tuba player is like a chosen person and takes secret pride in his position in a concert or marching band.

¶6   Tuba playing is not for the weak. It takes a mighty blow and more lip action than any other instrument requires to get just a tiny peep out of a tuba. And since marching bands usually equip their tuba players with sousaphones, which rest on the shoulder rather than in the lap, the tuba player must have a strong left shoulder as well as good lips and lungs. The first few days of band camp, new tuba players are the tiredest of campers with the sorest of shoulders and limpest of lips.

¶7   But in spite of the effort it takes to maintain this special musical relationship, most tuba players feel as I do: humbled by, proud of, and infatuated with their

instrument. You can probably see why Bertha is a very
special part of my life.

Transitions

Several times during the discussion of making sentences into paragraphs and
paragraphs into compositions, we have mentioned a smooth flow from one sentence into the next or a smooth flow from one paragraph into the next.
Transitions are words or phrases or structural devices that smoothly link units
of writing. Coordinating and subordinating conjunctions and introductory words
or phrases like *First* and *On the other hand* are good examples. Sometimes,
though, combining two or three phrases or combining two or three clauses can
eliminate the need for transitions.

- INSTEAD OF: Leatrice studied her history, and she worked so hard at it
  that she couldn't sleep.
- BETTER: Leatrice studied her history so hard she couldn't sleep.

The box below presents a list of common transitional expressions, classified
according to how they join. If content alone is not enough to make a sentence
flow smoothly into the next sentence and a paragraph flow smoothly into the
next paragraph, these expressions are invaluable.

Transitions to show **added material** include the following: additionally,
also, and, another, besides, equally, further, furthermore, in addition, moreover, next, too, with.

Transitions to show **cause, purpose, or result:** accordingly, as a result,
because, because of this, consequently, for, for this purpose, for this reason, in effect, of course, possibly, probably, so, therefore, thereupon, thus,
to this end, with this object.

Transitions to show **difference:** although, but, conversely, either, even
so, even though, however, in contrast, in other words, nevertheless,
nonetheless, nor, notwithstanding, on the contrary, on the other hand, or,
otherwise, still, unlike, yet.

Transitions to give **examples:** for example, for instance, in fact, one kind
of, specifically, that, that is, to illustrate, to name a few, which, who, whose.

Transitions to show **likeness:** also, by coincidence, in comparison, in like
manner, likewise, moreover, similarly.

Transitions to show **order of importance:** in the first place, more important (not importantly).

Transitions to show **place:** above, below, beyond, close, farther, here,
nearby, opposite, over, there, to the left, to the right, under.

> Transitions to show **time:** after, afterward, at the same time, before, during, earlier, finally, first (second, third, etc.), immediately, in the meantime, later, meanwhile, next, now, shortly, simultaneously, since, soon, then, thereafter, when, while.
>
> Transitions to show **summarizing:** accordingly, as has been noted, as I have said, finally, for the most part, I must say, in brief, in conclusion, indeed, in other words, in short, in summary, on the whole, that is, therefore, to be sure, to summarize, to sum up.

To sum up, transitions like these help make your writing smooth and coherent, but they must not be overdone.

Conjunctive adverbs, which are also transitional words, are listed on page 310, as are transitional phrases.

And there are certain structural devices that also may aid in transition.

Repetition

- Mrs. Murphy thinks we have forgotten her. She thinks we have forgotten how hard she works to help her students master English. She thinks we have forgotten her just because we haven't mentioned her for a while. We have not forgotten her.

Parallel Construction

- I came, I saw, I conquered (comma splices okay here in series of short main clauses).
- Begin one paragraph with, "I suspected I'd never be a famous artist when . . . " Start the next one with, "I was pretty well convinced I'd never make it when . . . " And start the last paragraph with, "Now I know I'll never be famous because . . . "
- Incidentally, my explanation of "Begin one . . . ," "Start the . . . ," "And start the . . . " also illustrates parallel construction.

Asking a Question

- She's too tall, don't you think?—too tall to play the part of Little Miss Muffet.

EXERCISE 2.8 Turn back to Jerie's composition on page 96. Circle the transitional expressions.

Answers on page 141.

EXERCISE 2.9 Using transitions or transitional devices, combine sentences or make a smooth passage from one sentence to the next.

1. Mrs. Murphy, the English teacher, and Ms. Larue, the history teacher, were having lunch together in the faculty dining room. Neither one had fixed a lunch to bring to school. Neither one had had time.

2. "I have a student named Carla. I'm concerned about her," said Mrs. Murphy. "She never gets her homework in on time. Often she doesn't hand it in at all. She is failing. I know she is bright."

3. "I have a young man I'm worried about," said Ms. Larue. "He always does poorly on tests. He seems fascinated by history. That is, he is interested while he is in class. Then he must lose all interest. He must never think of history after school."

4. "They sound very much alike. I wish we could do more for students like these two," said Mrs. Murphy. "I hope to help Carla Careless. I'm going to recommend that she make an appointment with a tutor in the Learning Center."

5. "Did you say Careless? My student is Calvin Careless." Ms. Larue said this excitedly. "Carla must be the twin sister he has mentioned. I have repeatedly asked him to see me in my office. We could talk about his history grade. Finally he has made an appointment."

6. "These two sound almost identical. Opposite-sex twins can't be identical. Maybe we can give them both help."

Answers on page 141.

EXERCISE 2.10 Without rearranging the order, put the sentences below together into a smooth-reading whole by adding transitions or using transitional devices.

It's a beast walking upright like a man, seven to nine feet tall. It has a large head, almost no neck, a face like a gorilla, huge arms, and a covering of hair.

"You've never seen one. That doesn't mean it doesn't exist," said Tom Steenburg, of Water Valley, Alberta.

He explains he has never seen a wolverine.

He knows they do exist.

He believes there is definitely something prowling the Canadian Rockies.

It leaves huge human-like footprints.

Its existence needs to be proved; its existence needs to be disproved.

Evidence of the sasquatch, the hairy, man-like creature called Bigfoot, was first found by a fur trader named David Thompson.

He reported sighting huge footprints near Jasper, Alberta, in 1811.

Hundreds of people later reported seeing Bigfoot.

No evidence has held up scientifically.

Steenburg keeps looking.

He checks reports of sightings.

He separates the obvious fakes from those he can't explain.

He hopes that Bigfoot will come his way.

He hopes Bigfoot will die a peaceful death from lack of evidence.

Possible answers on page 142.

Consistent Point of View

Now (time), I shall try to make a smooth transition to another (added material) device that's (example) helpful in the writing process: consistent point of view. **Point of view** is nothing more than the position from which the subject is viewed, or the person through whose eyes the subject is told about, that is, the person who is doing the talking, who is telling the story. If you write about the world as a toddler sees it, the point of view is from about two feet off the ground. If an ex-convict tells a story of bad conditions in prison, the first-person account, seen through his or her eyes, would be authentic and realistic.

In choosing the person who is doing the talking, you have your choice of first person (*I* or *we*), second person (*you*), or third person (*he, she, it,* or *they*). Don't shift from one point of view to another within the same composition without good reason. A common fault is flipping from third to second person for no valid reason, as in "*They* had to be careful shooting the rapids after the spring thaw. *You* needed to be a good swimmer."

Most English classes call for high-informal writing, usually done in first or third person, once in a great while in second. Formal writing (the style preferred in academic journals or scientific reports) is almost always in third person.

EXERCISE 2.11 Correct, above the line, mistakes in point of view in the following sentences.

1. As we relived the Renaissance in Ms. Larue's class, we realized you couldn't afford to miss a single class.

2. Students should be sure they vote in the Student Senate election. It's the only way we can participate in decision making at the college.

3. If you want Peter for president, we are all going to have to campaign for him.

4. Mrs. Murphy feels the job of Student Senate president is important, and they sometimes wish faculty members could vote in student elections.

5. When the election is over, let's hope we all get behind the winner, whether you voted for that person or not.

Answers on page 142.

Clear Logic

Good writing requires checking and double-checking all the way. Double-check to be sure that your reasoning is logical and not something that will cause the reader to lose faith in you. I frequently mark "faulty logic" in the margin of student papers when a conclusion is reached on a basis that is not reasonable.

- "Watching sexually suggestive acts on TV can build desire in teenagers. If the teenager is not aware of some form of contraceptive, he or she may become pregnant from watching programs like this." I must have overdone my advice to avoid sexism in your writing. *He* may become pregnant? From watching TV?

- "I am sending you this as a surprise. Let me know if you don't get it." Impossible, of course, because if I don't get it, I won't know that you sent it to me as a surprise and that I didn't get it.

- "All the English teachers at our school have a master's degree. Mr. Jones has a master's degree. Therefore, he teaches English." Maybe all the math teachers and all the history teachers have master's degrees too.

- "The board of trustees raised the salary of the president 10 percent. Since then, the cost of books has gone up 10 percent." The two may be completely unrelated, but the implication is that the first event caused the second. Be careful not to plant false implications.

- And be careful not to make sweeping statements that you couldn't possibly back up, like "Everyone should be required to take at least two years of Latin."

EXERCISE 2.12 In the blanks tell why each sentence deserves to be marked "faulty logic."

1. Teenagers are not mature enough to hold responsible jobs. _____

_____

2. Right after the president was elected, unemployment rose 10 percent.

_____

3. My next-door neighbor is kind to animals, but he can't find a job.

_____

4. People born in July become rich and famous. Since I was born in July, I

have a great future to look forward to. _____

_____

5. There is too much violence on TV because there are murders and hijack-

ings and armed robberies every time you turn around. _____

_____

Answers on page 143.

Before we move on, we'll pick apart one more small composition and put it back together again. This one is based on a column by Erma Bombeck. We'll call it, "Questioning Advertising." I have mixed up the order, and Exercise 2.13 will involve putting it back in order. Here it is, mixed up, further proof that a composition can be perfect grammatically but perfectly impossible otherwise.

¶1   After he left, I stood there at the door with a five-year subscription to *The Bleeding Gums Journal* in hand; and my husband asked, "Why didn't you just tell him you didn't want the magazine?"

¶2   Not only am I assaulted by magazine ads, but a salesman came to my door the other day and asked, "Are you interested in saving 50 cents a copy on each magazine you receive?"

¶3   It's hard to imagine running a successful business by asking dumb questions that any moron would know the answer to. But that's advertising. I guess it works or they wouldn't keep on doing it.

¶4   "Because that wasn't the question." See how it works?

¶5   Hardly a day goes by that I don't pick up a magazine which screams at me, "Do You Want a Healthy Head of Hair?" or "Are You Sick of Cockroaches in Your Cupboards?" or "Do You Want to Lose 12 Pounds in Three Days?" Some weirdos may consider dandruff a turn-on and cockroaches cute little pets; and, hey, I'd settle for three pounds in 12 days. But the answers are pretty obvious.

¶6   Am I supposed to say, "No, I want to get in my car, use gas and time I don't have, run down to the corner drugstore whenever I want a magazine, buy the magazine before it's sold out, and pay an extra $60 a year for the privilege"?

EXERCISE 2.13 It's hard to imagine an outline from which the mixed-up composition above could have come. So make an outline which will give these paragraphs a thesis and unity.

Possible answer on page 143.

QUIZ YOURSELF ON STEP TWO Fill in the blanks.

1. Compositions may be divided into what three parts for the sake of outlining? _____ _____ _____

_____ **2.** To make each sentence flow smoothly into the next sentence and each paragraph flow smoothly into the next paragraph, you should use   (a) transitions.   (b) transactions.   (c) transformations.

—— **3.** What is point of view?   (a) the person who is acted upon.   (b) the person who is doing the talking.   (c) the person who uses logic.

4. What is wrong with the logic of the student who said, "Watching sexually suggestive acts on TV can build desire in teenagers. If the teenager is not aware of some form of contraceptive, he or she may become pregnant from watching programs like this."

_____

_____

Answers on page 144.

Step Three: From Better Composition to Best

Many Combinations, Your Choice

We have now studied techniques of the writing process. As you can see, within a unified composition there are many elements of clarity, coherence, and creativity to be put together in almost infinite combinations to produce the best possible composition—or anything else you may be writing.

Writing can be a very enjoyable process. It is too bad that so many students become intimidated by the prospect of a writing assignment at such an early age. My advice is to learn the basics, learn where to look up the many things you can't keep in mind (often you don't know what you need to know until you start writing), find your own sources of material (remember, you have within you many interesting ideas), develop your own style, learn to rewrite and correct, and then relax and enjoy writing.

The following are 10 of the best compositions my students have produced, one developed by each of the methods we have discussed. Don't be dismayed if your writing doesn't seem to be that good right away. You'll get there. Practice is the secret. Rewrite and then rewrite some more. Nobody has said learning to write well is easy. But it can be done; it can be fun—at least more fun, I hope, than you thought it was going to be.

Ten Student Compositions, the Best

1. Success

by Joon S. Park

1 Success—the word probably has a different meaning to
2 every individual. Here is one definition of success, part
3 of my heritage from my father.

4 Before I left Korea for the United States, my father
5 told me that he wanted to have a father-to-son talk with
6 me. He said, "Joon, maybe we will not have enough time to
7 talk again. You are going to study in a country far away.
8 You are going to build your life and your future; you will
9 be looking for success.

10 "Joon, I can say after 50 years' experience that
11 success is not money, as you may think. It is not power,
12 as you may have heard. It is not status, as you may feel.

13 "Success is happiness. You are as successful as you
14 are happy, and you are as happy as you are helpful to
15 others. I know a lot of people who have power or money or
16 status, but they are not happy in their lives because
17 money, power, or status is their goal in life. They can
18 always find people who have more than they, so they push
19 to get more and more, and never find success. Money and
20 power and status can be your instruments, but they should
21 never be your goals.

22 "Joon, you will always find people who have more of
23 the material things than you do. But more important, there
24 are always people who possess less than you. So smile when
25 you have problems because I am sure you can find someone

26 who is in worse trouble than you and who needs your help.

27 Helping others will bring you much more happiness than

28 money or power or status.

29   "Joon, by encouraging you to get a good education, I

30 am asking you to improve your life. I am also asking you

31 just as sincerely to be content with your life and to help

32 others who are less fortunate. That's the way to find

33 peace of mind and happiness.

34   "Life is like a garden after a rain storm. There is

35 mud, and that is ugly, and sometimes your shoes seem to

36 stick in it. But if you can look at the flowers, the

37 beauty of life, and find ways to contribute, not just to

38 seek for yourself, you will find happiness and success.

39   "Joon, do not forget this conversation if you want to

40 be a successful man. I pray that God will take care of

41 you."

42   I have not forgotten what you told me, Dad. I will

43 try to live by it.

EXERCISE 2.14 Fill in the blanks.

1. What is the controlling idea, the thesis? _____

_____

2. Where is the thesis located, at the beginning of the composition or at the
   end? _____

3. Which of the 10 methods of development is/are predominant?

_____

4. What pattern/patterns of organization (chronological, by importance,
   spatial) predominate? _____

5. What are the strong or weak points of the introduction and the conclusion?

_____

_____

6. What can you say about the writer's use of words, including transitions, and effectiveness of sentences? _____

_____

7. What are the strong or weak points of the whole composition?

_____

_____

Answers on page 144.

2. The Attic
by Kathie Pearlstein

1   When I felt the call to high adventure, nothing in my
2 childhood matched the excitement of a trip to the attic.
3 Ours was not the kind of attic where things were stored to
4 be retrieved for later use, or the kind that was cleaned
5 in the spring. It was a final resting place for several
6 generations of family memorabilia, with an accumulation of
7 other miscellaneous junk added whenever the lower floors
8 began to overflow. This stuff was merely carried up the
9 stairs and deposited, never to be seen again.
10   Our attic was hot. It was dirty. And, because it was
11 not fully floored, it was dangerous.
12   Although it was not locked, it was forbidden.
13 Therefore, my expeditions had to be planned and executed
14 with the care of a covert CIA operation. Obviously, I
15 couldn't just say, "See you in a couple of hours, Mom. I'm
16 going up to the attic." But once I had decided I was

17 going, I could feel the excitement mount.

18 Still vivid in my mind is my last secret pilgrimage.

19 I feigned getting ready to go outside to play and watched

20 carefully until Mother was busy in some other part of the

21 house.

22 Then, when all the conditions were right, I crept to

23 the stairs and carefully made my ascent on shaky knees,

24 certain that I would be discovered every time a floorboard

25 squeaked.

26 When I reached the top, I looked back for the first

27 time, half expecting to see Mother at the foot of the

28 stairs, but no one was there. I quickly reached for the

29 doorknob, opened the door, stepped inside, closed the door

30 behind me, and waited for my eyes to adjust to the

31 dimness, my heart pounding. Once more I had safely

32 traveled the hazardous road to adventure.

33 As I looked around, the old vacuum cleaner with its

34 sinister-looking black bag caught my attention, and I had

35 a strange feeling in my stomach. I forced myself to look

36 directly at it. I knew it was broken. I looked at the

37 cord; it wasn't even plugged in. Comforting myself with

38 that knowledge, I firmly turned my back on it.

39 I walked slowly to the piece of string hanging from

40 the single bulb on the rafters and pulled on the light.

41 The dusty bulb glowed dimly, the eerie light deepening the

42 shadows along the eaves and seeming to give life to the

43 old lamps, furniture, and boxes scattered about. For a

44 second, I thought I saw the headless dressmaker's form

45 move; but, of course, I knew that wasn't possible. I had

46 made peace with that old dummy before. It was just felt

47 panels and a wire frame; it had never had a head; it
48 couldn't move.

49   I began to pick my way through cobwebs and around an
50 old dressing table, with its three cloudy mirrors watching
51 my progress, to one of my favorite pieces in the whole
52 attic, an old trunk of Mother's, probably packed and put
53 there shortly after I was born. It was very large and
54 randomly filled with old papers, letters, clippings,
55 cards, and clothing. I had looked into it before so I knew
56 what to expect even before I raised the heavy lid. I
57 opened it and quickly took out the things on top. Then I
58 sat down on the floor for some serious snooping.

59   Digging through the papers, I came upon a packet of
60 notes. I removed the ancient, twisted rubber band that was
61 holding them together and concentrated on deciphering the
62 hurried cursive handwriting. I was so intent on figuring
63 out what they said that it took some time before I
64 realized their impact. They were beautiful, romantic love
65 notes addressed to my mother and written by my father. I
66 couldn't believe it. My father wrote these? To my mother?

67   As I sat there reading them, and trying to imagine my
68 parents as lovers, out of the corner of my eye I saw
69 something move. I sat very still, holding my breath, but I
70 could not turn to look fully in the direction of the
71 movement.

72   After a minute or two, I jumped to my feet, stuffed
73 things back into the trunk, slammed the lid, and ran down
74 the stairs. I didn't even bother to be sure the coast was
75 clear.

76   That year I got very busy, and I never returned to

77 the attic in that same way. In fact, it was not until

78 Mother died that I found myself once again face to face

79 with those old spirits above the stairs, and remembered

80 that last visit that seemed connected somehow to the end

81 of my childhood.

EXERCISE 2.15 Fill in the blanks.

1. What is the controlling idea, the thesis? _____

_____

2. Where is the thesis located, at the beginning of the composition or at the
end? _____

3. Which of the 10 methods of development is/are predominant?

_____

4. What pattern/patterns of organization (chronological, by importance,
spatial) predominate? _____

5. What are the strong or weak points of the introduction and the conclusion?

_____

_____

6. What can you say about the writer's use of words, including transitions,
and effectiveness of sentences? _____

_____

7. What are the strong or weak points of the whole composition?

_____

_____

Answers on page 145.

3. Finally, I Found Her

by Tussy French

1 My search for the perfect woman began when I was
2 eight. A new girl joined our third-grade class, and she
3 was pretty. As soon as she sat down, I sent her a note: "I
4 love you. Do you love me?" She smiled and sent a note back
5 asking if I had enough money to pay for her lunch in the
6 cafeteria. I nodded, and she gave me a wider smile.

7 At lunch, she asked if I would carry her books home
8 for her. I did, and when we got to her house, I asked if I
9 could kiss her. She agreed provided we went back of the
10 garage so her mother wouldn't see us. We kissed, and she
11 ran into the house.

12 For a whole week I bought her lunch, carried her
13 books, kissed her in back of the garage, and floated home.
14 I was in love.

15 The next Monday I had only enough money for my own
16 lunch. Too embarrassed to tell her that, I gave her what I
17 had and went without lunch. Tuesday I had to tell her I
18 couldn't give her any more money. She stomped away. In the
19 middle of the morning, I saw another boy giving her money.
20 I followed them as he walked her home, carrying her books;
21 and I suffered my first broken heart as they disappeared
22 behind the garage. That evening I confided in my father
23 and asked him for extra money. He explained that times
24 were hard, and that I probably would be better off without
25 that little lady who loved me only for my lunch money.
26 Lesson Number One.

27 Several years later, as I was making my first foray
28 into the world of the gainfully employed, I fell in love

29 with a beautiful, sexy blue-eyed blonde who worked in the
30 same office. She had eyes for me when I had the
31 wherewithal to take her fashionably to dinner, but she
32 cheated on me constantly, always looking for someone who
33 had more to offer. Once she went out with a guy we both
34 knew, and I asked her what she saw in him. He wasn't a
35 nice guy like me. Her answer was simple and to the point:
36 "He has a Corvette." Well, of course; if he has a
37 Corvette, he must be a wonderful person. Before long she
38 officially dumped me for a bookkeeper who had inherited a
39 corporate accounting firm from his uncle. So I chalked up
40 Lesson Number Two in the art of being revered only for
41 what could be wheedled out of my wherewithal.

42   Female jocks intimidate me. I had known this muscular
43 miss for some time when I bumped into her one day in front
44 of a supermarket. I'd always liked her but could never get
45 to first base with her. "You look like a giant Pillsbury
46 dough boy," she said, poking her index finger into my
47 protruding belly. Not knowing what else to do, I giggled
48 stupidly, fully aware that I was in bad shape—still am. "I
49 know you want me," she said, stuffing her groceries into
50 her backpack, "so I'll tell you what. If you can catch me,
51 you can have me."

52   I just stood there panting as she leaped over three
53 shopping carts and vanished beyond the hills of joggers'
54 highs. I never saw her again.

55   Intellectual snobs are not for me either. Late one
56 afternoon as I sat at one of the few small tables in the
57 crowded cappuccino bar of my favorite book store, a
58 handsome, well-dressed intellectual female approached me

59 and asked to share my table. I knew she was intellectual

60 because as she sipped her cappuccino, she kept flashing

61 conspicuously in front of me the cover of the book she had

62 just bought: *An Intellectual's Guide to the Common Man.*

63 Finally she asked me how much formal education I'd had,

64 and when I told her, None, but that informally I had

65 learned to read and write, she spat a bunch of big words

66 at me and headed for another table.

67   Once in my life I succeeded in getting a date with a

68 glamour girl, but she was unreal. Her chief interest was

69 in how she would next have her wig styled. She had false

70 eyelashes. She had false fingernails. Her sweater was

71 enhanced with unbiological bulges. She faked an interest

72 in me, but I soon lost mine in her.

73   I finally found the perfect woman. It was not love at

74 first sight—we had been friends for years. It was not a

75 sizzling romance nor even a strong physical attraction,

76 but as we learned to love one another, our love kept

77 growing—it still is. She isn't out for material gain, or

78 for setting records, or for showing off, or for faking.

79   She has a habit of bringing home animals and old

80 folks who are lost. She thinks I'm wonderful even though I

81 don't have a Corvette. Her infectious smile makes everyone

82 around her feel important.

83   I'm a lucky man. Finally I found her, the perfect

84 woman, and she's my wife.

EXERCISE 2.16 Fill in the blanks.

1. What is the controlling idea, the thesis? _____

2. Where is the thesis located, at the beginning of the composition or at the end? _____

3. Which of the 10 methods of development is/are predominant?

_____

4. What pattern/patterns of organization (chronological, by importance, spatial) predominate? _____

5. What are the strong or weak points of the introduction and the conclusion?

_____

_____

6. What can you say about the writer's use of words, including transitions, and effectiveness of sentences? _____

_____

7. What are the strong or weak points of the whole composition?

_____

_____

Answers on page 146.

4. To Smile or Not to Smile
by Charlotte Michalski

1   If your smile is marred by stained teeth, fractured
2   enamel, a wide diastema (space between teeth), toothbrush
3   abrasion, or a misshapen tooth, two procedures in
4   dentistry may interest you: crowning and bonding.
5   Crowning and bonding can achieve the same cosmetic
6   results, but the processes are entirely different.
7   Crowning has been around for several centuries, but
8   the art was greatly improved in the early 1900s. Modern

9   methods of bonding, also known as the acid-etch technique,

10 came into being in the 1980s and have rapidly gained

11 popularity due to improved quality of materials and

12 techniques.

13   With crowning, a local anesthetic must be used while

14 the tooth is reduced to a peg-like stub. An impression is

15 taken and sent to a dental laboratory, where the

16 artificial body of the tooth is fabricated. When the crown

17 is ready, the dentist cements it to the remaining stub of

18 the tooth. Unlike crowning, bonding requires no

19 anesthesia, little or no drilling, but instead just the

20 preparation of the enamel with a mild acidic solution.

21 Then tooth-colored resin (the bonding compound) is applied

22 to the roughened surface of the tooth and shaped, and the

23 material is light-cured (intense white light causes the

24 material to harden) and polished.

25   Crowning is usually necessary when there is little

26 left of a tooth due to decay or fracture. A crown insures

27 protection of the root and the remaining tooth structure.

28 Bonding is preferred when there is adequate tooth

29 structure and the enamel is strong enough to support the

30 bonding compound.

31   Crowning requires at least two office visits. During

32 the first (a fairly long appointment), the dentist

33 prepares the tooth, makes the impression for the

34 laboratory, and installs a temporary protective cap;

35 during the second, the crown is cemented in place.

36 Bonding, on the other hand, can be completed in one visit,

37 usually not more than an hour, although return

38 appointments may be required for minor adjustments.

39   Crowns have been known to last 30 years or more, but
40 the usual life expectancy is five to eight years. Bonding
41 hasn't yet had the test of time, but there have been cases
42 where it has lasted more than 10 years. The care the
43 patient gives the crown or the bonding determines the time
44 it lasts. The average bonding job is about one-third the
45 cost of crowning.
46   Both processes have done a great deal toward
47 eliminating unsightly dental problems. Thanks to crowning
48 and bonding, one way or another you can turn that frown
49 upside down. Smile.

EXERCISE 2.17 Fill in the blanks.

1. What is the controlling idea, the thesis? _____

_____

2. Where is the thesis located, at the beginning of the composition or at the
   end? _____

3. Which of the 10 methods of development is/are predominant?

_____

4. What pattern/patterns of organization (chronological, by importance,
   spatial) predominate? _____

5. What are the strong or weak points of the introduction and the conclusion?

_____

_____

6. What can you say about the writer's use of words, including transitions,
   and effectiveness of sentences? _____

_____

7. What are the strong or weak points of the whole composition?

_____

_____

Answers on page 147.

5. Living, a Risky Business
by Marianne Pescho

1 Remember when taking a risk meant something like sky
2 diving from 5,000 feet up or going over Niagara Falls in a
3 barrel? Those were the good old days. Life was simple. We
4 were naive. We were happy.

5 Then someone decided we needed to be better informed
6 about the risks of living. We have gone from uninformed to
7 educated to over-educated to neurotic and finally to
8 paranoid.

9 Let's start at the beginning, the beginning of your
10 day, that is. You open one eye to see what time it is. You
11 have just taken your first risk of the day. That innocent-
12 looking alarm clock on the night stand could be emitting
13 radiation from the luminescent dial.

14 So go brush your teeth. Did you let the water run for
15 at least three minutes before rinsing? There could be lead
16 seeping from the pipes into your water supply, you know.

17 Now that you're up, how about doing some exercises?
18 If you don't, your energy and your state of mind and your
19 bone density will sag and your blood pressure and your
20 cholesterol will soar. Of course, as of yesterday,
21 scientists are thinking that too-low cholesterol may be as

22 bad as too-high. Maybe a cup of coffee will help? Naw,

23 that'll just make you nervous and your heart will start to

24 race. The jury is still out on decaf—is it safe or is

25 cancer brewing in every cup?

26   Time for the breakfast of champions. No, not a diet

27 coke and an Excedrin. Or even the leftover Danish wrapped

28 in aluminum foil. Don't you know that Alzheimer's patients

29 have too much aluminum in their brains?—something to keep

30 in mind when you reach for that wrap of many uses or when

31 you crack an egg into an aluminum fry pan. Anyhow, do you

32 really want to heat up leftovers? Can you be absolutely

33 sure the door on your microwave is sealed properly?

34   Forget breakfast. Time to head for the shower. Look

35 at all those electrical appliances in the bathroom: razor,

36 blow dryer, curling iron, radio. Wonder if this room is

37 grounded. Of course, if you manage to escape

38 electrocution, you probably will absorb enough harmful

39 chemicals from the water to do you in. Or maybe you'll

40 slip while getting out of the shower. Accidents, you know,

41 are the leading cause of death in the home. Before you

42 apply your deodorant, read the label. Almost all

43 deodorants contain aluminum.

44   So you're a bit chilly after the shower? Well, turn

45 up the heat. But has your furnace been checked lately? It

46 could be leaking carbon monoxide. That gas being odorless,

47 you'll never know. How about radon? Any cracks in your

48 basement that might be oozing radiation?

49   Time to get dressed. Is that plastic bag still on the

50 suit you picked up from the dry cleaner? Haven't you heard

51 those bags need to come off as soon as you get your

52 clothes home; otherwise, toxic chemicals build up inside
53 them. And don't leave it lying around for some child to
54 suffocate in. Really, don't you know what's happening in
55 your world?

56   Well, at least you're now somewhere between educated
57 and paranoid, and you've been up only an hour. What's that
58 you say? You feel you've taken enough risks for one day so
59 you're going back to bed?

60   Wait a minute. Haven't you heard about the chance of
61 broken bones from falling out of bed and the hazards of
62 radiation from electric blankets? Risky business, you say?
63 Better not take the chance. And to think it's only 8 a.m.

EXERCISE 2.18 Fill in the blanks.

1. What is the controlling idea, the thesis? _____

_____

2. Where is the thesis located, at the beginning of the composition or at the
end? _____

3. Which of the 10 methods of development is/are predominant?

_____

4. What pattern/patterns of organization (chronological, by importance,
spatial) predominate? _____

5. What are the strong or weak points of the introduction and the conclusion?

_____

_____

6. What can you say about the writer's use of words, including transitions,
and effectiveness of sentences? _____

_____

7. What are the strong or weak points of the whole composition?

_____

_____

Answers on page 147.

---

6. Teaching Second-Class Citizenship
by Irv Oslin

1 Trash cans are placed near the entrances of most
2 campus buildings so that students can discard chewing gum,
3 candy wrappers, plastic cups, unwanted notes, and other
4 forms of refuse. At some schools, students might as well
5 drop their First Amendment rights there too.

6 We thought the *Tinker* vs. *Des Moines* case in 1969
7 guaranteed school papers freedom from censorship. That
8 decision said that schools run with public money, which
9 would include most high schools and many colleges, had to
10 extend First Amendment rights to student publications. It
11 established that student newspapers were a public forum
12 and that, even though the publications were financed by
13 the schools, administrators could not deny students the
14 same rights of free expression enjoyed by people in the
15 "real world."

16 Then along came *Hazelwood* in 1988. That case decreed
17 that a high school principal was within his rights when he
18 withheld stories on the pregnancy experiences of three of
19 the school's students and on the impact of divorce on
20 students at the school. Freedom of the school press was
21 set back a couple of centuries.

22   We had a close call at our school, but we lucked out.

23 The staff of *High Point,* the award-winning student

24 newspaper of Cuyahoga Community College's Eastern Campus,

25 found itself in hot water when it published a headline

26 "Board passes tuition increase, raise in president's

27 salary." The board of trustees had indeed, with the

28 stupidest timing possible, at the same meeting both passed

29 a tuition increase and raised the president's salary. It

30 certainly looked as if the students were being asked to

31 pay more tuition so that the president could live in

32 higher style.

33   The administration called the adviser on the carpet,

34 tried to get her to fire the editor (me), and assigned an

35 administrative staff member to read and approve all copy

36 prior to publication. The administration even went so far

37 as to have its censor accompany staff members to the

38 printer, lest they attempt any unauthorized last-minute

39 copy changes.

40   But when the editor brought the matter to the

41 attention of the local media, the administration backed

42 off.

43   *Hazelwood* reinforced the point of view that, since

44 student newspapers are published in the school's name and

45 at the school's expense, administrators should have

46 control over what is published. However, if the

47 administration of a college is doing its job, if it is

48 functioning effectively, it should have no fear of

49 criticism from its students. It should, instead, consider

50 itself successful for having produced students who are

51 critical thinkers.

52   Certainly it would be unreasonable to expect
53 administrators to allow students to publish anything they
54 wanted to. But capable journalism professors should be
55 able to guide students into making responsible decisions
56 of what is and is not libelous, what is and is not fair,
57 and what is and is not appropriate for publication; and
58 administrators should keep their hands off. The school
59 newspaper should be a proving ground for journalists-to-be
60 and for any student interested in clear, accurate writing.

61   Some schools do better by their future automobile
62 drivers than by their future journalists, first
63 instructing them in safety and traffic regulations, then
64 allowing them to put what they have learned into practice.
65 What sort of journalists can we hope to produce if we
66 aren't willing to give them practical experience? Where
67 will we be if the Bob Woodwards and Carl Bernsteins of
68 tomorrow first have to clear their stories with future
69 Richard Nixons?

70   Attempts to censor school newspapers send a clear
71 message to students: The Constitution guarantees certain
72 rights to every American citizen—except you. Please
73 deposit your Constitutional rights in the trash cans at
74 the door. By the way, we need to order larger trash cans.

EXERCISE 2.19 Fill in the blanks.

1. What is the controlling idea, the thesis? _____

_____

2. Where is the thesis located, at the beginning of the composition or at the
  end? _____

3. Which of the 10 methods of development is/are predominant?

_____

4. What pattern/patterns of organization (chronological, by importance, spatial) predominate? _____

5. What are the strong or weak points of the introduction and the conclusion?

_____

_____

6. What can you say about the writer's use of words, including transitions, and effectiveness of sentences? _____

_____

7. What are the strong or weak points of the whole composition?

_____

_____

Answers on page 148.

---

7. Out of the Fog
by Ruby L. Scott

1 The warmth of a bright, sunny, fun-filled day is
2 being drawn below the horizon by the coming darkness.
3 Enticed to arise from its bed in the cool dampness of the
4 swamp, the fog moves slowly, but with definite purpose. It
5 will creep toward the surrounding land, and as it becomes
6 more fully awake, it will become denser and move more
7 rapidly. When it has built sufficiently to take possession
8 of the land by dropping as an impenetrable blanket, it
9 will have reached its goal. Here it will remain, to enjoy
10 whatever havoc may be caused, until the sun again comes up
11 to brighten a new day. In the manner of fog, alcohol
12 descends on man.

13   Man will have his sunny day. There will be friends,

14 laughter, and nothing to make him apprehensive about

15 evening's approach. There will be no indication that this

16 day cannot last forever, and he will try to make each

17 moment count. Even when the sun begins its descent, man

18 continues the merriment. He has not seen the fog and

19 therefore can see no cause for alarm. The sun sinks lower

20 and lower.

21   When he first becomes aware of the awakening fog, he

22 is not concerned because he feels he is in control. After

23 all, man is master of the universe and should have nothing

24 to fear. He has no concept of the power of the fog, once

25 awakened, until finally there is no turning back. There is

26 no choice given; he must proceed along the course which

27 leads directly to the heart of the grandfather of all

28 fogs.

29   Man is now engulfed in a cloud heavy enough to

30 obliterate his senses and impair his reasoning. He has

31 eyes that cannot see and ears that will not hear. He does

32 not know which way to turn. His mind refuses to function

33 and he has truly lost his way. He stumbles along an

34 unfamiliar path and is totally unaware of the obstacles he

35 will encounter or the hazards that await him. He is only

36 vaguely aware of his family, who have slipped into the

37 darkness with him but have been left to feel their way

38 alone. How can he help them when he cannot help himself?

39   He detects a glimmer in the distance. Is the sun

40 actually beginning to eat its way through the vapor? He

41 moves forward hopefully. He can now see that the sun has

42 been released by the horizon, like a balloon, to float

43 toward the sky, giving off its light as it ascends. As the

44 light grows brighter, the fog begins its retreat, back to

45 the swamp where it will lie dormant until it is once more

46 aroused.

47   Man looks around and finds his family, which had been

48 lost only to him. He finds some of himself that had been

49 unknown to him, but he is pleased. He finds something that

50 he had lost in the deep fog, his self-respect. This new

51 man can now gather his family, and together they can walk

52 into the sunshine of a bright new day.

53   Alcohol no longer clouds his brain. He has come out

54 of the fog.

EXERCISE 2.20 Fill in the blanks.

1. What is the controlling idea, the thesis? _____

_____

2. Where is the thesis located, at the beginning of the composition or at the

end? _____

3. Which of the 10 methods of development is/are predominant?

_____

4. What pattern/patterns of organization (chronological, by importance,

spatial) predominate? _____

5. What are the strong or weak points of the introduction and the conclusion?

_____

_____

6. What can you say about the writer's use of words, including transitions,

and effectiveness of sentences? _____

_____

7. What are the strong or weak points of the whole composition?

_____

_____

Answers on page 149.

8. Those Damned Cigarettes

by Harold L. Gaines Jr.

1   It was one of those long hot August nights. I sat in
2 my car listening to the incessant chatter of the police
3 dispatcher barking orders. I was an intern with the local
4 newspaper while I was in college. I had been covering the
5 police beat for three weeks now.

6   I took a long drag on my cigarette and immediately
7 started coughing. "Those damned things will kill me some
8 day," I thought.

9   The air was stale from the smoke of my cigarette. I
10 glanced at my watch. It was 3 a.m.

11   Suddenly the radio barked, "A worker at 2513 Ansel
12 Rd. Unit Five respond Code Three." A worker—police lingo
13 for an active fire. I decided to go. Maybe I could get a
14 story.

15   Flames were leaping from the window of an eighth-
16 floor apartment. I knew this was low-income housing for
17 the elderly.

18   In the eerie glow of the flashing red lights, the
19 firemen, putting on oxygen tanks, grabbing axes, and
20 shouting instructions, apparently couldn't hear the
21 screams over the roar of the fire trucks. If I were going

22 to get a story, I'd have to get up there.

23 The elevator wasn't working, so I started up the
24 stairs. I got to the third floor, breathing heavily; the
25 fourth floor, panting; the sixth floor, completely out of
26 breath. I stopped to rest. Then I heard those hideous
27 screams again. I had to keep going.

28 The seventh floor, my lungs screamed for air! Then I
29 started coughing. "Those damned cigarettes!" I thought.

30 Two firemen ran past me. Thank goodness they would
31 get there first. I could cancel the hero act and just be a
32 reporter again. I pulled out my pad and pencil, lit a
33 cigarette, and walked the remaining stairs.

34 I tried to keep out of the way as the firemen, now
35 several of them, connected hose to standpipe and began
36 dousing the tiny apartment. When the fire was out, I asked
37 if I could go in. I stamped out my cigarette and went
38 through the charred doorway. My stomach wretched as I saw
39 vividly the cause of the fire and the source of the
40 screaming.

41 My story was buried in the depths of Section Two.
42 "Mrs. Aretha Davis, 89, burned to death early this morning
43 at Elders' Haven, 2513 Ansel Rd. The fire was confined to
44 her apartment. Evidence pointed to the fact that Davis, a
45 victim of severe arthritis, had been smoking in bed. She
46 has no survivors."

47 The story satisfied my editor but didn't begin to
48 tell the horror. Mrs. Davis sat on the side of her bed
49 smoking a cigarette. She dropped her cigarette into a pile
50 of clothes on the floor and was too crippled to pick up
51 the cigarette or to move away from the fire.

52   She just sat there screaming while her cigarette
53 caught the clothes on fire, then the bed, then her whole
54 body.

55   When I finally got to bed, I couldn't sleep. I'll
56 never forget those awful screams. I started coughing
57 again. Those damned cigarettes.

EXERCISE 2.21 Fill in the blanks.

1. What is the controlling idea, the thesis? _____

_____

2. Where is the thesis located, at the beginning of the composition or at the
end? _____

3. Which of the 10 methods of development is/are predominant?

_____

4. What pattern/patterns of organization (chronological, by importance,
spatial) predominate? _____

5. What are the strong or weak points of the introduction and the conclusion?

_____

_____

6. What can you say about the writer's use of words, including transitions,
and effectiveness of sentences? _____

_____

7. What are the strong or weak points of the whole composition?

_____

_____

Answers on page 149.

9. Relativity
by Brendan J. M. O'Haire

1   Fear is relative. Some people are scared to death of
2 the dentist. Others lie awake nights worrying about
3 nuclear fallout. I have a friend who won't leave the house
4 on the 13th of any month, a victim of triskaidekaphobia.
5 There's acrophobia, fear of heights; agoraphobia, fear of
6 crowds; claustrophobia, fear of being closed in;
7 hydrophobia, fear of water; and necrophobia, fear of
8 death, to name a few more.

9   Me, I had Englishcompositionaphobia. I was terrorized
10 by having to write an English composition. That is, until
11 I had real fear to compare it with.

12   I work as a security guard at a nursing home. So does
13 Charlie, a college student like me. Or rather, unlike me.
14 He's small; I'm big. He's unreliable about showing up for
15 work on Thursdays; I'm there when I'm supposed to be and
16 lots of other times to sub for people like Charlie. Maybe
17 he bowls on Thursdays. I don't know.

18   I was called in on a recent Thursday to sub for
19 Charlie. The nursing home is in an "old money"
20 neighborhood and is full of older folks still possessed of
21 lots of money, art works, and jewelry, all protected by us
22 part-time security guards. To assure the safety of the
23 residents and their valuables, we are equipped with a
24 radio, a flashlight, a large ring of keys, and a
25 nightstick. No guns. The management reasons that the sight
26 of guns might disturb some of our clients, and one good
27 loud gunshot might send half the population into cardiac
28 arrest.

29   Charlie's duty this particular Thursday was roving

30   guard, the guy most in danger of being mugged because he

31   is the most visible and he is the one with keys to all the

32   doors. A clear Thursday night in October when you have

33   been called in on your day off is a good one for letting

34   your mind wander, for thinking about school, English, what

35   to write about. Maybe this is why I didn't see him until

36   he jumped out from his hiding place.

37   Cool electricity cascaded down my back. All the

38   lights, even the moon, took on a luminous greenish tinge.

39   The only part of my body not trying to figure out what to

40   do with all that extra adrenaline was my right arm. It had

41   pulled my nightstick halfway out of its holster before the

42   rest of me realized that Joe here wasn't playing by the

43   same rules I was. He had decided to bring along a gun.

44   His planning had been good: the timing (he obviously

45   knew Charlie's schedule), the hiding place, his dark

46   clothes. But he had a couple of problems. His hiding spot

47   meant that he would meet the guard face to face. He was

48   expecting someone not quite 5'5 and 140 pounds; he got

49   someone 6'2 and 260 pounds.

50   The look on his face as he stared into my chest and

51   then slowly raised his eyes to meet mine was beyond

52   description. You could see that four-letter word take

53   possession of his brain.

54   The realization that something had gone seriously

55   wrong with his plan slowed him down for only a moment. We

56   had a classic standoff. A clock would have argued that

57   only a few seconds passed; he and I knew different. We got

58   to know each other very well. If he even blinked, I'd do

59 my level best to break his neck. If I moved, he would open
60 a new freeway through my stomach.

61   After what seemed like hours of silent negotiation,
62 we came to an unspoken agreement. He turned and ran. I did
63 not follow. I wasn't about to test my luck at holding off
64 a gun with nothing but an overgrown twig.

65   His luck held. The police never caught him.

66   Now I can sit down and write an English paper with
67 only the least bit of trembling. I just think back to that
68 night when the moon changed color and bolts of electric
69 adrenaline shot through my body.

70   Heck, literary death isn't nearly as frightening as
71 some of life's other alternatives.

EXERCISE 2.22 Fill in the blanks.

1. What is the controlling idea, the thesis? _____

_____

2. Where is the thesis located, at the beginning of the composition or at the
end? _____

3. Which of the 10 methods of development is/are predominant?

_____

4. What pattern/patterns of organization (chronological, by importance,
spatial) predominate? _____

5. What are the strong or weak points of the introduction and the conclusion?

_____

_____

6. What can you say about the writer's use of words, including transitions,
and effectiveness of sentences? _____

_____

7. What are the strong or weak points of the whole composition?

_____

_____

Answers on page 150.

---

10. Do Unto Others . . .

by Ronald Lee Franklin

1   It could have been just about any stinkin' hot July
2   afternoon in Ohio—but it wasn't. It was the first day of
3   the rest of my life, or my living death, to be more
4   accurate.

5   My little brother Reginald was bugging me to drive
6   him to the beach. Little brother, that's a laugh. He was
7   six foot, husky like me, but he wasn't old enough to get a
8   driver's license.

9   My fiancée Sharon was over, and we were sharing a
10 Pepsi and trying to ignore Reginald by turning the music
11 up louder and louder.

12 "Pullease, Ron," he begged. "I'm dyin'."

13 Me, one of the best athletes in the state—All
14 Scholastic Basketball Team, All-East Senate leading
15 scorer, a dozen colleges coming up with scholarships—and
16 all I'd done all summer was drive Reginald.

17 "Maybe we should, Ron," said Sharon. She was
18 beautiful. "Remember, we were talking last night about the
19 Golden Rule?"

20 "Yeah, Ron. I'd do unto *you* whatever you needed."
21 Reginald picked up on things real quick.

22   "Oh, okay. Load up the wieners and the charcoal, and
23 ask Raymond if he wants to go." Raymond was my older
24 brother. "We'll stop by Sharon's and pick up her
25 swimsuit."

26   We piled into my graying, arthritic Dodge, and 45
27 minutes later were at Mentor Headlands Park. Lake Erie
28 around Cleveland wasn't famous for its pure water, but
29 even a swim in impure water would be cooler than none.

30   As soon as we hit the beach, we headed for the water.
31 I swam out to a yacht about 50 yards off shore and asked
32 the owner if it would be all right to dive from his boat.
33 He said okay. The others joined me, and we were having a
34 great time. That's when I did my jackknife off the bow of
35 the boat.

36   I hit something. There were a few seconds of shock
37 before reality struck. I couldn't move. I was paralyzed.
38 Was this a dream? Why was I under water in this dark, cold
39 limbo?

40   Time stood still. I thought I wasn't going to make
41 it. For some reason, I started counting. I got to 59. I
42 felt my body being snatched up from the water. I was being
43 dragged to shore. My brothers had realized my predicament.

44   I remember the sandy water lifting my legs off the
45 beach, legs I could no longer feel. Somehow I hung on
46 until the Coast Guard got there. . . .

47   I woke up in a hospital. Then there was another
48 hospital. Three operations in a year. And transfer to a
49 skilled-nursing hospital, where I have lived for 13 years.

50   Six months strapped into a Stryker frame. Lying
51 there, face to the floor, no rest because I was turned

52 every two hours. Always in tears and depressed. I couldn't

53 believe this sick, quadriplegic body was Ron Franklin. Why

54 me, God? Where the hell are you, God?

55   In the beginning, friends came regularly; they used

56 to have to step over each other. Gradually they stopped

57 coming. It was just my family and Sharon. Reginald has

58 been great. So has Sharon, but I told her it wouldn't

59 work. I needed help with washing, eating, dressing,

60 writing, telephoning—every activity of daily living—and I

61 still do, even though I'm in a wheelchair and a real bed

62 now.

63   It took eight years of wallowing in self-pity before

64 I began to realize I was lucky to be alive. It wasn't my

65 time to go. God must have spared me for some reason. He

66 knows what He's doing.

67   I decided to take a stab at college, a course or two

68 at a time. The local transit company provides a special

69 bus for people in wheelchairs, so I get to nearby Cuyahoga

70 Community College one day a week. Other days someone from

71 the college comes to me. And I dictate homework to

72 volunteers at the hospital, as I am doing now. The day I

73 mastered turning pages by myself was another first day of

74 my life. There have been many.

75   I try to focus my attention on things other than my

76 physical condition. It's what's in the head and the heart

77 that counts. I hope to go to law school. I know so much

78 more about human beings now than I did before the

79 accident, and I find I can communicate successfully.

80   It may sound corny, but I try to follow the Golden

81 Rule every day. It makes me feel good, and then, as I

82 found out, you never know when you may need someone to do
83 unto you.

EXERCISE 2.23 Fill in the blanks.

1. What is the controlling idea, the thesis? _____

_____

2. Where is the thesis located, at the beginning of the composition or at the

end? _____

3. Which of the 10 methods of development is/are predominant?

_____

4. What pattern/patterns of organization (chronological, by importance,

spatial) predominate? _____

5. What are the strong or weak points of the introduction and the conclusion?

_____

_____

6. What can you say about the writer's use of words, including transitions,

and effectiveness of sentences? _____

_____

7. What are the strong or weak points of the whole composition?

_____

_____

Answers on page 151.

QUIZ YOURSELF ON STEP THREE Write a composition with a subject and thesis of your choice, using one of the 10 methods of development and one of the three patterns of organization we have discussed. Be prepared to show your outline and your rough draft. Choose your method of development and your pattern of organization with care, and select words and construct sentences for the most effective, most creative result. Be sure your introduction and your conclusion are strong. But above all, use your own style and try to enjoy the writing.

Answers to Exercises

Answers to Exercise 2.1, Page 74

Suitable thesis statements are **2, 3, 6, 8,** and **10.** The others are unsuitable; they are just topics and not the point you want to make about the topics (not complete sentences) or else general facts that everyone knows and would agree with.

Possible Answers to Exercise 2.2, Page 75

1. There should be an easy, nonincriminating method for students to evaluate their instructors.

2. One of the benefits of enlisting in the armed services is the possibility of furthering your education.

3. Many parents would be horrified if they thought they were abusing their children, yet they constantly make the kids feel as if they are inferior beings. This is emotional abuse at its worst.

4. Why does there have to be so much violence—even glorified violence—in children's television? Why can't there be more educational programs, interesting enough for children to want to watch?

5. More students would use the library if there were a section where chairs were more comfortable and where snacks were permitted.

Possible Answer to Exercise 2.4, page 79

I. Introduction. In order to maintain high standards of education, schools should devise an easy, nonincriminating method for students to evaluate their instructors.

II. Body.
   A. Present non-system is wrong.
      1. Students are not encouraged to evaluate the instruction they are receiving; usually there is no procedure to do so.
      2. Students are fearful their grade will be jeopardized if they criticize the instructor.
   B. There is great need for evaluation so that ineffective instructors can improve or be dismissed.
      1. Bad instruction may permanently discourage students from getting an education.
      2. Bad instruction can adversely affect the reputation of an otherwise good college.
   C. There is need for a fair system for student input.

1. Student evaluation is the best way for administrators who hire faculty to know the truth about instructors' capabilities.
2. A system is needed whereby students won't be penalized by an instructor they complain about, but also whereby an instructor's career can't be jeopardized by a disgruntled student's unjustified complaint.
3. A "middleman" is needed; it could be a Student Government committee to receive complaints (guaranteeing the student's anonymity and encouraging only valid complaints) and to forward them to the instructor and to proper administrator.
4. Student-evaluation-of-faculty forms should be readily available through the same Student Government committee, to be forwarded to the instructor and the administrator.
   D. The system should also to be used for recognizing outstanding instructors and encouraging them to continue outstanding work.
III. Conclusion. There is a real need for a good student-evaluation-of-faculty system as an incentive for bad teachers to improve and outstanding teachers to remain outstanding, thereby improving the quality of education for the student.

Answers to Quiz Yourself on Step One, Page 86

1. They are alike in that the purpose of both is to develop a controlling idea coherently. They are different in that the paragraph is made up of sentences, and the composition is made up of paragraphs (which, of course, are made up of sentences). **2.** Thesis or thesis statement. **3.** a. **4.** b. **5.** b. **6.** c. **7.** c. **8.** F. **9.** F. **10.** F.

Answers to Exercise 2.8, Page 102

I'd—but I had, no (repetition of), when, before—while—after, In fact, finally, then, But after that, In five days, So much for, at least, but, Instead of, And.

Answers to Exercise 2.9, Page 103

1. Mrs. Murphy, the English teacher, and Ms. Larue, the history teacher, were having lunch together in the faculty dining room <u>because</u> neither one had had time <u>before</u> school to fix her lunch.
2. "I have a student named Carla <u>whom</u> I'm concerned about," said Mrs. Murphy. "She never gets her homework in on time, <u>and</u> often she doesn't hand it in at all. She is failing, <u>yet</u> I know she is bright."
3. "I have a young man I'm worried about <u>too</u>," said Ms. Larue, "<u>because</u> he always does poorly on tests. He seems fascinated by history <u>during</u> class, <u>but</u> he must lose all interest in history after school."

4. "<u>I must say</u>, these two sound very much alike. I wish we could do more for students like them," said Mrs. Murphy. "<u>For instance</u>, I hope to help Carla Careless <u>by recommending</u> that she make an appointment with a tutor in the Learning Center."

5. "Did you say Careless? <u>By coincidence</u>, my student's name is Careless <u>too</u>—Calvin Careless," Ms. Larue <u>said excitedly</u>. "<u>So</u> Carla must be the twin sister he has mentioned. <u>After</u> my repeatedly asking him to see me in my office, <u>finally</u> Calvin has made an appointment to see me <u>so</u> we can talk about his history grade."

6. "These two sound almost identical, <u>don't they? Of course</u>, opposite-sex twins can't be identical. <u>But</u> possibly we can give them both help."

Possible Answers to Exercise 2.10, Page 103

Types of transitions are in boldface:

It's a beast walking upright like a man, seven to nine feet tall, with (**added material**) a large head, almost no neck, a face like a gorilla, huge arms, and a covering of hair. "Just because (**cause**) you've never seen one doesn't mean it doesn't exist," said Tom Steenburg, of Water Valley, Alberta, explaining (**combining clauses**) that he has never seen (**repetition**) a wolverine but (**difference**) knows they do indeed (**summary**) exist. And (**added material**) he believes there is definitely something prowling the Canadian Rockies that (**example**) leaves huge human-like footprints, something (**repetition**) whose (**example**) existence needs either (**difference**) to be proved or (**difference**) to be disproved.

The first (**time**) person to find evidence of the sasquatch, the hairy, man-like creature called Bigfoot, was a fur trader named David Thompson, who (**example**) reported sighting huge footprints near Jasper, Alberta, in 1811. Since then (**time**), although (**difference**) hundreds of people have reported seeing Bigfoot, no evidence has held up scientifically.

Meanwhile (**time**), Steenburg keeps looking, checking reports of sightings, separating the obvious fakes from those he can't explain (**combining clauses**). And (**added material**) he keeps hoping (**parallel construction with "Steenburg keeps looking"**) that Bigfoot will either (**difference**) come his way or (**difference**) die a peaceful death from lack of evidence.

Answers to Exercise 2.11, Page 104

1. As we relived the Renaissance in Ms. Larue's class, we realized <u>we</u> couldn't afford to miss a single class.

2. Students should be sure they vote in the Student Senate election. It's the only way <u>they</u> can participate in decision making at the college.

3. If you want Peter for president, <u>you</u> are all going to have to campaign for him. OR If we <u>want</u> . . .

4. Mrs. Murphy feels the job of Student Senate president is important, and <u>she</u> sometimes wishes faculty members could vote in student elections.

5. When the election is over, let's hope we all get behind the winner, whether <u>we</u> voted for that person or not.

Answers to Exercise 2.12, Page 106

1. A generalization that certainly is not always true.
2. Hardly the new president's fault, but that's what is implied.
3. Two completely unrelated facts.
4. A faulty premise that all people born in July become rich and famous.
5. Same thing said twice.

Answer to Exercise 2.13, Page 107

I. Introduction = thesis: Advertising sometimes asks dumb questions, but it must work.
II. Body.
  A. Examples of dumb questions in ads.
  B. Even salesmen at the door ask dumb questions.
III. Conclusion. It works—he sold me.

Here is the composition in good order.

¶3   It's hard to imagine running a successful business by asking dumb questions that any moron would know the answer to. But that's advertising. I guess it works or they wouldn't keep doing it.

¶5   Hardly a day goes by that I don't pick up a magazine which screams at me, "Do You Want a Healthy Head of Hair?" or "Are You Sick of Cockroaches in Your Cupboards?" or "Do You Want to Lose 12 Pounds in Three Days?" Some weirdos may consider dandruff a turn-on and cockroaches cute little pets; and, hey, I'd settle for three pounds in 12 days. But the answers are pretty obvious.

¶2   Not only am I assaulted by magazine ads, but a

salesman came to my door the other day and asked, "Are you interested in saving 50 cents a copy on each magazine you receive?"

¶6   Am I supposed to say, "No, I want to get in my car, use gas and time I don't have, run down to the corner drugstore whenever I want a magazine, buy the magazine before it's sold out, and pay an extra $60 a year for the privilege"?

¶1   After he left, I stood there at the door with a five-year subscription to *The Bleeding Gums Journal* in hand; and my husband asked, "Why didn't you just tell him you didn't want the magazine?"

¶4   "Because that wasn't the question." See how it works?

Answers to Quiz Yourself on Step Two, Page 107

1. Introduction, body, and conclusion. **2.** a. **3.** b. The first sentence is okay. The second sentence makes the mistake of saying that a male can become pregnant and that either male or female can become pregnant from watching TV.

Answers to Exercise 2.14, Page 110

1. Success is happiness found in helping others.
2. Three short clauses in the third paragraph (success is not money, it is not power, it is not status) build up to the thesis in the fourth paragraph: success is happiness, and you're as successful as you are happy, and you're as happy as you are helpful to others.
3. Definition (of success), with some comparison and contrast (some people's idea of success versus Joon's father's idea).
4. The pattern flows from wrong to right, from what not to do to what to do, from what isn't important to what is important. The pattern of organization is by order of importance, ending in the fact that Joon is going to try to live up to his father's ideals.
5. The first two sentences are weak. They could well be left off. A more interesting beginning might be, "Joon, maybe we will not have time to talk again . . ." That would arouse my curiosity more than saying, "Here is my definition of success." I like the conclusion very much. You can

visualize this kid in a foreign land far away from home and family, resolving to live by his father's philosophy, and being comforted by it.

6. The use of words and sentences is good, partly, I suppose, because English is Joon's second language (no doubt his father's too, but his father probably wasn't speaking English). The reader feels that the simplicity of words and sentence structure makes the message clearer, and the emotions seem to come more directly from the heart. Paragraph 3 is especially interesting with its three balanced subordinate clauses: as you may think, as you may have heard, as you may feel. There is a lack of transitional expressions, but that lack is hardly missed as the reader follows from one simple idea to the next one. The repetition of the direct address ("Joon, . . .) is realistic and ties the paragraphs together.

7. One of the strong points is the effective definition of success told in such a simple way. Another is ending with direct address back to Dad and the son's saying he'll try to live by the father's words. You can feel the son's emotion. The reader is so moved by the father-son relationship that the great wisdom in the father's definition of success comes very much alive. I do think, however, that the beginning could be made more interesting.

Answers to Exercise 2.15, Page 114

1. As a child, I found our attic a forbidden magical storehouse of treasures.

2. It is never expressed, but it comes across clearly to the reader.

3. Description, held together by narration.

4. Spatial.

5. Both are very good. Kathie expresses her excitement in the first sentence and gives the reader a sense of excitement too. Telling in the second sentence what the attic was not (not the kind of attic that was for temporary storage or the kind that was frequently cleaned) makes clearer what kind of attic it really was. Then a general description leads to a detailed description of the attic and of her feelings.

   The conclusion brings a delightful description to a fitting end, with the purposes in telling the story made clear (not nostalgia alone, but also, with her last trip to the attic, a symbolic end to her childhood).

6. Kathie's use of descriptive words is excellent: the vacuum cleaner's sinister-looking black bag, three cloudy mirrors watching her progress, dusty bulb glowing dimly. She has a knack of turning ordinary language into concrete language to make the reader see, hear, and feel what she does: shaky knees, floorboard squeaks, eyes adjust to the dimness, strange feeling in her stomach, eerie light gives life to the old furniture, the headless dressmaker's form moves, she picks her way through cobwebs.

She doesn't need too many transitions; this is a good example of narration used to carry the content along smoothly. With a couple of *when*s, *then*s, and *but*s, plus *and, although, therefore, obviously, still, as, for a second,* and *before,* she carries off a smooth progression from up the stairs to down the stairs, with her vivid description in between.

She varies sentence length to help establish the mood. For example, in the seventh paragraph, she walks slowly to the piece of string . . . The sentences are long and slow. Then she thinks she sees the dress-maker's form move. The pace is increased to match her heartbeat, with five short main clauses.

7. The strong points are her simple but vivid descriptive words (call to high adventure, final resting place, hot, dirty, dangerous, hazardous road), her concrete language (see question 6), her strong verbs (deposit-ed, executed, feigned, crept, forced), and her happy but serious child-like tone as she puts this superb description into a narrative framework. The title, however, could be more exciting.

Answers to Exercise 2.16, Page 117

1. After much searching and becoming acquainted with many types of women, I finally found the perfect woman, my wife.

2. At the end.

3. Classification. Tussy puts the women he has known into categories: gold digger, jock, intellectual snob, fake glamour girl, and, finally, his wife.

4. A mixture of spatial (as if he were looking from left to right at the women he has known) and chronological (the reader assumes the women are discussed in chronological order, from the writer's third-grade attraction to his present-day wife) and, of course, order of impor-tance, from grade school puppy lover to present loving wife.

5. The introduction, I believe, arouses the reader's interest, probably by having the writer begin at such an early age his search for the perfect woman. The narration at the start about the new girl in the class and the writer's falling in love is fun. After going through the various cate-gories of women he has spurned or been spurned by, Tussy ties things up neatly with reference again to the perfect woman.

6. Tussy has a way with interesting words: floated home, stomped away, suffered my first broken heart, dumped me, chalked up, intimidate me, stuffing her groceries into her backpack, vanished beyond the hills of joggers' highs, kept flashing the cover of the book, spat a bunch of big words, faked an interest in me (all strong verbs). He uses alliteration (finally I found, little lady who loved me only for my lunch money, first foray, what could be wheedled out of my wherewithal, muscular miss, unbiological bulges) and metaphor (giant Pillsbury dough boy). His use

of words fits his tongue-in-cheek tone. He makes the most of the Corvette, referring to it at the end. He uses symbolic language: she has a habit of bringing home animals and old folks who are lost (this stands for the fact, is another way of saying, that she is very kind and loving). The transitions beginning the second through fifth paragraphs involve time, as do *once in my life* and *finally,* helping chronology carry the classification along. The order is logical and coherent; the sentence structure, varied and interesting.

7. The strong points are his effective use of words and the underlying sense of humor.

Answers to Exercise 2.17, Page 120

1. Two dental procedures, crowning and bonding, may be of interest to people whose smile is marred by dental defects.

2. In the first sentence.

3. Comparison and contrast, using alternating or point-by-point development. There is also some how-to, or process, development.

4. Chronological, from beginning to end of the procedures.

5. I believe Charlotte makes potentially tedious procedures as interesting as possible. Her introductory and concluding references to smiling lighten the subject and tie the composition together well.

6. Her use of words is appropriate to the serious subject. Certainly, creative use of words (as in the preceding composition about the perfect woman) would be out of place here. Few transitions (with crowning, unlike crowning) are necessary because the alternating method of comparison and contrast moves smoothly from point to point of each method. Sentence structure is okay, with varied length of sentences.

7. She did a good job with what could have been a boring subject.
   (Charlotte, I must tell you, is now in dental school.)

Answers to Exercise 2.18, Page 123

1. We are paranoid over the risks of living.

2. At the end of the second paragraph (still at the beginning of the composition).

3. Examples (with just a touch of comparison and contrast at the start, with the simplicity of knowing what was risky in the good old days contrasted to our paranoia now).

4. Chronological.

5. The introduction grabs the reader's attention enough to make him or

her want to read on, wondering what risks today could compare with sky diving or going over Niagara Falls in a barrel. The conclusion wraps the composition up well by referring to the thesis, our paranoia over the risks of living.

6. Marianne constructs her sentences for the best effect: Those were the good old days. Life was simple. We were naive. We were happy. Short simple sentences emphasize the lack of worry then. Then her sentence structure becomes varied, and questions and answers are used as an interesting technique. She uses parallel construction to good advantage: from uninformed to educated to over-educated to neurotic and finally to paranoid, and energy sags while blood pressure soars (good verbs). Her use of words is good: open one eye, jury still out on whether cancer is brewing in the decaf cup, forget breakfast, room grounded, somewhere between educated and paranoid.

7. The strong points are her interesting examples and her attitude toward her subject, poking fun at our worrying about so many things that it takes up all our time. She picks her words effectively too.

    (Marianne now has an M.A. in counseling and human services.)

Answers to Exercise 2.19, Page 126

1. Censorship of school newspapers is wrong.

2. It is never expressed in just the six words, "Censorship of school newspapers is wrong." But it is strongly suggested in the first paragraph, hinted at in the writer's tone throughout the composition, clearly stated in the third-from-last paragraph (Administrators should keep their hands off), and restated in a clever way in the last paragraph, which refers to the first paragraph and ties beginning to end.

3. Argumentation.

4. Partly chronological (from the earlier court case to the later case to what goes on in schools today), partly in order of importance (from candy wrappers to the possible need for larger trash cans for bigger issues).

5. The introduction attracts the reader's attention with a picture of Constitutional rights being dropped into a trash can: he or she wants to read on. The conclusion returns to the picture of the trash can, giving the composition added coherence. Irv is creative in his use of language and images. Both introduction and conclusion are strong.

6. Each paragraph seems to flow smoothly into the next, partly through the use of effective transitions and partly through logical arrangement of the subject matter. The writer's words are serious but quite clear, appropriate for a serious topic. Sentences are varied in length and structure, but not too complicated, which could easily have been the case in deal-

ing with this somewhat complex topic.

7. The strongest point is the way the argument is presented: a clever beginning, a brief history of court cases, a personal experience, a look at the other side of the question (perhaps the school that pays for the newspaper *should* have a right to censor it), making clear that the other side is not valid, showing how lack of censorship should work ideally, and a clever conclusion reinforcing the description at the start. The weakest point is the title. I would be more attracted by something like "Please Drop Your Constitutional Rights in the Trash Can."

(Irv, incidentally, is having fun with freedom of the press as editor and publisher of *Hoot,* Columbus, Ohio's biweekly cartoon newspaper, and as featured columnist for the weekly *Columbus Guardian.*)

Answers to Exercise 2.20, Page 129

1. Being an alcoholic is like being in a deep fog.

2. In the last sentence of the first paragraph and in the last two sentences of the last paragraph.

3. Analogy.

4. Chronological and spatial (from outside the fog into it and back out again), with good description throughout.

5. The introduction arouses interest and builds suspense. The first and the third-from-last paragraphs are beautifully descriptive. The first paragraph, with alcohol descending on man like fog, and the last, with man coming out of the fog, add excellent coherence to the composition.

6. Somehow the choice of words is outstanding in painting a picture of fog slowly overtaking man (being drawn, moves slowly, creep), then moving faster (become denser, move more rapidly, take possession, reached its goal), and finally receding (sun has been released, it ascends, light grows brighter, fog begins its retreat). Transitions are good, but the smooth flow is mainly the result of the logical progression of the action.

7. The strongest asset of the composition is its description, so vivid that the reader lives the situation. It could have been written only by someone who has "been there."

(This is true. Ruby's life was turned around by Alcoholics Anonymous. She survived cardiac arrest, cancer, a stroke, and four heart attacks. "God has kept me alive for some purpose," she says, "and I don't intend to die until I get the okay from Him." She works in alcohol-abuse treatment.)

Answers to Exercise 2.21, Page 132

1. Smoking is very dangerous, on two counts: possibility of death from lung cancer, possibility of death from accidental fire.

2. It is never expressed except in "Those damned cigarettes," which appears at the beginning, in the middle, and at the end.

3. A beautiful cause-and-effect paper but told in narrative style.

4. Chronological.

5. The introduction contains a good, brief description of the quiet August night almost immediately contrasted with the excitement of the fire. It makes the reader want to go on. The conclusion presents another contrast: that of the newspaper item contrasted with the actual situation. The composition comes to a fitting and effective close with the final "Those damned cigarettes."

6. Use of both words and sentences is extremely good: quiet mood at first, excitement mounting, the breathlessness of the smoker, the horror of the scene, the matter-of-factness of the newspaper account, and the recurring coughing and condemnation of cigarettes. The narrative progression makes the need for transitional words and phrases minimal.

7. The unusual subject matter itself is one of the strong points. Add to that the writer's attitude toward his subject, a tone of condemnation toward all smoking but particularly his own, and you have an interesting combination that will appeal to almost any audience. His description is brief but eloquent.

Answers to Exercise 2.22, Page 135

1. Fear is relative. Something you really feared may turn out to be comparatively harmless.

2. At the beginning, repeated at the end.

3. If I asked this on a quiz, I'd accept either comparison and contrast or narration. I would consider it to be more narration—it tells a rather fascinating story.

4. Chronological.

5. The introduction makes you want to read on to find out what fear the writer has. The conclusion is strong, emphasizing how his fear of writing compositions was put in perspective.

6. His use of words is excellent. Especially good is his description of the confrontation, with the would-be mugger silently realizing he is up against a much bigger problem than he had anticipated. Brendan's feelings as his adrenaline began to surge are well conveyed to the reader.

Sentences are longer in the descriptions leading up to the climax, shorter when the action is at its height. As is often the case in narrative compositions, transitions are few because the action carries the story along without the necessity for special connectors.

His language is vivid: cool electricity cascaded, luminous greenish tinge, extra adrenaline, not playing by the same rules, see that four-letter word take possession of his brain, classic standoff, hours of silent negotiation, unspoken agreement, overgrown twig.

7. His story is told in an interesting manner. His language is strong. His controlling idea is one we can all relate to. He has expressed it well— fear *is* relative.

Answers to Exercise 2.23, Page 139

1. The only way to achieve mental peace after becoming tragically handicapped physically is to turn outside oneself.

2. It is never expressed, but it becomes evident in the last four paragraphs in which the writer is telling how he overcame his vast self-pity.

3. I am using this as an example of a process, a how-to, paper because it so beautifully tells how Ron overcame his mental handicap. The process is blended into the narration, a beautiful story. However, this certainly isn't a run-of-the-mill process paper, telling how to change a washer in a faucet or how to make money in the stock market. It is also cause and effect.

4. A chronological pattern predominates although the story also builds from least to most important.

5. The introduction lets the reader know immediately that something terribly important is going to happen. Then the scene turns to the ordinary aspects of a hot July afternoon, with the writer sharing a Pepsi and turning up the music and resisting his brother's pleas for a trip to the beach. The contrast is good. The end is effective because the whole how-to-survive piles up there.

6. The writer uses dialogue well at the start to get the story moving. His language is interesting and descriptive: graying, arthritic Dodge; a swim in impure water; cooler than none; body being snatched up from the water; sandy water lifting my legs off the beach; friends used to have to step over each other. The story flows without the use of too many transitions. His short sentences describing his feelings as he realizes what has happened to him are excellent: I hit something. I couldn't move. Was this a dream? Time stood still.

7. The reader can't help but feel that the main strength of this composition is Ron Franklin himself. He tells his story in such a simple, thoroughly understandable way that the reader feels instant empathy.

(Seeing Ron buzz cheerfully around campus in his wheelchair, one would never suspect he spent years overcoming self-pity. Not only is he blessed with, or has he cultivated, a wonderful sense of humor, but he has a beautiful tenor voice and often is invited to sing at school or community functions. When last heard from, he was working on his master's degree in rehabilitation counseling, hoping later to study law.)

3 Words

Words, the building blocks of writing, are grouped into **eight parts of speech:** nouns, verbs, pronouns, adjectives, adverbs, prepositions, conjunctions, and interjections.

Nouns: Step One

Definition of a Noun

A **noun** is a word that names a person, place, or thing, but we must include such "things" as animals, ideas, qualities, conditions, emotions, and actions.

Nouns

- Persons = *Mary, sister, boy*
- Things = *car, Oldsmobile*
- Ideas = *belief, opinion*
- Conditions = *poverty, perfection*
- Actions = *arrival, betrayal, completion*

- Places = *New York, downtown*
- Animals = *dog, Rottweiler*
- Qualities = *dishonesty, courage*
- Emotions = *love, excitement*

Main Uses of Nouns

Nouns are used in sentences as subjects, objects, appositives, and predicate nouns.

1. Subject. The subject tells who or what does something, is something, or has something done to it. The verb tells that the subject has indeed done something, or is something, or has had something done to it. In subject-verb explanations in this book, subjects are underlined once, verbs twice.

- Subject does something: <u>Mary</u> <u>reads</u> every evening.
- Subject is something: <u>Mary</u> <u>is</u> my friend.
- Subject has something done to it: <u>Mary</u> <u>was pushed</u> out of line by the rude student.

2. Object. The object answers the question what?, whom?, to what?, to whom?, for what?, or for whom? after a verb or a preposition.

- Answers question *what?* after verb: <u>Mary</u> <u>reads</u> *mysteries*.
- Answers question *whom?* after verb: <u>Mary</u> <u>likes</u> her *teacher*.
- Answers question *what?* after preposition: <u>Mary</u> <u>carried</u> a stack of *books*.
- Answers question *whom?* after preposition: <u>Mary</u> <u>studied</u> with her *sister*.
- Answers question *to whom?* after verb: <u>Mary</u> <u>gave</u> the *boy* her books.

See page 181 for the use of nouns as object complements.

3. Appositive. An appositive is a noun, call it noun #2, which is placed after noun #1, and which renames noun #1 in a different way, giving more information about noun #1.

- Mary, my *friend,* will soon leave for college.
- My very best friend, *Mary,* won the scholarship.

4. Predicate Noun. The predicate noun (also called a subject complement) follows a being verb like *is* and renames the subject in a different way, giving more information about it.

- <u>Mary</u> <u>is</u> a good *student.*
- <u>Mary</u> <u>became</u> my *friend* the first day of school.

EXERCISE 3.1 Over the underlined nouns write **s** for subject, **o** for object, **ap** for appositive, or **pn** for predicate noun to describe correctly their uses. Prepositions and verbs involved in this exercise are in italics to help you find **s, o, ap,** and **pn.**

1. A <u>sneeze</u>, a violent <u>expulsion</u> *of* <u>air</u> *through* the <u>nose</u>, *is* the <u>result</u> *of* <u>irritation</u> *of* sensory <u>nerves</u> *in* the <u>nose</u>.

2. The <u>nose</u> *is* involuntarily *removing* the <u>irritation</u>.

3. You can't keep your eyes open *during* a <u>sneeze</u>; just try it! A protective <u>reflex</u> *takes over.*

4. You may have heard that a <u>sneeze</u> *is* a near-death-like <u>state</u> when bodily <u>functions</u> *are* momentarily *suspended;* this *is* a <u>myth</u>, a <u>superstition</u>.

5. But don't suppress your sneezes; one <u>man</u> *ruptured* his <u>eardrums</u> when he *held back* a <u>sneeze</u>.

6. Just be sure you sneeze *into* a <u>tissue</u>; otherwise, <u>droplets</u> full *of* <u>germs</u> *travel* as far as 12 feet *from* the <u>sneezer</u>.

7. And the <u>germs</u> *may remain in* the <u>air</u> *for* <u>days</u> after the droplets evaporate.

8. Another <u>superstition</u> *is* that evil spirits are expelled when a <u>person</u> sneezes.

9. That is why we *wish* <u>Gesundheit</u>, <u>health</u>, *to* the <u>sneezer</u>. So close your eyes, enjoy a good sneeze, and God bless you.

Answers on page 231.

Nouns: Step Two

Six Kinds of Nouns

1. Common Nouns. Common nouns name a member or members of a class of persons, places, or things. They begin with a lowercase letter (not capitalized) unless they begin a sentence.

- A well-known *poet* who lives in the *city* won a *prize*.

2. Proper Nouns. Proper nouns name specific persons, places, or things. They begin with an uppercase (capital) letter.

- Poet *Gwendolyn Brooks* of *Chicago* won the *Pulitzer Prize*.

3. Collective Nouns. Collective nouns name a group (a collection), usually of people, sometimes of animals and things. They may be either common or proper nouns but are more often common.

- The *Class* of '99 saw a *flock* of birds flying over the *audience*.

4. Concrete Nouns. Concrete nouns can be perceived by the senses (people, places, and things that can be seen, heard, touched, smelled, or tasted). They may be either common or proper nouns.

- *Jo* was moved by the *music,* but it was *fumes* from the *onion* that caused her *tears*.

5. Abstract Nouns. Abstract nouns name intangible qualities (ideas that can not be seen or heard or touched or perceived by any of the other senses). They are usually common nouns.

- *Fear* decreases where *freedom* and *truth* are cherished *values*.

6. Predicate Nouns. Any of the five kinds of nouns can be used as predicate nouns, nouns that come after verbs like *is* (being verbs, also called linking verbs) and restate the subject.

- Her <u>story</u> <u>was</u> the *truth;* <u>witnesses</u> <u>were</u> her *sister* and the *class*.

So, all nouns are either common or proper. All nouns are also either abstract or concrete. Some nouns are collective. Any of the five other types may be used as a predicate noun.

Regular nouns form the plural by adding *s* to the singular. For a complete rundown on ways to change singular nouns to plural, see pages 381-385.

EXERCISE 3.2 Underline the nouns in the following sentences, and after every sentence write what type each noun is; there will be two or three types for each noun. The number of blanks will give you a clue to how many nouns to look for. A hint: one noun is two words, *Business Office.*

1. Peter, a student at our college, had a problem; and as he and his three friends sat in the cafeteria drinking a cup of coffee, he asked the opinion of the group. _____ _____

   _____ _____ _____ _____

   _____ _____ _____ _____

2. He said he had been in the bookstore buying a notebook when he saw a girl from his last class slip a pen into the pocket of her jacket.

   _____ _____ _____

   _____ _____ _____

3. Then she picked up a second pen, and that was all she paid for as she went out. _____

4. The four students agreed that honesty is the best policy, but Kate said maybe the girl needed the pen and didn't have the money.

   _____ _____ _____

   _____ _____ _____

5. Leatrice said she would have given the girl money to pay for the pen, and Roberto said he would have told the manager.

   _____ _____ _____

   _____ _____ _____

6. The students decided to all chip in and pay for the pen and then confront the girl, knowing that their trust in her would be destroyed if she didn't tell the truth. _____ _____

   _____ _____ _____

7. When they tried to pay the manager, he told them that the girl was not a thief; she had felt such guilt that when she saw him later in the Business Office, she paid him for the pen.

_____ _____ _____

_____ _____ _____

Answers on page 232.

QUIZ YOURSELF ON NOUNS Fill in the blanks.

____ **1.** Nouns are words that (a) always begin a sentence. (b) name persons, places, or things. (c) connect two main clauses.

____ **2.** T or F. Nouns can be subjects and objects.

____ **3.** Collective nouns name (a) groups. (b) people whose hobby is collecting something. (c) fund-raisers.

4. What kind of nouns are always capitalized? _____

5. When are other nouns always capitalized? _____

6. Abstract nouns name intangible qualities that can not be perceived directly through the _____

Answers on page 233.

Verbs: Step One

Verbs are probably the most troublesome part of speech. There are several reasons. First, there are too many irregular verbs, verbs that do not conform to the rules. Second, a verb has to agree in person and number with its subject in a sentence. This is a problem in present tense and in the past tense of the verb *be*. And third, verbs also have principal parts, tense, voice, and mood. It's enough to put any person in a tense mood, but we'll try to help you make sense out of verbs. It can be done; you can do it.

Definition of a Verb

A **verb** is a word or a group of words telling that the subject does something (action) or is something (being) or has something done to it (passive voice).

- <u>John</u> <u>throws</u> the football (action).
- <u>John</u> <u>is</u> the quarterback (being).
- The <u>football</u> <u>is thrown</u> by John (passive voice).

EXERCISE 3.3 The subject is underlined once. Underline the verb twice. Sentences 3, 8, 9, and 10 contain two-word verbs, with the words *were, are, can,* and *is* serving as helping verbs

1. <u>Graffiti</u> are messages or pictures drawn on walls for the public to see.
2. <u>Human beings</u> probably decorated their cave walls with graffiti from the beginning of time.
3. <u>Graffiti from about 320 B.C.</u> were discovered by American archaeologists in Greece just a few years ago.
4. <u>Men and women more than 2,000 years ago</u> wrote clever, dumb, trivial, and profound sayings on their walls.
5. <u>The Italian word meaning *to scratch*</u> gave us the word *graffito;* <u>the plural</u> is *graffiti*.
6. <u>A good graffito</u> has humor, sometimes with an unpleasant bite.
7. <u>Vandals</u> often use spray paint for their graffiti.
8. <u>We</u> are bombarded every day by walking graffiti (buttons) and rolling graffiti (bumper stickers) as well as graffiti on walls.
9. <u>Buttons</u> can be custom-made graffiti, with picture or message to suit the wearer.
10. A bumper sticker: "Careful when passing. <u>Driver</u> is chewing tobacco."

Answers on page 233.

Subject-Verb Agreement

Since subject-verb agreement is the biggest verb problem, we'll tackle it first. Subject-verb agreement is a big problem caused by a small rule: **the verb of a sentence must agree with the subject of the sentence in person** (first, second, or third) **and number** (singular or plural). Person shows whether the subject is speaking (*I* am or *we* are), spoken to (*you* are), or spoken about (*he, she,* or *it* is or *they* are). *I, he, she,* and *it* are singular, one person; *we* and *they* are plural, more than one person. *You* is used for both singular and plural.

In other words, if the subject is first-person singular, the verb must be first-person singular; if the subject is third-person plural, the verb must be third-person plural.

Verb Agrees With Subject in Person and Number				
	Singular Subject	**Singular Verb**	**Plural Subject**	**Plural Verb**
First person	I	walk	we	walk
Second person	you	walk	you	walk
Third person	he, she, it	walks	they	walk

A confusing fact of life in standard English is that plural nouns usually end in *s*, but present tense (happens now) third-person singular verbs end in *s*. A verb already ending in *s*, like *kiss*, adds *es* in the third-person singular.

- The <u>boy</u> <u>*walks*</u>. The subject *boy* is third-person singular (a kind of *he* from the *he, she, it* category), so the third-person singular verb *walks* must be used.

- The <u>boys</u> <u>*walk*</u>. The subject *boys* is third-person plural (from the *they* category) so the third-person plural verb *walk* must be used.

- His <u>mother</u> always <u>kisses</u> him goodnight. Add *es* in the third-person singular because the verb itself, *kiss*, ends in *s*.

EXERCISE 3.4 Fill in the blanks with the present tense of the verb in parentheses that will agree in person and number with the subject. The subject is underlined. No helping verbs are used, so each answer will be just one word.

1. The <u>skunk</u> (belong) _____ to the weasel family.

2. <u>Skunks</u> (look) _____ like black cats with white stripes on the back.

3. The <u>skunk</u> (walk) _____ as if it were wearing shoes that were too tight.

4. For the skunk's protection, <u>glands</u> near the tail (contain) _____ a

fluid with a strong, unpleasant odor, which the <u>animal</u> (squirt) _____ with considerable force at its enemies; it rarely (miss) _____.

5. <u>Skunks</u> (make) _____ their home in a hollow tree or (dig)

_____ burrows, often under a building.

6. <u>They</u> (help) _____ farmers because <u>they</u> (live) _____ on insects,

rodents, and reptiles that eat farm products.

7. Skunk <u>fur</u> (wear) _____ well, but animal activists (appeal)

_____ to consumers not to buy a fur coat of any kind.

8. <u>Skunks</u> (make) _____ excellent pets—after a <u>veterinarian</u> (deodorize)

_____ them.

9. Usually, though, when a <u>skunk</u> (turn) _____ its back on you, run!

Answers on page 233.

Here are **nine rules for making verbs agree with their subjects.**

1. Use a plural verb with a compound subject joined by *and*.

See Rule 4, page 162, for compound subjects joined by *or*.

- The <u>camel</u> <u>and</u> the <u>horse</u> <u>*are*</u> beasts of burden.

That seems simple enough, but some subjects that look compound take singular verbs. If the two (or more) elements of the compound subject are considered to be only one item, use a singular verb.

- <u>Liver and onions</u> <u>*is*</u> not my favorite dish (one dish).
- The <u>president and commander-in-chief</u> <u>*was*</u> at the head of the parade (one person).

2. Use a singular verb with singular indefinite pronouns.

Anyone, anybody, everyone, everybody, someone, somebody, either, and *neither* always take a singular verb and a singular pronoun in reference to them. See page 205 for more on indefinite pronouns.

- <u>Neither of them</u> <u>*does*</u> his (not *their*) work well.
- <u>Everyone</u> <u>*takes*</u> her (not *their*) time.

Also use a singular verb with the singular indefinite pronouns and with adjectives like *each, every,* and *many a* even when they are part of a compound subject.

- <u>Everyone</u> from your office <u>and</u> <u>everybody</u> from mine <u>*is*</u> invited.

- Each (or Every) boy and girl *works* at his or her own speed, and many a first-grader and second-grader *succeeds* because of this policy.

EXCEPTION: The indefinite pronoun *each* does *not* make the verb singular when it *follows* a plural or compound subject.

- Camels and horses each *have* their advantages as beasts of burden; they each *are* of great help to their owners. The boy and the girl each *realize* this. BUT Each boy and girl *realizes* this.

3. Watch out for plural-looking singular subjects.

- Ninety-three degrees *is* a camel's body temperature at night; 105 degrees *is* its temperature during the day. (I knew you'd want to know.)
- Eight inches of snow *was* our record.
- Measles *is* a serious disease for adults.
- *Better Homes and Gardens is* my favorite magazine.
- Brooks Brothers *is* a store specializing in men's clothes.

4. Use a verb that agrees with the subject closer to the verb in what might be called either-or subjects (two or more subjects joined by *or, either or, neither nor,* or *not only but also*).

- Either the teachers or the principal *is* wrong.
- Either the principal or the teachers *are* wrong.

It usually sounds better to put the plural subject next to the verb, as in the second example, although both are correct. Also correct: Either *they* or *I am* wrong.

5. Be sure a being verb (a linking verb) agrees with its subject, not with its predicate noun (which restates the subject).

- Semicolons *are* a problem.
- A problem *is* semicolons.

(Both examples are correct.)

6. In determining subject-verb agreement, disregard words intervening between subject and verb. Expressions coming between the subject and the verb that begin with such words as *in addition to, with, along with, together with, without, as well as, except, unlike,* and *rather than* do not affect subject-verb agreement.

- The little girl, along with her four cousins, *is* at the zoo.
- The twins, unlike their mother, *love* to be with other people.

7. Make the subject and the verb agree even if inverted word order is involved.

- *Attached is* a <u>letter</u> in addition to a dozen brochures for you to distribute.
- Where *are* your <u>dictionary</u> and your <u>thesaurus</u>?

In *here is, here are, there is,* and *there are* constructions, the subject comes after the verb.

- Here *are* the <u>papers</u> she handed back; there *is* <u>mine</u>.

There and *it* sometimes serve as unique introductory words called expletives.

- There *are* six <u>students</u> ready to take the exam. (Six <u>students</u> *are* ready to take the exam.)
- It *is* a painful fact <u>that I have a toothache.</u> (<u>That I have a toothache</u> *is* a painful fact. You will learn later that a subordinate clause like *That I have a toothache* can be a subject.)

8. When the subject is what I call a portion word followed by a prepositional phrase beginning with *of,* such as *all (any) of, a fraction (half) of, a handful of, a majority (minority) of, more (most) of, a percentage (proportion) of, none (some) of,* or *a range of,* use a singular verb if the word after *of* is singular, a plural verb if the word after *of* is plural.

- A <u>majority</u> of the district *votes* in presidential elections.
- A <u>majority</u> of the students *vote* in presidential elections.

EXCEPTION: When *one of* is followed by a plural, the verb remains singular, to agree with *one.*

- One of us *has* to make the decision.
- One of the cars *gets* 40 miles to the gallon.

BUT after the expression *one of those who,* the verb is usually plural, agreeing with the object of the preposition *of.*

- He is one of those teachers who *make* learning fun.

AND With the two subjects *a number* and *the number, a number* is usually plural; *the number* is usually singular.

- A <u>number</u> of courses *are* available.
- The <u>number</u> of courses *is* limited.

9. A collective noun (a noun that looks singular but represents a group of persons or things) may take either a singular or a plural verb. If the noun means one unit, use a singular verb; if it means separate persons or things, use a plural verb.

- The <u>faculty</u> at our college *is* excellent.
- The <u>faculty</u> at our college all *have* their different interests.

A WORD OF CAUTION: If you decide a collective noun (or any noun) is singular and use a singular verb with it, be sure that any pronoun you use to take the place of the noun is also singular. With a plural subject, use not only a plural verb but also a plural pronoun.

- WRONG: The <u>legislature</u> <u>*waits*</u> too long to pass <u>their</u> tax bills.
- RIGHT: The <u>legislature</u> <u>*waits*</u> too long to pass <u>its</u> tax bills.

EXERCISE 3.5 Fill in the blanks. All of the verbs are present tense of the verb *be*.

1. The verb of a sentence must agree with the subject of the sentence in both person and _____.

____ 2. Classes that are already filled   (a) is   (b) are   the worst thing you can encounter during registration.

____ 3. The worst thing that you can encounter during registration   (a) is (b) are   classes that are already filled.

____ 4. Every man and woman on the committee   (a) is   (b) are invited.

____ 5. Everyone   (a) is   (b) are   invited.

____ 6. Six feet   (a) is   (b) are   short for a basketball player.

____ 7. Either the teacher or the students   (a) is   (b) are   wrong.

____ 8. Either the students or the teacher   (a) is   (b) are   wrong.

____ 9. The instructor, as well as four of her students,   (a) is   (b) are going to the exhibition.

____10. What proportion of the classrooms   (a) is   (b) are   filled?

____11. What proportion of the classroom   (a) is   (b) are   filled?

Answers on page 233.

EXERCISE 3.6 Circle the correct verb of the two that are underlined. The rule that applies is given in parentheses to help you.

1. Peter, as well as Kate and Leatrice, <u>remembers/remember</u> registering for classes. (6)

2. Peter met Kate and Leatrice in the registration line when Peter said, "The

hardest part of starting college <u>is/are</u> the long lines." (5)

3. "Yes," agreed Kate, "the long lines <u>is/are</u> the hardest part for sure." (5)

4. Wait and wait some more <u>is/are</u> typical of registration at most colleges. (1)

5. "Where <u>is/are</u> the cafeteria and the coffee machine?" Leatrice asked Kate. (7)

6. "The committee <u>seems/seem</u> to be helpful," said Kate. "I bet either that woman or those men <u>knows/know</u>. I'll hold your place in line." (9), (4)

7. "Neither those men nor that woman <u>knows/know</u>," said Leatrice, returning to the line. (4)

8. After Peter registered, he came back to Leatrice and said, "Here <u>is/are</u> a cup of coffee and cream and sugar for you. A number of drinks <u>is/are</u> available from the vending machine around the corner, but in the cafeteria the number of drinks available <u>is/are</u> small. Corned beef and cabbage <u>is/are</u> their special today." (7), (8), (8), (1)

9. Peter also handed Kate a cup of coffee and said, "Each of you two <u>needs/need</u> a cup of coffee. Yes, the two of you each <u>needs/need</u> something to keep you awake. (1), (1)

10. "<u>Is/Are</u> 60 cents enough?" asked Leatrice as she and Kate offered to pay. (3)

11. "No charge," said Peter, and the three immediately became good friends. Everyone <u>knows/know</u> coffee and kindness <u>makes/make</u> fast friends. (2), (1)

Answers on page 233.

EXERCISE 3.7 Circle the correct verb of the two that are underlined. After the sentence, place in parentheses the number of the rule that applies.

1. In some classes, a majority of the students <u>seems/seem</u> already to know each other, but Peter and Roberto first met in their computer class.

2. Peter and Roberto <u>is/are</u> now good friends.

3. They are both tall, but even Roberto's six feet three inches <u>is/are</u> not enough to get him onto the basketball team.

4. Roberto's cousin, shorter than the captain and the point guard, <u>measures/measure</u> six feet five inches. In a trophy case <u>is/are</u> his most-valuable-player award and the game ball.

5. Each forward and guard <u>plays/play</u> so hard that a popular form of enter-

tainment for the students <u>is/are</u> the Saturday-night games.

6. Roberto, along with 10 of his classmates, <u>hopes/hope</u> to become a computer programmer; he, unlike the others, <u>runs/run</u> the lab for the class every evening.

7. The class <u>is/are</u> bright, but every guy and girl <u>seems/seem</u> to need help.

8. Both Peter, who wants to major in journalism, and Roberto <u>works/work</u> hard, and neither one <u>gets/get</u> bad grades.

9. Neither of the two of them <u>wastes/waste</u> much time playing.

10. Everyone <u>thinks/think</u> Roberto is helpful in the lab.

11. Not only the computer instructors but also his English teacher <u>relies/rely</u> on his knowledge of computers.

Answers on page 234.

You need to know the correct forms of the irregular verbs *be, have,* and *do* because these three verbs are not only much used in their own right but also are among the verbs most used as auxiliary or helping verbs to form other tenses. The box below presents their present-tense (happens now) forms.

Present Tense					
Be		**Have**		**Do**	
I am	we are	I have	we have	I do	we do
you are	you are	you have	you have	you do	you do
he, she,	they are	he, she,	they have	he, she,	they do
it is		it has		it does	

The third-person singular verb is a problem in some types of spoken American English: He *go* (instead of *goes*) to school every day. But *do* and *be* are perpetual offenders. One common problem with the verb *do* occurs in the third-person singular present tense when *he does* (or *she does* or *the thing does,* etc.) is made into a contraction.

- NONSTANDARD: He *don't.* (This says *He do not.*)
- STANDARD: He *doesn't.* (This says *He does not.*)

Other problems are misuse of the verb form *be* instead of the correct form of the present tense, *am, is,* or *are,* and use of the negative *ain't,* always unacceptable in standard English.

- NONSTANDARD: I *be* busy. He *be* busy. We *be* busy. You *be* busy. They *be* busy. I *ain't* busy. He *ain't* busy.

- STANDARD: I *am* busy. He *is* busy. We *are* busy. You *are* busy. They *are* busy. I'*m not* busy. He *isn't* busy.

EXERCISE 3.8 Fill in the blanks with the correct present-tense form of the verb in parentheses.

1. I (be) _____ sure you (be) _____ aware that the camel (be) _____ the "ship of the desert," but did you know that riding camels (make) _____ some people seasick because of the swaying motion?

2. Dromedary camels (have) _____ one hump, but the Bactrian camel (have) _____ two humps.

3. The hump (be) _____ a lump of fat (not a place where water is stored, as is commonly believed) that helps give the camel energy if it (have) _____ no food.

4. While camels (do) _____ many useful things for people, a camel (do) _____ bad things too, like kicking and spitting at people.

5. When a camel (get) _____ hungry enough, it (eat) _____ almost anything it (have) _____ access to—bones, fish, meat, leather, and even its owner's tent.

6. The desert people of Africa and Asia (have) _____ many of the world's camels.

Answers on page 234.

EXERCISE 3.9 In the blank write the correct form of the incorrect italicized verb. Put all verbs in present tense.

1. Algebra *do* _____ seem to have some logic to it; sometimes I think English *don't* _____.

2. Mr. Perez, the algebra instructor, *say* _____ he *were* _____ going to give us a test tomorrow.

3. We *be* _____ going to get out of class right after the test tomorrow because he *don't* _____ want to be late to a meeting he has to go to downtown.

4. Fortunately, teachers *hasn't* _____ many all-day meetings to go to.

5. It *am* _____ hard on the teachers to have to be in two places at once; they *has* _____ enough to do as it is.

Answers on page 234.

EXERCISE 3.10 Circle the correct form of the verb. In No. 1, also place a check in the appropriate blank.

1. Some of these exercises <u>are/be</u>, in my opinion, ____ stupid. ____ educational. ____ strictly for the birds. ____ all of the above.

2. A good student <u>doesn't/don't</u> bother to do exercises that sound silly; students <u>hasn't/haven't</u> a lot of extra time.

3. Believe me, it <u>is/be</u> very hard to make up exercises.

4. You <u>are/be</u> good not to complain. I hope we still <u>are/be</u> friends.

Answers on page 234.

You should also become acquainted with *be, have,* and *do* in the past tense (happened at a time in the past that is over before now). *Be* presents special problems because of its irregularity in the past tense.

Past Tense

	Be		Have		Do	
I was	we were	I had	we had	I did	we did
you were	you were	you had	you had	you did	you did
he, she,	they were	he, she,	they had	he, she,	they did
it was		it had		it did	

EXERCISE 3.11 In the blank write the correct form of the past tense of the verb in parentheses.

1. As a traveler in foreign countries, you probably (be) _____ eager to read signs written in "fractured" English.

2. A Bulgarian resort (have) _____ this sign near the entrance: "Women wearing topless suit will be put into the hands of the authorities."

3. Near the same resort (be) _____ a sign declaring, "Accidents are prohibited on this road."

4. Sign makers for an East Berlin department store (do) _____ their share of fracturing too, with "Visit our bargain basement one flight up."

5. This one (be) _____ in Kiev: "Ladies are requested not to have children in the bar."

6. A Budapest hotel (have) _____ this warning: "All rooms not denounced by twelve o'clock will be paid for twicely."

7. If you are looking for fractures of the language, look what a hotel in Leningrad (do) _____: "The passenger must get free the room before two o'clocks of the day they are abandoning. In other case, as the passenger fracture the day he must the administration pay for full."

Answers on page 234.

Principal Parts of Verbs

Understanding the principal parts of verbs is necessary in order to use verbs properly. The principal parts, either alone or with auxiliaries, form all the tenses. The various tenses show time: something happens now, something happened yesterday, or something will happen tomorrow.

Present, Past, and Past Participle. The three principal parts of a verb are the present (the stem of the infinitive: *to do* = infinitive; *do* = stem), the past, and the past participle (always used with an auxiliary like *has* or *have* if it is used as a real verb). Many grammarians consider the present participle, the form ending in *ing,* a fourth principal part; it is also always used with an auxiliary.

Regular and Irregular Verbs. Life for both students and their instructors would be much simpler if all verbs were regular, but in the English-speaking world there are far too many irregular verbs. Actually, there is an overabundance of irregular verbs in every language.

In a **regular verb** the past tense and the past participle are the same word, formed by adding *ed* to the present—or just *d* if the present ends in *e,* or *ied* after dropping the *y* if the present ends in *y.* In some verbs, the final consonant is doubled before adding the *ed.* The present participle always ends in *ing.*

Principal Parts, Regular Verbs

Present	look	bake	cry	stop	occur
Past	looked	baked	cried	stopped	occurred
Past participle	looked	baked	cried	stopped	occurred
Present participle	looking	baking	crying	stopping	occurring

A good dictionary lists the principal parts of an **irregular verb** immediately after the listing of the verb. If the principal parts are not shown, the verb is regular.

For your convenience, a list of common irregular verbs and their principal parts (present, past, past participle) follows.

arise, arose, arisen

awake, awoke or awaked, awaked or awoken

be, was, been

beat, beat, beaten

become, became, become

begin, began, begun

bend, bent, bent

bite, bit, bitten

blow, blew, blown

break, broke, broken

bring, brought, brought

build, built, built

burst, burst, burst

buy, bought, bought

catch, caught, caught

choose, chose, chosen

come, came, come

cost, cost, cost

creep, crept, crept

cut, cut, cut

deal, dealt, dealt

dig, dug, dug

dive, dived or dove, dived

do, did, done

draw, drew, drawn

drink, drank, drunk

drive, drove, driven

eat, ate, eaten

fall, fell, fallen

feed, fed, fed

feel, felt, felt

fight, fought, fought

find, found, found

fly, flew, flown

forbid, forbade or forbad, forbidden

forget, forgot, forgotten

freeze, froze, frozen

get, got, got or gotten

give, gave, given

go, went, gone

grow, grew, grown

hang (suspend), hung, hung

hang (execute), hanged, hanged

have, had, had

hear, heard, heard

hide, hid, hidden

hold, held, held

hurt, hurt, hurt

keep, kept, kept

know, knew, known

lay (place, put), laid, laid

lead, led, led

leave, left, left

lend, lent, lent

let, let, let

lie (rest, repose), lay, lain

light, lit or lighted, lit or lighted

lose, lost, lost

make, made, made

meet, met, met

pay, paid, paid

read, read, read (present pronounced *reed,* past and part participle *red*)

ride, rode, ridden

ring, rang, rung

rise, rose, risen

run, ran, run

say, said, said

see, saw, seen

sell, sold, sold

send, sent, sent

set, set, set

shake, shook, shaken

shine, shone or shined, shone or shined

shoot, shot, shot

shrink, shrank or shrunk, shrunk

shut, shut, shut

sing, sang, sung

sink, sank, sunk

sit, sat, sat

slay, slew, slain

sleep, slept, slept

speak, spoke, spoken

spend, spent, spent

spin, spun, spun

spring, sprang, sprung

stand, stood, stood

steal, stole, stolen

stick, stuck, stuck

sting, stung, stung

strike, struck, struck

strive, strived or strove, strived or striven

swear, swore, sworn

swim, swam, swum

swing, swung, swung

take, took, taken

teach, taught, taught

tear, tore, torn

tell, told, told

think, thought, thought

throw, threw, thrown

wake, woke or waked, woken or waked or woke

wear, wore, worn

win, won, won

wring, wrung, wrung

write, wrote, written

You will probably want to refer to the above list in future writing. However, you should learn the principal parts of the irregular verbs *be, have,* and *do* because they are so frequently used.

	Principal Parts		
	Be	**Have**	**Do**
Present	be (am, is, are)	have (has)	do (does)
Past	was (were)	had	did
Past participle	been	had	done
Present participle	being	having	doing

EXERCISE 3.12 Fill in the blanks with the correct past tense, past participle, or present participle of the italicized verb in parentheses. For your information, auxiliary verbs are underlined.

1. Martin Luther King Jr. (past tense *be*) _____ a black American Baptist minister, the best known of the leaders who (past tense *bring*) _____ civil rights to the attention of the American people.

2. He <u>had</u> (past participle *win*) _____ the Nobel Peace Prize in 1964 because he <u>had</u> (past participle *lead*) _____ nonviolent civil rights demonstrations.

3. Born in Atlanta, Ga., in 1929, he <u>had</u> (past participle *do*) _____ so well in school that he <u>had</u> (past participle *skip*) _____ both the ninth and the 12th grades before entering Morehouse College at age 15.

4. He (past tense *decide*) _____ to be a minister; his father and his grandfather <u>had</u> both (past participle *be*) _____ ministers.

5. Segregation in this country <u>had</u> (past participle *do*) _____ a great deal of harm, so what he (past tense *do*) _____ (past tense *be*) _____ to fight nonviolently against racial injustice.

6. Others before him <u>had</u> (past participle *have*) _____ some results, but he felt he <u>was</u> (present participle *have*) _____ more success when he <u>was</u> (present participle *teach*) _____ nonviolent rebellion.

7. In 1963 at a civil rights rally, he (past tense *give*) _____ his famous "I Have a Dream" speech, which was so eloquent that others <u>have</u> (past participle *give*) _____ it many times since.

8. He <u>is</u> (past participle *remember*) _____ most because he (past tense *live*) _____ according to his very high standards of justice.

9. We all <u>have</u> (past participle *have*) _____ deep regrets that in 1968 his life (past tense *come*) _____ to an end at the hands of a killer, an escaped convict who the following year <u>was</u> (past participle *sentence*) _____ to 99 years in prison.

10. Martin Luther King Jr. <u>could have</u> (past participle *do*) _____ so much more for humanity <u>had</u> he not (*be*) _____ the victim of violence while he <u>was</u> (present participle *preach*) _____ nonviolence.

Answers on page 234.

EXERCISE 3.13 The past tense and the past participle of the verb are underlined. Circle the correct one.

  1. He <u>went/gone</u> out about three o'clock. His mother said he had <u>went/gone</u> to the store for her.
  2. He has <u>did/done</u> that every Friday for years. He <u>did/done</u> it last week too.
  3. She <u>took/taken</u> the vegetables he bought and made a salad; she has <u>took/taken</u> it out of the refrigerator.
  4. I'll bet you have <u>saw/seen</u> enough of these past tense–past participle exercises. I <u>saw/seen</u> that you were getting tired of them.

Answers on page 234.

REMEMBER: The past tense stands alone; the past participle needs an auxiliary or helper, like *has* or *was* or *will be*. In regular verbs, the past tense and the past participle are the same word. I *talked* (past tense); I have *talked* (past participle) or I had *talked*. In irregular verbs, however, you must be careful not to use one when you mean the other.

  • CORRECT: I *went* (past tense), I *have gone* or I *had gone* (past participle with auxiliary).
  • NOT: I *have went* or I *had went*.

The present participle is always the stem of the infinitive (present) + *ing;* and the present participle, when used as a real verb, always takes an auxiliary.

- I am *going;* they will be *going.*

Auxiliary Verbs

To change verbs from one tense (time) to another, **auxiliary** (or helping) **verbs** are used. We have seen how the past and present participles can not be used without an auxiliary. The verb + its one or more auxiliaries form a **verb phrase,** a verb of more than one word.

The verbs that are used as auxiliary verbs are among the worst offenders when it comes to irregularity.

Auxiliary Verbs
....

be + *am, is, are, was, were, been*
have + *has, had*
do + *does, did*
can + *could*
shall + *should*
will + *would*
may + *might* and *must*
has to + *have to, ought to, used to*
Sometimes: *get* + *got* and *keep* + *kept*

Some of these auxiliary verbs do not have a past participle but have only the present and past forms (*may, might; can, could*); others have only the present form (for example, the past form of *must* changes completely: I *must* go today; I *had to* go yesterday).

Combinations of these auxiliaries with verbs make short (He *is studying*) or long (He *should have been studying*) verb phrases. Words may come between auxiliaries and verbs.

- *Has* <u>he</u> *been studying* hard? He *has* <u>not</u> *been studying* enough. He *has,* <u>I'm afraid,</u> *failed.*

BE CAREFUL: If you join two verb phrases with a conjunction, be sure to include entire verb phrases if needed for clarity.

- WRONG: The government *has* or *will issue* new stamps.
- RIGHT: The government *has issued* or *will issue* new stamps.

Verb Tenses

Tense shows time in a verb. The form of the verb changes depending on whether the action or being that the verb shows happens now, happened in the past, or will happen in the future, whether the action or being is completed or is ongoing.

1. Simple Tenses. The three simple tenses are present, past, and future.

- PRESENT: We *study* (now).
- PAST: We *studied* (at a time in the past which is over before now).
- FUTURE: We *will study* (sometime after now).

See Chapter 7, pages 413-414, for the use of *shall* versus *will* (and *should* versus *would*).

2. Perfect Tenses. The three perfect tenses are formed by adding the simple tense of the auxiliary verb *have* (in the proper person and number) to the past participle of the verb.

- PRESENT PERFECT: I *have* (he *has*) *studied* two hours already (at a time in the past but up to now).
- PAST PERFECT: I *had studied* two hours when the fire alarm sounded (at a time in the past but before a specific time in the past).
- FUTURE PERFECT: I *will have studied* eight hours by the time the library closes (will have taken place before a specific time in the future).

3. Progressive Tenses. Present, past, and future progressive tenses are formed by adding the simple tense of the auxiliary verb *be* (in the proper person and number) to the present participle of the verb to indicate ongoing action or being.

- PRESENT PROGRESSIVE: I *am studying* for a French exam (now, ongoing).
- PAST PROGRESSIVE: I *was studying* when an hour-long phone call interrupted (at a time in the past, ongoing, but over before now).
- FUTURE PROGRESSIVE: I *will be studying* every day before the exam (sometime after now, ongoing).

4. Perfect Progressive Tenses. Present, past, and future perfect progressive tenses follow the same pattern.

- PRESENT PERFECT PROGRESSIVE: I *have been studying* two hours (ongoing at a time in the past but up to now).
- PAST PERFECT PROGRESSIVE: I *had been studying* two hours when the phone rang (ongoing at a time in the past but before a specific time in the past).
- FUTURE PERFECT PROGRESSIVE: I *will have been studying* French two years before I go to France (ongoing but will have taken place before a specific time in the future). This tense is a bit awkward and, ongoing or not, it is often replaced by the future perfect, *I will have studied* French . . .

That wasn't so bad, was it? But don't change channels; we'll be right back with more, after this break for tense identification.

EXERCISE 3.14 In the blanks following the italicized verbs, write what tense of the verb has been used.

1. Wednesday night Leatrice *had come* _____ into the computer lab to write her history paper.

2. Roberto *helped* _____ her get started.

3. "I *am* _____ sure that I *will need* _____ more help as I go along," she *said* _____.

4. "No problem," *replied* _____ Roberto. "I *have* already *finished* _____ my history paper."

5. "*Save* _____ what you *have written* _____ as you *go* _____ along," Roberto *announced* _____ to the students in the lab. "Computers *have* _____ a mind of their own, and if for any reason they *have* _____ a system error or if the power *goes* _____ off, you *will have lost* _____ everything you *haven't saved* _____."

6. Roberto *was keeping* _____ busy because many students *had* _____ questions to ask him.

7. "Don't be a victim of the 'save-it-soon syndrome,'" he again *announced*
    _____ to all the students. "I *am begging* _____ you not to
wait to save your work until you *have finished* _____ just one
more page."

8. A printer *needed* _____ more paper; a student *asked* _____
how to underline; an instructor *requested* _____ permission to use
a computer.

9. The lights in the computer lab *blinked* _____. The power *had*
failed _____ for a split second.

10. Some students *had* not *saved* _____ their work for a while; they
moaned _____. Leatrice *was moaning* _____ loudest. "I
was going _____ to save after I *had finished* _____ this
page," she *said* _____, almost in tears. "I *lost* _____ more
than half my paper."

11. "*Relax* _____, Leatrice," *said* _____ Roberto. "When you
left _____ your seat to use the dictionary, I *saved* _____
your composition for you. So you *will* not *have lost* _____ more
than a sentence."

12. "Roberto, you *are* _____ absolutely wonderful," said Leatrice, hug-
ging him. "I *will* never *do* _____ that again."

Answers on page 234.

Verbs: Step Two

The kinds and characteristics of verbs may seem somewhat overwhelming at
first, but this section will help you better understand verbs and the way they act.
    Grammarians usually categorize verbs as either real verbs (finite) or verbals
(nonfinite). **Real verbs** are the action or being (also called linking) verbs that
can serve as the predicate of a sentence (what is said about the subject). Verbals
are not verbs at all. See pages 187-189.

Kinds of Real Verbs

There are two kinds of real verbs: **action verbs** and **being verbs.** Tlese are the real verbs that can be predicates of sentences. (To be a sentence, a group of words must have a subject and a real verb and must express a complete thought.)

1. Action Verbs. Action verbs express some kind of activity, physical or mental.

- PHYSICAL ACTIVITY: The <u>Chinese</u> <u>invented</u> eyeglasses. <u>Children</u> often <u>break</u> their glasses playing ball.
- MENTAL ACTIVITY: Their <u>parents</u> <u>forgive</u> them.

Action verbs come in two styles: transitive and intransitive.

Transitive Verbs—Objects. Transitive verbs are action verbs that have objects. A transitive verb must have a **direct object** to complete its meaning. The direct object is a noun or a noun substitute that answers the question what? or whom? after the verb.

- WHAT? The <u>Chinese</u> <u>invented</u> *eyeglasses.* <u>Children</u> often <u>break</u> their *glasses* and sometimes their *teeth* playing ball.
- WHOM? Their <u>parents</u> <u>forgive</u> *them.*

A transitive verb has, by definition, a direct object, but it may also have a noun or noun substitute as an **indirect object.** Certain verbs show that the direct object may be "done" to or for someone: *give* or *take, bring* or *send* or *show, lend* or *buy* or *sell* are a few of the most common ones. The person or thing to or for whom, or which, the direct object is *given* or *taken* or *brought* or *sent,* etc., is the indirect object. **A verb can not have an indirect object without also having a direct object.** The indirect object always answers one of the following questions about the direct object: to whom?, for whom?, to what?, or for what?

- TO WHOM? Our <u>doctor</u> <u>gave</u> *us* a prescription. *Prescription* is the direct object of the verb *gave; us* is the indirect object.
- FOR WHOM? The <u>parents</u> <u>did</u> their *son* a *favor;* <u>they</u> <u>bought</u> *him* new glasses. *Favor* is the direct object of the verb *did; son* is the indirect object. *Glasses* is the direct object of the verb *bought; him* is the indirect object.
- TO WHAT? The <u>pitcher</u> <u>gave</u> the *ball* quite a curve. *Curve* is the direct object of the verb *gave; ball* is the indirect object.
- FOR WHAT? The <u>hole</u> in the fence <u>caused</u> the *city* much trouble.

Trouble is the direct object of the verb *caused; city* is the indirect object.

NOTE: Usually a prepositional phrase beginning with *to* or *for* may be substituted for the indirect object: Our doctor gave a prescription *to us.* The parents did a favor *for their son;* they bought new glasses *for him.* The pitcher gave quite a curve *to the ball.* The hole in the fence caused much trouble *for the city.*

The third kind of object that a transitive verb may have is an **object complement,** a noun or adjective that renames or describes and gives more meaning to the direct object. Transitive verbs like *call* or *name* or *consider, make* or *elect, color* or *paint,* or other verbs of "appointing" or "fixing up" may have an object complement to give more meaning to the direct object. **A verb can not have an object complement without also having a direct object.**

- The <u>players</u> <u>called</u> their coach a *dictator* and <u>voted</u> the team captain the most valuable *player. Dictator* is a noun object complement that renames and gives more meaning to the direct object *coach,* and *player* is a noun object complement that renames and gives more meaning to the direct object *captain.*
- After <u>he</u> <u>painted</u> the fence *black,* <u>he</u> <u>pulled</u> the wire *tight. Black* is an adjective object complement that describes and gives more meaning to the direct object *fence. Tight* is an adjective object complement that describes and gives more meaning to the direct object *wire.*

So, there are two kinds of real verbs: action verbs and being verbs. There are two kinds of action verbs: transitive verbs, which must have a direct object, and intransitive verbs, which do not have a direct object. Transitive verbs, which must have a direct object, may or may not also have an indirect object preceding the direct object, or they may or may not also have an object complement following the direct object. The following outline will show that transitive verbs have the most complicated life story of all verbs:

I. Real Verbs.
  A. Action verbs.
    1. Transitive verbs: must have **direct object.**
      a. May also have **indirect object** preceding direct object.
      b. Or may also have **object complement** following direct object.
      c. Must be in either **active or passive voice** (see pages 182-183).
    2. Intransitive verbs: do not have direct object.
  B. Being (also called linking) **verbs** (see pages 185-186): have a subject complement. There are two kinds.
    1. Predicate noun.
    2. Predicate adjective.

NOTE: All real verbs, both action and being, are in indicative or imperative or subjunctive mood (see pages 186-187).

  II. Verbals (not verbs at all—see pages 187-189).
    A. Gerunds.
    B. Infinitives.
    C. Participles.

EXERCISE 3.15 Write **d.o., i.o.** or. **o.c.** above the underlined words to show whether they are direct object, indirect object, or object complement. Of the three object complements, two are nouns and one is an adjective.

1. A belief based on fear or ignorance, inconsistent with what is true and rational, is called a <u>superstition</u>.

2. Every human society has had <u>superstitions</u>, but some groups have called <u>superstitions</u> <u>heresy</u>.

3. Many superstitions concern important <u>events</u> in a person's life, such as the belief that a pregnant woman must eat the right <u>food</u> or she will give her <u>child</u> an unwanted <u>birthmark</u>.

4. There is the belief that carrying a newborn baby upstairs before carrying it downstairs will bring the <u>baby</u> <u>success</u>.

5. And some think Friday the 13th brings <u>us</u> bad <u>luck</u>, not to mention walking under a ladder or having a black cat cross our path.

6. Some Japanese call <u>four</u> an unlucky <u>number</u>. Many buildings there have no fourth <u>floor</u>. Their word for *four* sounds like their word for *death,* so naturally they call that <u>number</u> <u>unlucky</u>.

7. So give <u>me</u> your rabbit's <u>foot</u>, and forget silly <u>superstitions</u>.

Answers on page 235.

Transitive Verbs—Voice. Only transitive verbs have **voice,** a form of the verb that shows whether the subject acts or is acted upon.
  A verb in **active voice** shows that the subject is doing the acting.

- <u>Bill</u> <u>*threw*</u> the ball. Bill, the subject, is doing the acting.

A verb in **passive voice** shows that the subject is being acted upon. Passive voice consists of the appropriate auxiliary of the verb *be* + the past participle of the verb being made passive.

- The <u>ball</u> <u>*was thrown*</u> by Bill. The ball, the subject, is being acted upon by Bill, who becomes the object of the preposition *by.*

It is usually preferable to use active voice because it is more direct (shorter, quicker) and more vivid than passive voice. But there are times when passive voice cannot be avoided:

- When you do not know who or what did the acting: The ball <u>game</u> <u>*was called*</u> (passive voice) on account of darkness. You would have to know *who* called the game in order to have the subject do the acting: The <u>umpire</u> *called* (active voice) the game on account of darkness.
- When you want to emphasize the action instead of the person who did the acting: The locker <u>room</u> <u>*was wrecked*</u> (passive voice) by vandals. The fact emphasized is that the locker room is ruined, not who did it. If you want to emphasize who did it, use active voice: <u>Vandals</u> <u>*wrecked*</u> (active voice) the locker room.

EXERCISE 3.16 Rewrite the following sentences, changing all active-voice verbs to passive voice and passive-voice verbs to active.

1. A meeting was held by Student Government last week. _____

_____

2. The president called the meeting to order. _____

_____

3. The secretary read the minutes, and the members approved them.

_____

4. The condition of the baseball field was discussed by the team captain.

_____

_____

5. A motion to adjourn to the ball field was made by Peter. _____

_____

6. Team members were pitching the ball to each other. _____

_____

7. The team captain noticed the litter on the field. _____

_____

8. A committee to clean up the field was appointed by Student Government.

_____

_____

Answers on page 235.

Intransitive Verbs. Intransitive verbs are the second kind of action verb. They have **no objects;** they do not need an object to complete their meaning.

- The <u>coach</u> <u>*collapsed*</u>. Team <u>members</u> <u>*shrieked*</u>. The <u>custodian</u> <u>*came*</u>; <u>he</u> just <u>*stared*</u>. The cut phone <u>wires</u> <u>*dangled*</u> from the wall.

Why English Students May Become Prematurely Gray

Some verbs are **transitive only.**

- The <u>pitcher</u> <u>*persuaded*</u> the catcher to go for the police; the <u>catcher</u> <u>*got*</u> his bike.

Some verbs are **intransitive only.**

- The <u>police</u> <u>*arrived*</u>; the <u>shortstop</u> <u>*fainted*</u>.

But some verbs can be either **transitive or intransitive.**

- Intransitive: The <u>coach</u> <u>*shouted*</u>. His <u>glasses</u> <u>*dropped*</u>.
- Transitive: The <u>custodian</u> <u>*shouted*</u> instructions. One <u>policeman</u> <u>*dropped*</u> his glasses.

EXERCISE 3.17 The underlined words are all verbs. Circle the intransitive verbs.

1. Mrs. Murphy, as you <u>know</u>, <u>teaches</u> English at our college. She <u>has</u> <u>taught</u> there 11 years.
2. The students <u>like</u> her because she <u>explains</u> concepts clearly and because she <u>smiles</u> a lot.
3. She also <u>gives</u> students their papers back quickly and <u>grades</u> fairly.

4. She <u>encourages</u> students to come to her office, and if they <u>have</u> a problem, she always <u>helps</u>.

5. At the end of the day, she <u>relaxes</u>, <u>cooks</u> dinner for her husband and two children, and then <u>starts</u> the next day's class preparation.

Answers on page 235.

---

2. Being Verbs. Being verbs (also called linking verbs) are real verbs which tell that the subject is, appears or seems to be, or becomes something—or that the subject is in some condition. Naturally, *be* is the most common being verb, along with *appear, seem,* and *become,* but often verbs of the senses (*look, sound, smell, taste,* and *feel*) are used as being verbs. Being verbs do not have direct objects, but they have subject complements. A **subject complement** is a word that completes the subject, either by restating it or describing it. There are two kinds of subject complements.

Predicate Nouns. Predicate nouns follow a being verb and complete the subject by restating it, by renaming it in a different way.

- The first <u>glasses</u> <u>were</u> magnifying *lenses* inserted in frames. *Glasses* is the subject; *were* is the being verb; *lenses* is the predicate noun renaming the subject *glasses*.

Predicate nouns may also be words that have been substituted for nouns, such as predicate pronouns, phrases, or clauses.

- The guilty <u>one</u> <u>was</u> *he*. The pronoun *he* is a predicate pronoun renaming the subject *one*.
- His <u>hobby</u> <u>was</u> *playing tennis*. The phrase *playing tennis* is used as a predicate noun renaming the subject *hobby*.
- The <u>child</u> <u>became</u> *what he had always wanted to be*. The clause *what he had always wanted to be* is used as a predicate noun renaming the subject *child*.

Predicate Adjectives. Predicate adjectives follow being verbs and complete the subject by describing it.

- A <u>portrait</u> of a gentleman wearing glasses <u>looked</u> *strange* to the people of 14th-century Italy. *Portrait* is the subject; *looked* is the being verb; *strange* is the predicate adjective describing *portrait*.
- By the 1600s <u>glasses</u> <u>had become</u> somewhat *common*. *Glasses* is the subject; *had become* is the verb; *common* is the predicate adjective describing *glasses*.

- If you are not wearing glasses, spoiled <u>food</u> <u>may look</u> *tasty* even though <u>it</u> <u>smells</u> *bad* and <u>tastes</u> *worse*. *Food* is the subject of the main clause; *may look* is the verb; *tasty* is the predicate adjective describing *food*. In the subordinate clause after the subordinating conjunction *even though,* the subject is *it; smells* and *tastes* are the compound verb; *bad* and *worse* are the predicate adjectives describing *it.*

- <u>You</u> <u>will</u> surely <u>feel</u> *bad* if you eat spoiled food. *You* is the subject; *will feel* is the verb; *bad* is the predicate adjective describing *you.* Despite popular misuse, it is still preferred *not* to use the adverb *badly* here because a subject complement, a predicate adjective, not an adverb, is needed to complete the subject after a being verb.

- All adjectives in the predicate of a sentence are, of course, not predicate adjectives. The predicate adjective must modify the subject. The word *good* is a predicate adjective in the sentence "Her painting is good," but it is a plain adjective modifying the predicate noun *painter* in the sentence "She is a good painter."

EXERCISE 3.18 Underline the predicate nouns and predicate adjectives in the following sentences. Over the word write **p.n.** or **p.a.**

1. Mrs. Murphy's stew smelled good and tasted better.
2. She is an excellent cook, and her husband feels confident that she is an excellent teacher too.
3. She is also a tennis player; her game is only mediocre, but she could become skillful with more practice.
4. She feels bad because she can't find more time to play.
5. She works hard and seems busy all the time.

Answers on page 235.

Verbs: Step Three

Mood of Verbs

Mood is not just something students get into when confronted by pages and pages of grammar rules. Don't be too harsh on verbs; they have moods too. There are three of them:

1. Indicative Mood. This mood is not a troublemaker. The verb in indicative mood states a fact or opinion or asks a question.

- I *think* studying helps. It *does. Do* you *agree?*

2. Imperative Mood. This mood also causes little trouble. The verb in imperative mood states a command, directions, or a request.

- *Study* your assignment; *do* Exercise 1; please *bring* it to class tomorrow. The subject of each sentence is *you* understood.

3. Subjunctive Mood. This mood causes a great deal of trouble. It is, in most cases, a matter of using *be* instead of the normal present tense or of using *were* instead of *was.* Or it may be a case of dropping the *s* from the third person singular verb. Use the subjunctive mood in clauses of conditional or contrary-to-fact situations, necessity, or demand; but don't be surprised if the subjunctive is not long for this world—so few people use it.

- CONTRARY TO FACT: If I *were* queen, I would make English simpler.
- NECESSITY: It is necessary that he *think* before speaking.
- DEMAND: Students should demand that their wishes *be* considered.

EXERCISE 3.19 Identify the mood of the underlined verbs in the following sentences by writing above them **ind, imp, or sub** for indicative, imperative, or subjunctive.

1. <u>Stop</u>, <u>look</u>, and <u>listen</u>.
2. We <u>should demand</u> that crossing gates and signals <u>be</u> in good working order.
3. It <u>is</u> stupid to try to beat a train to the crossing.
4. If I <u>were</u> in a hurry, I <u>would try</u> to save time some other way.
5. It <u>is</u> vital that we <u>be</u> more aware of the dangers of grade crossings.

Answers on page 235.

Verbals

Verbals are not verbs at all; they deserve to be in this section only because grammarians persist in calling them nonfinite verbs. They are words that came from verbs, still look like verbs, are often confused with verbs, but are not used as verbs. They are used rather as adjectives, adverbs, or nouns. **They cannot be used as the real verb of a sentence.**

Verbals include gerunds, infinitives, and participles; and, like the real verbs from which they evolved, they may have particles (see page 190), subjects, objects, complements, and adverb modifiers. A verbal plus such an addition is known as a **verbal phrase.**

1. Gerunds. Gerunds are verbals that end in *ing* and are used as nouns.

- *Reading* and *writing* are necessary skills in today's world. The two gerunds *Reading* and *writing* are the compound subject of the verb *are*.
- Therefore, *fitting* glasses is an important profession. *Glasses* is the direct object of the gerund *fitting; fitting* is the simple subject of the sentence; the gerund phrase *fitting glasses* is the complete subject.
- Because of glasses, many people with faulty vision can enjoy *sketching* and *painting*. The gerunds *sketching* and *painting* are direct objects of the verb *can enjoy.*

2. Infinitives. Infinitives are verbals that are made up of the word *to* plus the present form of the verb (called the stem of the infinitive). They are usually used as nouns but sometimes as adjectives or adverbs.

- *To be* stylish was the goal of the person who wore a monocle, a glass held up to a single eye by face muscles. *Stylish* is the complement, a predicate adjective, of the infinitive *To be*. The infinitive phrase *To be stylish* is used as a noun, the subject of the sentence, subject of the verb *was*.
- Glasses *to fit* the wearer's precise needs came later. *Glasses* is the subject of the infinitive *to fit. Glasses to fit the wearer's precise needs* is the complete subject of the verb *came. Needs* is the direct object of the infinitive *to fit*. The infinitive phrase *to fit the wearer's precise needs* is used as an adjective modifying the word *Glasses.*
- *To correct* astigmatism, Sir George Airy, a British astronomer, devised a cylindrical lens in 1827. *Astigmatism* is the direct object of the infinitive *To correct*. The infinitive phrase *To correct astigmatism* is used as an adverb modifying the verb *devised,* telling why.

IMPORTANT: The *to* in an infinitive is sometimes understood but not expressed.

- When two or more infinitives are used in parallel construction, the *to* may be omitted after the first infinitive: I want *to* read the material, [to] make an outline of important points, and [to] study from that outline.

- The word *to* is sometimes understood but not expressed in an infinitive: I will help you [to] find a job.

3. Participles. Participles come in two time frames, past and present. Past participles usually end in *ed, n,* or *t.* Like gerunds, present participles end in *ing;* but present participles never are used as nouns, as gerunds always are. Participles can be used as real verbs in verb phrases; but as verbals, participles and participle phrases are used as adjectives.

- PAST PARTICIPLES: Easily *broken,* rimless spectacles, *invented* in 1840, are less popular than eyeglasses *surrounded* by plastic rims. *Broken* and *invented* are both adjectives modifying *spectacles; surrounded* is an adjective modifying *eyeglasses.* The participle phrases, used as adjectives, are *Easily broken, invented in 1840,* and *surrounded by plastic rims.*

- PRESENT PARTICIPLES: Contact lenses, *fitting* against the eyeball, are popular among glasses wearers *wanting* a "glassesless" look. *Fitting* is an adjective modifying *lenses; wanting* is an adjective modifying *wearers; look* is the direct object of the present participle *wanting.* The participle phrases, used as adjectives, are *fitting against the eyeball* and *wanting a "glassesless" look.*

EXERCISE 3.20 Above each of the underlined verbals, write what type it is: **ger** for gerund, **inf** for infinitive, and **par** for participle.

1. <u>Attending</u> a circus is one of the greatest pleasures of childhood.
2. Circus-type acts go back to ancient Rome's games, which featured chariot races and men <u>racing</u> around a track <u>standing</u> on the bare backs of two horses.
3. The modern circus, <u>featuring</u> trick horseback <u>riding</u> and live music, developed in England in the mid 1700s.
4. About a half century later, circus people began <u>to perform</u> in America.
5. People flocked <u>to see</u> <u>traveling</u> menageries of exotic animals, including the first elephant <u>to arrive</u> in the United States in 1796.
6. Sideshows offered fat ladies, <u>tattooed</u> men, midgets, and giants.
7. Parades of brightly <u>painted</u> wagons have been discontinued because of <u>crowded</u> city streets; tents have given way to auditoriums.

Answers on page 236.

Phrasal Verbs

Phrasal verbs are verbs used with a preposition or an adverb, but the verb and the other word combined become, essentially, a single word, a verb. The other word is called a **particle.**

- He *struck out* twice in the last inning.
- Fortunately my employer *backed* me *up.*

QUIZ YOURSELF ON VERBS Fill in each blank with the letter that makes the sentence correct.

_____ 1. A verb is a word that   (a) always has a direct object.   (b) always tells that the subject does or is something or has something done to it.   (c) never changes form.

_____ 2. A verb agrees with its subject   (a) in person and number.   (b) plus any preposition in the sentence.   (c) because it is a polite part of speech.

_____ 3. The principal parts of verbs are   (a) direct, indirect, and object complement.   (b) present, past, and past participle.   (c) always regular.

_____ 4. T or F. Compound subjects always take plural verbs, with no exceptions.

_____ 5. Auxiliary verbs are used in forming   (a) tense.   (b) nonsense. (c) pretense.

_____ 6. Combinations of auxiliary verbs and verbs make   (a) verb phrases. (b) phrasal verbs.   (c) verbal phrases.   (I won't blame you if you miss this one.)

_____ 7. A verbal   (a) is a kind of gerbil.   (b) can be used in place of a verb.   (c) is not a real verb at all.

_____ 8. Tense in verbs show   (a) time.   (b) how relaxed the student is. (c) whether the subject is singular or plural.

_____ 9. T or F. In regular verbs the past tense and the past participle are the same word.

_____10. Being verbs have two types of subject complements: (a) praise and flattery.   (b) indicative and imperative.   (c) predicate nouns and predicate adjectives.

Answers on page 236.

CALVIN & HOBBES by Bill Watterson

Pronouns: Step One

Definition of a Pronoun

A **pronoun** is a word that is used instead of a noun.

- Jack and Jill are getting married. Kate says *she* (takes the place of *Kate*) is going to *their* (takes the place of *Jack and Jill's*) wedding, *which* (takes the place of *their wedding*) will be the only event of *its* (takes the place of *the wedding's*) kind ever held in the gazebo.

Can you imagine a day without pronouns? Pronouns make life much less monotonous for us. Without pronouns, we would have to say, "Bob's alarm woke Bob up, and Bob climbed out of Bob's bed, brushed Bob's teeth, put on Bob's clothes, and ate Bob's breakfast. Bob's parents let Bob drive Bob's parents' car to school because the weather was cold."

See how handy pronouns are?—words that take the place of nouns. Another definition for you: the noun the pronoun takes the place of is called the **antecedent** of the pronoun.

If we had used pronouns, as we normally would have, the paragraph about Bob would have read, "Bob's alarm woke *him* up, and *he* climbed out of *his* bed, brushed *his* teeth, put on *his* clothes, and ate *his* breakfast. *His* parents let *him* drive *their* car to school because *it* was cold." The antecedent of *he, him,* and *his* is Bob. The antecedent of *their* is Bob's parents'; the antecedent of *it* is the weather.

There are several kinds of pronouns, and some change form depending on how they are used. **Pronouns must agree in person** (first, second, or third), **number** (singular or plural), **and gender** (masculine, feminine, or neuter) **with their antecedents and must change case according to their use in the sentence** (used as subject or object or to show possession). You can see why pronouns are sometimes a bit of a problem.

Changes in Form of Personal Pronouns

The changes in the form of **personal pronouns,** pronouns which refer to specific persons or things, is illustrated below (*you* is repeated to indicate its singular and plural forms).

1. Person. Person tells whether the pronoun is the speaker (first person), the person spoken to (second person), or the person or thing spoken about (third person).

> **First** = *I, we* (*I* is always capitalized.)
>
> **Second** = *you, you*
>
> **Third** = *he, she, it, they*

2. Number. Singular means one person or thing. Plural means more than one person or thing.

> **Singular** = *I, you, he, she, it*
>
> **Plural** = *we, you, they*

Personal Pronouns

	Singular	Plural
First person	I	we
Second person	you	you
Third person	he, she, it	they

3. Gender. There is a gender change only in third-person singular, the other persons and numbers (*I, you, we, you, they*) being unisex.

> **Masculine** = *he*
>
> **Feminine** = *she*
>
> **Neuter** = *it*

Before recent women's rights activities, most writers were content to use the masculine *he* to mean either *he* or *she:* If a student wants to make good grades, *he* has to study. Now, to **avoid sexism,** writers often use *he or she:* If a student wants to make good grades, *he or she* has to study. This can become very awkward if used several times in the same sentence: A student should do his or her

MOTHER GOOSE & GRIMM   **by Mike Peters**

paper by himself or herself if the paper is to reflect what he or she knows and what he or she can express. Sometimes you can **use the plural** to avoid this: *Students* should do their papers by themselves if the papers are to reflect what students know and what they can express.

4. Case. Now we come to case of personal pronouns: the form of the pronoun changes depending on whether the pronoun is used as a subject, as an object, or to show possession.

> **Subjective** (nominative) = Use this form for subject or subject complement (predicate pronoun): *I, you, he, she, it, we, you, they.*
>
> **Objective** = Use this form as object of verb, subject and object of verbal, or object of preposition: *me, you, him, her, it, us, you, them.*
>
> **Possessive** (genitive) = Use this form to show ownership: *my, your, his, her, its, our, your, their* (used as adjectives), and *mine, yours, his, hers, its, ours, yours, theirs* (used as pronouns).

Case of Pronouns

	Subjective	**Objective**	**Possessive**
First person singular	I	me	my
Second person singular	you	you	your
Third person singular	he, she, it	him, her, it	his, her, its
First person plural	we	us	our
Second person plural	you	you	your
Third person plural	they	them	their

Use the possessive forms shown above when the possessive pronoun is used as an adjective before a noun, as in *my* book, *his* brother.

Use the possessive forms below when the possessive pronoun is used as a pronoun with no noun following, as in The book is *his,* OR The problem is *yours,* not *mine.*

First person singular	mine
Second person singular	yours
Third person singular	his, hers, its
First person plural	ours
Second person plural	yours
Third person plural	theirs

EXERCISE 3.21 Fill in the blanks with the appropriate pronouns. In each sentence pronouns are used as the subject of the verb *needed,* to show possession before the noun *mother,* and as object of the preposition *for.* These uses are followed by the possessive pronoun used alone, not modifying a noun. The first blanks should be filled with *I, my, me,* and *mine.*

1. First-person singular: _____ needed help, so _____ mother cared for _____. The problem was _____.

2. Second-person singular: _____ needed help, so _____ mother cared for _____. The problem was _____.

3. Third-person singular masculine: _____ needed help, so _____ mother cared for _____. The problem was _____.

4. Third-person singular feminine: _____ needed help, so _____ mother cared for _____. The problem was _____.

5. Third-person singular neuter: _____ needed help, so _____ mother

cared for _____. The problem was _____ (correct but not commonly used).

6. First-person plural: _____ needed help, so _____ mother cared for _____. The problem was _____.

7. Second-person plural: _____ needed help, so _____ mother cared for _____. The problem was _____.

8. Third-person plural: _____ needed help, so _____ mother cared for _____. The problem was _____.

Answers on page 236.

EXERCISE 3.22 In the following two paragraphs, find the personal pronouns and their antecedents. The number of pronouns you find should correspond to the number of blanks; write each pronoun followed by its antecedent.

Not often does an important religious body revoke charges it has held against a man for more than 300 years. This is what happened to the famous Italian astronomer and physicist Galileo. Through his experiments, he became convinced that the earth revolved around the sun, instead of vice versa. This contradicted the church's belief that the earth was the center of the universe. In 1633 the Roman Catholic Church forced Galileo to renounce his beliefs and sentenced him to house arrest, thereby saving him from being burned at the stake. Most people of today feel that revoking the charges is a long-overdue acknowledgment of an error, and they are happy it was finally corrected.

I tried very hard to get a couple of feminine pronouns into the first paragraph, but I learned by calling the library that Galileo never married. When his father died, however, Galileo, the oldest of many brothers and sisters, took care of them as well as of his mother. She must have been very proud of him. If you want to know why Galileo was famous, keep reading. Another exercise will be along before too long, and it will tell more about him.

1. _____   2. _____
3. _____   4. _____
5. _____   6. _____
7. _____   8. _____
9. _____   10. _____
11. _____ 12. _____
13. _____ 14. _____
15. _____ 16. _____
17. _____ 18. _____

Answers on page 236.

Pronouns: Step Two

Avoiding Problems With Case

The personal pronouns *you* and *it* cause very little trouble because they do not change form. However, the rest of the personal pronouns as well as *who* and *whom* can be difficult. They change form depending on whether the pronoun is used as **subject or object or to show possession.**

1. Subjective Case. Use subjective case (*I, he, she, we, they, who*) for pronouns that are subjects of clauses or sentences, and for predicate pronouns.

- SUBJECTS: *I* bought a copy of the anthology. *He* was not included. *They* did not know why. *Who* is he anyway?
- PREDICATE PRONOUNS: The man included was not *he*. The teacher was *I*.

2. Objective Case. Use objective case (*me, him, her, us, them, whom*) for direct and indirect objects of real verbs and objects of prepositions as well as for subjects and objects of most verbals.

- Stop *him* (direct object of verb *stop*).
- I gave *her* (indirect object of verb *gave*) my book (*book* = direct object of verb *gave*).
- The competition is between *you* and *me* (two objects of the preposition *between*).

ALWAYS WRONG: Between you and I.

ALWAYS RIGHT: Between you and me.

Use objective case for the subject and object of an infinitive.

- I wanted *him* to get glasses. *Him* is the subject of the infinitive *to get*.
- I did not want to worry *her. Her* is the direct object of the infinitive *to worry*.
- I wanted to get *him* glasses. *Him* is the indirect object of the infinitive *to get* (*glasses* is the direct object of the infinitive).
- My parents caused *me* to be successful; they often fancied *me* to be *him*. If the infinitive *to be* has a subject alone, or if it has both subject and object, use objective case.

BUT if the infinitive *to be* has an object but no subject, use the subjective case for the object.

- She is often thought to be *I*. The infinitive *to be* has an object *I* but no subject.

Use objective case for the object of a participle.

- John, pushing *him* away, said nothing about the broken glasses. *Him,* the direct object of the participle *pushing,* is in objective case.

If you think you may still have trouble with *I, he, she, we, they* (subjective) versus *me, him, her, us, them* (objective), and with *who* (subjective) versus *whom* (objective), you are not alone.

Here's a hint: If you are in doubt about which case of the pronoun to use, rearrange the sentence to make clear what function the pronoun serves. If you can substitute *he* for the in-doubt pronoun, you should use *who* or some other pronoun in subjective case; if you can substitute *him,* it should be *whom* or some other pronoun in objective case.

SHOE   by Jeff MacNelly

- It is William Shakespeare (*who* or *whom*) we are indebted to for hundreds of famous quotations. We are indebted to <u>him</u> (not to <u>he</u>), so use *whom,* object of the preposition *to.*

- The board included (*whoever* or *whomever*) they thought to be important. They thought <u>him</u> to be important, so use *whomever,* subject of the infinitive *to be.*

- BUT: The board included (*whoever* or *whomever*) was important. <u>He</u> was important, so use *whoever,* subject of the verb *was.*

- They save places for *whoever* or *whomever* has done significant work. <u>He</u> has done significant work, so use *whoever,* subject of the verb *has done.* The whole clause *whoever has done significant work* is the object of the preposition *for.*

Here's another hint: We all delight in catching a television newsperson saying something like, "The president's spokesperson gave this information to another reporter and *I.*" Objects of prepositions (*to*) must be in objective case (*me*). When in doubt, leave the other person out: ". . . gave this information to I"? No way.

- I hope you can go to the program with Jerry and *I.* Leave out the other person. You would never say "I hope you can go to the program with *I.*"

3. Possessive Case. Possessive case can be mastered—almost—if you just remember that some pronouns in possessive case are used as adjectives and some are used as pronouns.

- *My* dog is friendlier than *your* dog. *My* is a possessive pronoun used as an adjective modifying *dog; your* is a possessive pronoun used as an adjective modifying *dog.*

- *Mine* is friendlier than *yours. Mine* is a possessive pronoun used as a pronoun whose antecedent is *my dog; yours* is a possessive pronoun used as a pronoun whose antecedent is *your dog.*

HOWEVER (and this is the reason for the *almost* above), there are two rules that are a bit troublesome:

Use possessive case before a gerund for both pronouns and nouns.

- *Their* wanting to include a broader range of feature stories led to *his* relaxing the moral standards of the magazine.
- *Benjamin Franklin's* inventing bifocals in 1784 caused an increase in the manufacture of glasses.
- The *door's* closing alerted the police.

The possessive pronoun *its* never takes an apostrophe.

- The skunk sometimes makes *its* home in a hollow tree.

Save the apostrophe for the contraction meaning *it is*.

- *It's* a cute animal, but *its* bite can cause rabies.

EXERCISE 3.23 In the blank, write the pronoun in the proper case for third-person singular masculine (*he, him,* or *his*).

1. In 1564 Galileo Galilei was born in Pisa, Italy, where later _____ (possession) father enrolled _____ (direct object of verb *enrolled*) in the university's medical program and tried to encourage _____ (direct object of the infinitive *to encourage*) in every way.

2. The father, wanting _____ (direct object of the present participle *wanting*) in the field of medicine, was disappointed when Galileo preferred mathematics to medicine and decided to teach math at the University of Pisa.

3. This position required _____ (subject of infinitive *to teach*) to teach courses in astronomy.

4. On the basis of his research, _____ (subject of verb *rejected*) rejected the theory that the sun and all the planets revolve around the earth and concluded that all the planets, including the earth, revolve around the sun.

5. Publication of his findings won _____ (indirect object of verb *won*) wide

renown, but the church punished _____ (direct object of verb *punished*)
for holding beliefs that it opposed.

6. In 1633 the church sentenced _____ (direct object of verb *sentenced*) to
life imprisonment but, because of _____ (possession before gerund
becoming) becoming ill and nearly blind, allowed _____ (subject of
infinitive to *serve*) to serve his imprisonment under house arrest.

7. The charges against _____ (object of preposition *against*) were revoked
in 1992, 428 years after his death.

8. It was _____ (subject complement of verb *was*) who built a powerful
telescope, learned that the moon's surface is not smooth, and discovered
four moons circling Jupiter.

9. _____ (subject of verb *came*) also came to the conclusion that all objects
fall at the same rate of speed regardless of their size and weight, later
proved true if the objects fall in a vacuum.

Answers on page 236.

EXERCISE 3.24 Fill in the blanks with pronouns in the proper case.
Choices are given for some; others should be obvious.

1. Dr. Jefferson teaches journalism. Peter has _____ for Introduction to
Mass Communications.

2. He is the instructor (who or whom) _____ Peter likes best. (Don't forget
the *he-him* substitution hint: Peter likes *he* or *him* best?)

3. He is the instructor (who or whom) _____ is adviser to the campus
newspaper, and between you and (I or me) _____, he's a good one.

4. He has no trouble making students like _____ because he does many
exciting things with (the students) _____.

5. Kate is taking Mass Communications from Dr. Jefferson too, but _____
has no intention of making journalism _____ career even though it is (he

or him) _____ (who or whom) _____ has taught _____ many interesting facts about the media.

6. Nursing would have (its, it's) _____ advantages as a career for (Kate) _____ because she has been interested in _____ since _____ childhood.

7. If anyone would make a good nurse, it is (she, her) _____.

Answers on page 237.

Avoiding Problems With Antecedent Agreement

Problems with pronoun-antecedent agreement are probably as prevalent as cases of wrong case. The rule is that **a pronoun must agree with its antecedent** (the noun it takes the place of) **in person, number, and gender.**

- *John* admitted *he* was to blame. The antecedent *John* is masculine third-person singular; therefore, use the personal pronoun *he.*
- A good *doctor* (singular antecedent) has sympathy for *his* or *her* (not *their*) patients. OR Make the antecedent plural: Good *doctors* have sympathy for *their* patients.
- It is *I who* am to blame. The relative pronoun *who* takes on the first-person singular characteristics of, or agrees with, the antecedent *I;* therefore, use the first-person singular verb *am.*

Obviously, singular antecedents are referred to by a singular pronoun, a rule that's easy to obey in the case of *John-he* but one that is *often* violated in the case of the singular indefinite pronouns (see page 205).

- WRONG: <u>Anyone</u> who thinks life is easy will change *their* mind.
- RIGHT: <u>Anyone</u> who thinks life is easy will change *his or her* mind, OR <u>All</u> who think life is easy will change *their* mind. Change *their* to *his or her* because *Anyone* is singular, or make the subject plural.
- WRONG: <u>Everyone</u> who is invited to join the club thinks *they* are special.
- RIGHT: <u>Everyone</u> who is invited to join the club thinks *he or she* is special. OR <u>All</u> who are invited to join the club think *they* are special. Change *they* to *he or she* because *Everyone* is singular, or make the subject plural.

  BUT DON'T BE RIDICULOUS: After <u>everybody</u> sings the last hymn, the ushers will pass among *him* with the collection plate.

REWORD: After everybody sings the last hymn, the ushers will pass among the worshipers with the collection plate.

HOWEVER, usage is changing. I predict that before this book is very old, *Everyone does their thing* will be an acceptable exception to the rule.

For pronoun-antecedent agreement with collective nouns, follow the same rules that apply to subject-verb agreement.

Use a singular pronoun if the antecedent is considered one entity, and use a plural pronoun if the antecedent is considered separate individuals.

- The <u>staff</u> makes *its* selections largely on the basis of news items.
- The <u>staff</u> have *their* special duties.

Use a plural pronoun with two or more antecedents joined by *and.*

- <u>He and I</u> wish *we* could be in your club.

With two or more antecedents joined by *or* or *nor,* make the pronoun agree with the antecedent closer to it.

- The <u>senators</u> or the <u>president</u> gets *his* way. The pronoun agrees with the closer antecedent, *president;* but sometimes rewriting, putting the plural subject closer to the verb and pronoun, sounds better: The <u>president</u> or the <u>senators</u> get *their* way.

EXERCISE 3.25 Fill in the blanks with pronouns that agree with the underlined antecedents in person, number, and gender.

1. Although <u>most of us</u> pay _____ income <u>tax</u>, _____ do not always pay _____ happily.

2. The first income <u>tax</u> was imposed by <u>rulers</u> in Italy in 1451; _____ made _____ unpopular rulers, and _____ was repealed.

3. In 1799 British <u>citizens</u> were taxed to pay _____ share of the war against France.

4. In the United States the first federal income tax was levied in 1862 to help pay for the Civil War even though every <u>mother</u> probably thought _____ had paid enough in loss of family.

5. The 16th Amendment in 1913 gave <u>Congress</u> the right to impose federal income tax, and _____ has been doing so ever since.

6. A teenage <u>boy</u> with a job must pay _____ share; a working <u>mother</u> pays _____ share; older <u>people</u> pay _____ share; <u>everyone</u> does _____ part.

7. Although <u>we</u> all try to make _____ payments on time so the government won't make _____ pay a penalty, there is always <u>somebody</u> who doesn't get _____ check in the mail by the deadline.

8. If <u>you</u> try to avoid paying income tax, _____ tax will be higher when the government catches up with _____.

9. <u>I</u> always send _____ a couple of weeks before the deadline to put _____ mind at ease.

10. <u>Everybody</u> should be glad to pay _____ fair share.

Answers on page 237.

EXERCISE 3.26 Circle the underlined words that make the sentences correct.

1. Jane, as well as her two sisters, <u>does/do</u> <u>her/their</u> part to make my life easier.
2. Jim and his two brothers <u>does/do</u> <u>his/their</u> part too.
3. A sympathetic teacher should listen to <u>his or her/their</u> students.
4. Anyone can make good grades if <u>he or she/they</u> <u>studies/study</u>.
5. Every boy and girl in the class <u>is/are</u> trying <u>his or her/their</u> best.
6. Each mother and father <u>is/are</u> proud of <u>his or her/their</u> child.
7. The Women's Committee <u>is/are</u> planning <u>its/their</u> program.
8. The Women's Committee <u>is/are</u> trying to use <u>its/their</u> separate talents to get the job done.
9. Neither the other members nor the chairperson <u>makes/make</u> <u>her/their</u> views very well known.
10. Neither the chairperson nor the other members <u>makes/make</u> <u>her/their</u> views very well known.

Answers on page 237.

Avoiding Problems With Unclear Reference

When either of two nouns could be the antecedent of a pronoun, the reader may be thoroughly confused. Rewrite the sentence to **make the reference** (antecedent the pronoun refers to) **clear.**

- UNCLEAR: John became very angry with James when he finished his speech. Who finished his speech, John or James?
- CLEAR: John became very angry with James when John finished his speech. OR When John finished his speech, he became very angry with James.
- UNCLEAR: Jan spent all her spare time teaching the child at home when she was in her 30s. When who was in her 30s? The child?
- CLEAR: When Jan was in her 30s, she spent all her spare time teaching the child at home.

Pronouns: Step Three

A Half Dozen Kinds of Pronouns

1. Personal Pronouns. We have pretty well mastered the personal pronouns (those that refer to specific persons or things) and the way they change person and number and gender and case and the way they sometimes don't get along agreeably with their antecedents.

2. Intensive or Reflexive Pronouns. From a select group of the personal pronouns—and there seems to be no logical reason for the ones selected (some are possessive case; others are objective case)—come the *self* pronouns, which may be either intensive or reflexive pronouns, the pronouns formed by adding *self* or *selves* to *my, your, him, her, it, our, your,* and *them.*

Use **intensive pronouns** for emphasis.

- I *myself* want to do that job.
- I want to do that job *myself.*

Use **reflexive pronouns** as objects of verbs, verbals, or prepositions, showing that someone or something is acting on or for itself.

- I hurt *myself* (direct object of verb *hurt*).
- I bought *myself* some new bandages (indirect object of verb *bought*).
- Bandaging *myself* was difficult (direct object of gerund *bandaging*).

- I felt sorry for *myself* (object of preposition *for*).

IMPORTANT WARNING: Do not use a *self* pronoun unless the person or thing to which it refers has been expressed in the same sentence.

- WRONG: Helen and *myself* are going to the library to study. The pronoun *I* has not been used in the sentence, so don't use *myself*.
- RIGHT: Helen and *I* are going to the library to study.
- WRONG: She gave the book to Helen and *myself*.
- RIGHT: She gave the book to Helen and *me*.
- RIGHT: I felt it an insult to *myself* that <u>she</u> did all the work *herself*.
- RIGHT: The <u>dogs</u> were wandering all by *themselves* in the woods.
- EXCEPTION: Bandaging *myself* was difficult.

3. Indefinite Pronouns. We have met indefinite pronouns in connection with subject-verb agreement and pronoun-antecedent agreement. They do not refer to any specific person, persons, thing, or things; many have no particular antecedent. The most common indefinite pronouns are *somebody* (not any particular person), *someone, something, anybody, anyone, anything, everybody, everyone,* and *everything.* Indefinite pronouns also include *nobody, no one, nothing, another, each, one, each one, other, either,* and *neither.*

The indefinite pronouns listed above are all **singular,** but popular usage will probably before long dictate change, at least in making the use of a plural pronoun (*their*) with *everyone* and *everybody* acceptable.

- NONSTANDARD: <u>Everybody</u> should bring *their* notebooks.
- STANDARD: <u>Everybody</u> should bring *his or her* notebook. OR Change to plural: <u>All</u> students should bring *their* notebooks.

The following indefinite pronouns are always **plural:** *both, few, many, others,* and *several.*

- Even though my students seem ambitious, <u>few</u> get *their* homework done ahead of time.

The indefinite pronouns *all, any, more, most, none,* and *some* may be **either singular or plural** depending on whether the noun they are taking the place of is singular or plural.

- The <u>guests</u> are from all walks of life. *Some* (*guests* = antecedent, plural) *are* classmates of the host.
- The <u>paint</u> is two years old. *Some* (*paint* = antecedent, singular) *is* too sticky to use.

4. Relative Pronouns. Relative pronouns—*that, what(ever), which(ever), who(ever), whom(ever),* and *whose*—are noun substitutes that introduce subordinate clauses and may also serve as subjects or objects or possessives in the subordinate clauses. (Subject = *who;* object = *whom;* possessive = *whose.)*

- Jack, *who* ran for class president, is the one *whom* we voted for. *Who* is a relative pronoun introducing the subordinate clause *who ran for class president* and serving as the subject of the subordinate clause. *Whom* is a relative pronoun introducing the subordinate clause *whom we voted for* and serving as the object of the preposition *for.*

- The daily newspaper, *which* contains local and national news, takes hours to read all the way through. *Which* is a relative pronoun introducing the subordinate clause *which contains local and national news* and serving as the subject of the subordinate clause.

- But the newspaper *that readers consult in the morning* is an important part of their day. *That* is a relative pronoun introducing the subordinate clause *that readers consult in the morning* and serving as the object of the verb *consult* (readers consult *that*).

MORE ON RELATIVE PRONOUNS: The relative pronoun is often omitted if the meaning is clear without it:

- The dictionary is the book (that) most readers consult.
- He is the one (whom) we saw reading it.
- BUT It was John *who* was selected. *Who* is the subject of the subordinate clause *who was selected* and can't be omitted.

To decide whether to use *that, which,* or *who* for people or things, the rule is use *which* for things, *who* for people, and *that* for either. But don't use *that* if you know the antecedent is people; use *who.* Use *which* for introducing nonessential clauses. *That* is still preferred to introduce essential clauses, but *which* is no longer outlawed. For which clauses are essential and which are nonessential, see page 317.

5. Interrogative Pronouns. Relative pronouns become interrogative pronouns when they are used as questions.

- *Whom* can you see? *Whom* = object of the verb *can see. You* = subject. Don't forget the *he-him* test: You can see *he?* No. You can see *him,* so use *whom.*

- *Whatever* happened to your plans? *Who* canceled them? In this case *Whatever* = subject of the verb *happened. Who* = subject of the verb *canceled.*

- Joe canceled the plans. *What* plans? *Which* Joe? By *whose* authority?

6. Demonstrative Pronouns. Demonstrative pronouns, which point out, cause relatively little trouble. There are four of them: *this, that* (both singular), *these,* and *those* (both plural).

- The books you have selected have two due dates. *These* are due in two weeks; *those,* in three weeks. *This* circulates; *that* doesn't.

The only problem that demonstrative pronouns may cause occurs when they are used as adjectives before the words *kind(s)* and *sort(s).* Use the singular *this* and *that* with the singular *kind* and *sort,* and use the plural *these* and *those* with the plural *kinds* and *sorts.*

- WRONG: You have to be careful with *these* kind of pronouns.
- RIGHT: You have to be careful with *this* kind of pronoun (or *these* kinds of pronouns).

EXERCISE 3.27 In the blanks, correct the underlined mistakes.

1. The woman told her daughter <u>she</u> had made a mistake in the recipe. (Who made the mistake? Use a direct quotation to make this clear.) The woman told her daughter, "_____ ."

2. My boss and <u>myself</u> will attend the meeting. _____

3. Everyone must finish <u>their</u> work by 4 p.m. _____

4. After I have cooked dinner in my microwave oven, I always set <u>it</u> on the table to cool. _____

5. When you finish the report, give it to Jake or <u>myself</u>. _____

6. Of 15 girls in the class, there were only six <u>that</u> passed. _____

7. Don't waste your time on <u>these kind</u> of books. _____

Answers on page 237.

QUIZ YOURSELF ON PRONOUNS Fill in the blanks.

1. A pronoun is a word that _____ .

____ 2. An antecedent is   (a) a noun that follows another noun.   (b) a noun that a pronoun takes the place of.   (c) a noun that has no verb.

____ 3. T or F. Personal pronouns change according to person, number, and gender.

_____ **4.** The case of the pronoun changes according to whether the pronoun is   (a) a legal case, a case of mistaken identity, or a briefcase. (b) a phrase, a clause, or a sentence.   (c) a subject, an object, or a possessive word.

5. The cases of pronouns are   (a) _____ , (b) _____ , and   (c) _____ .

_____ **6.** Which is always right? Keep this between you and   (a) *I.* (b) *me.*

7. Usually don't use the pronoun *myself* unless the pronoun _____ is also in the sentence.

_____ **8.** Which is correct? I was pleased by   (a) him   (b) his   coming to see me.

9. The rule that applies to No. 8 is, Use _____ case before a gerund.

_____**10.** T or F. A pronoun must agree with its antecedent in person, number, and gender.

Answers on page 237.

Adjectives: Step One

Definition of an Adjective

An **adjective** is a word that modifies a noun or a pronoun. To **modify** a noun or a pronoun means to describe it (tell what kind of or what appearance) or to limit it (tell how many, which, or whose). For clarity, adjectives should be placed as close as possible to the words they modify. In the following examples, adjectives are italicized.

- *E. A. Robinson's* definition says poetry has *two outstanding* characteristics: poetry is *undefinable;* poetry is *unmistakable. E. A. Robinson's* tells whose <u>definition</u>; *two* tells how many and *outstanding* tells what kind of <u>characteristics</u>; *undefinable* and *unmistakable* tell what kind of <u>poetry</u>.

- I was *poor,* so I bought *this small red* book of *his* poems instead of *the huge leather-bound poetry* book. *Poor* describes the pronoun <u>I</u>; *this* tells which <u>book</u>, and *small* and *red* tell the appearance of the <u>book</u>; *his* tells whose <u>poems</u>; *the* tells which <u>book</u>; *huge* and *leather-bound* tell the appearance of the <u>book</u>; and *poetry* tells what kind of <u>book</u>.

Eight Kinds of Adjectives

Into the two sentences in the examples above are jammed all kinds of adjectives. There are eight kinds of adjectives that you need to know about.

1. Descriptive adjectives are those that tell what kind the noun or pronoun is, how the noun or pronoun looks, or how many of the noun or pronoun we are dealing with (*two, outstanding, undefinable, unmistakable, poor, small, red, huge, leather-bound*).

2. Three of the descriptive adjectives listed above are also used as **predicate adjectives:** Poetry is *undefinable* and *unmistakable*. I was *poor*. Predicate adjectives follow a being verb and describe the subject. Predicate adjectives (and predicate nouns) are called subject complements.

3. Possessive adjectives are sometimes nothing more than the possessive personal pronouns *my, your* (singular), *his, her, its, our, your* (plural), and *their* used before nouns to show ownership.

- *Your* poetry is quite good in *its* own way. *Your* modifies *poetry* telling whose poetry; *its* modifies *way* telling whose way.

A possessive adjective may also be a possessive noun used before another noun to show ownership.

- Most *poets'* talents are not recognized as early in life as *Mozart's* musical abilities were. *Poets'* is a noun in the possessive case modifying the noun *talents* and telling whose, thereby qualifying as an adjective. *Mozart's* is a proper noun in the possessive case modifying the noun *abilities* and telling whose, thereby also qualifying as an adjective.

4. Adjectives may come **from indefinite, interrogative, and demonstrative pronouns** as well as possessive pronouns when the pronouns are used to modify a noun.

- *Many* students have problems with square roots (indefinite).
- *Which* students are going to be math majors (interrogative)?
- *These* students are sociology majors (demonstrative).

5. Nouns don't have to be in the possessive case to modify another noun. Of course we know that nouns by definition don't modify nouns, so the following are merely **descriptive adjectives originating from nouns.**

- I bought a *poetry* book. *Poetry* is usually a noun, but here it is an adjective modifying *book* and telling what kind.

- We have a *gas* fireplace. *Gas* is usually a noun, but here it is an adjective modifying *fireplace* and telling what kind.

6. You have undoubtedly noticed that adjectives can be made from proper nouns and therefore can be called **proper adjectives;** proper adjectives need to be capitalized.

- My friend is a *Cleveland* novelist.
- *Homer's* epic poems made him a great *Greek* poet.

7. Also, **participles,** as we know, are used as adjectives.

- *Studying* for her midterm, Karen fell asleep, her head *propped* on her elbows. *Studying* modifies *Karen; propped* modifies *head.*

8. And don't forget the **articles,** *a, an,* and *the,* adjectives of a special breed. *The* is a **definite article,** limiting the noun it modifies to one in particular, someone or something previously noted.

- *The* poet read aloud for two hours = a particular poet.

A and *an* are **indefinite articles,** limiting the nouns they modify to any one or all of a class or group, someone or something not previously noted.

- *A* poet must be creative = any poet, all poets. Use *an* instead of *a* before a noun beginning with a vowel sound.

NOTE: We also need examples of adjectives modifying pronouns.

- I selected *this* one, and he insisted on buying it for *poor little* me. *This* modifies the indefinite pronoun *one,* and *poor* and *little* modify the personal pronoun *me.*

EXERCISE 3.28 Circle all the adjectives in the following paragraphs. Don't forget the articles *a, an,* and *the* and possessive pronouns and nouns used as adjectives.

¶1   The weather was quite warm but not too hot. The windows of the car were partly open, but the big dog in the car, barking frantically, had some kind of problem. Peter, tossing a bright red Frisbee back and forth with friends in the big field by the north parking lot, thought the dog might be sick or in great discomfort for some other reason.

¶2   "That's Mrs. Murphy's car," said Peter. "I'm going to tell her that her dog must be very ill."

¶3   Quickly Peter went inside and asked Mrs. Murphy if he could interrupt her English class.

¶4   "Your dog is really upset about something," he said. "I saw his brown leash on the front seat and would have taken him out; however, he growled ferociously at me."

¶5   "Class, work on the next exercise while I see what's wrong with my dog. I had to bring him to school today because no one was at my home to let him out. I took him for a walk between third and fourth periods, but possibly he needs another outing sooner than I thought."

¶6   She walked out of the main building with Peter. "My 15-year-old son taught him to guard our car. That's why he wouldn't let you come very close. . . . Oh, my goodness," she said, laughing. "I know what's wrong with Leo. He wants to play Frisbee. That's his favorite game. I'll introduce you to him; then he'll let you open the car door. I'd sincerely appreciate your letting him play with you for a little while."

¶7   Mrs. Murphy went back to her second-floor classroom and explained briefly to the curious class what had happened outside. Peter came in at the end of class and said excitedly, "Wow, Leo was the best Frisbee player on the whole field!"

Answers on page 237.

Adjectives: Step Two

Comparison of Adjectives

Although most adjectives have never been to college, many have degrees. **Degree** is the form an adjective takes when comparison is involved. Only descriptive adjectives (and not all of them) can be compared: *high, higher, highest; exciting, more exciting, most exciting*.

There are three degrees.

1. **Positive degree** describes a person or thing.
   - Poetic language is brief.
   - Janice is beautiful.

2. **Comparative degree** compares two persons or things.
   - Poetic language is briefer than prose.
   - Janice is more beautiful than her sister.

3. **Superlative degree** compares three or more persons or things.
   - Poetic language is the briefest of all methods of expression in the language.
   - Janice is the most beautiful girl in the class.

One-syllable adjectives go from the plain adjective (positive degree), to the adjective + *er* (comparative degree), to the adjective + *est* (superlative degree): *cold, colder, coldest.*

Three-or-more-syllable adjectives go from the plain adjective, to the adjective preceded by *more* or *less,* to the adjective preceded by *most* or *least: desirable, less desirable, least desirable.*

Some two-syllable adjectives form comparisons by *er, est;* others, by *more most.*

   - RIGHT: *Lively, livelier, liveliest*
   - RIGHT: *Loving, more loving, most loving*

Just don't make the mistake of using both *er* and *more* or both *est* and *most.*

   - WRONG: Poets are never *more happier* than when they are studying human beings' *most strongest* emotions.

And don't make the mistake of comparing certain absolute adjectives that cannot be compared—there is no better or best with them; they are already there.

FRANK & ERNEST   **by Bob Thaves**

- WRONG: *more correct, deader, more perfect, squarer, most unique*
- RIGHT: *more nearly correct*

Where have you heard this before? There are EXCEPTIONS to the rules for showing degree.

- One-syllable: *pleased,* BUT NOT *pleaseder, pleasedest,* BUT RATHER *more pleased, most pleased*

Dictionaries show irregular comparative and superlative forms of adjectives and adverbs.

- *Good, better, best*
- *Bad, worse, worst*
- *Many, more, most*

If a person or thing is being compared to others in the group to which it belongs, add an *other* or an *else*.

- Wordsworth's poetry is better than that of any *other* Romantic poet.
- His imagery is better than anyone *else's*.

Make comparisons parallel; compare things that are alike.

- WRONG: Wordsworth's poetry has more imagery than Shelley. Here you are comparing poetry to a person, not to a person's poetry.
- RIGHT: Wordsworth's poetry has more imagery than Shelley's.

ONE MORE NOTE: Comparison of adjectives often causes trouble with the case of pronouns following the comparison if words are understood but omitted.

- Poets are more creative than . . . *I* or *me?* Use the case of the pronoun that would be correct if all the words were there . . . *I* (am).

- We admired no other teacher as much as (we admired) *her*.

If using the pronoun alone sounds strange (He is as tall as *I*), include the omitted words.

- He is as tall as *I* am.

QUIZ YOURSELF ON ADJECTIVES Fill in the blanks.

____ **1.** The function of adjectives is to modify nouns or pronouns. In English grammar, *to modify* means   (a) to add a verb to.   (b) to describe or limit.   (c) to make a subject agree with.

2. The three most popular adjectives, *a, an,* and *the,* are called

_____.

____ **3.** T or F. A participle, a word ending in *ing* and coming from a verb, can be used as an adjective.

4. Like nouns, adjectives can be either common or _____.

5. Comparison of adjectives is saying a noun can be a certain way

(positive degree), or it can be more that way than another noun

(comparative degree), or it can be the most that way of several

nouns (_____ degree).

6. An example of the three degrees in the comparison of adjectives is

high, _____, _____. An example of irregular

comparison is *good,* _____, _____.

7. Another example of the three degrees in comparison is *intelligent,*

_____, and _____.

Answers on page 238.

Adverbs: Step One

Definition of an Adverb

An **adverb** is a word that modifies (describes or limits) a verb, an adjective, or another adverb. In addition, adverbs may modify phrases, clauses, verbals, or whole sentences.

Six Kinds of Adverbs

There are six kinds of adverbs. Five kinds answer questions; one kind is transitional.

1. When? He came to the meeting *late*. *Late* modifies the verb *came*, telling when. Other **adverbs of time** include *when, already, early, formerly, now, recently,* and *soon*. Nouns of time can be used as adverbs: He said he would come *today*; it rained *Thursday*.

2. Where? I looked *everywhere* for my jacket. *Everywhere* modifies the verb *looked*, telling where. Other **adverbs of place** include *where, here, there, anywhere, elsewhere, away, back, up,* and *down*.

3. Why? **Adverbs of cause** include *accordingly, consequently, hence, therefore,* and *wherefore*.

4. How? *How* adverbs abound: Milton wrote *powerfully*. Other **adverbs of manner** include *aloud, cheerfully, fast, haltingly, impishly, little by little* (a phrasal adverb, more than one word), *nervously,* and *zealously*. Many adverbs are the adjective + an *ly* ending.

5. **Adverbs of degree** answer questions of **frequency** (How often? or How many times?) and **extent,** (To what extent? or How much?).

- ADVERBS OF FREQUENCY: He rewrote the poem *frequently, twice* in one week. *Frequently* and *twice* modify the verb *rewrote*. Other adverbs of frequency include *always, ever, hourly, maybe, often, once, perhaps, periodically, recurrently, repeatedly,* and *sometimes;* their negative counterparts *hardly, infrequently, never, rarely, scarcely,* and *seldom;* and phrasal adverbs like *once in a while, over and over,* and *year after year*.

- ADVERBS OF EXTENT: Poetry written in Old English is *extremely* difficult to read. *Extremely* modifies the adjective *difficult*. Some other adverbs of extent are *almost, always, at least, barely, just, more, most, much, nearly, only, probably, quite, rather, really, somewhat, too, truly,* and *very*.

The **negative** adverbs *no* and *not* and the **affirmative adverb** *yes* seem to belong more to frequency or extent adverbs than anywhere else. An adverbial *yes* or *no* often modifies a whole sentence or main clause:

- *Yes,* you may go; *no,* it is not snowing.

More often than not (that's a phrasal adverb of frequency), the adverb *not* modifies a verb, making it negative.

- I will *not* tell (*not* modifies the verb *will tell*).

Other examples of *no* and *not:*

- He could go *no* farther; he had walked briskly but *not* enthusiastically. *No* modifies the adverb *farther; not* modifies the adverb *enthusiastically.*

Don't use a **double-negative.**

- WRONG: When Milton began to lose his eyesight, his friends were afraid he would <u>not</u> be able to write <u>no</u> more poetry.
- RIGHT: . . . <u>not</u> be able to write <u>any</u> more poetry.
- WRONG: His blindness did <u>not</u> affect his poetry, <u>I *don't* believe</u>.
- RIGHT: <u>I believe</u> his blindness did <u>not</u> affect his poetry OR His blindness did <u>not</u> affect his poetry, I <u>believe</u> OR <u>I don't believe</u> his blindness affected his poetry.

6. Conjunctive adverbs, the only adverbs that do not answer a question, are transitional words or phrases that usually join main clauses into a bigger sentence.

- I would like to go to bed; *however,* I still have work to do.
- I played last night; *consequently,* I am behind in my homework..

Conjunctive Adverbs

accordingly	furthermore	likewise	otherwise
also	hence	meanwhile	specifically
besides	however	moreover	still
briefly	incidentally	nevertheless	then
consequently	indeed	next	therefore
finally	instead	nonetheless	thus
			too

Some conjunctive adverbs may be used in other ways.

- I told you *specifically* (adverb of manner modifying verb *told*) to take the *next* (adjective modifying noun *train*) train.

EXERCISE 3.29 Turn back to Exercise 3.28 about Leo, the Frisbee whiz, page 210. This time, underline the adverbs. Don't forget conjunctive adverbs.

Answers on page 238.

Adverbs: Step Two

Formation of Adverbs

Some adverbs have the same form as their adjective counterparts.

- Still waters run *deep. Deep* is an adverb of manner modifying the verb *run*.
- Be careful when you are in *deep:* water. Here, *deep* is an adjective modifying the noun *water.*
- Run *faster. Faster* is an adverb of manner modifying the verb *run.*
- Of the two, the *faster* horse will qualify. Here *faster* is an adjective modifying the noun *horse.*
- He always came to work *early. Early* is an adverb of time modifying the verb *came.* The *early* bird often gets the wormy jobs. Here, *early* is an adjective modifying the noun *bird.*

Many adverbs are adjectives with an *ly* added.

- A so-called *honest* (adjective modifying the noun *politician*) politician does not always behave *honestly* (adverb modifying the verb *behave*) after he is elected to office.

BE AWARE that all words ending in *ly* are not adverbs: *friendly, lively, lonely, lovely, manly* = adjectives.

Some adverbs have no relation to adjectives: *how, now, thus.* Even nouns can be used as adverbs!

- I arrived an *hour* late: *hour* modifies *late* telling to what extent.

Comparison of Adverbs

The comparison of adverbs is similar to the comparison of adjectives; many can be compared, with positive, comparative, and superlative degree.

- One-syllable adverbs: *soon, sooner, soonest; fast, faster, fastest.*
- Adverbs of more than one syllable: *willingly, more willingly, most willingly; nearly, more nearly, most nearly.*

BUT Many adverbs cannot be compared: *then, there, not.*

Adverbs: Step Three

What Adverbs Modify

Adverbs are quite versatile and can modify in seven ways: six different sentence elements and whole sentences themselves.

1. Verbs. He stared *curiously* at the old man: modifies the verb *stared*. The old man sat *still* in his chair: modifies the verb *sat*.

2. Verbals. He seemed to regard me *curiously* when I spoke: modifies the infinitive to *regard*.

3. Adjectives. His heart was *curiously* weak for the heart of such a young man: modifies the predicate adjective *weak*. He had been in *very* poor health since he was a child: modifies the adjective *poor*.

4. Adverbs. Yet he had run *curiously* well in the track meet for never having had any training: modifies the adverb *well; well* modifies the verb *had run*.

5. Phrases. His thinking was *curiously* off the track: modifies the prepositional adjective phrase *off the track*. The monkey was living *high* in the tree: modifies the prepositional adverb phrase *in the tree*.

6. Clauses. But his actions were *curiously* as we had predicted: modifies the subordinate clause *as we had predicted*. He did the job *only* because his brother insisted: modifies the subordinate clause *because his brother insisted*.

7. Sentences. *Curiously,* no one seemed to care: modifies the whole sentence. *Unfortunately,* he was unqualified for the job: modifies the whole sentence.

QUIZ YOURSELF ON ADVERBS Fill in the correct answers.

_____ 1. Adverbs modify   (a) nouns and pronouns.   (b) verbs, adjectives, and other adverbs.   (c) conjunctions and prepositions.

2. Many adverbs are adjectives with what two letters added? _____ All words ending in these two letters are not adverbs, however.

_____ 3. T or F. Adverbs do not have positive, comparative, and superlative degree the way adjectives do.

4. The young man ran *well* in the race now that he was finally *well* after recovering from pneumonia. Is the first *well* an adjective or an adverb? _____ Is the second *well* an adjective or an adverb? _____

_____ 5. T or F. Adverbs can modify words, phrases, clauses, and even whole sentences.

6. An example of the three degrees in the comparison of adverbs is *soon,* _____, and _____. An example of irregular comparison is *well,* _____, _____.

7. Another example of the three degrees in comparison is willingly, _____, _____.

Answers on page 238.

QUIZ YOURSELF ON ADJECTIVES AND ADVERBS Above the line, identify each of the underlined words as either an adjective or adverb, and draw a line to the word or words that each modifies.

1. Garrett Morgan (1877–1963) is <u>famous</u> for <u>two</u> inventions that have <u>really</u> changed <u>the</u> <u>modern</u> world.

2. He and <u>his</u> brother Frank developed <u>a</u> <u>breathing</u> apparatus that was <u>the</u> precursor of <u>the</u> <u>gas</u> mask.

3. There was <u>not</u> <u>much</u> interest in it until there was <u>a</u> <u>bad</u> explosion in <u>a</u> tunnel being dug for <u>a</u> <u>city</u> <u>water</u> intake in <u>Morgan's</u> <u>adopted</u> home of Cleveland, where Morgan had moved from <u>his</u> birthplace in Kentucky.

4. <u>Eleven</u> men were trapped in <u>the</u> shaft, and <u>10</u> men were killed trying to rescue them.

5. Morgan went into <u>the</u> tunnel with <u>a</u> dozen of <u>the</u> <u>breathing</u> masks and brought <u>out</u> six of <u>the</u> men <u>alive</u>.

6. <u>Later</u>, he saw <u>a</u> collision between <u>a</u> <u>horse-drawn</u> wagon and <u>a</u> car, and <u>the</u> <u>traffic</u> signal <u>slowly</u> began to take shape in <u>his</u> <u>inventive</u> mind.

7. <u>The</u> <u>first</u> models were <u>clumsily</u> operated by hand, with <u>a</u> lever <u>changing</u> <u>the</u> light from green to red and <u>causing</u> <u>a</u> "<u>Stop</u>" sign to descend.

8. You can see that Garrett Morgan has <u>greatly</u> affected <u>our</u> lives.

Answers on page 238.

Prepositions: Step One

Definition of a Preposition

A **preposition** is a word that shows the relationship of a noun or noun substitute (the object of the preposition) to another word or words in the sentence. Often the relationship is one of location (*above*) or time (*after*), but cause (*due to*) or manner (*according to*) or other relationships (*with* and *except*) may be involved.

Prepositions are always part of prepositional phrases. A prepositional phrase consists of the preposition, its object, and modifiers of the object.

- The poet John Milton was educated <u>by</u> his learned, wealthy father until the young boy turned 12. (The prepositional phrase *by his learned, wealthy father* is used as an adverb modifying the verb *was educated.*)

- His father helped him financially so that he could lead a life <u>of</u> scholarly pursuits (the prepositional phrase *of scholarly pursuits* is used as an adjective modifying the noun *life.*)

Some words used as prepositions may be used as other parts of speech too. For example, the same word may be either an adverb or a preposition. If it has an object, it is a preposition.

- He came aboard (adverb modifying the verb *came.*)
- He came aboard the ship (preposition with *ship* its object).

Prepositions

aboard	before	down	off	throughout
about	behind	during	on	till
above	below	except	onto	to
across	beneath	excepting	out	toward
after	beside	for	outside	under
against	besides	from	over	underneath
along	between	in	past	until
amid	beyond	inside	plus	up
among	but (*except*)	into	regarding	upon
around	by	like	round	with
as	concerning	near	since	within
at	despite	of	through	without

Phrasal Prepositions
(prepositions of more than one word)

according to	by reason of	in spite of
ahead of	by way of	instead of
along with	due to	on account of
apart from	except for	out of
aside from	in addition to	together with
as for	in back of	to the side of
as to	in case of	up to
as well as	in front of	with reference to
away from	in lieu of	with regard to
because of	in place of	with respect to
by means of	in regard to	with the exception of

And, yes, it *is* all right to end a sentence with a preposition—if *not* ending in a preposition results in an awkward construction.

- AWKWARD: For what is a grammar book good?
- QUITE OKAY: What is a grammar book good for?

DON'T FORGET: The object of a preposition is in objective case.

- Keep it between you and *me* (never *I*).
- Give it to Pedro and *me* (never *I*).

"We admired the content of your essay, Mr. Rodney, but found the grammar typical of a kind up with which we here at Charing House will not put."

EXERCISE 3.30 Underline the prepositions in the following paragraph, and circle their simple objects (without modifiers). Some prepositions have compound objects (more than one). There are two phrasal prepositions. Four italicized words look like prepositions but are not. Can you figure why just for your own information?

If you ever want *to* shoot the rapids, you should do it in a whitewater kayak. Whitewater kayaks are made of plastic or of fiberglass and are built for quick maneuvering on river rapids. The kayakers sit one in front of the other in cockpits in an enclosed deck. A kayak paddle has a blade at each end. If you have done this *before,* you know it is a thrilling sport, but brush up on your swimming skills *before* you go so nothing unpleasant will happen before the end of the trip. Between you and me, I think this would be a great sport except for the fact that there are no rapids near my town, or anywhere *near.*

Answers on page 239.

QUIZ YOURSELF ON PREPOSITIONS Fill in the blanks.

_____ **1.** Prepositions show the relationship between   (a) a subject and a verb.   (b) a noun or noun substitute and another word in the sentence.   (c) a linking verb and a subject complement.

_____ **2.** A preposition   (a) always   (b) sometimes   (c) never   has an object.

_____ **3.** A preposition   (a) always   (b) sometimes   (c) never   is part of a prepositional phrase.

_____ **4.** A phrasal preposition is   (a) the same as a prepositional phrase. (b) a preposition that is being phased out of the language. (c) nothing more than a preposition of more than one word.

_____ **5.** T or F. Prepositions sometimes confuse us by being used as other parts of speech too.

Answers on page 239.

Conjunctions: Step One

Definition of a Conjunction

A **conjunction** is a word that connects words, phrases, or clauses.

Three Kinds of Conjunctions

The three kinds of conjunctions play a big part in making our writing (and talking) flow smoothly.

1. **Coordinating conjunctions** connect words, phrases, and clauses of equal value. There are seven coordinating conjunctions: *and, but, for, nor, or, so,* and *yet.*

- WORDS: <u>Homer</u> *and* <u>John Milton</u> wrote epic poems.
- PREPOSITIONAL PHRASES: Homer wrote <u>about the Trojan War</u> *and* <u>about the adventures of Odysseus</u>.
- SUBORDINATE CLAUSES: <u>Because Homer lived in Greece about 800 B.C.</u> *and* <u>because Milton lived in England in the 1600s</u>, comparing the two poets is quite interesting.
- MAIN CLAUSES (sentences combined to form a bigger sentence): <u>Homer was blind,</u> *and* <u>Milton lost his eyesight too.</u>

2. **Correlative conjunctions** connect words, phrases, and clauses of equal value, but correlative conjunctions consist of pairs of words. There are five of them: *both . . . and, either . . . or, neither . . . nor, not only . . . but also,* and *whether . . . or.*

- *Neither* Milton's great epic *nor* Homer's two epics are likely to become outdated.
- *Not only* are Homer's and Milton's works classed among the world's greatest epic poetry, *but* they *also* have characters with which every man and woman can identify.

3. **Subordinating conjunctions** connect subordinate clauses with main clauses (they connect clauses of unequal value). In the following examples, the main clauses are underlined, and the subordinate clauses begin with the italicized subordinating conjunction.

- <u>Poet John Milton's eyesight failed</u> *because* as a boy he had often studied all night.
- *After* he became blind in 1654 at the age of 46, <u>he was still able to do his work</u> *if* someone assisted him.

Subordinating Conjunctions

after	by the time	once	unless
although	even though	provided (that)	until
as	how	since	when
as far as	if	so	whenever
as if	inasmuch as	so as	where
as much as	in order that	so that	whereas
as soon as	in that	than	wherever
as though	no matter how	though	whether
because	now that	till	while
before			why

DON'T FORGET: Relative pronouns (see page 206) can also connect subordinate clauses with main clauses.

CONTRARY TO POPULAR BELIEF (or at least contrary to the belief that many students bring to college with them): You may start a sentence with a conjunction, (*and, but, because,* etc.). See the three examples which follow.

- *Because* subordinate clauses sometimes end up standing alone as incomplete sentences, teachers may discourage students' starting sentences with a subordinating conjunction.

- *Yet* it's quite all right to start a sentence with a conjunction, subordinating or correlative or coordinating.

- *But* don't start too many sentences with *and* or *but,* or you will sound like a breathless child talking.

EXERCISE 3.31 Underline the conjunctions in the following paragraph, and write the type (coordinating, correlative, or subordinating) above each. You should find 14.

Even though puppets are inanimate doll-like figures, they appear to be human beings or animals because the puppeteer makes them move. Although puppetry is thousands of years old, probably first having been used in religious ceremonies, it is alive and well today. Both marionettes and rod puppets have movable body parts, controlled by strings or wires from above the stage in the case of marionettes and by rods from below the stage in the case of rod puppets. Hand puppets are usually glove-like figures that fit over the hand, so changing position of the fingers makes the puppet appear to move. A ventriloquist's dummy is a complex type of hand puppet, but both strings and small rods inside the dummy must still be operated by hand. Either on stage or on television, puppets are fun; they are not only entertaining but are also educational, for some teachers use them to make schoolwork more interesting. A good puppeteer can make his creations come alive.

Answers on page 239.

QUIZ YOURSELF ON CONJUNCTIONS Fill in the blanks.

1. What do conjunctions do? _____

2. What are the three kinds of conjunctions? _____

_____   _____

3. While I don't recommend memorizing rules unnecessarily (you can look
them up when you need them), I believe it pays in understanding sentences to learn the seven coordinating conjunctions. What are they?

_____ _____ _____ _____ _____ _____ _____

_____ **4.** Coordinating conjunctions connect sentence elements of
(a) equal   (b) unequal   value.

_____ **5.** Subordinating conjunctions connect sentence elements of
(a) equal   (b) unequal   value.

Answers on page 239.

Interjections: Step One

Definition of an Interjection

An **interjection** is an exclamation or outcry that expresses a strong emotion, or a word that provides a milder sort of transition in conversation. Interjections are usually followed by an exclamation point, but the milder ones may be followed by a comma. Other parts of speech may become interjections if they are used in an exclamatory way.

- *My!* (normally a possessive pronoun). *Wow!* (can be a noun or a verb).
- *Ah,* here comes the doctor now (the milder transitional type).

QUIZ YOURSELF ON INTERJECTIONS In the following sentences, insert an interjection of your choice, using an exclamation mark if it is truly exclamatory or a comma if it is merely transitional. Capitalize the first word after the interjection if you have used an exclamation mark; don't capitalize it if you have used a comma.

_____ **1.** I am absolutely stunned!

_____ **2.** you are hurting me.

_____ **3.** what do you know about that?

_____ **4.** can't you see you've gone far enough?

_____ **5.** what do you think you are doing?

Possible answers on page 239.

Sentence Elements Used as Parts of Speech: Step One

Same Word Used as Several Parts of Speech

In English, as in all languages, the same word may be used as several different parts of speech. The best example that I could come up with of one word used as many parts of speech was the word *out,* for which I found uses as six of the eight parts of speech.

- NOUN: He made an *out* in the third inning.

CALVIN & HOBBES   **by Bill Watterson**

- VERB: The truth will *out*. The obsolete product was soon phased *out* (*phase out* = a phrasal verb).

- ADJECTIVE: We waited too long to make a reservation, so flying is *out* (predicate adjective modifying the gerund *flying*).

- ADVERB: I had stayed home so long that it was a pleasure to go *out* (adverb modifying the infinitive *to go* and telling where).

- PREPOSITION: He pushed me *out* the door.

- INTERJECTION: I said get out of here. *Out!*

Sentence Elements Used as Parts of Speech: Step Two

Phrases Used as Parts of Speech

A **phrase** is a group of grammatically related words without a subject *or* without a predicate *or* with neither subject nor predicate. In addition to verb phrases, which can be used only as verbs (see page 176), there are three kinds of phrases.

1. Prepositional phrases are usually used as adjectives or adverbs, rarely as nouns.

- Poet John Milton was a follower *of Puritan beliefs* (used as an adjective modifying the noun *follower*).

- Religious faith is apparent *in his poetry* (used as an adverb modifying the predicate adjective *apparent*).

- Later, however, he no longer went to *church* (used as an adverb modifying the verb *went*).

- *After lunch* is too late (used as a noun, subject of the sentence).

2. Verbal phrases are also used as parts of speech. Just as there are three kinds of verbals, there are three kinds of verbal phrases.

A **gerund phrase** is always used as a noun.

- *Milton's <u>working</u> hard* was the reason for his success (subject of the sentence).

An **infinitive phrase** may be used as a noun, an adjective, or an adverb.

- *<u>To combine</u> writing and politics* was Milton's ambition (noun, subject of the main clause).
- His ability *<u>to write</u> prose* (adjective modifying the noun *ability*) was well known.
- But he struggled *<u>to achieve</u> his political goal* (adverb modifying the verb *struggled,* telling why).

A **participle phrase** is always used as an adjective.

- *<u>Displeased</u> by his Puritanical strictness,* his first wife, *<u>being</u> very young,* went back to her parents a month after their marriage. (*Displeased* is a past participle; *being* is a present participle; both participle phrases modify the noun *wife.*)

3. Absolute phrases are used as no particular part of speech but modify an entire main clause (sentence). They usually consist of a noun or pronoun followed by a participle + modifiers.

- *His first wife having come back to him two years later,* (absolute phrase modifying the entire main clause that follows), Milton became the father of three daughters.

Clauses Used as Parts of Speech

A **clause** is a group of grammatically related words with a subject and a real verb. There are two kinds of clauses.

1. A **main (independent) clause** is a simple sentence that has become part of a bigger sentence. A simple sentence has one subject and one verb and expresses a complete thought. However, either the subject or the verb or both may be compound (may have more than one part, the parts usually joined by *and* or *or*). When it becomes part of a bigger sentence, the simple sentence changes its name from sentence to main clause.

A main clause may be used (rarely) as a part of speech when it is in a "quoted" context.

- *"Treat others as you want to be treated"* is good advice (used as noun, subject of the sentence).

2. A **subordinate (dependent) clause** is a group of related words with a subject and a real verb but <u>not</u> expressing a complete thought. The thought is not complete because the subordinate clause begins with a subordinating conjunction or a relative pronoun and needs a main clause to complete its meaning. A subordinate clause is always used as a noun, an adjective, or an adverb.

- NOUN: *That poetry can be both calming and stimulating* is readily apparent in a study of English poets (subject of the sentence).
- ADJECTIVE: Milton's second wife died in childbirth; his third wife, *who was devoted to him,* made his last years happy (modifies the noun *wife*).
- ADVERB: *After they had been married nine unhappy years,* Milton's first wife had died (modifies the verb *had died* telling when).

QUIZ YOURSELF ON SENTENCE ELEMENTS USED AS PARTS OF SPEECH The underlined words are used as what parts of speech?

1. Are you getting weary <u>of adjectives and adverbs</u>? _____

2. <u>Learning about them</u> can be very useful. _____

3. <u>If you want to be a writer</u>, you need these facts. _____

4. You must know <u>what goes into sentences</u>. _____

5. This chapter will help you if you want <u>to succeed in college</u>.
_____

6. In fact, it will make your time <u>on the job</u> as well as your days <u>at school</u> easier. _____

7. Students <u>trying hard</u> often lose sleep. _____

Answers on page 240.

QUIZ YOURSELF ON CHAPTER 3 Proofread the following paragraphs for mistakes in subject-verb agreement, tense, use of past participle, pronoun-antecedent agreement, and case of pronouns. Change the passive *had been turned around* to active voice. Find a *was* that needs to be put in the subjunctive mood. Make corrections above the lines.

1   Florence Nightingale (1820–1910) was an English nurse

2 who modern nursing owes a great deal to. It was her who

3 first brought sanitary nursing conditions to hospitals.

4 She had went to Russia to nurse English soldiers whom were

5 wounded in the Crimean War. Neither she nor her fellow

6 nurses was prepared for conditions at the army hospital.

7 She, along with her coworkers, were unhappy to find half-

8 starved soldiers with wounds that hasn't been washed or

9 bandaged. The nursing staff were willing to work hard, but

10 there was almost no medical supplies. Every nurse was

11 unhappy with their job, and a number of them was ready to

12 go home. But in about six months the situation had been

13 turned around by Nurse Nightingale. She and her nurses

14 have washed, bandaged, and fed the patients, scrub floors,

15 made mattresses, and obtained medical supplies. If there

16 was anything else she could have done, she would have did

17 it. Later she done a great deal to improve public health

18 nursing in England. She will have been considered the

19 founder of modern nursing—all this from the daughter of

20 wealthy parents who wanted her to be nothing more than

21 socially prominent.

Answers on page 240.

Answers to Exercises

Answers to Exercise 3.1, page 155

1. <u>sneeze</u>, subject of verb *is;* <u>expulsion</u>, appositive, renames *sneeze;* <u>air</u>, object of preposition *of;* <u>nose</u>, object of preposition *through;* <u>result</u>, predicate noun, renames *sneeze;* <u>irritation</u>, object of preposition *of;* <u>nerves</u>, object of preposition *of;* <u>nose</u>, object of preposition *in.*

2. <u>nose</u>, subject of verb *is removing;* <u>irritation</u>, object of verb *is removing.*

3. <u>sneeze</u>, object of preposition *during;* <u>reflex</u>, subject of verb *takes over.*

4. <u>sneeze</u>, subject of verb *is;* <u>state</u>, predicate noun, renames *sneeze;* <u>functions</u>, subject of verb *are suspended;* myth, predicate noun, renames subject *this;* superstition, appositive, renames *myth.*

5. man, subject of verb *ruptured;* eardrums, object of verb *ruptured;* sneeze, object of verb *held back.*

6. tissue, object of preposition *into;* droplets, subject of verb *travel;* germs, object of preposition *of;* sneezer, object of preposition *from.*

7. germs, subject of verb *may remain;* air, object of preposition *in;* days, object of preposition *for.*

8. superstition, subject of verb *is;* person, subject of verb *sneezes.*

9. Gesundheit, object of verb *wish;* health, appositive, renaming *Gesundheit;* sneezer, object of preposition *to.*

Answers to Exercise 3.2, page 157

1. Peter, a student at our college, had a problem; and as he and his three friends sat in the cafeteria drinking a cup of coffee, he asked the opinion of the group. Peter = proper, concrete. Student = common, concrete. College = common, concrete. Problem = common, abstract. Friends, cafeteria, cup, and coffee = common, concrete. Opinion = common, abstract. Group = common, collective, concrete.

2. He said he had been in the bookstore buying a notebook when he saw a girl from his last class slip a pen into the pocket of her jacket. Bookstore, notebook, girl = common, concrete. Class = common, collective, concrete. Pen, pocket, jacket = common, concrete.

3. Then she picked up a second pen, and that was all she paid for as she went out. Pen = common, concrete.

4. The four students agreed that honesty is the best policy, but Kate said maybe the girl needed the pen but didn't have the money. Students = common, concrete. Honesty = common, abstract. Policy = common, abstract, predicate. Kate = proper, concrete. Girl, pen, money = common, concrete.

5. Leatrice said she would have given the girl money to pay for the pen, and Roberto said he would have told the manager. Leatrice = proper, concrete. Girl, money, pen = common, concrete. Roberto = proper, concrete. Manager = common, concrete.

6. The students decided to all chip in and pay for the pen and then confront the girl, knowing that their trust in her would be destroyed if she didn't tell the truth. Students, pen, girl = common, concrete. Trust, truth = common, abstract.

7. When they tried to pay the manager, he told them that the girl was not a thief; she had felt such guilt that when she saw him later in the Business Office, she paid him for the pen. Manager, girl = common, concrete.

Thief = common, concrete, predicate. Guilt = common, abstract. Business Office = proper, concrete. Pen = common, concrete.

Answers to Quiz Yourself on Nouns, page 158

1. b.   **2.** T.   **3.** a.   **4.**   Proper.   **5.** When they start a sentence.   **6.** Senses.

Answers to Exercise 3.3, page 159

1. <u>Graffiti</u> <u>are</u> messages or pictures drawn on walls for the public to see (being verb).

2. <u>Human beings</u> probably <u>decorated</u> their cave walls with graffiti from the beginning of time (action verb).

3. <u>Graffiti from about 320 B.C.</u> <u>were discovered</u> by American archaeologists in Greece just a few years ago (verb in passive voice).

4. <u>Men and women of more than 2,000 years ago</u> <u>wrote</u> clever, dumb, trivial, and profound sayings on their walls (action verb).

5. <u>The Italian word meaning *to scratch*</u> <u>gave</u> us the word *graffito; the plural* <u>is</u> *graffiti* (action verb, being verb).

6. <u>A good graffito</u> <u>has</u> humor, sometimes with an unpleasant bite (action verb).

7. <u>Vandals</u> often <u>use</u> spray paint for their graffiti (action verb).

8. <u>We</u> <u>are bombarded</u> every day by walking graffiti (buttons) and rolling graffiti (bumper stickers) as well as graffiti on walls (verb in passive voice).

9. <u>Buttons</u> <u>can be</u> custom-made graffiti, with picture or message to suit the wearer (being verb).

10. A bumper sticker: "Careful when passing. <u>Driver</u> <u>is chewing</u> tobacco" (action verb).

Answers to Exercise 3.4, page 160

1. belongs.   **2.** look.   **3.** walks.   **4.** contain, squirts, misses.   **5.** make, dig.   **6.** help, live.   **7.** wears, appeal.   **8.** make, deodorizes.   **9.** turns.

Answers to Exercise 3.5, page 164

1. Number.   **2.** b.   **3.** a.   **4.** a.   **5.** a.   **6.** a.   **7.** b.   **8.** a.   **9.** a.   **10.** b.   **11.** a.

Answers to Exercise 3.6, page 164

You should have circled the following verbs: **1.** remembers.   **2.** is.   **3.** are.   **4.** is.   **5.**

are. **6.** seems, know. **7.** knows. **8.** are, are, is, is. **9.** needs, need. **10.** Is. **11.** knows, make.

Answers to Exercise 3.7, page 165

You should have circled the following verbs: **1.** seem (8). **2.** are (1). **3.** is (3). **4.** measures (6), are (7). **5.** plays (1), is (5). **6.** hopes (6), runs (6). **7.** is (9), seems (1). **8.** work (1), gets (2). **9.** wastes (2). **10.** thinks (2). **11.** relies (4).

Answers to Exercise 3.8, page 167

1. I am, you are, camel is, riding makes. **2.** camels have, camel has. **3.** hump is, it has. **4.** camels do, camel does. **5.** camel gets, it eats, it has. **6.** people have.

Answers to Exercise 3.9, page 167

1. does, doesn't. **2.** says, is. **3.** are, doesn't. **4.** haven't. **5.** is, have.

Answers to Exercise 3.10, page 168

1. are. **2.** doesn't, haven't. **3.** is. **4.** are, are

Answers to Exercise 3.11, page 169

1. were. **2.** had. **3.** was. **4.** did. **5.** was. **6.** had. **7.** did.

Answers to Exercise 3.12, page 174

1. was, brought. **2.** won, led. **3.** done, skipped. **4.** decided, been. **5.** done, did, was. **6.** had, having, teaching. **7.** gave, given. **8.** remembered, lived. **9.** had, came, sentenced. **10.** done, been, preaching.

Answers to Exercise 3.13, page 175

1. went, gone. 2. done, did. 3. took, taken. 4. seen, saw.

Answers to Exercise 3.14, page 178

1. had come = past perfect. **2.** helped = past. **3.** am = present, will need = future, said = past. **4.** replied = past, have finished = present perfect. **5.** Save = present (*you* is the understood subject), have written = present perfect, go = present, announced = past, have = present, have = present, goes = present, will have lost = future perfect, have saved = present perfect. **6.** was keeping = past progressive, had = past. **7.** announced = past, am begging = present progressive, have finished = present perfect. **8.** needed = past, asked = past, requested = past. **9.** blinked = past, had failed = past perfect. **10.** had saved = past perfect, moaned = past, was moaning = past progressive, was going = past progressive, had finished = past perfect, said = past, lost = past. **11.** Relax = present (*you* is the understood subject), said = past, left = past, saved = past, will have lost = future perfect. **12.** are = present, will do = future.

Answers to Exercise 3.15, page 182

1. superstition (d.o.). **2.** superstitions (d.o.), superstitions (d.o.), heresy (o.c., noun). **3.** events (d.o.), food (d.o.), child (i.o.), birthmark (d.o.). **4.** baby (i.o.), success (d.o.). **5.** us (i.o.), luck (d.o.). **6.** four (d.o.), number (o.c., noun), floor (d.o.), number (d.o.), unlucky (o.c., adjective). **7.** me (i.o.), foot (d.o.), superstitions (d.o.).

Answers to Exercise 3.16, page 183

1. Student Government held a meeting last week (active voice).

2. The meeting was called to order by the president (passive).

3. The minutes were read by the secretary and approved by the members (passive).

4. The team captain discussed the condition of the baseball field (active).

5. Peter made a motion to adjourn to the ball field (active).

6. The ball was being pitched by team members to each other (passive).

7. The litter on the field was noticed by the team captain (passive).

8. Student Government appointed a committee to clean up the field (active).

Answers to Exercise 3.17, page 184

You should have circled the following words: **1.** know, has taught. **2.** smiles. **3.** grades. **4.** helps. **5.** relaxes.

Answers to Exercise 3.18, page 186

1. good, better (both p.a.). **2.** cook (p.n.), confident (p.a.), teacher (p.n.). **3.** player (p.n.), mediocre (p.a.), skillful (p.a.). **4.** bad (p.a.). **5.** busy (p.a.).

Answers to Exercise 3.19, page 187

1. imp, imp, imp. **2.** ind, sub. **3.** ind. **4.** sub, ind. **5.** ind, sub.

Answers to Exercise 3.20, page 189

1. Attending = gerund (noun, subject of verb *is*).   **2.** racing and standing = present participles (both adjectives, modifying noun *men*).   **3.** featuring = present participle (adjective, modifying noun *circus*), riding = gerund (noun, direct object of participle *featuring*).   **4.** to perform = infinitive (noun, direct object of verb *began*).   **5.** to see = infinitive (adverb, modifying verb *flocked*), traveling = present participle (adjective, modifying *menageries*), to arrive = infinitive (adverb, modifying adjective *first*).   **6.** tattooed = past participle (adjective, modifying noun *men*).   **7.** painted = past participle (adjective, modifying noun *wagons*), crowded = past participle (adjective, modifying noun *streets*).

Answers to Quiz Yourself on Verbs, page 190

1. b.   **2.** a.   **3.** b.   **4.** F.   **5.** a.   **6.** a.   **7.** c.   **8.** a.   **9.** T.   **10.** c.

Answers to Exercise 3.21, page 194

1. I needed help, so my mother cared for me. The problem was mine.

2. You needed help, so your mother cared for you. The problem was yours.

3. He needed help, so his mother cared for him. The problem was his.

4. She needed help, so her mother cared for her. The problem was hers.

5. It needed help, so its mother cared for it. The problem was its (correct but not commonly used).

6. We needed help, so our mother cared for us. The problem was ours.

7. You needed help, so your mother cared for you. The problem was yours.

8. They needed help, so their mother cared for them. The problem was theirs.

Answers to Exercise 3.22, page 195

1. it, body.   **2.** his, Galileo's   **3.** he, Galileo.   **4.** his, Galileo's.   **5.** him, Galileo.   **6.** him, Galileo.   **7.** they, people.   **8.** it, error.   **9.** I, writer of this book.   **10.** I, writer of this book.   **11.** his, Galileo's.   **12.** them, brothers and sisters.   **13.** his, Galileo's.   **14.** she, mother.   **15.** him, Galileo.   **16.** you (+ you understood "keep reading"), reader of this.   **17.** it, exercise.   **18.** him, Galileo.

Answers to Exercise 3.23, page 199

1. possessive case *his,* objective case *him,* objective case *him.*   **2.** objective case *him.*   **3.** objective case *him.*   **4.** subjective case *he.*   **5.** objective case *him,* objective case *him.*   **6.** objective case *him,* possessive case *his,* objective case *him.*   **7.** objective case *him.*   **8.** subjective case *he.*   **9.** subjective case *He.*

Answers to Exercise 3.24, page 200

1. him, direct object of verb *has*.   **2.** whom, direct object of verb *likes*.   **3.** who, subject of verb *is;* me, object of preposition *between*.   **4.** him, direct object of infinitive *to like* with *to* understood; them, object of preposition *with*.   **5.** she, subject of verb *has;* her, possessive pronoun used as adjective modifying *career;* he, subject complement = predicate pronoun; who, subject of verb has *taught;* her, indirect object of verb *taught* with direct object = *facts*.   **6.** its, possessive pronoun modifying *advantages;* her, object of preposition *for;* it, object of preposition *in,* antecedent *nursing;* her, possessive pronoun modifying *childhood*.   **7.** she, subject complement = predicate pronoun.

Answers to Exercise 3.25, page 202

1. our, we, it.   **2.** it, them, it.   **3.** their.   **4.** she.   **5.** it.   **6.** his, her, their, his or her.   **7.** our, us, his or her.   **8.** your, you.   **9.** mine, my.   **10.** his or her.

Answers to Exercise 3.26, page 203

You should have circled these words: **1.** does, her.   **2.** do, their.   **3.** his or her.   **4.** he or she, studies.   **5.** is, his or her.   **6.** is, his or her.   **7.** is, its.   **8.** are, their.   **9.** makes, her.   **10.** make, their.

Answers to Exercise 3.27, page 207

1. "I made a mistake." OR "You made a mistake."   **2.** I.   **3.** his or her.   **4.** the dinner.   **5.** me.   **6.** who.   **7.** these kinds OR this kind.

Answers to Quiz Yourself on Pronouns, page 207

1. is used instead of a noun.   **2.** b.   **3.** T.   **4.** c.   **5.** subjective, objective, possessive.   **6.** b.   **7.** *I.*   **8.** his.   **9.** possessive.   **10.** T.

Answers to Exercise 3.28, page 210

You should have circled the following: **¶1:** The, warm, hot, The, the, open, the, big, the, barking, some, tossing, a, red, the, big, the, north, parking, the, sick, great, some, other. **¶2:** Mrs. Murphy's, her, ill. **¶3:** her, English. **¶4:** Your, upset, his, brown, the, front. **¶5:** the, next, wrong, my, my, a, third, fourth, another. **¶6:** the, main, My, 15-year-old, our, my, laughing, wrong, his, favorite, the, car, your, a, little. **¶7:** her, second-floor, the, curious, the, the, best, Frisbee, the, whole.

Answers to Quiz Yourself on Adjectives, page 214

1. b.   **2.** articles.   **3.** T.   **4.** proper.   **5.** superlative.   **6.** higher, highest; better, best.   **7.** more intelligent, most intelligent.

Answers to Exercise 3.29, page 217

The following should be underlined: **¶1:** quite, not, too, partly, frantically, bright, back, forth. **¶2:** very. **¶3:** Quickly, inside. **¶4:** really, out, however, ferociously. **¶5:** today, out, possibly, sooner. **¶6:** very, close, then, sincerely. **¶7:** back, briefly, outside, in, excitedly.

Answers to Quiz Yourself on Adverbs, page 219

1. b.   **2.** ly.   **3.** F.   **4.** adverb, adjective.   **5.** T.   **6.** sooner, soonest; better, best.   **7.** more willingly, most willingly.

Answers to Quiz Yourself on Adjectives and Adverbs, page 219

1. famous = adj. modifying proper noun *Garrett Morgan;* two = adj. modifying noun *inventions;* really = adv. modifying verb *changed;* the = article adj. modifying noun *world;* modern = adj. modifying noun *world.*
2. His = possessive pronoun adj. modifying noun *brother;* a = article adj. modifying noun *apparatus;* breathing = adj. modifying noun *apparatus;* the = article adj. modifying noun *precursor;* the = article adj. modifying noun *mask;* gas = adj. modifying noun *mask.*
3. not = adv. modifying adj. *much;* much = adj. modifying noun *interest;* a = article adj. modifying noun *explosion;* bad = adj. modifying noun *explosion;* a = article adj. modifying noun *tunnel;* a = article adj. modifying noun *intake;* city = adj. modifying noun *intake;* water = adj. modifying noun *intake;* Morgan's = proper possessive adj. modifying *home;* adopted = adj. modifying noun *home;* his = possessive pronoun adj. modifying noun *birthplace.*
4. Eleven = adj. modifying noun *men;* the = article adj. modifying noun *shaft;* 10 = adj. modifying noun *men.*
5. the = article adj. modifying noun *tunnel;* a = article adj. modifying noun *dozen;* the = article adj. modifying noun *masks;* breathing = adj. modifying noun *masks;* out = adv. modifying verb *brought;* the = article adj. modifying noun *men;* alive = adj. modifying noun *men.*
6. Later = adv. modifying verb *saw;* a = article adj. modifying noun *collision;* a = article adj. modifying noun *wagon;* horse-drawn = adj. modifying noun *wagon;* a = article adj. modifying noun *car;* the = article adj. modifying noun *signal;* traffic = adj. modifying noun *signal;* slowly = adv. modifying verb *began;* his = possessive pronoun adjective modifying noun *mind;* inventive = adj. modifying noun *mind.*
7. The = article adj. modifying noun *models;* first = adj. modifying noun *models;* clumsily = adv. modifying verb *were operated;* a = article adj. modifying noun *lever;* changing = participle adj. modifying noun *lever;* the = article adj. modifying noun *light;*

causing = participle adj. modifying noun *lever;* a = article adj. modifying noun *sign;* "Stop" = adj. modifying noun *sign.*

8. greatly = adv. modifying verb *has affected;* our = possessive pronoun adj. modifying noun *lives.*

Answers to Exercise 3.30, page 222

If you ever want *to* (part of the infinitive *to shoot*) shoot the rapids, you should do it in a whitewater kayak. Whitewater kayaks are made of plastic or of fiberglass and are built for quick maneuvering on river rapids. The kayakers sit one in front of the other in cockpits in an enclosed deck. A kayak paddle has a blade at each end. If you have done this *before* (adverb modifying verb *have done*), you know it is a thrilling sport, but brush up on your swimming skills *before* (subordinating conjunction introducing subordinate clause *before you go*) you go so nothing unpleasant will happen before the end of the trip. Between you and me, I think this would be a great sport except for the fact that there are no rapids near my town, or anywhere *near* (adverb modifying adverb *anywhere*).

Answers to Quiz Yourself on Prepositions, page 223

1. b.   **2.** a.   **3.** a.   **4.** c.   **5.** T.

Answers to Exercise 3.31, page 225

1. Even though, subordinating.   **2.** or, coordinating.   **3.** because, subordinating.   **4.** Although, subordinating.   **5.** and, coordinating.   **6.** Both . . . and, correlative.   **7.** or, coordinating.   **8.** and, coordinating.   **9.** so, coordinating.   **10.** but, coordinating.   **11.** both . . . and, correlative.   **12.** Either . . . or, correlative.   **13.** not only . . . but also, correlative.   **14.** for, coordinating.

Answers to Quiz Yourself on Conjunctions, page 226

1. connect words, phrases, and clauses.   **2.** coordinating, correlative, and subordinating.   **3.** and, but, for, nor, or, so, yet.   **4.** a.   **5.** b.

Possible Answers to Quiz Yourself on Interjections, page 227

The answers might be as follows: **1.** Oh! I . . .   **2.** Ouch! You . . .   **3.** Well, what . . .   **4.** No! Can't . . .   **5.** Hey, what . . .

Answers to Quiz Yourself on Sentence Elements Used as Parts of Speech, page 230

1. adverb (prepositional phrase modifying adjective *weary*). **2.** noun (gerund phrase used as subject of verb *can be*). **3.** adverb (subordinate clause modifying verb *need*). **4.** noun (subordinate clause used as direct object of verb *must know*). **5.** noun (infinitive phrase used as direct object of verb *want*). **6.** adjective (prepositional phrase modifying noun *time*); adjective (prepositional phrase modifying noun *days*). **7.** adjective (participle phrase modifying noun *Students*).

Answers to Quiz Yourself on Chapter 3, page 230

2. English nurse <u>whom</u>; It was <u>she</u>. **4.** She had <u>gone</u>; soldiers <u>who</u> were wounded. **6.** fellow nurses <u>were</u>. **7.** <u>was</u> unhappy. **8.** wounds that <u>hadn't</u>. **9.** staff <u>was</u>. **10.** there <u>were</u>. **11.** <u>her</u> job. a number of them <u>were</u>. **13.** Nurse Nightingale had turned the situation around (<u>active</u> voice). **14.** <u>had</u> washed; <u>scrubbed</u> floors. **16.** if there <u>were</u> (subjunctive mood). would have <u>done</u>. **17.** she <u>did</u> a great deal. **18.** She <u>is</u> considered.

4 Sentences

Step One: Writing Correct Sentences

Definition of a Sentence

A **sentence** is a group of words containing a subject, a real verb, and a complete thought and ending with a period, a question mark, or an exclamation point.

A **subject** is a noun, or a word or words substituting for a noun, telling who or what does something or is something or has something done to it.

- *I* go to school. My *teachers* are good. Too many *students* are turned off by uncaring teachers.

A **real verb** tells us that the subject does something (action) or is something (being) or has something done to it (passive voice). There are many words that look like real verbs but aren't because they would not make sense as the verb in the sentence.

To check that you have a real verb, test it with a subject. Say the word *I* or *she* or some other subject in front of it: I *writing* a book. She *to write* a book.

These don't make sense; *writing* and *to write* are not real verbs.

He *writes*. She *wrote*. I *am writing*. They *will be writing*. All of these make sense. These are real verbs.

A sentence must not only have a subject and a real verb, but it must also express a **complete thought.** The listener or reader must get sensible meaning from the words.

- COMPLETE: Ms. Larue is our history teacher. She is so nice! Don't you wish she were your teacher? Listen. (*Listen* is a one-word sentence, subject *you* understood, real verb *listen,* complete thought expressed: You know what the speaker or writer means.)
- INCOMPLETE: Although Ms. Larue is our history teacher. If she taught math. Wish you could know her. She and I good friends.

Use a **period,** a **question mark,** or an **exclamation point** to end a sentence. You need to decide what the purpose of the sentence is to determine which of the three marks of punctuation you need to end any particular sentence.

Put a period at the end of a declarative sentence. A **declarative sentence** is a statement.

- Wolfgang Amadeus Mozart was a famous Austrian composer.

Usually put a period at the end of an imperative sentence. An **imperative sentence** is a command or request.

- Play his music for me.

You may end an imperative sentence with an exclamation point if strong emotion is expressed.

- Stop! Go away!

The subject of imperative sentences is *you* understood: *You* play his music for me. *You* stop! *You* go away!

Put a question mark at the end of an interrogative sentence. An **interrogative sentence** is a question.

- Is that true that he was just a boy when he composed this music?

Put an exclamation point at the end of an exclamatory sentence. An **exclamatory sentence** is an expression of strong emotion, a sharp or sudden utterance, or an outcry.

- How beautiful his piano concertos are!

EXERCISE 4.1 In the blank write the appropriate abbreviation for the type of sentence: **dec** for declarative, **int** for interrogative, **exc** for exclamatory, and **imp** for imperative. Place the correct mark of punctuation at the end of each sentence.

_____ **1.** Wolfgang Amadeus Mozart was born in Salzburg, Austria, in 1756 ___

_____ **2.** What a tremendous amount he accomplished in the 35 years of his life _____

_____ **3.** The beloved "Minuet" was composed when he was just five; he heard music in his head and played it while his father wrote it down _____

_____ **4.** Where did he get such talent _____

_____ **5.** His father was choirmaster to the Archbishop of Salzburg, and his sister, five years older, was a prodigy _____

_____ **6.** Imagine what Mozart's life must have been like _____

_____ **7.** Do you suppose he ever played childhood games _____

_____ **8.** Did you know he played the clavier, or German harpsichord, and the organ and the violin _____

_____ **9.** Also note that his sister played the clavier and sang _____

_____**10.** What a family they must have been _____

Answers on page 287.

Avoiding Three Serious Sentence Errors

You will be well on your way to a command of the English language if you can learn, *now,* to avoid the three following serious sentence errors:

1. **Fragment (FR)** = an incomplete sentence, a part of a sentence pretending to be a complete sentence.
2. **Comma splice (CS)** = two sentences connected with a comma, spliced together with just a comma.
3. **Fused sentence (FS)** = two sentences connected with nothing, fused together with nothing in between.

Although we can sometimes get by with less-than-perfect sentences in conversation, because a listener can't tell whether we have put a period, a semicolon, a comma, or nothing between sentences, *writing* faulty sentences can quickly make a person appear ignorant. Ignorance of the three common sentence errors is not bliss.

Error One: The Fragment. If a "sentence" does not contain all three of these—a subject, a real verb, and a complete thought—it is not a sentence. It is a **fragment.** Subjects are underlined once, verbs twice.

- NO SUBJECT: One day in English class accidentally <u>wrote</u> a fragment.

- ADD A SUBJECT TO MAKE A SENTENCE: One day in English class <u>Mrs. Murphy</u> accidentally <u>wrote</u> a fragment.

- NO REAL VERB: One day in English class <u>Mrs. Murphy</u> accidentally writing a fragment. An *ing* word can't be a real verb unless it has an auxiliary with it: *is writing, was writing, will be writing.*

- ADD A REAL VERB TO MAKE A SENTENCE: One day in English class <u>Mrs. Murphy</u> accidentally <u>was writing</u> a fragment OR <u>had written</u> a fragment OR <u>wrote</u> a fragment.

- YOU MAY HAVE A SUBJECT AND A REAL VERB BUT NO COMPLETE THOUGHT: When <u>Mrs. Murphy</u> accidentally <u>wrote</u> a fragment one day in English class. Here, although you have a subject and a real verb, you need more information to have a complete thought.

- ADD A MAIN CLAUSE (a sentence) TO GIVE MEANING TO THE INCOMPLETE THOUGHT: When Mrs. Murphy accidentally wrote a fragment one day in English class, *the students all laughed.*

A group of words that contains a subject and a real verb but does not express a complete thought until it is attached to another sentence that gives it meaning is a **subordinate (or dependent) clause.** Standing by itself, it is a fragment and makes no sense. It needs to be attached to a complete sentence that gives it meaning, making it part of a bigger sentence.

Subordinate-clause fragments (italicized below) are often caused by putting the period in too soon.

- WRONG: *As soon as class was over.* Mrs. Murphy went to lunch.

To fix this, connect the subordinate clause, which doesn't make sense by itself, to the main clause (*Mrs. Murphy went to lunch,* a complete sentence) which follows it.

- RIGHT: As soon as class was over, Mrs. Murphy went to lunch.

Or subordinate clause fragments may be caused by putting in a semicolon, which is usually like a period, where it doesn't belong.

- WRONG: She went to the library; *because she needed to grade papers.* To fix this, take out the semicolon and connect the subordinate clause, which simply doesn't make sense by itself, to the main clause (*She went to the library,* a complete sentence) which precedes it.

- RIGHT: She went to the library because she needed to grade papers. The subordinate clause, attached to the main clause, now makes sense.

NOTE: When a subordinate clause is attached to a complete sentence, the complete sentence, now part of a bigger sentence, changes its name to main clause. A **main (or independent) clause** is nothing more than a simple sentence (a subject and a verb and a complete thought) that has become part of a bigger sentence. Remember, though, that in a simple sentence either subject or verb or both may be compound (may have more than one part, the parts usually joined by *and* or *or*).

You can also usually fix a subordinate-clause fragment by removing the **subordinating conjunction,** the word that introduces the subordinate clause. Without the subordinating conjunction, a subordinate-clause fragment becomes a sentence.

A list of subordinating conjunctions is presented in the box below. These are the words that are so often responsible for fragments.

Subordinating Conjunctions

after	by the time	once	unless
although	even though	provided (that)	until
as	how	since	when
as far as	if	so	whenever
as if	inasmuch as	so as	where
as much as	in order that	so that	whereas
as soon as	in that	than	wherever
as though	no matter how	though	whether
because	now that	till	while
before			why

When a subordinating conjunction is placed before a sentence, it automatically turns a perfectly good sentence into a subordinate clause because, by the very nature of the subordinating conjunction (*When* the party is over OR *Because* you are tall), another sentence is needed to complete the meaning. But remove the subordinating conjunction, and you have a complete sentence: The party is over. You are tall.

The following expressions are all subordinate clauses: After we study late. . . , As we study late. . . , Because we study late. . . , Before we study late. . . , Since we study late. . . , When we study late. . . , Whenever we study late. . . , While we study late . . .

There are two ways to make these subordinate clauses into complete sentences:

1. Leave off the subordinating conjunction, and your sentence is *We study late.*

2. Add a sentence, *we have to have something to eat,* and you have a bigger sentence that makes sense: (*When we study late, we have to have something to eat*). *We have to have something to eat* becomes a main clause in the bigger sentence.

If a **relative pronoun** (*that, what, whatever, which, whichever, who, whoever, whom, whomever, whose*) introduces the subordinate clause, the relative pronoun cannot always be removed to change the subordinate clause into a sentence (as a subordinating conjunction can) because the relative pronoun may have a function in the subordinate clause other than just introducing it.

- It was Mrs. Murphy who taught us to write complete sentences. *Who taught us to write complete sentences* is the subordinate clause; obviously, removing *who,* the subject of the subordinate clause, does not make the subordinate clause a complete sentence.

A good way to test for a fragment is to pretend someone is saying the words to you. Is the meaning clear? It won't be clear if what has been said is a fragment.

- NOT CLEAR: When the weather is better.

It will be clear if it is a complete sentence.

- CLEAR: I'll make the trip when the weather is better.

Although fragments most often are not acceptable in formal writing, **there are a few times when using a fragment is acceptable and desirable.**

- To ask questions: *When? Where?*
- To answer questions: *Not now. In the garage.*
- To show a sudden emotion: *Oops! No way! You bumbling idiot!*
- To write realistic dialogue (because people often don't speak in complete sentences): Marcia slapped Harry across the face and muttered, "*Low life. Out. Out of my life forever. Time to call it quits.*"
- To provide emphasis: Mrs. Murphy is one of the best teachers in our school. *Absolutely. No question.*"

If you understand the preceding facts about fragments, you are well on your way to writing complete sentences.

EXERCISE 4.2 Write **C** (for Correct) in the blank if the words express a complete thought, **W** (for Wrong) if they do not.

_____ **1.** Witchcraft is the use of supernatural powers.

_____ **2.** Usually harms people.

_____ **3.** A witch receives magic powers from evil spirits.

_____ **4.** Many people from earliest times of recorded history to the present time, everywhere in the world.

_____ **5.** Even today believe in witches and in the evil powers of witches.

_____ **6.** European witchcraft involves the devil.

_____ **7.** The word *witch* from an Anglo-Saxon word meaning *wise one* or *magician*.

_____ **8.** Originally a witch either a man or woman with supernatural powers.

_____ **9.** Now, however, witches are more often women.

_____**10.** Men with magical powers *sorcerers, warlocks,* or *wizards*.

Answers on page 287.

EXERCISE 4.3 Underline the simple subject once, the verb twice.

1. Believers in witchcraft attribute tremendous power, often quite dangerous power, to witches and warlocks.

2. A witch or a warlock may make a small wax or wooden image of the victim.

3. She or he then puts something from the victim's body, such as fingernail clippings or hair, into the image.

4. The treacherous person practicing witchcraft then destroys the image by cutting it, burning it, or sticking pins into it.

5. The victim supposedly suffers severe pain or even death.

6. A person really deep into practicing witchcraft and wanting to make another person suffer sometimes casts a spell by muttering the victim's name and reciting a magic formula.

7. People lacking knowledge of agriculture and disease once blamed witches and warlocks for any unexplained misfortune, such as illness, a sudden death, or a crop failure.

8. These wicked witches and warlocks cast spells on churns to prevent butter from forming.

9. Oct. 31 was the favorite day for these supernatural beings to hold meetings.

10. Children of all ages and all beliefs about witchcraft dress as goblins and ghosts every Halloween.

Answers on page 288.

NOTE: A **simple sentence** is a sentence that has one subject and one verb, but either the subject or the verb or both may be compound (may have more than one part).

You should also keep in mind that words that explain, describe, or limit other words are called **modifiers.** The **complete subject** consists of the simple subject (the noun or noun substitute alone) plus its modifiers; the **predicate** consists of the real verb plus its modifiers and its **complements,** words that complete its meaning. In the following examples, the simple subject and verb are circled; the complete subject is underlined once, the predicate twice.

- Sweet, patient Mrs. Murphy, our English teacher, is getting quite a workout in these exercises (one subject, one verb).
- Mrs. Murphy and Mr. Perez are my favorite teachers (compound subject).
- They explain things clearly and treat students fairly (compound verb).
- They and my other teachers listen to our problems and always help us (both compound subject and compound verb).

EXERCISE 4.4 Circle all simple subjects and all verbs, marking them **s** or **v.** Sentences may have compound subjects and/or compound verbs.

1. Witches have existed, at least in people's minds, since the beginning of time and have appeared in literature from the beginning of writing.

2. The *Odyssey* and the Bible contain references to witchcraft.

3. Circe, a witch in Homer's epic poem, had the power to turn people into animals.

4. The Old Testament contains several references to witches and witchcraft, including the following sentence from Exodus 22:18.

5. "Thou shalt not suffer a witch to live."

6. Witch-hunters hundreds of years later accepted such biblical statements as gospel and persecuted persons accused of witchcraft.

7. Those persons accused of witchcraft were often tortured and were sometimes even killed.

8. Tests of a woman's guilt included tying her arms and legs and throwing her into deep water.

9. A witch's floating on the surface was considered a sign of guilt.

10. What good was innocence to a drowning, falsely accused witch?

Answers on page 289.

EXERCISE 4.5 Using the answers to Exercise 4.4, go over the sentences, this time underlining the complete subject once, the predicate twice.

Answers on page 290.

Reversing the position of subject and verb, as was done in No. 10, forms a **question** and sometimes makes finding the subject and the verb more difficult. If the verb has an auxiliary (helper), the subject is usually relocated between the two parts of the verb. Verbs sometimes acquire an auxiliary when being made into a question.

- The <u>cat</u> <u>is</u> sick. <u>Is</u> the <u>cat</u> sick? (simple reversal of position of subject and verb).

- The <u>cat</u> <u>is lying</u> in the sun. <u>Is</u> the <u>cat</u> <u>lying</u> in the sun? (relocation of subject between two parts of verb).

- <u>I</u> <u>buy</u> cat food every week. <u>Do</u> <u>I</u> <u>buy</u> cat food every week? (addition of auxiliary *do*).

Also, the position of subject and verb is sometimes reversed for emphasis.

- Wise <u>is</u> the <u>student</u> with a dictionary by his or her side at study time. (Emphasis is on the word *wise*.)

EXERCISE 4.6 Underline the simple subject once and the verb twice in these sentences. Part of each example is a question except No. 6, in which the order is reversed for emphasis.

1. Joan of Arc was burned at the stake. Why was Joan of Arc burned at the stake?

2. She was a witch. Was she really a witch?

3. Were many women killed as witches? Between 1484 and 1782, about 300,000 women were killed by the Christian Church for practicing witch-craft.

4. Where did the most famous witch-hunt in American history occur? The most famous witch-hunt in American history occurred in Salem, Mass.

5. Who stirred public feeling against witches? Cotton Mather, a colonial preacher, stirred public feeling against the supposed evil deeds of witches.

6. Disgraced for life were many women in the town of Salem.

7. Is voodoo anything like witchcraft? Voodoo is like witchcraft in many ways.

8. Witchcraft is becoming of more interest as a religion. Why is witchcraft becoming of more interest as a religion?

9. Have witches been meeting? Witches have been meeting in groups of 13 known as covens.

10. Education has lessened the fear of witches. Will further education lessen the fear of witchcraft even more?

Answers on page 290.

Remember the definition of a sentence: a group of words containing a subject, a real verb, and a complete thought and ending with a period, a question mark, or an exclamation point. We have learned how to avoid fragments by including the three ingredients necessary for a sentence: a subject, a real verb, and a complete thought. But what if a sentence ends in a comma, or what if there is no mark of punctuation at the end of a sentence separating it from the next sentence?

Aha, we have just described the remaining two serious sentence errors, the comma splice and the fused sentence. First we will redefine these two errors; then we'll tell how to correct them. The comma splice and the fused sentence are corrected in the same four ways.

Error Two: The Comma Splice. A **comma splice** is the sentence error of connecting two sentences with a comma. The first sentence needs to be ended with something more than a comma.

- CS: We sometimes stay in the cafeteria too long, we're late for class. The ways to correct a comma splice are listed below, under "fused sentence" because comma splices and fused sentences are corrected in the same four ways.

Error Three: The Fused Sentence. A **fused sentence** is the sentence error of connecting two sentences with nothing in between. The first sentence needs to be ended with something more than a "nothing."

- FS: We sometimes stay in the cafeteria too long we're late for class.

IMPORTANT: **The same four ways may be used to correct comma splices and fused sentences:**

1. **Insert a period** (or it could be a question mark or an exclamation point) at the end of the first sentence and an uppercase (capital) letter at the beginning of the second sentence.

- We sometimes stay in the cafeteria too long. We're late for class.

2. **Insert a semicolon** between the two sentences, and begin the second sentence with a lowercase (small) letter.

- We sometimes stay in the cafeteria too long; we're late for class.

NOTE: **In 99 cases out of 100, the semicolon is used like a period to end a sentence.** But another sentence always follows the semicolon when it is used this way, and the two sentences (now main clauses) become one bigger sentence. A semicolon is preferred over a period when the two sentences are closely related in meaning.

3. **Insert a comma and a coordinating conjunction** (*and, but, for, nor, or, so, yet*) between the sentences.

- We sometimes stay in the cafeteria too long, and we're late for class.

4. **Subordinate one of the sentences to the other** (making one into a subordinate clause, shown here in italics).

- *Because we sometimes stay in the cafeteria too long,* we're late for class (main clause).

NOTE: Not all comma splices and fused sentences can be corrected by subordination.

• The new student has pretty brown eyes she is from Albuquerque. It would not make sense to say *Because* or *If* or *When* or *Although* the new student has pretty brown eyes, she is from Albuquerque.

EXERCISE 4.7 In the blank write **C** if the sentence is correct; write **FR** for fragment, **CS** for comma splice, or **FS** for fused sentence. Three contain a correct sentence followed by a fragment; mark those **FR.** Be sure you know why you marked each one as you did.

_____ **1.** Joseph Pulitzer (1847–1911) was a great American publisher who was born in Hungary.

_____ **2.** And came to the United States when he was 17, having been persuaded by a recruiter to come to this country to join the Union Army in the Civil War.

_____ **3.** Although he could not speak English when he arrived, he learned quickly penniless, after the war he went to St. Louis, Mo., where he got a job as a reporter for a German-language newspaper.

_____ **4.** In four years he became part owner of the paper. Which he sold just before moving to New York City to become European correspondent for the *Sun*.

_____ **5.** In 1878 he went back to St. Louis there he bought the dying *Dispatch,* combined it with the *Evening Post,* and began amassing a fortune as publisher of the St. Louis *Post-Dispatch*.

_____ **6.** Five years later he bought the ailing New York *World* soon he had turned it into a profitable, influential paper.

_____ **7.** He was elected to the United States House of Representatives but resigned after little more than a year, he was in ill health and became almost totally blind during the last years of his life.

_____ **8.** When he died, he left $1,000,000 to the Columbia University Graduate School of Journalism. Which he had founded with a $1,000,000 gift in 1903.

_____ **9.** Also endowed a fund for the Pulitzer Prizes.

_____**10.** The annual Pulitzer Prizes recognize contributions in journalism. As well as fiction, biography, poetry, history, music, drama, and art.

Answers on page 291.

EXERCISE 4.8 In the blank write **C** if the sentence is correct; write **FR** for fragment, **CS** for comma splice, or **FS** for fused sentence. Be sure you know why you marked each one as you did.

_____ **1.** Zippers should not be called zippers they are really slide fasteners.

_____ **2.** The first slide fastener was devised in 1892 by Whitcomb L. Judson, a Chicago inventor.

_____ **3.** Who immediately sensed its possibilities and started gathering capital for production of this potentially useful gadget.

_____ **4.** A series of teeth that meshed when a slider passed over them.

_____ **5.** It was not until 1913 that Gideon Sundback, a Swedish technician, perfected the slide fastener, the Hookless Fastener Co. was born.

_____ **6.** The Hookless Fastener Co. originated Talon fasteners these replaced buttons, hooks and eyes, buckles, and snaps on articles as diverse as clothing, luggage, furniture upholstery, tents, and footwear.

_____ **7.** During World War I, sales rocketed, slide fasteners were put on soldiers' money belts.

_____ **8.** "Zipper" was the trade name registered in 1924 for galoshes made by the B. F. Goodrich Co., they were equipped with Talon fasteners.

_____ **9.** Unique uses of zippers, as slide fasteners are now universally called, just as refrigerators have been called Frigidaires and photocopying is often called Xeroxing.

_____ **10.** The Waldorf-Astoria Hotel in New York once ordered 95-foot zippers to connect sections of carpeting; a hat maker devised a single strip of material that was easy to pack and could then be unpacked and zipped to make a lady's hat.

Answers on page 291.

EXERCISE 4.9 In the blank write **C** if the sentence is correct; write **FR** for fragment, **CS** for comma splice, or **FS** for fused sentence. Then correct the sentences above the line. Mark the "sentence" **FR** if it includes both a complete sentence and a fragment. There are three each **FR, CS,** and **FS** and one correct, **C.**

_____ **1.** A brilliant agricultural chemist, George Washington Carver born about 1864 of slave parents in Missouri.

_____ **2.** When he was just a baby, he and his mother were stolen by raiders, his master bought him back in exchange for a race horse.

_____ **3.** He worked his way through school and graduated from Iowa State College later he got his master's degree there.

_____ **4.** He was a member of the Iowa State faculty until he joined Tuskegee Institute in Alabama, where he spent the rest of his life.

_____ **5.** Where his work to revolutionize the agriculture of the South won him international fame.

_____ **6.** He encouraged farmers to grow peanuts and sweet potatoes instead of cotton. Which was exhausting the soil.

_____ **7.** Soon the farmers were growing more of these two crops than people could eat he began making useful products from them.

_____ **8.** From peanuts he made cheese, milk, coffee, soap, and ink from sweet potatoes he made flour, candy, vinegar, molasses, and rubber.

_____ **9.** In 1940 he gave his life savings of $33,000 to found the George Washington Carver Foundation for Agricultural Research at Tuskegee Institute, a museum of his discoveries is there.

_____ **10.** He was given many honors, he died in 1943.

Answers on page 292.

EXERCISE 4.10 In the blank write **C** if the sentence is correct; write **FR** for fragment, **CS** for comma splice, and **FS** for fused sentence. Mark the "sentence" **FR** if it includes both a complete sentence and a fragment. Then correct the sentences above the line.

_____ **1.** Tattooing the practice of making permanent designs on the body.

_____ **2.** It is done by pricking deep holes in the skin coloring matter is then placed in the holes.

_____ **3.** A popular custom among soldiers and sailors of many countries.

_____ **4.** No one knows when or where tattooing started, some Egyptian mummies of 1300 B.C. show blue tattoo marks under the skin.

_____ **5.** The Japanese and the Burmese some of the most elaborate tattooing in the world.

_____ **6.** Tattooing is also popular in Southeastern New Guinea, in that part of the world tattoos on girls are looked on as signs of beauty.

_____ **7.** Although in the United States all kinds of people sport tattoos.

_____ **8.** Most people who get tattooed consider their new look a method of self-expression, many consider their tattooed bodies a walking art form.

_____ **9.** Beginning tattooers, who often have degrees in art, usually learn their needle work from established tattooers. Often their fathers.

_____ **10.** The tattooed even have conventions; at which they trade ideas for designs and select Mr. Tattoo and Ms. Tattoo.

_____ **11.** Tattoos can be removed with laser beams.

Answers on page 293.

EXERCISE 4.11 Sometimes instead of assigning exercises in the text, I ask students to make up their own. Then they trade papers and correct the mistakes. These are the five sentences that one of my students, Sunthorn Phetcharat, wrote for a fellow student to correct. Pretend he has traded papers with you, and correct his exercise in the blanks below.

1. In Thailand, teachers more like second parents than faculty members.
2. Students in Thailand show their teachers great respect, students always do exactly what their teachers say.
3. American teachers are more friendly, students get to know them better.
4. In Thailand schools, students from fourth grade through high school must wear uniforms they consist of short pants for the boys and not-too-short skirts for the girls.
5. Boys' hair must be cut very short with the weather so hot, I never minded the short hair or the short pants.

1. _____
2. _____
3. _____
4. _____
5. _____

Possible answers on page 293.

Some grammarians lump the comma splice and the fused sentence into one error called a **run-on sentence,** but it is possible to write a sentence that runs on and on that is grammatically correct. Dividing the two errors of "sentences stuck together incorrectly" into CS and FS is more precise than calling both sentence errors run-ons.

QUIZ YOURSELF ON STEP ONE Fill in the blanks.

1. Why is learning about sentences important to you? _____

_____

_____

2. What is the definition of a sentence? _____

_____

3. What is the definition of a subject? Of a verb? _____

_____

_____

4. What are the three most common and most serious sentence errors?

(a) _____ (b) _____ (c) _____

5. Two of the three serious sentence errors are cured in the same four ways. What are the two errors?

(a) _____ (b) _____

6. What are the four ways to cure them?

(a) _____ (c) _____

(b) _____ (d) _____

7. What is a main (or independent) clause? What is a subordinate (or dependent) clause? _____

_____

_____

8. A subordinate clause standing alone with no main clause is which sentence error? _____

9. What is a predicate? _____

10. What is an imperative sentence? What is the subject of an imperative sentence? What mark of punctuation usually goes at the end of an imperative sentence? _____

_____   _____

_____**11.** T or F. You have to memorize all the rules of English because after you finish this course, you can not refer to this book ever again.

Answers on page 294.

Step Two: Writing Effective Sentences

Using Sentences With Different Structures

Sentences can be categorized not only according to their purpose (declarative, interrogative, exclamatory, and imperative) but also according to their structure (according to how many main clauses and how many subordinate clauses they contain). Knowing the various ways in which you may put clauses together to create effective sentences helps you a great deal in writing. It gives you a choice. It gives you control over your writing. There are four types of sentences according to structure.

1. Simple Sentence. A **simple sentence** has one main clause—that is, one simple subject and one real verb. There may also be modifiers and complements to make up the complete subject and the predicate. In the following examples, the simple subjects and verbs are circled, the complete subjects underlined once, and the predicates underlined twice.

- Mozart, the masterful composer of sonatas, concertos, symphonies, and operas, traveled extensively in Europe.

BUT DON'T FORGET: In a simple sentence either the subject or the verb or both may be compound (may have more than one part, the parts usually joined by *and* or *or*).

- The six-year-old Mozart and his 11-year-old sister visited Vienna and played for the empress. This is still a simple sentence.

2. Compound Sentence. A **compound sentence** has two or more main clauses. A main clause (or independent clause) is nothing more than a simple sentence that has been joined to another clause to form one bigger sentence. In a compound sentence, two (or more) main clauses are connected to each other (within the bigger compound sentence) by a coordinating conjunction (*and, but, for, nor, or, so,* and *yet*) or by a semicolon or by a semicolon and a conjunctive adverb (see pages 309-310).

- The young Mozart took music lessons from his father, and at five the child had begun composing short pieces. The two main clauses are joined into a compound sentence by the coordinating conjunction *and.*

In a compound sentence, the main clauses are of equal importance to the reader. Writing a compound sentence is a way of showing the equality of two ideas—or more if there are more than two main clauses.

3. Complex Sentence. A **complex sentence** has one main clause and one or more subordinate clauses. A subordinate clause, also called a dependent clause, is a group of words including a subject and a real verb but introduced by a subordinating conjunction or a relative pronoun. Because of this introductory word, the subordinate clause depends on a main clause for meaning; it can't stand alone as a sentence. Joining the subordinate clause to the main clause makes a complex sentence. Subordinate clauses are italicized in the examples that follow.

- *Although Mozart lived to be only 35,* he is considered one of the greatest geniuses in musical history. The main clause gives meaning to the subordinate clause.

Complex sentences show an unequal relationship between the main clause and the subordinate clause. The main clause is more important; the subordinate clause still needs to be there, though, because it gives additional information about the main clause. In the sentence above, the important information is that Mozart is such a genius. The subordinate clause tells why this is so astonishing.

4. Compound-Complex Sentence. A **compound-complex sentence** has at least two main clauses and at least one subordinate clause.

- The Archbishop of Salzburg called the boy composer a fraud (first main clause), but Mozart composed a beautiful oratorio in a week (second main clause) *even though the archbishop had locked him in a room alone* (subordinate clause depends on the preceding main clause for its meaning).

Compound-complex sentences are useful when you want to keep several related ideas in the same sentence, but when some ideas are of greater but equal importance (the main clauses) and the other ideas (the subordinate clause or clauses) are of less importance but give additional information about the main clauses.

The Four Kinds of Sentences According to Structure

Simple sentence = one main clause: I worked.

Compound sentence = two (or more) main clauses: I worked, and I played.

Complex sentence = one main clause + one (or more) subordinate clauses: I worked *when the weather was good.*

Compound-complex sentence = two (or more) main clauses + one (or more) subordinate clauses: I worked, and I played *when the weather was good.*

EXERCISE 4.12 Underline main clauses once, subordinate clauses twice. Then indicate in the blank the type of sentence according to structure: **s** = simple, **cpd** = compound, **cpx** = complex, **cc** = compound-complex.

_____ **1.** The six-year-old Mozart and his 11-year-old sister visited Vienna and played for the empress.

_____ **2.** Whenever Mozart's father took him on a tour of European capitals, audiences were astounded by the young man's musical talent.

_____ **3.** Mozart began teaching music in Germany, and soon he met Aloysia Weber.

_____ **4.** After she became a successful singer, she rejected Mozart.

_____ **5.** He later married her younger sister, Constanze, who was also a singer, and for the rest of his life he had financial difficulty.

_____ **6.** Even though Mozart was composer to the emperor, he lived his life in poverty because he could not manage money well.

_____ **7.** The last decade of his life he frantically composed music and gave frequent concert tours.

_____ **8.** He is often considered the father of the modern concerto; he composed some 25 concertos for piano and orchestra.

_____ **9.** Life in his household must not have been tranquil, but his wife and his children apparently adored him and he adored them.

_____ **10.** Wolfgang and Constanze had six children; four died at an early age, but the two sons who survived to adulthood were talented musicians.

Answers on page 294.

EXERCISE 4.13 Using the answers to the 10 sentences of Exercise 4.12, repeated below, put one check over coordinating conjunctions that connect main clauses to other *main clauses* (be aware that coordinating conjunctions may connect words or phrases as well as clauses). Also put one check over semicolons connecting two main clauses. Put two checks over subordinating conjunctions, which always introduce subordinate clauses; and put two checks over the relative pronoun *who*, which introduces a subordinate clause.

s **1.** The six-year-old Mozart and his 11-year-old sister visited Vienna and played for the empress. (Main clause with compound subject and compound verb.)

cpx **2.** Whenever Mozart's father took him on a tour of European capitals, audiences were astounded by the young man's musical talent. (Subordinate clause, main clause.)

cpd **3.** Mozart began teaching music in Germany, and soon he met Aloysia Weber. (Two main clauses.)

cpx **4.** After she became a successful singer, she rejected Mozart. (Subordinate clause, main clause.)

cc **5.** He later married her younger sister, Constanze, who was also a singer, and for the rest of his life he had financial difficulty. (Main clause, subordinate clause, main clause.)

cpx **6.** Even though Mozart was composer to the emperor, he lived his life in poverty because he could not manage money well. (Subordinate clause, main clause, subordinate clause.)

s **7.** The last decade of his life he frantically composed music and gave frequent concert tours. (Main clause with compound verb.)

cpd **8.** He is often considered the father of the modern concerto; he composed some 25 concertos for piano and orchestra. (Two main clauses.)

cpd **9.** Life in his household must not have been tranquil, but his wife and his children apparently adored him, and he adored them. (Three main clauses, compound subject in second one.)

cc 10. <u>Wolfgang and Constanze had six children; four died at an early age,</u>
<u>but the two sons</u> <u>who survived to adulthood</u> <u>were talented musicians</u>.
(Three main clauses, the first with compound subject, and one subordinate clause. *Who survived to adulthood* is a subordinate clause inside the main clause *but the two sons were talented musicians.*)

Answers on page 295.

Knowing how to put clauses together and knowing which clauses to subordinate will help you write effective sentences. Be sure, however, that you end up with the more important ideas in main clauses and the less important ideas in subordinate clauses. In the following examples, the meaning of the sentence changes according to which clause you subordinate.

- She feels good because she dances every day (she feels good = main clause = more important idea). OR She dances every day because she feels good (she dances every day = main clause = more important idea).

EXERCISE 4.14 Combine the short, choppy simple sentences below into five effective sentences. You may want to leave one sentence as it is and, for the other four, combine main and subordinate clauses into compound, complex, and/ or compound-complex sentences. Add or change a few words if you need to.

Magazines are full of advice on how to invest your money.

This is usually not a big problem with students.

Many of you are working your way through college.

Your problem more often is how to get enough money for tuition and books.

You can wait to win the lottery.

You can look for a rich person to marry.

You can wait for Uncle Harry to die.

He is rich.

He is childless.

He is terminally ill.

Maybe he will leave you an inheritance.

The chance of coming into big bucks by any of these methods is slim.

The most reliable way to acquire money is to work for it.

Work hard and save just a little each month.

Some day you will need that advice on how to invest your money.

Possible answer on page 296.

EXERCISE 4.15 Combine the short, choppy simple sentences below into a half dozen or so effective sentences. You may want to leave one sentence as it is and, for the rest, combine main and subordinate clauses into compound, complex, and/or compound-complex sentences. Add or change a few words if you need to.

A generation or two ago, most college freshmen were 18-year-olds.

Most were from middle- to upper-income families.

Most were from the community.

Today education is exciting.

Classrooms are filled with a much more interesting mix.

There are high school seniors earning college credits early.

There are recent high school graduates.

There are senior citizens.

Some of these senior citizens missed college the first time around.

There are students of all ages in between.

Some students are financially secure.

Some are on financial aid.

Some are from the city and its suburbs.

Some are from Thailand or Liberia, Germany or Japan.

The world will benefit from this increased accessibility of education.

The classroom now has a more democratic and tolerant atmosphere.

Possible answer on page 296.

WARNING: Don't get *too* enthusiastic about combining clauses. Sometimes clauses need to be *un*combined if the sentence is too long to understand easily.

- TOO LONG TO BE EFFECTIVE: Mrs. Murphy and Mr. Perez, who teach English and algebra, respectively, and Ms. Larue and Dr. Jefferson, who teach history and journalism, respectively, ardently believe in students' rights, and a time or two they have spoken out in favor of students' causes so strongly that they have made their fellow faculty members and members of the administration angry, but the four of them believe, among other things, that students should be able to use the computer labs until midnight instead of 10 p.m., that they should be able to cash checks in the Business Office just as faculty can, that they should be able to eat in the same dining room and have the same food as the faculty, and that the choice spots in the parking lots should not be reserved for faculty, especially since sometimes some of the spots stand empty all day.

- MUCH BETTER AS TWO SENTENCES: Our English, algebra, history, and journalism teachers sometimes anger fellow faculty members and administrators because they stand up for student causes. Mrs. Murphy, Mr. Perez, Ms. Larue, and Dr. Jefferson believe computer labs should be open to students until midnight instead of 10 p.m., students should be able to cash checks in the Business Office, students should have the same dining facilities as faculty, and faculty should not have reserved parking spots.

Changing clauses or sentences into phrases often gets the reader to the point sooner and makes the reading smoother. An example is shown.

- BEFORE: Debbie was looking for two people to go out in the boat with her. She wanted to go water skiing. That was her favorite sport. Boating safety rules dictate that the skier must have two people in the boat, the driver and the observer. The observer watches the skier and tells the driver if the skier is in trouble.
- AFTER: Debbie wanted to go water skiing, her favorite sport; but she needed two other people, one to drive the boat and, to conform to boating safety rules, one to watch the skier for signs of trouble.

EXERCISE 4.16 Make the sentences in this exercise into a smooth-reading paragraph by changing clauses or sentences into phrases.

Debbie asked Lynn if she had time to drive the ski boat. Debbie could ski behind it. Lynn had had lots of experience driving her own boat. Lynn said she'd like to. Then Debbie asked Leesa if she would come along too. She could be the observer. Leesa said she had made plans to go the mall with her friend Angie. Leesa said she needed to shop for a bathing suit. Debbie said, "Don't you already have three bathing suits?" Leesa agreed. She said she needed one more. She needed it in case she should be invited to a swimming party. The other ones were all a year or more old. So Debbie asked Charlie if he would be the observer, and he said he would as soon as he finished cleaning the fish he had caught. He had caught nine perch and two lake trout. He said he was almost through. It would be only a few more minutes. Soon the three were out on the lake. They enjoyed being on the water. The two girls were also looking forward to the invitation they had just accepted. Charlie had invited them to a fish fry in his back yard.

Possible answer on page 297.

EXERCISE 4.17 Correct all errors in the following sentences. One sentence is correct.

1. In the last year of his life, 1791, Mozart asked by a mysterious stranger to write a funeral service, or requiem mass, for an Austrian nobleman.
2. Said he would because he needed the money.
3. He was convinced he was writing music for his own funeral he died, apparently of typhoid, before he had finished this great work.
4. One of his pupils who completed this masterpiece.
5. The day of Mozart's burial was stormy, no one attended the funeral.
6. Was that a fitting way to honor an outstanding musical genius
7. He buried in a pauper's cemetery
8. Constanze broke down from grief did not go to the funeral.
9. When she recovered and visited the cemetery, she could not find which grave was Wolfgang's
10. A monument to Wolfgang Amadeus Mozart was later erected over an empty grave; we will now put Mozart to rest. Forever.

Answers on page 297.

Using Words Clearly

There is little point in writing if what you write confuses your reader. To make certain your writing is easy to understand, certain faults should be avoided.

Faulty Parallelism. Avoid faulty parallelism, the unequal treatment of grammatically equal elements in a sentence.

- FAULTY PARALLELISM: I like *swimming* and *to play* tennis. Using the *ing* form of the verb first and then the infinitive for equal elements, two things that you like to do, throws the sentence out of balance.
- PARALLELISM: I like *swimming* and *playing* tennis. OR I like *to swim* and *to play* tennis.
- FAULTY PARALLELISM: Think before *you speak,* and look before *leaping.*
- PARALLELISM: Think before *you speak,* and look before *you leap.* OR Think before *speaking,* and look before *leaping.*
- FAULTY PARALLELISM: Topics will include *low cholesterol, take your blood pressure,* and *that getting plenty of exercise can be a big help.*
- PARALLELISM: Topics will include cholesterol, blood pressure, and exercise. OR Topics will include reducing cholesterol, taking blood pressure, and getting plenty of exercise.

Sometimes words should be repeated to make the parallel construction unmistakable.

- NOT QUITE PARALLEL: I like *to* swim and play tennis, but I couldn't do either *all* morning or afternoon.
- BETTER: I like *to* swim and *to* play tennis, but I couldn't do either *all* morning or *all* afternoon.

EXERCISE 4.18 In the blanks correct the faulty parallelism in the following sentences.

1. Relaxation is good for you because it restores your energy, that it relieves tension, and a big help to go to sleep. _____

_____

2. Sit quietly in a comfortable position with eyes closed, don't forget to relax muscles, and your mind being at rest. _____

_____

3. You will find relaxation can make you to be happier and having more success at your job. _____

_____

Answers on page 298.

Double Negatives. Avoid double negatives. Although we would undoubtedly understand that "I ain't got no money" means I'm broke, a double negative is a no-no in standard English. Use a single negative if you want the emphasis of a sentence to remain negative. To avoid saying the opposite of what you mean, be aware that, just as two negatives make a positive in math, double negatives in English do too.

- WRONG: He would <u>not</u> go <u>no</u> farther (means he would go farther).
- RIGHT: He would go no farther. OR He would not go any farther.

Another common fault occurs if you tack a negative expression onto the end of a negative sentence.

- WRONG: He will never make a go of it, I don't think (means I think he will make a go of it).
- RIGHT: He will never make a go of it, I think. OR I don't think he will ever make a go of it.

EXERCISE 4.19 In the blanks correct the double negatives.

1. A smile doesn't take no more energy than a frown. _____

_____

2. And when you frown, it doesn't make the people around you feel good, I don't think. _____

_____

3. Try smiling at a stranger, and you won't have nothing but good feelings when you see that person first look bewildered and then smile back at you.

_____

_____

Answers on page 298.

Inconsistent Verb Tense. Avoid inconsistent verb tense. Sometimes there is reason for shifting verb tense in midstream. Usually, though, if you start a sentence in present tense, don't shift to past tense in the middle.

- WRONG: I *walk* (present tense) into the room and *stumbled* (past tense) over the teacher's foot. One student *was discussing* (past progressive tense) adverbs while two others *whisper* (present tense) to each other.
- RIGHT: I *walked* into the room and *stumbled* over the teacher's foot. One student *was discussing* adverbs while two others *were whispering* to each other.
- TENSE SHIFT OKAY: Because my parents *taught* (past tense, action took place in the past) me to be tolerant, I *work* (present tense, action taking place in the present) hard for human rights.

EXERCISE 4.20 In the blanks correct inconsistent tense in the three sentences below.

1. Kate disliked exams because she knows she had been getting tense and

that she will forget what she knew. _____

_____

2. She does not need extra stress and was not happy when it will be time for

exams and term papers._____

_____

3. Leatrice got ready to study for her English test and finds all her notes are in

her locker at school._____

_____

_____

Answers on page 298.

Unnecessary Words and Redundancies. Avoid unnecessary words and redundancies. They are repetitious, not vital to the meaning. We all seem to speak and write using more words than we really need. Say it once, and then quit.

You've undoubtedly been warned to watch out for the following sneaky redundancies:

- *refer back* and *return back: back* is implied in the words refer and return by the prefix *re.*
- *six a.m. in the morning: a.m.* means morning.
- *free gift:* by definition, all *gifts* are free.
- *past history:* if it were present or future, it wouldn't be *history.*
- *each and every,* the identical-twin expressions, along with *any and all:* please, one to a customer—*each* or *every* but not both, *any* or *all* but not both.

There are many **redundant expressions** so common they sound right to us (parentheses enclose the unnecessary words):

(advance) reservations	a great future (ahead of him)
a(n actual) fact	(hot-)water heater
in (the city of) Chicago	a large(-size) reindeer
bald(-headed) man	in (the month of) December
a cease-fire (to end the fighting)	a (new) breakthrough
a (definite) commitment	paid (the amount of) $25
first(-ever)	throughout the (entire) meeting
five survivors (still alive)	tuition (fee)
(foreign) import	turquoise (blue-colored) sky

EXERCISE 4.21 Cross out the unnecessary words in the following expressions.

1. an old antique
2. a blue-colored car
3. in the year 1776
4. at 12 noon on Dec. 24
5. Her speech was about the subject of boats.
6. the fortune teller's advance predictions of the future
7. for a period of three hours

8. a large-size dog

9. returned back to the school

10. He was engaged in weeding the garden.

11. Perhaps he may change his mind.

12. is of a square shape

13. a tall man who stood seven feet tall

14. a hot summer night in July

15. a highly regarded man of good reputation

Answers on page 299.

Once in a while repetition is used effectively for emphasis.

- He got up early that morning. He got up early because he knew he had to confront her. He got up early because he had to somehow build up his courage before he saw her.

But usually avoid repetition and wordiness, both of which your instructor will be watching for. **Tight** (concise) **writing** saves time, not always for the writer because it's hard to write concisely, but certainly for the reader. Lord Chesterfield is said to have sent this gem to a friend: "I'm sorry that I have written you a five-page letter; I didn't have time to write a one-page letter."

SHOE by **Jeff MacNelly**

Unnecessarily Complex Words. Avoid unnecessarily complex words, perhaps even worse offenders than unnecessary words. This writing fault goes by several names, including foggy writing, gobbledygook, and bafflegab.

Too often a phenomenal change occurs when a student sits down to write an English assignment: his or her personality is altered completely. No longer can the writer communicate in ordinary terms. Polysyllabic words issue forth in convoluted sentences that overflow into tedious paragraphs, and a monster is born. The instructor is *not* impressed.

If a short word does the job just as well as a long word, use the short one. If your friend *lives next door,* don't complicate matters by having him *reside in an adjacent domicile.* Mark Twain commented that he never wrote *metropolis* because, being paid by the word, he got just as much for *city.*

If you have trouble expressing yourself in a natural way in writing, pretend that, instead of writing, you are *talking* about your subject with a friend. Now, it may be hazardous to your grade-point average to write as you talk—because our everyday talk is often in nonstandard American English—but sometimes this pretense can bring your language back down to earth.

If once in a while, however, a five-syllable word expresses just the shade of meaning you are looking for, go for it; use it unashamedly. Writing all one-syllable words would make exceedingly dull reading. Variety puts spice in your writing, but a great deal of variety can be had by using ordinary rather than extraordinary words. And your reader will thank you. A **thesaurus,** a book of synonyms, is an excellent investment for the writer who wants a bigger choice of words.

BORN LOSER   **by Art & Chip Sansom**

I have in my files hundreds of examples of atrocious writing. Government, businesses, and educational institutions (yes, colleges) are guilty. Because such writing is sometimes so bad, a new profession has been born: consultants are invited by companies and institutions to conduct workshops to teach employees how to write clearly.

A federal government official (obviously before the workshop) had this to say about inflation: "It is a very tricky policy problem to find the particular calibration and timing that would be appropriate to stem the acceleration in risk premiums created by falling income without prematurely aborting the decline in the inflation-generated risk premiums. This is clearly not an easy policy path to traverse." (Clearly not easy!)

The following memo was once circulated among the faculty of *our* college:

- "In order to provide for full articulation and integration of day, evening, and Saturday programs and to improve ongoing communications to night and Saturday populations, Curriculum and Instruction administrative availability will be extended. . . " (What did it mean? Only that the dean's office was going to stay open longer.)

I like the way in which Arthur Kudner told his son not to be awed by big words:

- Big long words name little things; all big things have little names, such as *life* and *death, peace* and *war,* or *dawn, day, night, hope, love, home.* Learn to use little words in a big way. It is hard to do, but they say what you mean. When you don't know what you mean, use big words. They often fool little people.

Arthur Kudner, I learned by calling the public library, was a Michigan newspaper reporter and advertising man who died in 1944. His advice to his son is excellent. I have some excellent advice too. Use your school and public libraries. Libraries have reference librarians who are glad to look up all kinds of information for you.

EXERCISE 4.22 De-fog the following sayings by rewriting each one in understandable words in the space below it.

1. Members of an avian species of identical plumage congregate.

_____

2. It is bootless to become lachrymose over precipitately overturned lacteal

fluid. _____

_____

3. The stylus is more potent than the claymore. _____

_____

4. It is fruitless to attempt to indoctrinate a superannuated canine with innovative maneuvers. _____

_____

5. The temperature of the aqueous content of an unremittingly observed fluid-filled kitchen utensil does not reach 212 degrees Fahrenheit.

_____

_____

Answers on page 299.

EXERCISE 4.23 Combine the facts in the many sentences below into just a few correct, effective sentences. Use a mix of simple, compound, complex, and/or compound-complex sentences. Eliminate unnecessary words and unnecessarily complex words. Get in the habit of having a dictionary handy—and, of course, using it.

Academia began in Europe in the Middle Ages with *universitas*.

These were consortia of learned persons organized for a common purpose.

Our word *university* came from these venerable ancient institutions.

Harvard University is the oldest institution of this type in the United States.

It was founded in 1636.

It was founded in Newtowne, Mass.

Newtowne, Mass., as it was called then, is now called Cambridge, Mass.

At first Harvard was an institution of higher learning to prepare men for a religious career at the pulpit in the ministry.

It accepted only persons of the male sex.

Now it admits women of the female sex too.

There are many undergraduate programs.

There are also many graduate programs now.

_____

_____

_____

_____

_____

_____

_____

Possible answer on page 299.

QUIZ YOURSELF ON STEP TWO Fill in the blanks. For questions 1 through 4, write in the blank after each sentence which type of structure it is: simple, compound, complex, or compound-complex (one of each). Correct Sentences 5 through 7. Fill in the blanks for the rest.

1. Mrs. Murphy sometimes envies her colleagues because in other subjects

   instructors don't have to make up sentences for students to analyze and

   correct. _____

2. Mr. Perez, who will soon get his doctor's degree, sometimes envies the other teachers; he wishes he could grade their students' homework because he thinks the answers to English, history, and journalism assignments are more interesting reading than algebra answers.

_____

3. Dr. Jefferson has a Ph.D. from Columbia University School of Journalism, one of the best in the world. _____

4. Mrs. Murphy has a master's degree in English; Ms. Larue has a doctorate in history, but she prefers to be called Ms.

_____

5. Most instructors are glad to help students by answering questions and to recommend reference books. _____

_____

6. Carla Careless and her twin brother Calvin don't find no time to do homework on weekends. _____

_____

7. Calvin Careless sometimes wanders into class late and then will be discouraged because he missed important information. _____

_____

_____ **8.** *Ink pen* is an example of   (a) a redundancy.   (b) a subject and verb not agreeing.   (c) a compound subject.

_____ **9.** Tight writing is   (a) writing after drinking several whiskey sours.
(b) leaving out unnecessary words and sentences in your writing.
(c) writing standing up because your jeans shrank.

10. Which is harder, to write short or to write long? _____

_____**11.** T or F. If you have a choice between a big word and a small one that means the same thing, it is usually better to use the bigger one to give your reader assurance that you have an extensive vocabulary.

Answers on page 299.

Step Three: Writing Creative Sentences

In writing, there are many choices to be made. You, the writer, decide upon **your style,** the words you choose and the way you use them to express ideas. Be yourself. Don't hesitate to make creative choices. You are an individual. You are unlike any other person in the world. Your ideas are unique and important. You need not sacrifice creative sentences for correct or effective sentences. You can be creative within the bounds of correct, effective writing.

Choice of Emphasis in Sentences

By juggling the arrangement of the parts of a sentence, you may put the emphasis where you want it. There are four types of arrangement to help you do this.

1. In a **common sentence** (sometimes called a loose sentence), the major idea comes first and less important information follows. This is the most common order and is easy to read.

   - The merry-go-round is a popular children's ride at amusement parks, carnivals, and theme parks throughout the world.

2. In a **periodic sentence,** interest can be built up by placing a major idea last in the sentence, just before the period.

   - A popular children's ride at amusement parks, carnivals, and theme parks throughout the world is the merry-go-round.

3. In a **climactic sentence,** several ideas are arranged in order of their dramatic impact, from least to most.

   - The children climb on the brightly painted horses, hold tight as the merry-go-round starts to revolve, and squeal with delight as the horses begin to move up and down.

4. In a **balanced sentence,** main ideas are parallel, treated with equal emphasis.

   - The merry-go-round dates back to 1729 in England and 1799 in the United States, so it is the oldest amusement ride still in use.

EXERCISE 4.24 Write common, periodic, climactic, or balanced in the blank (one of each).

1. Peter, who had been worried about his biology grade, opened the envelope slowly, pulled out his report card, scanned it, and shouted, "I made a B!" _____

2. Biology was not easy for him. _____

3. As he studied for the exam and even after he had taken it, he hardly dared hope for a B. _____

4. He is a good student, and he always works hard. _____

Answers on page 299.

Choice of Words

Strong Verbs. In both active and passive voice, verbs are available in various strengths, all the way from watered down to industrial strength. Strong verbs make powerful writing.

- WEAK: She *came* into the room.
- STRONG: She *ambled* into the room. She *moseyed* into the room. She *shuffled* into the room. She *sauntered* into the room. She *strolled* into the room. She *sashayed* into the room. She *dashed* into the room. She *strode* into the room. She *swept* into the room. She *bounded* into the room. She *charged* into the room. She *lurched* into the room.

By picking appropriate strong verbs, you can often create the desired effect with an economy of words.

- MORE EXAMPLES: The prisoners were *shoehorned* into inadequate jails. The clouds *hopscotched* across the sky. The cat *unwound* from its nap. The door *squeaked* open.

Active Voice. Another verb choice that you have is the use of passive or active voice. In active voice, the subject does the acting. In passive voice, the subject is acted upon. Active voice is stronger.

- ACTIVE VOICE: The old man caught the fish.
- PASSIVE VOICE: The fish was caught by the old man.

Active verbs save words; they are more emphatic and more vigorous than passive verbs. Usually active verbs are preferable. But once in a while you may want to use passive voice, when you want to slow down the action or when you don't know who does the action.

- PASSIVE VOICE: The boat was propelled toward land by a soft breeze (passive construction slows the action).
- PASSIVE VOICE: The store was robbed again (you don't know by whom).

Specific Nouns, Adjectives, and Verbs. Just as strong verbs help paint the desired picture, so the use of specific nouns, adjectives, and adverbs instead of general or abstract words helps the reader receive a vivid impression.

- VAGUE: He spends all his spare time reading *books*.
- VIVID: He spends all his spare time reading *gory murder mysteries*.
- VAGUE: Sitting next to a *bad* kid in a restaurant can quickly devalue an expensive meal.
- VIVID: Sitting next to a *screaming, spoon-banging, table-thumping* kid in a restaurant can quickly devalue an expensive meal.
- VAGUE: He walked *slowly* toward the door of his boss' office.
- VIVID: He *walked hesitantly, worriedly, nervously, dejectedly, fearfully* (pick one) toward the door of his boss' office.
- VAGUE: He *has compassion* for the homeless.
- VIVID: He *spends four hours every Sunday serving soup* to the homeless.

Concrete Words. And just as strong verbs and specific nouns, adjectives, and adverbs are a way of showing as well as telling, so concrete words enhance your writing by painting a vivid picture. Concrete words are words that invoke the reader's senses, words that make the reader see, hear, smell, taste, or feel what the writer is talking about.

- The door slammed shut (sound) on the howling wind (sound) and the wet snow (feeling). The warmth (feeling) of a crackling (sound) fire (sight) and the spicy fragrance (smell) of Thanksgiving dinner cooking let him know that he was indeed home. In his mind he was savoring his mom's pumpkin-pies-past (taste) when she came out of the kitchen, arms outstretched (sight).

Connotative Words. Connotative words, words that make the reader think of similar things, can also be a powerful tool in writing. If you use the word *hearth*, the reader may immediately think *fireplace, warmth, home, family, good food, love*. If you use the word *gang*, the reader may think *bad kids, getting in trouble, cutting school, juvenile delinquents, danger, thugs*. You can get lots of mileage from connnotative words, but they must be used with care lest you send the reader off on roads you did not intend him to travel.

EXERCISE 4.25

1. Make the verb stronger: The women <u>were talking</u>. _____

2. Change to active voice: The Frisbee was caught by the wind and blown clear out to the street. _____

_____

3. Make the adjective more specific: The <u>next</u> song made her wish she had never come. _____

4. What senses are stimulated by the underlined words? Even as <u>his alarm went off</u>, he could tell that the <u>coffee was already perking</u> and the <u>bacon was almost ready</u>. _____

5. What is the connation to you of the underlined words? He came to a <u>fork in the road</u>. _____

6. What can strong verbs, active voice, specific words (nouns, adjectives, and adverbs), concrete words, and connotative words do for your writing?

_____

Possible answers on page 299.

Clichés. In the interest of writing creative sentences, avoid clichés, if not like the plague (a beautiful example of a cliché), at least like some other usually fatal illness. A cliché, according to the dictionary, is an expression that has become trite. Trite means worn-out by constant use, no longer having freshness or originality, hackneyed, stale.

Some of the worst clichés are the worn-out, used-over-and-over expressions found in business letters.

- Per our phone call, this is to inform you that we are in receipt of yours of Aug. 10. BETTER: We received your Aug. 10 letter.

EXERCISE 4.26 I often give my students this assignment: Write at least five sentences containing as many clichés as you can possibly fit in while still making some sense.

Possible answer on page 300.

SUBURBAN COWGIRLS   **by Janet Alfieri & Ed Colley**

Once in a great while a cliché, like a five-syllable word, is just right for your need—use it then, but otherwise clichés are not cute as a bug's ear. Avoid them, yes, like the plague.

Euphemisms. Almost as offensive as clichés are euphemisms. A euphemism is an inoffensive word or phrase used in place of an offensive one. We hate to think of dying, so what do our friends do? They *pass away* or *pass on*. Even more ridiculous, hospitals have been known to say a patient *did not fully achieve his wellness potential* or she *had a therapeutic misadventure resulting in a terminal episode.* He or she died. So did *inoperative combat personnel.*

My collection of euphemisms would fill a book—let me replace that cliché with a bit more truth: it would depend on the size of the book, but at least it would fill a big pamphlet.

EXERCISE 4.27 Write in the blanks what you think is the real meaning of these euphemisms.

1. airplane made premature impact with ground _____
2. petroleum transfer engineer _____
3. hoisting engineer _____
4. sanitary engineer _____
5. personal flotation devices _____
6. peacekeeper _____
7. handyman's special _____
8. previously owned car or gently worn clothes _____

9. hydroforce blast cup _____

10. physically challenged _____

11. waste reception center _____

12. food service technician _____

13. access controller _____

14. underutilized human resource _____

15. fiscally intensive _____

16. strategic misrepresentation _____

17. attitude adjustment emporium _____

18. motion caused by climatic disturbance at sea-air interface _____

19. having negative vulnerability to water _____

20. experiencing negative employee retention, dishired, involuntarily leisured

_____

21. entrenching instrument _____

22. rest room, comfort station _____

23. bath tissue _____

24. meaningful downturn _____

25. energetic disassembly _____

26. chronologically gifted, golden agers, seniors _____

27. deemphasizer _____

28. follicly endangered _____

29. having a protein spill _____

30. experiencing fuel starvation _____

31. the cornerstone of discommunication _____

Answers on page 300.

Malappropriate Language. By all means also avoid the discommunication brought on by malappropriate language, named after Mrs. Malaprop, a character in Irish dramatist Richard Sheridan's 1775 play, *The Rivals,* who was forever choosing the wrong word: "as headstrong as an allegory (alligator) on the banks of the Nile." While a person usually writes these inappropriate words with a straight face (a mild example right there: have you ever tried to write with a straight face instead of with a pen or a word processor?), the effect on the reader may be a case of the good old-fashioned knee-slapping, side-splitting, bent-double belly laughs.

We already have enough strange combinations that are acceptable: Nonstop flight—how will I ever get off? Watch your head—with cleverly concealed mirrors?

Watch your wording, or you will find yourself in one of Richard Lederer's books, *Anguished English,* and *More Anguished English.* Here are a few of his favorites, each one worthy of a "Pullet Surprise" (a Pulitzer Prize).

- "Abraham Lincoln's mother died in infancy, and he was born in a log cabin which he built with his own hands. When he was president, he wore only a tall silk hat."

- "Sir Frances Drake circumcised the world with a 100-foot clipper." The student had intended to use the word *circumscribed* or *circumnavigated.*

- Another misspelled *reaper,* with this result: "Cyrus McCormick invented the McCormick raper, which did the work of a hundred men."

c stock

- "Johann Bach wrote a great many musical compositions and had a large number of children. In between, he practiced on an old spinster which he kept up in his attic." A *spinster* is an older unmarried woman; a *spinet* is a small piano.

- From insurance forms: "In an attempt to kill a fly, I drove into a telephone pole" (maybe you should have tried a flyswatter). "My foot jumped from brake to accelerator, leaped across the road to the other side, and jumped into the trunk of a tree" (footloose?). "I had been driving for about 40 years when I fell asleep at the wheel and had an accident" (small wonder).

- From a church bulletin: "This being Easter Sunday, we will ask Mrs. White to come forward and lay an egg on the altar."

- From ads: "Four-poster bed, 101 years old. Perfect for antique lover." "Dog for sale, eats anything and is fond of children." "You can now have a bikini for a ridiculous figure."

- Sign at a restaurant-gas station: "Eat here and get gas." At a shopping mall: "Archery tournament. Ears pierced."

- An omitted letter: "Smile at someone who is hard to love. Say 'Hell' to someone who doesn't care much about you."

Dr. Lederer's examples of faulty communication (he has many more; he's an English teacher and author of books about our language) communicate a strong message: It is necessary to **proofread** carefully. If possible read aloud what you have written. And if you have time, proofread again. Then your malappropriate language won't come back to haunt you.

- Sign in a cemetery: "Persons are prohibited from picking flowers from any but their own graves."

Choice of Location of Words

Misbehaving modifiers, both misplaced and dangling, are almost as much fun as malappropriate language; this is not, however, the kind of fun that will improve your writing.

Misplaced Modifiers. Normally, for clarity, a modifier should be as close as possible to the word or words it modifies. A misplaced modifier is one that has become separated from what it modifies, thereby preventing clarity; and if it ends up beside another word, it may appear to be trying to modify that word, with sometimes humorous results. Check your modifiers to be sure they are in the proper company.

- MISPLACED: I like to make Easter baskets for children with chocolate bunnies on top.

C STOCK

- RIGHT: I like to make Easter baskets with chocolate bunnies on top for children. The prepositional phrase *with chocolate bunnies on top* is the modifier. It should be next to *baskets,* which it modifies, not *children.*

- MISPLACED: He stood in front of the alley, a narrow corridor between two buildings about 50 feet long and three feet wide. I'd hate to be in such a thin building in a severe wind.

- RIGHT: He stood in front of the alley, a narrow corridor about 50 feet long and three feet wide between two buildings.

- MISPLACED: She placed a babushka on her head and tied it very slowly, revealing the arthritis that had been troubling her under her chin.

- RIGHT: She placed a babushka on her head and tied it under her chin very slowly, revealing the arthritis that had been troubling her.

EXERCISE 4.28 Relocate modifiers, or revise the sentence so that what you *meant* to say is what the reader will see. These are from Dr. Lederer's collection. Write the corrections above the sentences.

1. Wanted: Man to take care of cow that does not smoke or drink.

2. For sale: Antique desk suitable for lady with thick legs and large drawers.

3. Remember in prayer the many who are sick of our church and community.

4. The concert was a great success. Special thanks are due to the minister's daughter, who labored the whole evening at the piano, which as usual fell upon her.

5. At our laundry, we do not tear your clothing with machinery. We do it carefully by hand.

6. After Gov. Baldwin watched the lion perform, he was taken to Main Street and fed 25 pounds of raw meat.

Answers on page 300.

B.C.   **by Johnny Hart**

Dangling Modifiers. A dangling modifier is a modifier that has become so far separated from what it is supposed to modify that what it is supposed to modify is not even in the sentence. This construction often involves a participle and is sometimes called a **dangling participle.**

- DANGLING: When only three, my mother died. She must be in the *Guinness Book of World Records* as the world's youngest mother!

- RIGHT: When *I* was only three, my mother died.

ding a ling a ling

C Stock

- DANGLING: While sitting in the bathtub, the phone always rings.
- RIGHT: While *I* am sitting in the bathtub, the phone always rings. You need to add to the sentence *who* is sitting in the bathtub. It probably is *not* the phone.

EXERCISE 4.29 Write revisions above the following sentences so that the dangling modifier no longer dangles but has something in the sentence to modify.

1. Not being able to work the computer very well, the computer instructor typed in the student's first paragraph.
2. With a broken leg, my mother will have to drive herself instead of having me chauffeur her.
3. Having flu and severe laryngitis, my dog was unable to go on his usual walk.
4. Being completely without clothes, I set out for another garage sale.
5. Having been hit by a car, the surgeon got ready to operate.

Answers on page 301.

Split Infinitives. You've heard the rules, Don't split an infinitive, and Don't end a sentence with a preposition. Usually an awkward sentence results from split infinitives, inserting a modifier between the *to* of an infinitive and its verb.

- AWKWARD: He promised to *very carefully* drive home.
- BETTER: He promised to drive home *very carefully*.

There are times, however, when placing the modifier between the two parts of the infinitive gives the intended emphasis better than placing the modifier before or after the whole infinitive.

- OKAY: He promised *really* to study this quarter.
- BETTER: He promised to *really* study this quarter.

I'm not even feeling guilty about the following line from page 269 because I think the emphasis is better with my split infinitive: He got up early because he had to *somehow* build up his courage before he saw her. In other words, it's okay to *occasionally* split an infinitive.

Sentences Ending With a Preposition. Sentences ending with a preposition are preferable to sentences that must be strangely and unnaturally arranged to avoid ending the sentence with a preposition.

- CORRECT: She is the teacher about whom I told you.
- MORE NATURAL AND QUITE ACCEPTABLE: She is the teacher I told you about.

EXERCISE 4.30 Make corrections above the line or leave sentences as they are to best handle (a split infinitive right there) the possible errors of splitting an infinitive or ending a sentence with a preposition.

1. About what was the baby crying?
2. He forgot to, even though he should have known better, tie the boat securely to the pier.
3. He would rather have been anywhere but in the predicament he was in.
4. Write a paragraph to thoroughly describe your feelings about compulsory military service.
5. That is the restaurant we met our daughter for dinner in.

Answers on page 301.

Although we usually don't want to split an infinitive or end a sentence with a preposition, there are times, as you have seen, when it is better to make an exception to the rule. Perhaps exceptions to the rule are a good thing to *finally* end this chapter *with*. Our language is far from cast in concrete, to use a cliché. You have creative choices. Don't forget, you want to develop **your** style.

QUIZ YOURSELF ON STEP THREE Fill in the blanks with the appropriate letter.

_____ **1.** T or F. Your writing will be more interesting if you vary the emphasis in your sentences, writing periodic, climactic, and balanced sentences as well as common sentences.

_____ **2.** Faulty parallelism is (a) the use of a long sentence followed by a short sentence. (b) expressing thoughts in incomplete sentences. (c) expressing grammatically equal sentence elements in an unequal manner.

_____ **3.** Which is usually better in your writing? (a) verbs in active voice. (b) verbs in passive voice.

_____ **4.** Strong verbs, specific words, concrete words, and connotative words (a) are obstacles to the ease of reading. (b) help paint a picture for the reader. (c) should be used rarely.

_____ **5.** *Proud as a peacock* is an example of (a) redundancy. (b) a cliché. (c) a euphemism.

_____ **6.** Calling a bald man *hair disadvantaged* is an example of (a) redundancy. (b) a cliché. (c) a euphemism.

_____ **7.** Which is a fault in writing? (a) tight writing. (b) trite writing.

_____ **8.** Usually a modifier should be as close as possible to (a) the subject of the sentence. (b) the verb. (c) what it modifies.

_____ **9.** (a) Sometimes a modifier is left high and dry without anything in the sentence to modify. (b) Sometimes the modifier is in the wrong place and appears to modify the wrong word. Which of these is a dangling modifier?

_____**10.** Style in writing is the words you choose and the way you use them. The most important key to developing your style is to (a) copy the style of a master writer. (b) ask a friend who has a big vocabulary to help you rewrite your composition. (c) be yourself.

Answers on page 301.

Answers to Exercises

Answers to Exercise 4.1, page 243

dec 1. Wolfgang Amadeus Mozart was born in Salzburg, Austria, in 1756__.__

exc 2. What a tremendous amount he accomplished in the 35 years of his life__!__

dec 3. The beloved "Minuet" was composed when he was just five; he heard music in his head and played it while his father wrote it down__.__

int 4. Where did he get such talent__?__

dec 5. His father was choirmaster to the Archbishop of Salzburg, and his sister, five years older, was a prodigy__.__

imp 6. Imagine what Mozart's life must have been like__.__

int 7. Do you suppose he ever played childhood games__?__

int 8. Did you know he played the clavier, or German harpsichord, and the organ and the violin__?__

imp 9. Also note that his sister played the clavier and sang__.__

exc 10. What a family they must have been__!__

Answers to Exercise 4.2, page 247

c 1. <u>Witchcraft</u> <u>is</u> the use of supernatural powers.

w 2. Usually <u>harms</u> people. (No subject. <u>Who</u> or <u>what</u> <u>harms</u> people?)

c 3. A <u>witch</u> <u>receives</u> magic powers from evil spirits.

w 4. Many <u>people</u> from earliest times of recorded history to the present time, everywhere in the world. (All subject, including words that explain the subject. No verb.)

w 5. Even today <u>believe</u> in witches and in the evil powers of witches. (No subject. <u>Who</u> <u>believes</u>?)

c 6. European <u>witchcraft</u> <u>involves</u> the devil.

w 7. The word <u>witch</u> from an Anglo-Saxon word meaning *wise one* or *magician*. (No real verb. *Meaning* looks like a verb but can't be the real verb for the subject <u>witch</u>; <u>witch</u> *meaning* doesn't make sense. Add the real verb <u>comes</u> after <u>witch</u>. Or change *meaning* to <u>means</u>: The word <u>witch</u>, from an Anglo-Saxon word, <u>means</u> *wise one* or *magician*.)

w 8. Originally a <u>witch</u> either a man or woman with supernatural powers. (No verb. Add the real verb <u>was</u> after the subject <u>witch</u>.)

c 9. Now, however, <u>witches</u> <u>are</u> more often women.

<u>**w**</u> **10.** <u>Men</u> with magical powers *sorcerers, warlocks,* or *wizards.* (No verb. Add the verb <u>are called</u> after powers.)

Answers to Exercise 4.3, page 247

1. <u>Believers</u> in witchcraft <u>attribute</u> tremendous power, often quite dangerous power, to witches and warlocks.

2. A <u>witch</u> or a <u>warlock</u> <u>may make</u> a small wax or wooden image of the victim.

3. <u>She</u> or <u>he</u> then <u>puts</u> something from the victim's body, such as fingernail clippings or hair, into the image.

4. The treacherous <u>person</u> practicing witchcraft then <u>destroys</u> the image by cutting it, burning it, or sticking pins into it. (Remember, a word ending in *ing* needs an auxiliary or helping verb with it to make it a real verb.)

5. The <u>victim</u> supposedly <u>suffers</u> severe pain or even death.

6. A <u>person</u> really deep into practicing witchcraft and wanting to make another person suffer sometimes <u>casts</u> a spell by muttering the victim's name and reciting a magic formula.

7. <u>People</u> lacking knowledge of agriculture and disease once <u>blamed</u> witches and warlocks for any unexplained misfortune, such as illness, a sudden death, or a crop failure.

8. These wicked <u>witches</u> <u>cast</u> spells on churns to prevent butter from forming.

9. <u>Oct. 31</u> <u>was</u> the favorite day for these supernatural beings to hold meetings.

10. <u>Children</u> of all ages and all beliefs about witchcraft <u>dress</u> as goblins and ghosts every Halloween.

Answers to Exercise 4.4, page 248

1. Witches have existed, at least in people's minds, since the beginning of time and have appeared in literature from the beginning of writing.

2. The *Odyssey* and the Bible contain references to witchcraft.

3. Circe, a witch in Homer's epic poem, had the power to turn people into animals.

4. The Old Testament contains several references to witches and witchcraft, including the following sentence from Exodus 22:18.

5. "Thou shalt not suffer a witch to live."

6. Witch-hunters hundreds of years later accepted such biblical statements as gospel and persecuted persons accused of witchcraft.

7. Those persons accused of witchcraft were often tortured and were sometimes even killed.

8. Tests of a woman's guilt included tying her arms and legs and throwing her into deep water.

9. A witch's floating on the surface was considered a sign of guilt.

10. What good was innocence to a drowning, falsely accused witch?

Answers to Exercise 4.5, page 249

1. Witches have existed, at least in people's minds, since the beginning of time and have appeared in literature from the beginning of writing.
2. The *Odyssey* and the Bible contain references to witchcraft.
3. Circe, a witch in Homer's epic poem, had the power to turn people into animals.
4. The Old Testament contains several references to witches and witchcraft, including the following sentence from Exodus 22:18.
5. "Thou shalt not suffer a witch to live."
6. Witch-hunters hundreds of years later accepted such biblical statements as gospel and persecuted persons accused of witchcraft.
7. Those persons accused of witchcraft were often tortured and were sometimes even killed.
8. Tests of a woman's guilt included tying her arms and legs and throwing her into deep water.
9. A witch's floating on the surface was considered a sign of guilt.
10. What good was innocence to a drowning, falsely accused witch?

Answers to Exercise 4.6, page 250

1. Joan of Arc was burned at the stake. Why was Joan of Arc burned at the stake?
2. She was a witch. Was she really a witch?
3. Were many women killed as witches? Between 1484 and 1782, about 300,000 women were killed by the Christian Church for practicing witchcraft.
4. Where did the most famous witch-hunt in American history occur? The most famous witch-hunt in American history occurred in Salem, Mass.
5. Who stirred public feeling against witches? (Here the interrogative pronoun *Who* is the subject, leaving subject and verb in normal order.) Cotton Mather, a colonial preacher, stirred public feeling against the supposed evil deeds of witches.
6. Disgraced for life were many women in the town of Salem. (Emphasis is on the word *Disgraced*.)
7. Is voodoo anything like witchcraft? Voodoo is like witchcraft in many ways.
8. Witchcraft is becoming of more interest as a religion. Why is witchcraft becoming of more interest as a religion?
9. Have witches been meeting? Witches have been meeting in groups of 13 known as covens.
10. Education has lessened the fear of witches. Will further education lessen the fear of witchcraft even more?

Answers to Exercise 4.7, page 252

c   **1.** *Pulitzer* is the subject; *was* is the verb. The subordinate clause beginning with *who* modifies *publisher* and is properly connected to the main clause. So this is a complete sentence.

fr   **2.** This "sentence" has no subject (<u>Who</u> came?), so it is a fragment.

fs   **3.** Here we have two sentences connected by nothing. A period or a semicolon is needed after *quickly* to correct this fused sentence.

fr   **4.** *Which* begins a subordinate clause (a fragment) that cannot stand alone pretending to be a sentence. Put a comma after *paper* instead of the period, make the *W* in *Which* lowercase, and connect the subordinate clause to the main clause that precedes it.

fs   **5.** Two sentences connected by nothing = a fused sentence. The first sentence ends after the first *St. Louis,* so either put a period there and start a new sentence, or use a semicolon, or subordinate the second sentence into a subordinate clause by changing the adverb *there* to the subordinating conjunction *where* preceded by a comma.

fs   **6.** Like No. 5, this is a case of two sentences connected by nothing, a fused sentence. The first sentence ends after *World.* Insert a period, a semicolon, or a comma and the coordinating conjunction *and.*

cs   **7.** This is a comma splice because two sentences are connected with a comma. Change the comma to a period or a semicolon. A semicolon would be better because the two main clauses are so closely related in meaning.

fr   **8.** The words beginning with *Which* are a subordinate clause, which, when standing alone, constitutes a fragment. The period after *Journalism* should be made a comma; this will connect the subordinate clause *which he had founded with a $1,000,000 gift in 1903* to the main sentence.

fr   **9.** This is a fragment, lacking a subject for the verb *endowed.*

fr **10.** The first part is a complete sentence, but the phrase after *As well as* is a fragment. Remove the period, and make the *A* in *As* lowercase. Not even a comma is needed.

Answers to Exercise 4.8, page 253

fs   **1.** You need to separate the two main clauses. Put a period, a semicolon, or a comma with a coordinating conjunction between *zippers* and *they*—or subordinate one of the clauses: Zippers should not be called zippers *because* they are really slide fasteners.

c   **2.** Simple subject *fastener,* real verb *was devised,* a complete thought. This is a complete sentence. Okay.

fr   **3.** This is a subordinate clause pretending to be a sentence. *Who* is the simple subject of the subordinate clause, and *sensed* and *started* form the compound verb of the subordinate clause; but the subordinate clause doesn't make sense by itself (does not express a complete thought). It depends on a main clause to give it meaning. Connect it to No. 2 above, putting a comma before *who*.

fr 4. Well, what *about* "A series of teeth. . . "? Something is missing. If "A series of teeth. . . " is the subject, you need a predicate: ". . . formed the first crude zipper." If "a series of teeth. . . " is meant to be the predicate, you need a subject: "The first crude zipper was. . . "

cs 5. You need to separate the first main clause ending with *fastener* and the second main clause beginning *the Hookless* with something stronger than a comma. Insert a period, a semicolon, or the coordinating conjunction *and* preceded by a comma.

fs 6. Stop the first main clause after *fasteners* with a period, a semicolon, or the coordinating conjunction *and,* preceded this time by a semicolon instead of a comma (for clarity) because of all the commas in the main clause that follows. Or perhaps subordinate the second main clause: ". . . fasteners, *which* replaced. . . "

cs 7. Separate the main clauses in one of the three ways discussed, or subordinate: Say ". . . rocketed *because* slide fasteners were put on soldiers' money belts."

cs 8. Separate the main clauses in one of the three ways discussed. Neither clause can be subordinated here.

fr 9. What about "Unique uses of zippers"? There appears to be a subject and modifiers but no real verb for the sentence, or rather the non-sentence.

c 10. It is perfectly proper to connect two closely related main clauses with a semicolon.

Answers to Exercise 4.9, page 253

fr 1. A brilliant agricultural chemist, George Washington Carver was born about 1864 of slave parents in Missouri.

cs 2. When he was just a baby, he and his mother were stolen by raiders. His master bought him back in exchange for a race horse. OR raiders, but his master bought him back . . .

fs 3. He worked his way through school and graduated from Iowa State College. Later he got his master's degree there. OR College, where later he got his master's degree.

c 4. He was a member of the Iowa State faculty until he joined Tuskegee Institute in Alabama, where he spent the rest of his life. Correct.

fr 5. His work to revolutionize the agriculture of the South won him international fame.

fr 6. He encouraged farmers to grow peanuts and sweet potatoes instead of cotton, which was exhausting the soil.

fs 7. Soon the farmers were growing more of these two crops than people could eat. He began making useful products from them. OR eat, so he began . . .

fs 8. From peanuts he made cheese, milk, coffee, soap, and ink. From sweet potatoes he made flour, candy, vinegar, molasses, and rubber. OR ink; from . . .

cs 9. In 1940 he gave his life savings of $33,000 to found the George Washington Carver Foundation for Agricultural Research at Tuskegee Institute. A museum of his discoveries is there. OR . . . Tuskegee Institute, where a museum of his discoveries is located.

cs 10. He was given many honors. He died in 1943. OR honors before he . . .

Answers to Exercise 4.10, page 254

fr 1. Tattooing is the practice of making permanent designs on the body.

fs 2. It is done by pricking deep holes in the skin; coloring matter is then placed in the holes. OR skin. Coloring matter . . .

fr 3. Tattooing is a popular custom among soldiers and sailors of many countries.

cs 4. No one knows when or where tattooing started; some Egyptian mummies of 1300 B.C. show blue tattoo marks under the skin. OR started. Some Egyptian mummies . . . OR started, but some Egyptian mummies . . .

fr 5. The Japanese and the Burmese have done some of the most elaborate tattooing in the world.

cs 6. Tattooing is also popular in Southeastern New Guinea, where tattoos on girls are looked on as signs of beauty.

fr 7. In the United States all kinds of people sport tattoos.

cs 8. Most people who get tattooed consider their new look a method of self-expression; many consider their tattooed bodies a walking art form. OR self-expression. Many consider . . . OR self-expression, and many consider . . .

fr 9. Beginning tattooers, who often have degrees in art, usually learn their needle work from established tattooers, often their fathers. (Connect phrase at end to preceding sentence by comma.)

fr 10. The tattooed even have conventions at which they trade ideas for designs and select Mr. Tattoo and Ms. Tattoo.

c 11. Tattoos can be removed with laser beams.

Possible Answers to Exercise 4.11, page 255

1. In Thailand, teachers are more like second parents than faculty members.
2. Students in Thailand show their teachers great respect; students always do exactly what their teachers say.

3. <u>Because</u> American teachers are more friendly, students get to know them better.

4. In Thailand schools, students from fourth grade through high school must wear uniform<u>s. They</u> consist of short pants for the boys and not-too-short skirts for the girls.

5. Boys' hair must be cut very <u>short; but</u> with the weather so hot, I never minded the short hair or the short pants.

Answers to Quiz Yourself on Step One, page 256

1. A knowledge of sentences helps me speak and write good English, which makes me appear educated, helps in college, helps in the job world, and helps in personal relations.

2. A sentence is a group of words containing a subject, a real verb, and a complete thought and ending with a period, a question mark, or an exclamation point.

3. A subject is a noun or words substituting for a noun telling who or what does something or is something or has something done to it. A verb tells that the subject does something or is something or has something done to it.

4. (a) fragment. (b) comma splice. (c) fused sentence.

5. (a) comma splice. (b) fused sentence.

6. (a) Add period. (b) Add semicolon. (c) Add comma and coordinating conjunction. (d) Subordinate main clause.

7. A main clause is a simple sentence (a subject, a verb, and a complete thought) that has become part of a bigger sentence. A subordinate clause is a group of words which has a subject and a verb but which does not express a complete thought until it is attached to a main clause that gives it meaning.

8. Fragment.

9. A predicate is the verb of a sentence plus the modifiers and complements of the verb.

10. An imperative sentence is a command or request. The subject of an imperative sentence is *you* understood. An imperative sentence usually ends with a period. However, if a strong emotion is expressed, it ends with an exclamation mark.

11. F.

Answers to Exercise 4.12, page 259

__s__ 1. <u>The six-year-old Mozart and his 11-year-old sister visited Vienna and played for the empress</u>. (Main clause with compound subject and compound verb.)

__cpx__ 2. <u>Whenever Mozart's father took him on a tour of European capitals</u>, <u>audiences were astounded by the young man's musical talent</u>. (Subordinate clause, main clause.)

__cpd__ 3. <u>Mozart began teaching music in Germany</u>, and <u>soon he met Aloysia Weber</u>. (Two main clauses.)

cpx   **4.** <u>After she became a successful singer</u>, <u>she rejected Mozart</u>. (Subordinate clause, main clause.)

cc   **5.** <u>He later married her younger sister, Constanze,</u> <u>who was also a singer,</u> <u>and for the rest of his life he had financial difficulty.</u> (Main clause, subordinate clause, main clause.)

cpx   **6.** <u>Even though Mozart was composer to the emperor,</u> <u>he lived his life in poverty</u> <u>because he could not manage money well</u>. (Subordinate clause, main clause, subordinate clause.)

s   **7.** <u>The last decade of his life he frantically composed music and gave frequent concert tours.</u> (Main clause with compound verb.)

cpd   **8.** <u>He is often considered the father of the modern concerto;</u> <u>he composed some 25 concertos for piano and orchestra.</u> (Two main clauses.)

cpd   **9.** <u>Life in his household must not have been tranquil,</u> <u>but his wife and his children apparently adored him,</u> <u>and he adored them.</u> (Three main clauses, compound subject in second one.)

cc   **10.** <u>Wolfgang and Constanze had six children;</u> <u>four died at an early age,</u> <u>but the two sons</u> <u>who survived to adulthood</u> <u>were talented musicians.</u> (Three main clauses, the first with compound subject, and one subordinate clause. *Who survived to adulthood* is a subordinate clause inside the main clause *but the two sons were talented musicians.*)

Answers to Exercise 4.13, page 260

s   **1.** <u>The six-year-old Mozart and his 11-year-old sister visited Vienna and played for the empress.</u> (Main clause with compound subject and compound verb. The two *and*s do not connect clauses. No checks.)

cpx   **2.** <u>Whenever Mozart's father took him on a tour of European capitals,</u> <u>audiences were astounded by the young man's musical talent.</u> (Subordinate clause, main clause.)

cpd   **3.** <u>Mozart began teaching music in Germany,</u> <u>and soon he met Aloysia Weber.</u> (Two main clauses.)

cpx   4. <u>After she became a successful singer,</u> <u>she rejected Mozart.</u> (Subordinate clause, main clause.)

cc   **5.** <u>He later married her younger sister, Constanze,</u> <u>who was also a singer,</u> <u>and for the rest of his life he had financial difficulty</u>. (Main clause, subordinate clause, main clause.)

cpx   **6.** <u>Even though Mozart was composer to the emperor,</u> <u>he lived his life in poverty</u> <u>because he could not manage money well</u>. (Subordinate clause, main clause, subordinate clause.)

s   **7.** <u>The last decade of his life he frantically composed music and gave frequent concert tours.</u> (Main clause with compound verb. The *and* here connects two parts of compound verb.)

cpd **8.** He is often considered the father of the modern concerto; he composed some 25 concertos for piano and orchestra. (Two main clauses.)

cpd **9.** Life in his household must not have been tranquil, but his wife and his children apparently adored him, and he adored them. (Three main clauses, compound subject in second one. The first *and* connects two parts of compound subject of second main clause.)

cc **10.** Wolfgang and Constanze had six children; four died at an early age, but the two sons who survived to adulthood were talented musicians. (Three main clauses and one subordinate clause. The *and* in the first main clause connects two parts of the compound subject. *Who survived to adulthood* is a subordinate clause inside the main clause *but the two sons were talented musicians.*)

Possible Answer to Exercise 4.14, page 261

1. Magazines are full of advice on how to invest your money, but this is usually not a big problem with you students who are working your way through college. (Connect two main clauses of equal importance with *but,* and add one subordinate clause beginning with *who* to make a compound-complex sentence).

2. Your problem more often is how to get enough money for tuition and books. (Okay to keep a simple sentence; strive for variety in sentence length and complexity).

3. Of course, you can wait to win the lottery, or you can look for a rich person to marry, or you can hope for an inheritance from rich, childless, terminally ill Uncle Harry. (Make the three main clauses, which are of equal importance, into a compound sentence, and change three other main clauses to three adjectives, *rich, childless, terminally ill.*)

4. But since the chance of coming into big bucks by any of these methods is slim, by far the most reliable way to acquire money is to work for it. (Subordinate one main clause, *since the chance. . .*, and connect it to the more important main clause, *the most reliable way. . .*, to make a complex sentence.)

5. So if you work hard and can manage to save just a little each month, some day you will need that advice on how to invest your money. (Again, subordinate one main clause, *if you work hard. . .*, and connect it to the more important main clause, *some day you will need. . .*, to make a complex sentence.)

Possible Answer to Exercise 4.15, page 262

1. A generation or two ago, a majority of college freshmen were 18-years-olds from middle- to upper-income families of the nearby community. (Leave the simple sentence but include ideas from two other main clauses, about income and community.)

2. Today education is exciting because classrooms are filled with a much more

interesting mix. (Subordinate one main clause with *because,* and add it to the main clause *Today education is exciting,* making a complex sentence.)

3. There are high school seniors earning college credits early and recent high school graduates; there are senior citizens who missed college the first time around, and there are students of all ages in between. (Make a compound-complex sentence with three main clauses and one subordinate clause, *who missed college the first time around.)*

4. Some students are financially secure, and some are on financial aid. (Join two main clauses with a comma and the coordinating conjunction *and,* forming a compound sentence.)

5. Some are from the city and its suburbs, and some are from as far away as Thailand or Liberia, Germany or Japan. (Same as the preceding sentence.)

6. Surely the world will benefit from this increased accessibility of education and from the atmosphere of democracy and tolerance in the classroom. (Combine two main clauses into one, making a simple sentence).

Possible Answer to Exercise 4.16, page 263

Lynn, experienced with motorboats, accepted Debbie's invitation to drive the boat so that Debbie could water ski. Leesa, when asked to be the observer, said she had made plans to go to the mall with Angie to shop for a bathing suit. Although she already had three, they were more than a year old. She needed a new one in case she were invited to a swimming party. Charlie said he would be the observer in just a few minutes, after he finished cleaning the nine perch and two lake trout he had caught. Soon the three were out on the lake enjoying themselves. The girls were also looking forward to the back-yard fish fry Charlie had invited them to.

Answers to Exercise 4.17, page 264

1. In the last year of his life, 1791, Mozart asked by a mysterious stranger to write a funeral service, or requiem mass, for an Austrian nobleman. (Real verb should be *was asked.)*

2. Said he would because he needed the money. (Add subject, *He.)*

3. He was convinced he was writing music for his own funeral he died, apparently of typhoid, before he had finished this great work. (Separate main clauses between *funeral* and *he* with period or semicolon.)

4. One of his pupils who completed this masterpiece. (Take *who* out of subordinate clause, making what was the subordinate clause into the predicate of the main clause.)

5. The day of Mozart's burial was stormy, no one attended the funeral. (Unfuse the two sentences with a period or a semicolon, or with a comma and the coordinating conjunction *and,* or subordinate the first main clause, *Because the day of Mozart's burial was stormy.)*

6. Was that a fitting way to honor an outstanding musical genius (How about a question mark at the end?)

7. He buried in a pauper's cemetery (You need a real verb, *was buried,* and a period at the end.)

8. Constanze broke down from grief did not go to the funeral. (Add a subject for the second main clause, changing sentence to *grief; she did not go. . . ,* or make the verb compound, *broke down from grief and did not go . . .*)

9. When she recovered and visited the cemetery, she could not find which grave was Wolfgang's (Just add a period.)

10. A monument to Wolfgang Amadeus Mozart was later erected over an empty grave; we will now put Mozart to rest. Forever. (Correct. It's all right to use the fragment *Forever* here for emphasis.)

Answers to Exercise 4.18, page 265

1. Relaxation is good for you because it restores your energy, relieves tension, and helps you sleep.

2. Sit quietly in a comfortable position with eyes closed, muscles relaxed, and mind at rest.

3. You will find relaxation can make you happier and make you more successful at your job.

Answers to Exercise 4.19, page 266

1. A smile takes no more energy than a frown. OR A smile doesn't take any more energy than a frown.

2. And when you frown, it doesn't make the people around you feel good, I think. OR And when you frown, I don't think it makes the people around you feel good.

3. Try smiling at a stranger, and you won't have anything but good feelings when you see that person first look bewildered and then smile back at you. OR . . . you will have nothing but good feelings . . .

Answers to Exercise 4.20, page 267

1. Kate dislikes exams because she knows she gets tense and forgets what she knows.

2. She does not need extra stress and is not happy when it is time for exams and term papers. OR She did not need extra stress and was not happy when it was time for exams and term papers.

3. Leatrice got ready to study for her English test and found all her notes were in her locker at school.

Answers to Exercise 4.21, page 268

Words in parentheses should be omitted. **1.** an (old) antique. **2.** a blue(-colored) car. **3.** in (the year) 1776. **4.** at (12) noon (on) Dec. 24. **5.** Her speech was about (the subject of) boats. **6.** the fortune teller's (advance) predictions (of the future). **7.** for (a period of) three hours. **8.** a large(-size) dog. **9.** returned (back) to the school. **10.** He was (engaged in) weeding the garden. **11.** (Perhaps) he may change his mind. **12.** is (of a) square (shape). **13.** a (tall) man (who stood) seven feet tall. **14.** a hot (summer) night in July. **15.** a highly regarded man (of good reputation) OR a (highly regarded) man of good reputation.

Answers to Exercise 4.22, page 271

1. Birds of a feather flock together. **2.** Don't cry over spilled milk. **3.** The pen is mightier than the sword. **4.** You can't teach an old dog new tricks. **5.** A watched pot never boils.

Possible Answer to Exercise 4.23, page 272

This is the way one student, Susan Phelps, handled this assignment.

1. Higher education began in Europe in the Middle Ages with the formation of *universitas,* groups of scholars working together for a common purpose.
2. Harvard, the oldest university in the United States, was founded in 1636 in Newtowne, which is now Cambridge, Mass.
3. At first it was a school to train ministers, men only, but now it also accepts women in its many undergraduate and graduate programs.

Answers to Quiz Yourself on Step Two, page 272

1. complex = one main, one subordinate. **2.** compound-complex = two main, three subordinate. **3.** simple = one main. **4.** compound = three main. **5.** Most instructors are glad to help students by answering questions and recommending reference books. **6.** Carla Careless and her twin brother Calvin don't find any time to do homework on weekends. **7.** Calvin Careless sometimes wanders into class late and then is discouraged because he has missed important information. **8.** a. **9.** b. **10.** short. **11.** F.

Answers to Exercise 4.24, page 275

1. climactic. **2.** common. **3.** periodic. **4.** balanced

Possible Answers to Exercise 4.25, page 277

1. were whispering, were chatting, were gossiping, were having a discussion, were debating, were arguing, were quarreling, were shouting, were yelling. **2.** The wind caught the Frisbee and blew it clear out to the street. **3.** haunting, loud, raucous, heavy-metal, nostalgic, patriotic, sentimental, sad, unharmonious, lilting, joyful. **4.** alarm went off = sound, feeling of what it's like to be rudely awakened; coffee perking and bacon frying = both sound and smell. **5.** two possible courses of action, decision to be made, only one road can be taken and what the other road is like will never be known, possibility of taking the wrong road. **6.** A careful choice of these words not only makes writing more concise but also helps the writer get his point across more clearly and helps give the reader pleasure.

Possible Answer to Exercise 4.26, page 277

Here is the way one student, Jeanne Oden, did the assignment.

When you become a grandparent, you'll have a thrill a minute and be happy as a lark. Other people's grandoffspring are a dime a dozen and have faces only a mother could love, but yours are good as gold and pretty as a picture. Although you worked like a Trojan raising your children and they sometimes made you mad as a wet hen, raising grandchildren is easy as pie, like falling off a log. As a grandparent, you are allowed to dispense sweets to the sweet, and when you get tired as a dog, you'll be happy as a clam to send the kid home to sleep like a baby, snug as a bug in a rug. That's when you'll know, sure as fate, the grandparent role fits you like an old shoe. If only you could have cut out the middleman (middle person?) and just had the grandchildren! (As you may suspect, Jeanne is a grandmother.)

Answers to Exercise 4.27, page 278

1. It crashed. **2.** gas station attendant. **3.** crane operator. **4.** trash collector. **5.** life preservers. **6.** nuclear missile. **7.** run-down house. **8.** used, second-hand. **9.** toilet plunger. **10.** handicapped. **11.** dump. **12.** waiter. **13.** doorman. **14.** unemployed. **15.** expensive. **16.** lie. **17.** bar. **18.** wave. **19.** waterproof. **20.** fired. **21.** shovel. **22.** toilet. **23.** toilet paper. **24.** recession. **25.** explosion. **26.** old folks. **27.** girdle. **28.** balding. **29.** vomiting. **30.** out of gas. (As you can see, there is no room in clear, creative writing for this.) **31.** the euphemism.

Answers to Exercise 4.28, page 283

1. Wanted: Man who does not smoke or drink, to take care of cow.
2. For sale: Antique desk with thick legs and large drawers, suitable for lady.
3. Remember in prayer the many of our church and community who are sick.
4. The concert was a great success. Special thanks to the minister's daughter, upon whom, as usual, fell the job of laboring the whole evening at the piano.
5. At our laundry, we do not tear your clothing with machinery. We wash it carefully by hand.
6. After Gov. Baldwin watched the lion perform, the lion was taken to Main Street and fed 25 pounds of raw meat.

Answers to Exercise 4.29, page 284

1. Because the student couldn't work the computer very well, the computer instructor typed in the first paragraph for her.
2. With my broken leg, I cannot chauffeur my mother, so she will have to drive herself.
3. Because I had flu and laryngitis, my dog was unable to go on his usual walk.
4. The sale being completely without clothes, I set out for another garage sale.
5. The child having been hit by a car, the surgeon got ready to operate.

Answers to Exercise 4.30, page 285

1. What was the baby crying about?
2. Even though he should have known better, he forgot to tie the boat securely to the pier.
3. Okay.
4. Okay.
5. That is the restaurant where we met our daughter for dinner.

Answers to Quiz Yourself on Step Three, page 286

1. T. **2.** c. **3.** a. **4.** b. **5.** b. **6.** c. **7.** b. **8.** c. **9.** a. **10.** c

5 Punctuation

_____

_____

_____

_____

Punctuation is one of the more logical aspects of the English language, a language in which _flammable_ and _inflammable_ mean the same thing, as do _fat_ chance and _slim_ chance, in which one _drives_ on a _parkway_ and _parks_ on a _driveway,_ and in which the _oughs_ in _cough, tough, though, through,_ and _bough_ are pronounced, respectively, as in _off, cuff, owe, you,_ and _ow_ meaning _ouch._

The purpose of all punctuation is increased clarity and ease of reading. We will consider 15 marks of punctuation as well as italics and the caret. There are far too many rules here for anyone to memorize; but after you have finished this chapter, you will know where to find help when you need it.

Step One: Most-Needed Punctuation

Use a period, a question mark, or an exclamation point to end a sentence. Use a period for many abbreviations. The semicolon is considered in Step One because its chief use is to end a main clause within a bigger sentence. The comma is also a part of Step One because, as we learned in the section on comma splices, it is frequently misused to end sentences and because its proper use is vital to clear writing.

THE FAMILY CIRCUS   by Bill Keane

11-26
©1993 Bil Keane, Inc.
Dist. by Cowles Synd., Inc.

"Why is something sent by ship called a cargo, but when it's sent by car it's a shipment?"

Periods

1. Use a period to end a **declarative sentence** (a statement).

- Pablo Picasso (1881–1973), the postimpressionist painter, was born in Spain, but he developed his art while living in France.

The following is also a declarative sentence and should end with a period even though it contains a question:

- "Did he invent cubism?" asked the student. The declarative sentence is "The student asked *something*." The *something* just happens to be a question, but the sentence is still a statement.

BUT: Do *not* put a period after the title of your composition, or any other title, even if the title is a complete sentence.

2. Use a period to end an **imperative sentence** (a command or request).

- Study Picasso, and learn that everything in life is a cube, a cone, or a cylinder.

If enough emotion is involved to make the command an exclamation, use an exclamation point.

- Help! Stop beating that dog!

3. Use a period also to form many **abbreviations.** Libraries have whole books of abbreviations. Most dictionaries have a section listing abbreviations and usually show, within the definition of a word, its abbreviation if that word is commonly abbreviated. We use abbreviations in our writing every day.

- <u>Mrs.</u> James <u>B.</u> Allen invited guests to her new home at 1375 <u>S.</u> Shore <u>Dr.</u> at 5 <u>p.m.</u> <u>Aug.</u> 16.
- She has vacationed in Frankfort, <u>Mich.,</u> for many years.

A section of Chapter 6 is devoted to a detailed consideration of abbreviations; see pages 386-392.

4. Use periods after numerals and letters in **listings and outlines.**

- a. Use a period after *a* in an outline or listing like this.
- b. And use a period after *b* in an outline or listing like this.

See Chapter 2, pages 77-78, for complete information on formal outlining.

5. Use proper **spacing.** Leave two spaces after periods at the end of sentences, only one space after periods that do not end sentences, as in abbreviations or after numerals in outlines or listings.

Question Marks

1. Place a question mark at the end of an **interrogative sentence** (a direct question).

- RIGHT (a direct question, requiring a question mark because the sentence is a question): Where was Picasso's father a professor of art?
- ALSO RIGHT, NO QUESTION MARK (an indirect question, requiring no question mark because the sentence is a statement): The student asked where Picasso's father was a professor of art.

2. Use a question mark after a **tag question,** a short direct question that is at the end of a declarative sentence.

- Picasso was a great painter, wasn't he?

PEANUTS   by Charles Schulz

If the short direct tag question falls within the sentence, set it off between commas and put the question mark at the end of the sentence.

- Picasso was great, wasn't he, in his use of color?

3. Use a question mark after a longer **question** that is **part of another sentence.**

- What were prime influences in his life? is the first question.
- The first question is, What were prime influences in his life?

4. Use a question mark after an **expression that is a question** but **not a complete sentence**.

- You said you are going to the art exhibit. When?
- Perhaps you should ask why? more often.

5. You do **not** need to use a question mark after a **request** or an order that is, out of courtesy, phrased as a question.

- Will you please study this work thoroughly in preparation for the exam.

6. You do need a question mark after the **title** of your composition or any other title if it is a question.

7. Usually a question mark requires **no additional punctuation.**

- WRONG: "Isn't this assignment too long?," asked the tired student.
- RIGHT: "Isn't this assignment too long?" asked the tired student.
- WRONG: The instructor replied, "Isn't this material important?."
- RIGHT: The instructor replied, "Isn't this material important?"

8. Use proper **spacing.** Leave two spaces after a question mark at the end of a sentence, one space after a question mark for a question within a larger sentence.

Exclamation Points

Use exclamation points after sentences or words spoken with emotion.

1. Use an exclamation point to end an **exclamatory sentence.**

- Picasso's work is so exciting!
- Don't tell me Picasso taught in Barcelona! Normally this would be an imperative sentence, a command or request; but here it is spoken with emotion, so it becomes an exclamatory sentence.
- That's where I was born! Normally this would be a declarative sentence, a statement; but here it is spoken with emotion, so it becomes an exclamatory sentence.

2. Use an exclamation point after an **exclamatory expression.**

- Bravo! What a painter!

3. Use an exclamation point after the **title** of your composition or any other title if it is an exclamation.

4. Usually an exclamation point requires **no additional punctuation.**

- WRONG: "Help!," she screamed.
- RIGHT: "Help!" she screamed.

NOTE: Do not use more than one exclamation point at a time.

- WRONG: "Help!!!!" she screamed.

5. Use proper **spacing.** Leave two spaces after exclamation points at the end of sentences and only one space after exclamation points that do not end sentences.

- His fellow workers screamed at him! He had cried Wolf! too many times.

EXERCISE 5.1 Fill in the blanks with a period, a question mark, an exclamation point, or **O** if no punctuation is needed.

1. Kate, who is from Boston, Mass _____, has decided she wants to be a nurse _____

2. After her first week of classes, she exclaimed, "Wow _____ _____ Are all my classes going to be this hard _____ _____"

3. Peter, who is from Poland, wrote his father that he was excited about becoming a journalist _____

4. Peter's father told him to study hard and to learn everything he could _____

5. Peter's secret goal is to get a job as a television newscaster like Mr _____ Peter Jennings or Ms _____ Barbara Walters _____

6. Roberto is from Toluca, Mexico, isn't he _____ _____ He helps students, doesn't he, with their Spanish homework _____ _____

7. "This is great _____ _____" exclaimed Roberto. "I got the job in the computer lab, and now I'm pretty sure I will have enough money to go on and get my bachelor's degree _____ _____

8. Leatrice, who is starting college in her hometown, wants to go away to school the last two years, doesn't she _____ _____

9. For tomorrow, will you please study the section on semicolons _____ _____

Answers on page 361.

Semicolons

We will consider semicolons next since they **almost always do the same job as periods,** i.e., end a sentence. But the sentences that semicolons end are main clauses within a bigger sentence.

- Truth in packaging should include truth in unpackaging; "To open, push here" really means "To break your nail, push here."

REMEMBER: A sentence changes its name to main clause (or independent clause) when it becomes part of a bigger sentence. A semicolon may be used after one main clause and before the next main clause within a bigger sentence.

The semicolon is the most misunderstood mark of punctuation in the world. Students say, "I never could understand semicolons, so I just never use them." I suppose it is possible to go through life without using any semicolons, but they are handy—make that *essential*—if you want to join two sentences that are closely related in subject matter into one bigger sentence.

The semicolon is called a weak period; 99 percent of the time it has a main clause before it and a main clause after it. So each time you are tempted to sprinkle semicolons here and there to flavor your writing, stop and think: Could I put a period there instead of the semicolon and be grammatically correct? No. 4 below is the one percent of the time when a period cannot be substituted for a semicolon.

1. Use a semicolon to join (into one bigger sentence) **main clauses** that are closely related.

- GRAMMATICALLY CORRECT: The cotton gin had a profound effect. This 1794 invention made cotton growing and slavery profitable. Here we have two closely related but separate sentences.
- BETTER: The cotton gin had a profound effect; this 1794 invention made cotton growing and slavery profitable. We now have the two closely related sentences turned into main clauses and joined into one bigger sentence by a semicolon.

2. Use a semicolon before a **conjunctive adverb** or a **transitional phrase** joining two main clauses into a bigger sentence. Main clauses can not (correctly) be joined to other main clauses with a comma plus a conjunctive adverb or transitional phrase. A semicolon is required.

The box below presents a list of some of the most common conjunctive adverbs and transitional phrases. These need semicolons before them when they join main clauses into a bigger sentence; usually they need commas after them.

Conjunctive Adverbs

accordingly	furthermore	likewise	otherwise
also	hence	meanwhile	specifically
besides	however	moreover	still
briefly	incidentally	nevertheless	then
consequently	indeed	next	therefore
finally	instead	nonetheless	thus
			too

Transitional Phrases (see also Chapter 2, pages 101-102)

after all	even so	in conclusion	on the contrary
as a result	for example	in contrast	on the other hand
at any rate	for instance	in fact	on the whole
at the same time	for the most part	in other words	that is
because of this	for this reason	in the first place	to illustrate
by the way	in addition	in the meantime	to summarize

DON'T FORGET: Usually a comma follows the conjunctive adverb or transitional phrase.

- Eli Whitney went to Georgia to become a tutor after he graduated from Yale; *however,* he found that someone else had been given his job.
- He decided to stay in Georgia instead of returning home to Massachusetts; *because of this,* he became interested in designing a machine to separate seeds from the cotton itself.

Then is often guilty of causing comma splices; however, it requires a semicolon (not just a comma) before it when it joins main clauses into a bigger sentence. Usually it does not require a comma after it as most of the other conjunctive adverbs do.

- In a few weeks he had invented a machine with which one man could clean 50 pounds of cotton a day; then he applied for a patent and began to manufacture his cotton gin in a factory in New Haven, Conn.

3. Use a semicolon before the **coordinating conjunctions** *and, but, for, nor, or, so,* and *yet* connecting main clauses when one or both of the main clauses they are connecting contain a comma or commas—if the semicolon helps make the sentence clear.

- SEMICOLON HELPFUL IN CLARITY: When Whitney's plans for the cotton gin were stolen, others began to design, manufacture, and sell similar machines; but even though Whitney very quickly sued, it was not until 1807, after 13 years of negotiations, that his patent rights were established.
- SEMICOLON PROBABLY NOT NEEDED: Meanwhile, his factory burned down, so he turned to the manufacture of firearms, making a fortune by standardizing parts to be assembled later. A semicolon before *so* would not be wrong, but it is probably not needed in spite of commas after *Meanwhile* and *firearms*.

4. Use a semicolon to separate items in a **series** when one of the items contains a comma within it. Use semicolons at the *main* points of separation for clarity. This is the one-percent use of semicolons when you could not substitute periods. Depending on where you put semicolons, there may have been from six to 11 people at the following meeting:

- Dr. Gold, the president, the provost, Dr. Stackelberg, the dean, Dr. Prange, Miss Ekstrom, the department secretary, Mrs. Van Tyne, a faculty member, and Dr. Humphreys met in Room 1234 (no semicolons, 11 people).
- Dr. Gold, the president; the provost, Dr. Stackelberg; the dean, Dr. Prange; Miss Ekstrom, the department secretary; Mrs. Van Tyne, a faculty member; and Dr. Humphreys met in Room 1234 (six people).
- Dr. Gold, the president; the provost; Dr. Stackelberg; the dean, Dr. Prange; Miss Ekstrom; the department secretary, Mrs. Van Tyne; a faculty member; and Dr. Humphreys met in Room 1234 (eight people; depending on where you put the semicolon, Mrs. Van Tyne can be either the department secretary or a faculty member).

Please don't go through life avoiding semicolons. Let's look at one more example of the use of semicolons for clarity at the main points of separation in a series.

- You will find more about Eli Whitney in newspapers of the time, which can be found in the archives of the library; in books on Civil War history, general United States history, and the history of the world's inventions; and in works of biography.

5. Do **not** use a semicolon to connect **elements of unequal grammatical rank,** such as a main clause and a subordinate clause. You can tell that a clause is subordinate if you say it aloud and it doesn't make sense standing alone. You will find that it begins with one of the subordinating conjunctions listed on pages 225 and 245 or relative pronouns listed on page 206.

- WRONG: After Eli Whitney died in 1825 at the age of 60; his fame spread. A semicolon cannot join a subordinate clause to a main clause; they are not of equal grammatical rank.
- RIGHT: After Eli Whitney died in 1825 at the age of 60, his fame spread. The comma is necessary because the subordinate adverb clause comes first, is introductory.
- RIGHT: Eli Whitney's fame spread after he died in 1825 at the age of 60. The comma is usually not necessary when the sentence is in normal order—subject, verb, subordinate adverb clause.
- WRONG: The world was changed in many ways because of Eli Whitney; a skilled mechanic, a dreamer, and an astute businessman. The words after the semicolon are not a main clause. Ninety-nine percent of the time semicolons have a main clause before them and a main clause after them.
- RIGHT: The world was changed in many ways because of Eli Whitney, a skilled mechanic, a dreamer, and an astute businessman.

6. Use proper **spacing** and **capitalization.** Leave one space after a semicolon. Do not capitalize the first word after a semicolon unless it is a proper noun or a proper adjective or the pronoun *I*.

EXERCISE 5.2 Circle any period that has been used where a semicolon might be better because the sentences are so closely related in meaning. You should find three.

Roberto's family is from Toluca, a resort and trading center about 45 miles southwest of Mexico City. The country of Mexico is divided into states, one of which is called Mexico. Toluca is capital of the state of Mexico. Toluca is an old city. It was founded in 1520. Its oldest church was built shortly after Cortés defeated the Aztec Indians and conquered Mexico for Spain in 1521. It was not until 300 years later that New Spain, as the country was called, became the independent country of Mexico. Toluca has developed into a commercial and communications center.

It is located in an important farming and cattle region.
Grain growing and livestock raising are important.
Roberto's father worked in a flour mill there until he
brought his family to the United States.

Answers on page 362.

EXERCISE 5.3 Insert semicolons where needed. Sometimes a comma needs to be replaced by a semicolon. One sentence is correct.

1. Five people went to the basketball game: Peter, a handsome fellow, Kate, a freckle-faced blonde, Roberto, a tall student, Leatrice, a slender girl, and Dr. Jefferson.

2. Nine people went to the basketball game: Peter, a handsome lad, Kate, a freckle-faced blonde, Roberto, a tall student, Leatrice, a slender girl, and Dr. Jefferson.

3. Leatrice's birthday is April 1, her sign is Aries.

4. Leatrice has developed good study habits she made the Dean's List last grading period.

5. To make the Dean's List you must have a 3.25 grade-point average, however, you can make a C once in a while if you make some A's to balance it.

6. Dr. Jefferson was given the Teacher of the Year Award, because of this, his graduate school honored him as Alumnus of the Year.

7. After he received his doctorate, Dr. Jefferson had a career as a newspaper reporter, covering the police beat for the *Daily News* three years before he started teaching, and one thing that makes him such a good journalism teacher is this practical experience, the other thing being that he really cares about his students.

Answers on page 362.

Commas

Some of us have learned that commas should be sprinkled everywhere in a sentence that we would pause if we were reading the sentence aloud. This works sometimes but is far from reliable; different people pause at different places for different reasons. There are many rules for the use of commas, yet certainly the trend is toward omitting those that aren't necessary for clarity. The most common uses are discussed here.

1. Use a comma before the **coordinating conjunctions** *and, but, for, nor, or, so,* or *yet* when the conjunction joins main clauses into one bigger sentence—unless the clauses are very short and the meaning is clear without the comma.

- RIGHT: Albert Einstein was born in Germany in 1879, and at the age of 14 he began to teach himself analytical geometry and calculus.
- RIGHT: He went to school in Munich but school bored him. A comma before *but* is preferred but is probably not necessary for clarity.
- WRONG: He received a diploma from the Swiss Federal Polytechnic School in Zurich and a doctor's degree from the University of Zurich *so,* he decided to become a Swiss citizen. The comma goes *before* the coordinating conjunction—not after it.

2. Use a comma between **items in a series.**

- Einstein's theory of relativity included new ideas regarding *time, space, mass, motion,* and *gravitation.* He *studied, researched,* or *tested* his theories. He announced important discoveries in *1915, 1950,* and *1953.*

Commas are used to separate a series of adjectives of equal value, called coordinate adjectives.

- A SERIES OF ADJECTIVES OF EQUAL VALUE: Einstein was a *bright, modest, generous* person.

But commas are not used between adjectives of unequal value, as in the example below.

- A SERIES OF ADJECTIVES OF UNEQUAL VALUE: Einstein often wore his old winter coat even in fairly warm weather.

TO TEST EQUALITY: Adjectives of equal value may be reversed in order; this does not work with adjectives of unequal value. You would not say his *winter old* coat. *Winter* is the more important adjective. Another test is to substitute *and* for the commas; if this makes sense, the adjectives are of equal value and need commas to separate them: Einstein was a *bright* and *modest* and *generous* person, but his coat was not *old* and *winter.*

- A SERIES OF PHRASES: He gave lectures at European universities, throughout the United States, and in many parts of Asia.

CAUTION: In a series, do not place a comma before the first item or after the last item, as in the following:

- WRONG: Einstein was interested in many subjects, such as, science, people, and music. Take out the comma before *science,* before the first item in the series. *Such as* requires a comma before it, not after it.
- RIGHT: Einstein was interested in many subjects, such as science, people, and music.
- WRONG: Einstein was a keenly analytical, generous, modest, person. Take out the comma after *modest,* after the last item in the series.
- RIGHT: Einstein was a keenly analytical, generous, modest person.

3. Use a comma **before *and* or *or* in a series.** This is always preferred but may be omitted if the meaning is absolutely clear without it.

- MEANING ABSOLUTELY CLEAR WITHOUT COMMA: Jane, Joan and Judy are coming. Jane, Joan or Judy will bring the cake.
- COMMA NEEDED FOR CLARITY: The items I bought at the flea market cost two dollars, one dollar and nine cents. Two items? OR The items I bought at the flea market cost two dollars, one dollar, and nine cents. Three items.

4. Use a comma after **introductory words,** including *yes, no,* interjections, conjunctive adverbs, and any word that is clearer with a comma than without; introductory phrases, including transitional phrases, long phrases, absolute phrases, and any phrase that is clearer with a comma than without; and introductory subordinate adverb clauses.

- INTRODUCTORY WORDS: *Yes,* Einstein was brilliant. *Well,* how else would he have known to leave Berlin just when Hitler was coming to power? *Indeed,* he had lived in Europe the first 54 years of his life.
- TRANSITIONAL PHRASE + CLARITY (could be misread without the comma): *By the way,* he won the Nobel Prize for physics in 1921.
- LONG INTRODUCTORY PHRASE: *After being invited to become director of the School of Mathematics of the Institute for Advanced Study at Princeton,* he moved to the United States in 1933.
- ABSOLUTE PHRASE = a phrase which does not modify any particular word in its sentence but rather is related to the whole sentence; absolute phrases usually consist of a noun or pronoun plus a participle with modifiers: *His humanitarianism being known throughout the world,* Einstein was invited to be president of Israel. He refused.
- INTRODUCTORY SUBORDINATE ADVERB CLAUSE: *Because he was not concerned about money,* he once used a $1,500 check for a bookmark and lost the book.

5. Use commas before and after **parenthetical expressions**—that is, before and after words, phrases, or clauses inserted in a sentence to add information, understanding, or emphasis, but whose removal from the sentence would not distort the meaning of the sentence. The word *naturally* in the following sentence is one. When parenthetical expressions are in the middle of a sentence, they require a comma before and after; at the end of the sentence, it is, *naturally,* impossible to put in the "after" comma.

- INTERJECTION: Einstein was, *alas,* a bit absent-minded.
- SUBORDINATE CLAUSE: He retired from his post at the Princeton Institute for Advanced Study in 1945 but, *as many scientists do,* kept on working.
- MAIN CLAUSE: He had been, *I forgot to tell you,* a professor at the University of Zurich.
- CONJUNCTIVE ADVERB (used parenthetically—as a transitional word—here, not joining two main clauses into a bigger sentence): His interests in his later years, *moreover,* included playing the violin and working for world peace.
- TRANSITIONAL PHRASE (to show contrast): He was also, *unlike many of his contemporaries,* a man with no high aspirations.

NOTE: *Too,* meaning also, is a parenthetical expression. Omit the comma before *too,* meaning also, when it occurs at the end of a sentence or clause.

- The Nazis had stripped Einstein of all his property and of his citizenship *too.*

Use a comma after *too,* meaning also, when it is the first word of a sentence or the first word after a semicolon.

- He was glad to make America his home; *too,* he was happy to become an American citizen.

Set off *too,* meaning also, between commas when it occurs in the middle of the sentence.

- Like many of his Jewish colleagues, he, *too,* could have become a victim of Hitler's anti-Semitism.

Do not use commas with the adverb *too* when it means excessively.

- Einstein's theories are *too* hard for most of us to understand.

6. Use commas before and after an **abbreviation** following a name, which is a type of parenthetical expression.

- Todd W. Locke, *M.D.,* could understand Einstein's theories, I'm sure.

- I hope you are not tired of hearing about Albert Einstein, *Ph.D.,* the subject of many of these examples.

- BUT Einstein's older son was Albert Einstein *Jr.;* if Einstein had had a relative who wanted to name *his* son Albert, that son would have been Albert Einstein *II.* The trend is to omit commas setting off *Jr., Sr.,* and *II* after the name. Even commas setting off *Inc.* are frequently omitted. If you know the preference of the person or the corporation, use that.

7. Use a comma to prevent **repetition** of clearly understood words, usually in parallel clauses joined by a semicolon.

- In the eyes of the world Albert Einstein was a brilliant scientist; in his own eyes, only a simple man. The semicolon prevents the repetition of *Albert Einstein was.*

8. Use commas before and after **nonessential** (also called nonrestrictive) **clauses, phrases, and appositives.**

Essential (also called restrictive) clauses, phrases, and appositives do *not* require commas.

Nonessential expressions, like parenthetical expressions, may be omitted from the sentence without changing the meaning of the sentence; but the omission of essential expressions changes the meaning of the sentence (they are essential to the meaning of the sentence). Nonessential clauses, phrases, and appositives need commas to show that the material between the commas could be left out without changing the meaning of the sentence.

- NONESSENTIAL CLAUSE (between the commas): Wilbur and Orville Wright, *who pioneered in making a heavier-than-air machine fly,* should have cities named after them. This nonessential clause can be omitted without distorting the meaning of the sentence.

- ESSENTIAL CLAUSE (no commas needed): Men *who pioneered in making a heavier-than-air machine fly* should have cities named after them. The clause *who pioneered in making a heavier-than-air machine fly* is essential to tell which? men. The meaning is not that *all* men should have cities named after them, just those who helped invent the airplane. The essential clause is necessary to make clear which? men. It can't be left out.

- NONESSENTIAL PHRASE (between the commas): It was the Wright brothers, *working in their bicycle-repair shop in Dayton,* who dreamed of being able to fly. The question who? dreamed—the Wright brothers—is already answered before the phrase; the nonessential phrase—it needs commas—can be omitted without distorting the meaning.

- ESSENTIAL PHRASE (no commas needed): It was two men *working in their bicycle-repair shop in Dayton* who dreamed of being able to fly. The question which? two men is not answered without the phrase—it was the two men *working in their bicycle-repair shop.* If the essential phrase is omitted, the meaning is distorted.

- NONESSENTIAL APPOSITIVE (between the commas): Wilbur Wright, *the inventor,* was more interested in flying than in repairing bicycles. *The inventor* is the appositive; it is nonessential and should be set off between commas. Which? inventor is fully identified by his name and omitting the appositive does not distort the meaning of the sentence.

- ESSENTIAL APPOSITIVE (no commas needed): The inventor *Wilbur Wright* was more interested in flying than in repairing bicycles. *Wilbur Wright* is the appositive; it is essential—needs no commas—because it is absolutely necessary to tell which? inventor. If it were omitted, the meaning of the sentence would be distorted: The inventor was more interested in flying than in repairing bicycles—which? inventor.

CAUTION: Many well-educated people wrongly omit the comma *after* a nonessential appositive, sometimes causing lack of clarity.

- Lift, the force that enables an airplane to leave the ground once in a while is misunderstood. A comma is needed after *ground* to separate the appositive *the force that enables an airplane to leave the ground* from the rest of the sentence, especially since airplanes need to leave the ground more than once in a while.

Even when clarity is not at stake, a nonessential appositive should have a comma before and after.

- WRONG: Charles Lindbergh, the American aviator made the first solo flight across the Atlantic in 1927.

- RIGHT: Charles Lindbergh, the American aviator, made the first solo flight across the Atlantic in 1927. The appositive *the American aviator* should be preceded *and followed* by a comma.

EXCEPTION: Once in a while an appositive that really is nonessential and *should* be set off between commas is treated as essential, with no commas, because it is so closely related to the noun it is an appositive for.

- Neither of the Wright brothers married; but if Orville Wright had had a wife, she probably would have frequently complained, "My husband *Orville* is always late for dinner." The appositive *Orville,* meaning the same thing as *husband,* is really nonessential because it is not needed to explain which? husband; but since the words *husband* and *Orville* seem to be one unit, the comma is usually omitted.

9. Usually use commas before and after **direct quotations** to separate "exact words spoken" (or "exact words thought") from the rest of the sentence.

- "We have accomplished our goal," Orville Wright thought to himself.
- Wilbur Wright often said, "I don't believe that airplanes will ever be able to fly at night."
- "I don't believe," Wilbur Wright often said, "that airplanes will ever be able to fly at night."

NOTE: An indirect quotation, a retelling of what was said without using the *exact* words of the speaker, does not require quotation marks or a comma: Wilbur Wright often said *that he didn't believe airplanes would ever be able to fly at night.*

ANOTHER NOTE: Periods and commas always belong *inside* (before) final quotation marks.

- "I didn't get a high school diplom<u>a</u>," said Wilbur, "because I didn't bother to go to the commencement exercis<u>es</u>."
- "I didn't get one eith<u>er</u>," Orville added, "because I took special subje<u>cts</u>."

B.C.   by Johnny Hart

10. Use commas to separate from the rest of the sentence an element of **direct address** (a name or names, sometimes with modifiers, designating the person, persons, thing, or things being spoken to, or addressed).

- Isn't it amazing, *all you frequent fliers,* that the Wright brothers didn't think the airplane would have much effect on the world?
- *Orville Wright,* what were you thinking during the 12 seconds of the first powered flight of man Dec. 17, 1903, at Kitty Hawk, N.C.?
- That same day, after Wilbur flew for 59 seconds, he probably thought, "*Good little airplane,* you did it!"

Immediately after Orville Wright's historic 12-second flight, his luggage could not be located.

11. Use commas to make street **addresses, cities, states, dates, and numerals** easy to read. Set off the name of a state between commas (a comma before and after) when the name of a city comes before it. Set off years between commas when the month *and* the day of the month come before the year.

- Wilbur Wright was born April 16, 1867, in Millville, Ind., and his brother Orville was born in Dayton, Ohio, Aug. 19, 1871. Don't forget the comma *after* the year and *after* the state.

NOTE: No comma is necessary if Orville Wright's birth date is written 19 Aug. 1871.

AND commas are not needed to set off the year unless both the month and the day of the month are given before the year; do not set off the state between commas unless the city is given before the state.

- CORRECT: Wilbur Wright set a record in September 1908 in North Carolina by staying in the air an hour and a quarter.

Read the year 1908 "nineteen eight," not "nineteen oh eight"; read the year 2001 "two thousand one," the year 2010 "twenty ten."

Insert a comma after each element of an address written within a paragraph.

- Orville Wright lived until 1948. If he had wanted to write to Einstein, he would have addressed the letter to Dr. Albert Einstein, 112 Mercer St., Princeton, N.J., and used a three-cent stamp with a picture of humorist Will Rogers on it. There were no zip codes until 1963.

In numerals of four or more digits, insert a comma after every third digit counting right-to-left from the decimal point. Do not put commas in years, house numbers, zip-code numbers, telephone numbers, serial numbers, or account numbers.

- The first flight in 1903 went 120 feet in 12 seconds; in 1905 the Wrights' airplane flew 126,720 feet (24 miles) in 2,283 seconds (38 minutes and three seconds).

A HINT TO SAVE SPACE AND ENERGY: In most cases you can omit the preposition *on* before a date and before days of the week.

- UNNECESSARY: Wilbur Wright died *on* May 30, 1912, of typhoid fever.
- INSTEAD: Wilbur Wright died May 30, 1912, of typhoid fever.
- UNNECESSARY: This library book about the Wright brothers is due on Thursday.
- INSTEAD: This library book about the Wright brothers is due Thursday.
- BUT: Wilbur Wright died *on* a Thursday. (I called the library to find out what day of the week May 30, 1912, was. Reference librarians can find almost anything and are glad to help.)

12. Use a comma after the **salutation** (Dear Clara,) of a personal letter (a colon follows the salutation of a business letter) and after the **complimentary close** (Yours truly,) of all letters.

13. Use a comma when necessary for **clarity.**

- COMMA NEEDED: The creativity Wilbur had had to have been a great asset.
- COMMA ADDED FOR CLARITY: The creativity Wilbur had, had to have been a great asset.

PEANUTS   by Charles Shulz

DON'T POOH-POOH THOSE "LITTLE CURVY MARKS": The classic example goes something like this: (no commas) Woman without her man is a beast (i.e., A woman without a man gets downright beastly). BUT: (with commas) Woman, without her, man is a beast (i.e., A man without a woman gets downright beastly). And consider these:

- Judge George Judd has quit, saying his salary is too low.
- OR Judge George Judd has quit saying his salary is too low.
- Prof. Prudence Pruitt rose, glasses in hand, demanded clearer records, brushed the papers off the table, and stalked out of the meeting.
- OR: Prof. Prudence Pruitt, rose glasses in hand, demanded clearer records, brushed the papers off the table, and stalked out of the meeting. Maybe she should have *put on* her rose-colored glasses.
- The restaurant has six private dining rooms, each assigned a waitress, that customers can reserve for an evening.
- OR: The restaurant has six private dining rooms, each assigned a waitress that customers can reserve for an evening.
- After all, rats eat, they fight, they bite, and they multiply.
- OR After all rats eat, they fight, they bite, and they multiply.
- ONE MORE: The king recently celebrated his 95th birthday, appearing at His Royal Highness' Annual Athletic Competition of gymnastics and unicycling, among thousands of young people in the streets dressed in shorts.
- OR The king celebrated his 95th birthday, appearing at His Royal Highness' Annual Athletic Competition of gymnastics, and unicycling among thousands of young people in the streets, dressed in shorts. (Goodness! If he unicycled around town in his underwear when he was 95, what do you suppose he'll do when he's 100?)

WHO SAYS ENGLISH ISN'T FUN?

A HINT: Media reporters are advised, "When in doubt, leave it out," in order to keep unconfirmed news from being spread. The same advice might well apply to the comma: When in doubt, leave it out *if* the meaning is clear without it. If clarity is at stake, you won't be in doubt. Then, put it in.

14. Use proper **spacing.** When typing, skip one space after a comma.

EXERCISE 5.4 Insert commas where needed. In the blank, write the number of the rule that applies, 1 through 13, discussed in the preceding examples.

_____ **1.** Kate parked her car in the school parking lot picked up her books and headed for class.

_____ **2.** Because she had a final exam in English she was thinking more about her schoolwork than about what she was doing.

_____ **3.** After class and she thought she had done well on the exam she looked for her car keys.

_____ **4.** She could not find them anywhere; however she thought she might have left them in the car.

_____ **5.** The car was not however where she thought she had parked it.

_____ **6.** "Joe I can't find my car," she said to the campus security guard after she had looked everywhere.

_____ **7.** "Maybe you parked in one of the other lots" suggested Joe.

_____ **8.** "No I'm sure it was this one."

_____ **9.** Joe began writing his report: Missing from Parking Lot A Cuyahoga Community College Eastern Campus 4250 Richmond Rd. Cleveland Ohio Monday March 26 at approximately 3 p.m.

_____**10.** Kate worried about what her Aunt Betty would say started toward the phone.

Answers on page 362.

EXERCISE 5.5 Insert commas to set off nonessential words, phrases, and clauses as suggested in Rule 8 on pages 317-318 in addition to any other commas as needed. Three sentences containing essential expressions will need no commas.

1. Before the missing car could be reported to the police Calvin Careless called Kate's aunt to say he was in Cincinnati where he had changed his mind about "borrowing" Kate's car.

2. Calvin a seemingly irresponsible student had decided to start his spring break early and take a nice trip; after all the keys were in the car.

3. A student who doesn't care about schoolwork sometimes doesn't bother to show up for final exams.

4. Calvin who apparently doesn't care about schoolwork sometimes doesn't bother to show up for final exams.

5. His twin sister Carla was alarmed when Calvin didn't come home.

6. The Careless twins who are very close look out for each other.

7. All students who are very close look out for each other.

8. Calvin who was feeling terrible about what he had done started the drive back home.

Answers on page 363.

QUIZ YOURSELF ON STEP ONE Fill in the blanks with the best answer.

_____ **1.** T or F. If the title of your composition is a complete sentence, put a period after it.

_____ **2.** T or F. It is all right to abbreviate personal titles (Dr., Prof., Ms., etc.) before the person's name.

_____ **3.** When typing, how many spaces should you leave after a period at the end of the sentence?   (a) one.   (b) two.   (c) three.

_____ **4.** When typing, how many spaces should you leave after a period that follows an abbreviation?   (a) one.   (b) two.   (c) three.

_____ **5.** T or F. You do not need a question mark after a request or an order that is, out of courtesy, phrased as a question.

_____ **6.** Semicolons almost always do the same job as what other mark of punctuation?   (a) periods.   (b) commas.   (c) apostrophes.

_____ **7.** T or F. A semicolon connects elements of unequal rank, such as a main clause and a subordinate clause.

8. The main use of semicolons is to join two _____ that are closely related in meaning.

_____ **9.** T or F. Main clauses are usually connected by just a comma.

_____**10.** T or F. Main clauses can be connected by a comma and a coordinating conjunction.

_____**11.** T or F. One rule in grammar to which there are no exceptions states that you should use a comma at any place where you would pause when reading the sentence aloud.

Answers on page 363.

Step Two: Much-Needed Punctuation

Apostrophes

On most keyboards apostrophes are identical to single quotation marks, but they serve vastly different purposes.

1. Use an apostrophe to form the **possessive case** (possessive case indicates "belonging to") of nouns and most indefinite pronouns. This is its most common use. Whether the words are singular or plural, make all words not ending in s possessive by adding apostrophe + *s*.

- Of the *airplane's* flights that December day in 1903, the fourth *flight's* 852 feet in 59 seconds was considered a miracle.
- Although five persons besides the Wrights witnessed the flights, *no one's* account of this historic event made Orville *Wright's* hometown newspaper the next day.
- one boy's hat
- the fox's tail
- the children's books
- the alumni's get-together
- Mrs. Perez's dog
- the geese's nest
- the men's room
- my two sisters-in-law's letters

Making words ending in s possessive raises the question of whether to use just an apostrophe or an apostrophe + s. Opinions differ. The simplest rule, one that will almost please almost all authorities almost all the time, is this: Make all words that end in s possessive by adding the apostrophe only. It does not matter whether the word ending in s is singular or plural, whether it is one syllable or more, or whether adding the s adds a syllable to the pronunciation. If it ends in s, use the apostrophe only, not the apostrophe and then another s.

- *Inventors'* work is often slow and painstaking.
- The Wright *brothers'* airplane was called the *Kitty Hawk* after the North Carolina town where the plane first became airborne.

- One *witness'* account called the flight "miraculous."
- Two other *witnesses'* accounts of what happened were different.

More Examples

- the boss' secretary
- the bosses' secretaries
- Mr. Jones' house
- the Joneses' house
- Keats' poems
- the wives' classes

- three foxes' tails
- Mrs. Perkins' cat
- many industries' losses
- the Perezes' yard
- Los Angeles' smog
- 10 pansies' leaves

Be aware that adding an apostrophe to an *s*-ending word sometimes adds a syllable to the pronunciation: *boss'* = two syllables, *wives'* = one syllable, *Keats'* may be either one or two syllables.

This Will Save You Time and Trouble

First write the word you want to make possessive. If the word does not end in *s,* add apostrophe + *s.* If it ends in *s,* add only the apostrophe. It isn't very hard to master possessives.

- one *boy*   one boy's mother
- one *book*   one book's cover
- one *day*   one day's work
- one *dollar*   one dollar's worth
- He took one month's vacation.
  BUT He took a one-month vacation.

- two *boys*   two boys' mothers
- two *books*   two books' covers
- five *days*   five days' work
- five *dollars*   five dollars' worth
- She took five months' vacation.
  She took a five-month vacation.

NOTE: Possessive pronouns do not take apostrophes; possession is built into the word: *my, mine, your, yours, his, her, hers, its, our, ours, your, yours, their, theirs, whose.*

Causing the most trouble is *its.* When the apostrophe is used (*it's*), the word formed always means *it is; it's* is a contraction, not a pronoun in possessive case. For the possessive, meaning *belonging to it,* always use *its* with no apostrophe.

- *It's* (it is) too bad that the dog hurt *its* (belonging to it) paw.

If two or more people own the same thing **(joint possession),** use an apostrophe after only the last person's name. To indicate separate possession, make each person's name possessive.

- Where would the world be without Orville and Wilbur's invention? (joint possession, one invention, the airplane).
- Where would the world be without Thomas Edison's and Alexander Graham Bell's inventions? (separate inventions).

BUT when a possessive pronoun (*my* in the following example) is used for one of the people in an example of joint possession, make the other person's name possessive too.

- It was John's and my idea to learn about inventors.

Awkward situations arise in making possessive a noun followed by an appositive. Make only the appositive possessive, and omit the comma that usually follows an appositive—or rewrite the sentence!

- Otto Lilienthal, a German glider pilot, inspired the Wright brothers. A comma belongs after the appositive *a German glider pilot* when it is not possessive).
- CORRECT: The Wright brothers became interested in flying by reading about Otto Lilienthal, *a German glider pilot's* exploits.
- OR REWRITE: The Wright brothers became interested in flying by reading about the exploits of Otto Lilienthal, a German glider pilot.

Usually use the possessive form of a noun or pronoun before a gerund (a verb form ending in *ing* but used as a noun, not a verb).

- *Wilbur's serving* as president of the Wright Company the last three years of his life may have contributed to *his becoming* ill.
- The Wright brothers are American heroes; *their inventing* the airplane is the reason for *our studying* their lives.

BUT BE REASONABLE: Don't use the possessive before the gerund if it sounds ridiculous.

- RIDICULOUS: They worked and worked on a gigantic two-winged machine; their hard work finally resulted in *this' flying*.
- INSTEAD: . . . their hard work finally resulted in this machine's flying.

Sometimes you should change the wording for smooth reading. Often a prepositional phrase beginning with *of, in,* or *at* is less awkward than the possessive of inanimate objects or of things already possessive.

- AWKWARD: Pop's' merchandise was damaged by fire. (Pop's was my favorite store.)
- BETTER: The merchandise at Pop's was damaged by fire.
- AWKWARD: The Kitty Hawk was exhibited at London's South Kensington's Science Museum's Aviation Department for 20 years before being placed in Washington, D.C.'s Smithsonian Institution.
- BETTER: The Kitty Hawk was exhibited in the Aviation Department of the Science Museum at South Kensington, London, before being placed in the Smithsonian Institution in Washington, D.C.
- AWKWARD: My car's tire's air was low, and my desk's leg broke.
- BETTER: The air in the tire of my car was low, and the leg of my desk broke.
- AWKWARD: One of my friends' grandfather knew Orville Wright.
- BETTER: The grandfather of one of my friends knew Orville Wright.

NOTE: As just illustrated, *of* phrases are frequently used to show possession (the *dog's* tail = the tail *of the dog*). The object of the preposition (*dog*) should usually not be in the possessive form (NOT the tail of the *dog's*). There are, however, some idiomatic exceptions.

- He was a friend of *Wilbur's*. He is a student of *mine*.
- BETTER: He was Wilbur's friend. He is my student. Avoid the idiomatic construction.

Form the **possessive of singular and plural abbreviations,** including acronyms and initialisms, the same way you form the possessive of singular and plural nouns: add apostrophe + *s* to those not ending in *s* and just an apostrophe to the those ending in *s*.

- the FBI's investigation
- one C.P.A.'s testimony
- Potter Co.'s policy
- a B.S.' requirements
- KISS' advice (Keep it simple, Stupid)
- one M.D.'s opinions
- two M.D.s' opinions
- Halle Bros.' building

In names of companies and institutions and publications, use the apostrophe as the company or institution or publication prefers. For holidays, use the apostrophe as it is ordinarily used, even though this may not be logical.

- *Reader's Digest*
- *Ladies' Home Journal*
- Stouffer's
- Marsh Bros. Ford
- Veterans Administration
- Sears Car and Truck Rental
- Women's Federal Bank
- Trotter Bros.' Ford
- Veterans Day
- Presidents' Day
- Mother's Day
- New Year's Day

Sometimes it is hard to tell whether an adjective is truly possessive or merely descriptive: He belonged to the *employees'* or *employees* union? More and more, words like this are being considered adjectives rather than possessives and are being written with no apostrophe. Follow your company's or your school's style, but if in doubt, use the possessive form.

2. Use an apostrophe to replace **missing letters or numbers.** Apostrophes replace the missing letters in contractions. Contractions should not be used in formal writing (scientific publications and academic journals), but they may be used (sparingly) in the type of writing most of us do—even in class assignments, which are on a high-informal level, unless your instructor tells you otherwise. Avoid those that are awkward (*there's been* = there has been, *could've* = could have). Some common contractions follow.

- I'll = I will (apostrophe replaces the *wi* in *will* that is left out).
- let's = let us (apostrophe replaces the *u* in *us* that is left out).
- doesn't = does not, don't = do not (apostrophe replaces the *o* in *not* that is left out).
- can't= can not (apostrophe replaces the *no* in *not* that is left out).
- he's = he is, there's = there is (apostrophe replaces the *i* in *is* that is left out).
- she'd = she would (apostrophe replaces the *woul* in *would* that is left out) or she had (apostrophe replaces the *ha* in *had* that is left out).

- they're = they are (apostrophe replaces the *a* in *are* that is left out).
- it's = it is (apostrophe replaces the *i* in *is* that is omitted).
- won't = will not (this unusual contraction is from the Middle English *wol not;* Middle English was spoken from 1100 to 1500).
- o'clock = of the clock (apostrophe replaces the *f* and the *the* that are left out). PREDICTION: I bet that the apostrophe in o'clock will, by the 22nd century at least, be dropped just as the apostrophe in Halloween has been. It started out Hallowe'en, meaning All Hallows Evening. BUT I doubt that I'll be around in 2100 to collect my bet.

BE CAREFUL: Put your contraction apostrophes in the right place—where the letters are missing. I have had many students write contractions (WRONG) *did'nt, is'nt,* instead of (RIGHT) *didn't, isn't.*

Use an apostrophe to show the omission of the first two numerals in years.

- He was in the class of '40, but he said he would have preferred life in the '20s.

3. There is a distinct tendency to overdose on apostrophes, but you sometimes need to use an apostrophe for **clarity** in forming certain plurals. Usually, however, do *not* use the apostrophe to form plurals.

An apostrophe and *s* are usually needed for clarity in making plurals of lowercase letters.

- He put too many *i*'s in *Mississippi.* Misreading might result from no apostrophe—too many *is*—in spite of the fact that the *i* is supposed to be italicized or underlined and the *s* not.
- Mind your *p*'s and *q*'s. This is clearer than Mind your *ps* and *qs.*

You usually need an apostrophe and *s* for clarity in making plurals of lowercase abbreviations (don't italicize the *s*).

- Even in informal writing, don't use too many *i.e.*'s.

Sometimes you need an apostrophe and *s* for clarity in making plurals of words used as illustrations (don't italicize the *s*).

- In singing scales he always missed his *ti*'s. This could be misread without apostrophe: *tis.*
- In the Bible there are too many *ye*'s and *thou*'s. This could be misread without apostrophes: *yes* and *thous.*
- BUT: Don't use so many *really*s in your writing. This is clear without apostrophe.

If you are making the plural from a singular word already containing an apostrophe, just add *s,* not an apostrophe and *s.* A good example occurs if you are referring to words as words.

- He had too many *can't*s in his vocabulary (not *can't*'s) but not enough *do*'s and *don't*s (not *don't*'s).

Do not use apostrophes to make numerals plural.

- The 1930s were years of depression.
- My typewriter sometimes sticks and prints a row of 3s.
- Our company is always late sending out W-2s.

Do not use an apostrophe to make plurals of capital letters or abbreviations ending in capital letters, unless the apostrophe improves clarity.

- CLEAR: The president and the dean were both Ph.D.s.
- CLEAR: The instructor asked all the students for IDs and IQs. In this unlikely event, he no doubt also asked how many TVs they had and how many were working toward B.A.s.
- CORRECT: I got two A's on my report card. As could possibly be misread without the apostrophe; Cs probably would be clear. But be consistent— if you write A's, also write C's.

4. Use proper **spacing.** The apostrophe is considered part of the word it is used with, so when typing, do not leave a space between the word and its apostrophe. There is no space between an apostrophe and another mark of punctuation that immediately follows.

- The idea was the girls', not the boys'.
- The idea was the counselors', but the campers claimed credit.
- Wasn't the idea really the parents'?

An apostrophe at the end of a sentence (*boys'* in the example above) looks just like a final single quotation mark (which should always go *outside* the period); but the apostrophe, being part of the word it is used with, goes inside other punctuation at the end of a sentence.

EXERCISE 5.6 Put in apostrophes where needed.

1. Kates Aunt Betty was upset about Kates carelessness, but she realized its hard to remember keys when one is in a hurry.

2. Calvin explained that his parents irresponsibility, including drug abuse, had left him and his sister in bad shape; the parents walking out on their children, leaving the rent unpaid, forced the twins to get jobs and find a small apartment.

3. Calvin had found that its hard to make Cs at school while working 40 hours a week as a maintenance persons assistants assistant, and Carlas working every evening as a waitress had certainly interfered with her getting As.

4. The apartments furnishings left much to be desired, resulting in Calvins sleeping on a mattress on the floor.

5. Carlas grades were average; Calvins were poor.

6. TVs distraction was no problem, though, because they couldnt afford one.

7. But they had looked into a B.S.s requirements and thought theyd eventually be able to get bachelors degrees.

8. "When I saw the keys in Kates car, I was overwhelmed with the thought of a few days vacation," said Calvin.

9. "Wasnt I stupid! Ive even lost my job."

10. When Kate and her aunt and uncle learned of Calvin and Carlas hardship, they did not press charges for Calvins having made such a bad mistake.

11. "Calvin and Carlas troubles arent entirely their fault. Lets try to help them," said Aunt Betty.

12. Kates uncle got Calvin a job running errands in his law firm, 30 hours work for more money than hed been making; Aunt Betty took Carla clothes shopping.

13. The two students gratitude was genuine.

14. Calvins goals now include law school, and Carlas include a career in fashion design.

Answers on page 363.

Double Quotation Marks

1. Use double quotation marks at the beginning and at the end of **direct quotations** (exact words spoken or thought or quoted from a book or other publication).

- EXACT WORDS SPOKEN: She said, "Please call me sometime." The periods always go inside final quotation marks.

- EXACT WORDS SPOKEN: "I'll call you next week," I replied. The commas always go inside final quotation marks.
- EXACT WORDS SPOKEN: "We need to talk about the next meeting," she added, "and when to have the election."
- EXACT WORDS THOUGHT: I thought, "Please do your homework instead of using the phone."
- EXACT WORDS QUOTED FROM A PLAY: In Act II of *Romeo and Juliet,* Juliet speaks her immortal words, "Parting is such sweet sorrow."

Periods and commas always go inside final quotation marks. Students have trouble accepting this fact.

A direct quotation, repeating the exact words someone has said or written, is usually more effective than an **indirect quotation,** retelling what someone has said or written without using the exact words. Direct quotations are placed within quotation marks; indirect quotations do not require quotation marks.

- DIRECT QUOTATION: "Hand in your papers after class," said Ms. Larue.
- INDIRECT QUOTATION: Ms. Larue told us to hand in our papers after class.
- DIRECT QUOTATION: "Mine will be late because I've been sick," said Kate.
- INDIRECT QUOTATION: Kate said hers would be late because she had been been sick.
- DIRECT QUOTATION: When Alexander Graham Bell's first telephone picked up a sound from Thomas Watson in the next room, Bell told Watson, "Don't change a thing."
- INDIRECT QUOTATION: When Alexander Graham Bell's first telephone picked up a sound from Thomas Watson in the next room, Bell told Watson not to change a thing.

Paraphrasing, restating in your own words what another person has said or written, is a third way of "quoting" someone, a technique often used to state difficult material more simply.

- ORIGINAL MATERIAL: "It is imperative that a total personnel effort be mounted to the end that our production quotas may be elevated to a more significant level," said the manager.
- PARAPHRASED MATERIAL: We all must work harder to produce more, according to the manager. No quotation marks are needed.

VERY IMPORTANT: No matter whether you are quoting directly, quoting indirectly, or paraphrasing—or even just using someone else's idea—you need to acknowledge your source. In a footnote, an end note, or within the text, let the reader know where you got the information. Don't be guilty of plagiarism.

2. Do *not* put **separate quotation marks** around each sentence in a paragraph that one person is speaking. Just put quotation marks at the beginning of the quotation and at the end.

- WRONG: The teacher continued, "Quotation marks, like other marks of punctuation, are to help the reader." "He or she might be terribly confused without quotation marks." "But too many quotation marks are completely confusing." "I have had students put in a separate set of quotation marks for each sentence in a paragraph, as demonstrated here." "The reader can't tell that one person is saying all of this." Put beginning double quotation marks before the first word that is quoted, *Quotation,* and end double quotation marks after the last word, *this.*

3. And if one person speaks **more than one paragraph** or something you are quoting (from a book) continues for more than one paragraph, put double quotation marks at the start of each paragraph and at the end of only the last paragraph.

- MORE THAN ONE PARAGRAPH BY ONE SPEAKER:

    "Mrs. Murphy," asked the student, "who invented the telephone?"
    (Now follows more than one paragraph by one speaker.)
    "Well," she replied, "the inventor was an American scientist named Alexander Graham Bell. He lived from 1847 to 1922. He grew up in Scotland. His father was a speech instructor, specializing in teaching deaf-mutes to speak.
    "Alexander attended the University of Edinburgh for one year and the University of London for one year, studying speech and hearing.
    "When his family moved to Canada, Alexander got a job teaching at a school for the deaf in Boston. Then he opened his own school for the deaf, later marrying one of his pupils."

Put beginning quotation marks at the beginning of each paragraph so the reader will know all paragraphs are still part of the same quote. But don't use final quotation marks until the end of the last paragraph; if you put them at the end of each paragraph, the reader will think the person speaking has finished and the next paragraph is a new speaker.

4. Use double quotation marks for **dialogue,** conversation between two or more people. Start a new paragraph each time the speaker changes, even if one paragraph consists only of "Ugh."

- DIALOGUE, TWO SPEAKERS: "Hello," I said, responding to the insistence of the phone's ringing.

    "Mrs. Taylor, how *are* you?" inquired a voice full of phony caring.
    "Fine," I replied. I wished I'd had the courage to add, "Who are *you,* and why do you care?"

> The syrupy-sweet voice continued, "Mrs. Taylor, you have been selected to invest your money in a sure thing, guaranteed to pay you a 25-percent annual return. Aren't you delighted?"
> "No."
> "Now, Mrs. Taylor. I know better than that."
> "Thank you for calling. I am going to hang up." And I did.
> "Why do junk calls always come at mealtime?" I thought. "Why does the telephone company charge to *not* list your number?"

5. Use double quotation marks (not single quotation marks, as many people wrongly do) before and after **short quoted expressions or words.**

- WRONG: My friend says her phone is 'a real bother'; she calls it 'the world's worst interrupter.' Double quotation marks should be used.
- RIGHT: In 1876 the British scientist William Thomson said Alexander Graham Bell's invention was "the greatest marvel hitherto achieved by the electric telegraph"; others said it was "miraculous." Periods and commas go inside final quotation marks even if the quotation is only one word. Colons and semicolons go outside final quotation marks.

6. "Set off" **long quotations** of prose or poetry (more than four typed lines of prose and more than three typed lines of poetry) instead of enclosing them in quotation marks. Setting off means indenting the quoted passages on both left and right margins.

> Authorities differ on the margin width and on the spacing of long quoted passages. Some say indent 10 spaces from the left; others say five from each side. Some say double space; others say single space. At least everyone seems to agree that quotation marks should not be used unless they were in the original material. Naturally you will follow the style that your instructor or your boss recommends. But I think it looks rather nice like this, don't you?

7. Put three or fewer lines of **quoted poetry** in quotation marks within the text, separated by slashes.

- Elizabeth Barrett Browning's famous sonnet asks, "How do I love thee? Let me count the ways. / I love you to the depth and breadth and height / My soul can reach . . . "

8. Enclose in double quotation marks (many people mistakenly use single quotation marks) **words used in a special sense** (nonstandard words, slang, words used with a double meaning, words used the first time that might be new to the reader). Periods and commas go inside the final double quotation marks, even if the quotation is only one word.

- Not realizing the potential of the telephone, many thought it was just a "flash in the pan" or downright "kooky."
- Perhaps the most unexpected phenomenon spawned by Bell's invention was "telemarketing," selling by telephone.

NOTE: If you use a word in a special sense or use a term the reader might not understand, put it in quotation marks *only the first time* it is used.

9. Use double quotation marks for **minor titles,** such as the titles of poems and articles; major titles, such as the titles of books and magazines in which poems and articles are published, should be italicized. See page 341 for a complete listing.

IMPORTANT: Don't enclose the title of *your* composition in quotation marks. Don't underline it, italicize it, or put it in all capital letters either. Don't put a period after a title even if it is a complete sentence; do put a question mark or an exclamation point if needed. The title of your composition would be enclosed in quotation marks only if it is referred to by someone else in his or her work or if you have used the title of an article, a poem, or a short story as the title of your composition.

- WRONG FOR THE TITLE OF YOUR COMPOSITION: "My Summer Vacation"
- RIGHT: My Summer Vacation
- RIGHT: (if you are writing about the poem by Gwendolyn Brooks and want to call your composition the name of the poem): "We Real Cool"

10. Use proper **spacing.** If no other mark of punctuation is involved, put double quotation marks up against words they enclose (no space). Sometimes, however, a comma or a sentence-ending punctuation mark is needed between the last word in the quotation and the final quotation mark.

- RIGHT: "The telephone is a mixed blessing," said Mrs. Murphy, "but I wouldn't want to be without it."

Use question marks with end quotation marks as follows: If what is inside the quotation marks is the question, put the question mark inside the quotation marks. If the whole sentence, but not what is inside the quotation marks, is the question, put the question mark outside the quotation marks. If both the quote and the whole sentence are questions, use only one question mark, the one inside the quotation marks.

- WRONG: Alexander Graham Bell said, "Do you think telephone wires are hollow?". Omit the period; the question mark is enough. The question mark belongs *inside* the final quotation marks because the quote is the question, not the whole sentence.

- WRONG: Did Alexander Graham Bell really say, "Do you think telephone wires are hollow?"? Even though both the sentence and the quote are questions, one question mark does the job. Use the one *inside* the quotation marks; omit the one outside the quotation marks.
- RIGHT: Alexander Graham Bell said, "Can you hear me?" The question mark belongs *inside* the final quotation marks because the quote, not the whole sentence, is the question.
- RIGHT: Did Alexander Graham Bell say, "The voice is transmitted by waves of electricity"? Here the sentence, not the quote, is the question, so the question mark goes *outside* the quotation marks.
- RIGHT: Is it true that all Bell heard in that first telephone "conversation" was a faint "twang"? The sentence, not the quote, is the question, so the question mark goes *outside* the quotation marks.
- RIGHT: Did Alexander Graham Bell say, "What hath God wrought?" Both the quote and the whole sentence are questions, but use only one question mark, the one *inside* the quotation marks.

Use exclamation points with quotation marks in the same way as question marks with quotation marks.

- I'm leaving if I hear one more "Shut up!"
- Don't tell me "Keep calm"!

A RULE TO REMEMBER: Whether to place question marks and exclamation points inside or outside final quotation marks depends on whether the quotation or the whole sentence is the question or the exclamation. But there is one rule to which there are no exceptions: **Periods and commas always go inside (before) final quotation marks, both double and single.** I am repeating this because students so often don't believe it. **Colons and semicolons always go outside (after) final quotation marks, both double and single.**

EXERCISE 5.7 Put in double quotation marks where they belong. Write very carefully so that it is clear whether the quotation marks belong before or after a period or other mark of punctuation. One sentence is correct.

1. Exactly what is a shooting star? you ask.
2. Let's pretend the tour guide at the Museum of Natural Science is answering this question. A shooting star is a meteor, a metallic or stony piece of matter from space that falls to earth, he says.
3. Did he say, It falls to earth from somewhere out in space?
4. Gracious! you say. What if someone gets hit by it?

5. Did you say, What if someone gets hit by it?

6. Did you hear the guide say that they become visible only when they enter the earth's atmosphere?

7. When they enter the earth's atmosphere, the guide says, friction heats them to about 4,000 degrees Fahrenheit, making them glow so that we can see them.

8. Do very many hit the earth? you ask.

9. No, the guide replies. You might like to read this article explaining the process.

10. He hands you a copy of Why Falling Stars Are Not Really Stars Falling from a recent news magazine.

11. There is an expression, a meteoric rise to fame, which refers to a new high in one's career.

12. Used in an opposite way in *King Richard II,* Shakespeare's expression was, I see thy glory like a shooting star / Fall to the base earth from the firmament.

Answers on page 364.

Single Quotation Marks

If you are typing, use the apostrophe key for single quotation marks.

1. Use single quotation marks for only one purpose: to enclose a **quotation** that appears **within another quotation** (the first quotation is already enclosed in double quotation marks). The single quotation marks clearly separate the second quotation from the first.

- DIRECT QUOTATION (within the first quotation): My son told his friend on the phone, "I overheard Mark say to John, 'A bunch of us aren't going to do our homework tonight.'"
- QUOTED EXPRESSION (within the first quotation): "The word *telephone* comes from Greek words meaning 'to speak from afar,'" Mrs. Murphy told the student.

NOTE: Single and double quotation marks are typed with no space between them.

- WORD USED IN A SPECIAL SENSE (i.e., slang or nonstandard use, within the first quotation): John said, "Mark, be our 'mouthpiece' and defend us for not doing our homework."
- MINOR TITLE (within the first quotation): The instructor said, "Call me if you have any trouble understanding 'A Rose for Emily,' the short story in the new anthology."

If it weren't for the fact that these direct quotations, quoted expressions, words used in a special sense, and minor titles occur within the first quotation, they themselves would be placed in double quotation marks.

2. If a **quotation within a quotation within a quotation** occurs, it is usually wise to rewrite the sentence. However, the rules of grammar do make provision for such an occurrence: Revert to double quotation marks for the third quotation.

- AWKWARD: My daughter complained, "Please don't keep saying, 'Hang up the phone and get started reading "The Killers."'"
- BETTER (use indirect quotations): My daughter complained about my constantly telling her to hang up the phone and to start reading "The Killers."

Many well-educated people, as we have said, make the mistake of using single quotation marks around short quoted expressions, words used in a special sense (such as slang or nonstandard use of words), or minor titles. All of these should be in double quotation marks unless, of course, these quoted words are within another quotation.

- WRONG (quoted expression): The telephone is sometimes called 'a teenager's best friend.' Use double quotation marks.
- RIGHT: The telephone is sometimes called "a teenager's best friend."
- RIGHT: She said, "The telephone is sometimes called 'a teenager's best friend.'" This is a quote within a quote.
- WRONG (word used in a special sense): My daughter has labeled one of her friends who is always on the phone a 'ding-a-ling.' Use double quotation marks.
- WRONG (minor title): Who wrote the poem 'Trees'? Use double quotation marks.
- RIGHT: The student asked, "Who wrote the poem 'Trees'?" And then she asked, "Who wrote 'How Do I Love Thee?'"

3. Use proper **spacing.** When typing, put single quotation marks up against the words they enclose (no space) unless an additional mark of punctuation is needed between the last word in the quotation and the final quotation mark. Single quotation marks are treated the same way double quotation marks are when other marks of punctuation are also involved. If single and double quotation marks come together, there should be no space between them.

EXERCISE 5.8 Put in double quotation marks and single quotation marks where they belong. Write very carefully so that it is clear whether the quotation marks belong before or after a period or other mark of punctuation.

1. The guide at the museum told us, This article, Why Falling Stars Are Not Really Stars Falling, says, Meteors which fall to earth without burning up are called meteorites.

2. A woman in the crowd said, My son asked, What are meteorites made from? Can you answer that?

3. There are two kinds of meteorites, replied the guide. So-called stony meteorites are made up of stony materials resembling minerals from volcanoes. Iron meteorites consist mainly of iron combined with nickel.

4. Fortunately, concluded the guide, most meteors burn up completely before they hit Spaceship Earth.

Answers on page 365.

Italics (Underlining)

When using a conventional typewriter (without italics) or writing by hand, underline words to be italicized.

- If your keyboard does not have italics or if you are writing by hand: Have you read <u>War and Peace</u>?
- If your keyboard has italics: Have you read *War and Peace*?

1. Italicize **major titles.** Major titles include the titles of works published separately, by themselves, separate entities, such as books, plays, magazines, newspapers, and pamphlets (but not chapters, articles, and poems, all of which are published within the major works). The title of a very long poem, published by itself (William Wordsworth's *The Prelude,* for example), is italicized.

Major titles also include the names of films; television and radio programs (but not the names of episodes); operas, musicals, long musical compositions, and albums (but not individual songs, which are often parts of a longer recording); software programs, disks, cassettes, and CDs; works of art, such as paintings and sculptures; and ships, trains, aircraft, spacecraft, and satellites.

Although they are usually published within a larger publication, comic strips are considered a separate entity, and their titles are italicized. Also, there is some disagreement on whether names of trains (the *Orient Express*) should be italicized (let's do), but there is general agreement that types and models of vehicles are not italicized.

- I'd rather ride in my Chevy Cavalier than fly in a Boeing 747 or even a Concorde.

2. This seems the logical place to list minor titles (of works published *within* major works) too. Enclose **minor titles in double quotation marks** (do *not* italicize). This would include chapter titles in a book as well as the titles of short stories, essays, articles, most poems (all but very long poems published by themselves), episodes of TV and radio programs (but not the names of the programs), songs, and parts of longer recordings.

- Edgar Allan Poe's 1843 short story "The Gold-Bug" had its origin in his article "Cryptography," published in *Graham's Magazine* in 1841.
- The song "Memory" from the musical *Cats* has a haunting melody.

EXCEPTIONS: Don't use either italics or quotation marks for the Bible, books of the Bible (Genesis 1:1), the Torah, or other holy books.

The box below presents a summary of which titles should be italicized and which should be placed in double quotation marks.

Italics for Titles of Major Works, Published by Themselves	Quotation Marks for Titles of Minor Works, Published Within Major Works
Books	Chapters
Magazines	Magazine articles
	Short stories (published in books or magazines)
Newspapers	Newspaper articles
	Essays (published in books, magazines, or newspapers)
Very long poems (published by themselves)	Short poems (published in books, magazines, or newspapers)
Plays	
Pamphlets	
Films	
TV and radio programs	Episodes of TV and radio programs
Operas, musicals, long musical compositions, albums	Songs, parts of longer recordings
Software programs, disks, cassettes, CDs	
Works of art: paintings, sculptures	
Ships, trains, aircraft, spacecraft, satellites	
Comic strips (even though published within larger work)	

To find out which words in titles should be capitalized, see Chapter 6, page 373.

3. Italicize a word when the word itself is used as an illustration, and do the same for a letter or numeral used as an **illustration.**

- Many people incorrectly use *an* instead of *a* before the word *historian;* most of us use too many *and*s.

Do not italicize the *s* that makes the word itself—or the numeral itself, in the example below—plural.

- My address has three *13*s in it; the street is spelled *Lukke* but pronounced *Lucky,* as if the first *k* were a *c* and the last two letters were *ky* instead of *ke.*

4. You may want to italicize or underline words you want to **emphasize,** but do it sparingly. Too many emphasized words lose their effect.

5. Italicize **foreign words** that have not yet become common English usage. Italicize scientific names of plants and animals. Consult your dictionary.

- *Mon ami,* this is a lovely party, *n'est-ce pas? Bon appétit.*
- His letter, full of clichés, invited me to a rendezvous at our alma mater (*clichés, rendezvous,* and *alma mater* have all been assimilated into our language and no longer require italicizing).

6. If any italicized numerals, symbols, letters, or words are to be made **plural,** do not italicize the *s* that makes them plural.

- Good advice is not to use many *I*'s in your writing, be wary of *very*s, don't use *&*s, and don't put too many *4*s in 1492.

7. If something **already in italics** needs to be italicized again, put it in regular (roman) print.

- I just bought a book called *All About the Word* Love *and More.*

EXERCISE 5.9 Underline what should be italicized in the following sentences. There are also some minor titles, which need to be enclosed in quotation marks. One sentence is correct.

1. Books on the summer reading list include David Copperfield and Tom Sawyer.

2. The English literature instructor suggested that the class watch Shakespeare's Macbeth on television instead of Murder She Wrote or L.A. Law.

3. An article in The New York Times called The Election Is Over gives the reader an idea of what will happen next.

4. Robert Frost's The Road Not Taken, which you can find in the text Sound and Sense, deals with the problem of making choices.

5. So many words rhyme with June that June seems to be a favorite month of poets.

6. Just as it is annoying to hear someone use too many you knows in speaking, it is hard on the reader to come across a basically in every paragraph.

7. A riddle I knew as a child went like this: "Railroad crossing, look out for the cars; can you spell this without any r's?" The answer, of course, was t-h-i-s.

8. The comic strip Peanuts shows Charlie Brown looking at the famous painting Mona Lisa and saying, "I think she knows something we don't know."

9. In the sinking of the Titanic in 1912, 1,517 pasengers and crew members lost their lives even though the steamship Carpathia rescued 706 persons.

10. When the crooked politician preached "Honesty is the best policy," by honesty he evidently meant not getting caught.

11. He based his sermon on Job, a book from the Bible.

12. My favorite part of the album Oklahoma is the title song, Oklahoma.

Answers on page 365.

Hyphens

It is little wonder that hyphens are a bit hard to handle—they serve two opposite functions: to join and to divide words.

1. Use a hyphen to **divide a word at the end of a line** of writing or type if the word is too long to fit on the first line. Do *not* put the hyphen at the beginning of the second line. Any division should take place between syllables. Never hyphenate a one-syllable word. A word book (a "dictionary" without definitions or pronunciations) is a handy guide to both spelling and division of syllables. Computers may do some very strange word division if they are not carefully supervised.

Try not to hyphenate proper names, and try not to separate a title like Mr. or Ms. or a person's initials from his or her last name by placing part on one line and part on the next line. Don't hyphenate one-syllable words. Don't hyphenate after only one letter. Divide hyphenated expressions only at the hyphen.

- WRONG: The best way to make a good grade in English is to fre-eze your attention on the instructor and take voluminous notes.

If the one-syllable word won't fit on the first line, move the whole word to the second line.

- WRONG: If you have taken your notes in shorthand, you should be a-ware of the importance of transcribing them as soon as possible.

If *aware* won't fit on the first line, move the whole word to the second line.

- RIGHT: It was clear to the bride that she should not let her mother-in-law interfere too much.

The hyphenated words would be harder to read like this: moth-er-in-law.

2. Use a hyphen to join **two or more words** that function as a **single** (compound) **adjective before a noun.** (Omit the hyphen if the first word of the compound adjective is an adverb ending in *ly*.)

- BEFORE THE NOUN: The teacher enjoys teaching inner-city students. These are not *inner* students nor *city* students. The hyphen brings the two words together into a single adjective.
- AFTER THE NOUN: The highly successful teacher enjoys teaching students from the inner city. There is no hyphen between *highly* and *successful* because of the adverb ending in *ly*. There are no hyphens between *inner* and *city* because they come after the noun *students*.

WARNING: Hyphenated compound adjectives before nouns can easily be overdone. There are many commonly used compound adjectives that are conventionally left unhyphenated even before the noun, as in "The high school teacher left the high school building to go to the real estate office to check real estate prices." According to the rule, *high school* and *real estate* should be hyphenated, but let's not. Use your judgment, remembering that too many hyphens spoil the flow of reading. On the other hand, some words are so commonly used together as a compound adjective that the hyphen stays in no matter whether they are before or after the noun (hands-on, two-faced). Check your dictionary.

3. Use **suspended hyphens** in a series of compound words in which one element of each word remains the same and the other element changes. Omit the element of the compound that remains the same in all but the last (or the first) item of the series.

- The band was made up of first-, second-, and third-grade students; the fourth- and fifth-grade students had their own group. Note proper spacing after suspended hyphens.
- Well-conceived, -planned, and -executed maneuvers win wars.

4. Use a hyphen to join **two or more words** that function as a **single** (compound) **noun or verb.** *Self, well,* and *ex* are usually joined to the following word by a hyphen.

- NOUNS: self-esteem, well-being, ex-wife, sixth-grader, one-year-old
- VERBS: double-cross, stir-fry, test-drive, hand-deliver
- ALSO: Women when they marry often use their maiden name connected by a hyphen to their married name.

If in doubt about compound words, consult a dictionary or word book. Similar compound expressions may be hyphenated, written as one word, or written as separate words. If the compound expression is not in the dictionary or word book, it is written as separate words.

5. Use a hyphen to join a **prefix** to a capitalized word or to numerals, as in un-American, anti-Semitic, mid-1990s, and post-Elizabethan.

6. Use a hyphen to make compound **numbers** like *twenty-one,* to write fractions like *two-thirds* (unless the spelled-out form is too awkward, as spelling out *425/593* would be), to separate the first five from the last four zip-code digits as in Cleveland OH 44122-6195, and to separate Social Security numbers after the third and fifth digit.

7. Use a hyphen for **clarity.**

- NOT: I liked the recreation (play facilities) of the pioneer village IF what you mean is, I liked the re-creation (rebuilding) of the pioneer village.

The trend is toward not hyphenating those awkward double-vowel combinations that always used to be hyphenated, like *reentry* and *semiilluminated.* But I certainly would not fault your putting a hyphen in a word like *re-echo* to prevent the reader's stumbling over *reecho.*

8. In an expression of more than one word which needs to be connected to another word or expression by a hyphen, hyphenate only the **last word** of the first expression.

- RIGHT: He spoke to the Madison County-based attorney.
- UNNECESSARY HYPHEN: He spoke to the Madison-County-based attorney.

Do not follow this last rule if the result is strange:

- He told his story to the blue apron-clad volunteer. Here you need also a hyphen between *blue* and *apron* to make it clear that the apron was blue and not the volunteer.

9. Use proper **spacing** and **capitalization.** Leave no space before and no space after a hyphen (unless, naturally, the hyphen divides a word at the end of a line). A common error is to use a hyphen with a space before and after it instead of a dash. See the section on dashes on pages 350-352.

Capitalize proper nouns and proper adjectives in a hyphenated expression. In a title or subtitle, capitalize the first and last words of a hyphenated expression and all other words except articles, conjunctions and prepositions of two or three letters, and the *to* of an infinitive.

- She was anti-Republican.
- The chapter title was "The Hazards of a Do-or-Die-for-the-Job Attitude."
- He couldn't decide whether to call his book *The How-to-Be-Your-Own-Plumber Handbook* or *Be Your Own Plumber: The Handbook of How-To.*

EXERCISE 5.10 Insert hyphens where they are needed.

1. Olympic contests took place as early as 776 B.C. in Western Greece, according to sports loving historians.

2. But there may have been much earlier Olympic like games because athletics had long had religious significance for the ancient Greeks.

3. For many years the Olympics were completely male oriented, not including female contestants or even permitting female spectators.

4. The Olympics were a once every four years happening, and the only event in the first 13 Olympics was a 200 yard footrace.

5. Winning these races boosted the self esteem of the runners.

6. Added to the then renowned running competition in 708 B.C. was the pentathlon: discus throw, javelin throw, long jump, sprint, and wrestling.

7. The four horse chariot race was added in 680 B.C. and a near deadly boxing wrestling sport in 648 B.C.

8. After the Roman Empire invaded Greece in the mid 100s B.C., the games began to lose their deep seated religious meaning.

9. By 394 A.D. the games were no longer race oriented events, so they were discontinued, not to be held again for more than 1,500 years.

10. Modern type games began in Athens in 1896, with long excluded women first competing in 1900 and winter games beginning in 1924.

Answers on page 365.

Colons

1. Use a colon to introduce a **list or series or** just one **example** to be emphasized, after a sentence or main clause. This is its most common use. Do not capitalize the first word after the colon if it does not begin a complete sentence unless the word is a proper noun or adjective.

- Some of the "firsts" in the development of the telephone are the following: the first telephone installed in a private home (1877); the first use of telephone numbers—operators no longer had to memorize names of subscribers (1879); invention of the pay phone (1889); opening of a telephone line between New York and San Francisco (1915); time-of-day service (late 1920s); dial-a-prayer, -suicide, -poem, etc. (1950s); and Ma Bell's death from divestiture (1984).

- The telephone has helped cause the decline of a flourishing art of days gone by: letter writing. A comma instead of the colon would be grammatically correct preceding the appositive *letter writing,* but the colon lends more emphasis.

WARNING: When the colon introduces a list or a series or an example, be sure a complete sentence precedes the colon. Otherwise, the colon is not needed.

- WRONG: Imagine how Alexander Graham Bell would feel if he knew about: car phones, call waiting, wake-up calls, answering machines, faxing, paging, and beeping. The words before the colon are not a complete sentence.

- RIGHT: Omit the colon in the above sentence. OR SAY, Imagine how Alexander Graham Bell would feel if he knew about the things we take for granted: car phones, call waiting, wake-up calls, answering machines, faxing, paging, and beeping. The sentence before the colon is complete.

2. You may want to use a colon after a sentence or main clause to **introduce** a **second sentence** that explains the first. Grammatically, a semicolon would also be correct here, but a colon gives more emphasis to the second sentence.

Authorities agree that the first word of the sentence that follows a colon should be capitalized if it is a proper noun or proper adjective or if it begins a quoted sentence. Authorities are divided on whether to capitalize the first word of the second sentence if it does not begin with a proper noun or adjective or begin a quoted sentence, but many say do not capitalize the sentence after the colon if it explains or amplifies the sentence before the colon.

- In 1968 welfare authorities decreed that the cost of minimum local telephone service could be included in payments to needy persons along with allowances for food and shelter: the (OR The) telephone had come into its own as a necessity of life. I would accept either the uppercase or the lowercase *t* as correct. Certainly, the more closely the second sentence explains the first, the less need there is for a capital letter.)

3. Use a colon between **numerals** in time references and numerals in biblical chapters and verses.

- He ran the mile in 5:24 (five minutes, 24 seconds).
- He arrived at the finish line at 3:23 p.m. For even hours, leave off the :00, not 3:00 p.m. but rather 3 p.m.
- He picked up his Bible, and turned to Psalm 107:1. A period is sometimes used instead of a colon to separate Bible chapters and verses.

4. Use a colon between **titles** and **subtitles.**

- After receiving two calls from robots and three other telephone solicitations today, I feel like writing a book titled *Alexander Graham Bell's Invention: A Blessed Event or a Bothersome Baby*. Always capitalize the first word of the subtitle. See Chapter 6, page 373, for capitalization of other words in titles and subtitles.

5. Use a colon after the **salutation** of a business letter.

- Dear Dr. Jones:

BUT: Use a comma after the salutation of a personal letter.

6. Use a colon after a short **introductory** command or **words** calling attention to what follows.

- COMMAND: Beware: Have a telephone installed in your home at your own risk.

• WORDS CALLING ATTENTION TO WHAT FOLLOWS:
  Note: No. 1:   Wanted: Assignments: Phone numbers:

Capitalize the first word following a colon, if it starts on a new line, even if it is not a complete sentence.

• Location of phones:
    In the kitchen behind the door.
    In the library.
    By the pool.

7. Use a colon to separate speaker from spoken lines in a **play script.**

• JAQUES: All the world's a stage.

8. Use proper **spacing.** Usually leave no space before the colon and two spaces after it. In the case of its use between numerals, leave no space before or after.

EXERCISE 5.11 Put colons in the following sentences where needed. Two sentences do not need colons.

1. At the zoo you will find many animals lions, tigers, elephants, bears, giraffes, and monkeys.
2. At the zoo you will find lions, tigers, elephants, bears, giraffes, and monkeys.
3. There is one animal that is of special interest to children the kangaroo.
4. For some animals, cages are not necessary grassy or wooded areas surrounded by deep ditches or moats allow them to behave more naturally.
5. The zoo is open from 930 a.m. to 530 p.m.
6. The first group of animals that might qualify as a zoo was in Paris, France, in 1804 scientific study of the animals was the purpose.
7. Please note Collections of wild animals have been kept by kings and very rich citizens since before the time of Christ.
8. Have you seen the book, *The Zoo A Place of Fun for All?*
9. The dairy farm is second only to the zoo as a favorite place for second-grade field trips.

Answers on page 366.

QUIZ YOURSELF ON STEP TWO Fill in the blanks with the best answer.

_____ **1.** The most common use for the apostrophe is   (a) to end a sentence.   (b) to form the possessive case.   (c) to enclose parenthetical material.

_____ **2.** Which is the proper location for the apostrophe in this contraction? (a) di'dnt.   (b) did'nt.   (c) didn't.

_____ **3.** T or F. Although the apostrophe is usually *not* used in the formation of plurals, it *is* needed for clarity in certain plurals.

4. Double quotation marks are used to set off _____ quotations.

_____ **5.** T or F. If one person speaks a whole paragraph of sentences, each sentence should be set off separately in double quotation marks.

_____ **6.** Double quotation marks are never needed for   (a) a very short quotation.   (b) an indirect quotation.   (c) dialogue.

_____ **7.** Periods and commas *always* go   (a) inside (before)   (b) outside (after) final quotation marks.

_____ **8.** There is only one use for single quotation marks: (a) to enclose words used in a special sense.   (b) to enclose minor titles.   (c) to enclose a quotation within another quotation.

_____ **9.** Italicize   (a) major works, works published separately, by themselves.   (b) minor works, works published within major works.

_____**10.** T or F. Hyphens are used both to join and to divide words.

_____**11.** The most common use of the colon is   (a) to end a paragraph. (b) to introduce a list or series.   (c) to end an abbreviation.

Answers on page 366.

Step Three: May-Be-Needed Punctuation

Dashes

Dashes and hyphens are often confused. Just remember that dashes do not divide or join words as hyphens do; dashes set something off from the rest of the sentence, and dashes are twice as long as hyphens. If your keyboard has no dash, two hyphens may be used to make one dash.

1. Use a dash (or a pair of dashes, one before and one after) to set off a **parenthetical expression.** Commas and parentheses can do the same job, but dashes give more emphasis to the set-apart expressions. Single words, phrases, and whole sentences may be set off by dashes, especially expressions to be emphasized and expressions containing commas themselves (for clarity).

- Commas can be comical—yes, I said comical—if they are used in the wrong places.
- Parenthetical expressions—thoughts inserted in a sentence to add information, understanding, or emphasis—can be removed without distorting the meaning of the sentence.

2. Use a dash to introduce an **abrupt change of thought.**

- Studying punctuation is so tiring—I can hardly wait till school is out.

3. Use a dash to introduce or follow a **list or series.**

- We've studied every kind of verb in existence—transitive verbs, intransitive verbs, action verbs, being verbs, strong verbs, weak verbs, and absurd verbs, to name a few. A colon instead of the dash would also be correct.
- Common nouns, uncommon nouns, proper nouns, improper nouns—we've studied them all.

4. Use proper **spacing** and **capitalization.** Usually leave no space before or after a dash (and no space between the two hyphens that are used to make a dash when keyboards have none).

- Punctuation is logical—if you use the word loosely—and certainly very helpful to the reader.
- Would you rather—? Oh, why don't we decide that later. Leave two spaces after the question mark; capitalize the separate sentence that follows. An ellipsis instead of the dash would also be correct. See pages 356-357.
- But I thought— How can you be sure you're right? No period is needed after the first interrupted sentence; leave two spaces after the dash, and capitalize the separate sentence that follows. An ellipsis instead of the dash would also be correct.
- Dashes—aren't they handy marks of punctuation?—can easily be overused. No capital is needed for *aren't*.
- Punctuation—it may be the death of me—will be 50 percent of the test. No capital is needed for *it* and no period after *me*.
- The largest campus—the business school is there, at 25 Maple St.—is

closing in January. No capital is needed for *the;* the period after *St.* is used because of the abbreviation.

• Although spelling is hard to master—it is so illogical—I'll keep on trying. Omit the comma, normally required, after *master.*

NOTE: When a dash comes at the end of a line, if you have a choice, type the dash at the end of the first line rather than at the start of the next line.

ONE LAST WORD: Use dashes sparingly—they are real eye-stoppers to the reader.

EXERCISE 5.12 Insert hyphens or dashes in the proper places. You should find three places where dashes belong—two where a dash goes both before and after a parenthetical expression and one where a dash goes before only. Perhaps you should write the word *dash* to be sure the difference is clear between your hyphens and your dashes.

1. Listen to the fish story of the year probably of the century.
2. Marty Huotari is the yarn spinning fisherman.
3. He was in his fishing shanty on Clam Lake in Northern Michigan, catching good sized perch through a 48 by 20 inch hole in the ice.
4. Suddenly something struck his worm baited No. 12 hook tied to a six pound test monofilament line. (According to the rule, a hyphen is needed in *No.-12 hook;* but it would look so strange and it is not needed for clarity, so leave it out.)
5. His yard long rod bent nearly double.
6. For one and one half hours alternately reeling in, then letting out line he struggled with the impossible to catch fish.
7. When he finally got a look at it, he saw a giant sized muskie, hooked in the jaw cartilage rather than in the sharp toothed mouth, where the line would have been quickly cut.
8. Huotari yelled for much needed help, but no one was near enough to hear.
9. Finally he brought the head of the fish through the hole in the shanty floor, reached down as far as he could, wrapped his arms around the fish it was tired too and rolled out the shanty door onto the ice with the fish in his arms.
10. It was a 50 inch, 36 pound muskie, which he believes is a world record catch on a six pound test line.

Answers on page 367.

Parentheses

Parenthetical material is usually "nonessential" (it can be omitted without distorting the meaning of the sentence); but it adds information, understanding, or emphasis to the word or words it explains. As we have seen, commas are a common mark of punctuation used to set off parenthetical material; dashes and, of course, parentheses are also used for this purpose. Dashes place the most emphasis on the parenthetical elements; parentheses provide moderate emphasis; commas are the least emphatic.

1. Use parentheses to enclose **explanatory** (parenthetical) **material.**

- It can be confusing deciding whether to use a capital (uppercase) letter or a small (lowercase) letter at the beginning of words in book titles.

As with dashes, the best advice is to use parentheses sparingly (they are disruptive to the reader).

2. Use parentheses to enclose numbers or letters in an **itemized listing.**

- Grammar Hot Line calls indicate the biggest problems are (1) apostrophes, (2) hyphens, (3) semicolons, (4) case of pronouns, (5) pronoun-antecedent agreement, and (6) subject-verb agreement.

3. Use parentheses to explain the meaning of **uncommon terms,** terms your reader may not know, the first time they are used.

- She was a victim of hypoglycemia (low blood sugar). Hypoglycemia is an insidious condition that robs its victims of much of their energy.

4. Use parentheses to enclose **directions** to the reader **and references.**

- The exam will cover Chapters 1 and 2. (Be sure to review the first 10 pages.)
- His lecture was excellent (with material from *The World Book Encyclopedia*).

5. Use parentheses for **stage directions** in a play script. You may use brackets instead, but be consistent—use one or the other. (See the next section for brackets.)

- MRS. MURPHY (enthusiastically, going to chalkboard): We're going to work on punctuation again today.
- CLASS (groaning): Not that again!

6. Use proper **spacing** and **capitalization.** Do not leave a space between the parentheses and the material they enclose.

- WRONG: There is so much to learn (more than I thought) about parentheses.
- RIGHT: There is so much to learn (more than I thought) about parentheses.

If you have placed a "sentence in parentheses" within a bigger sentence, do not capitalize the first word of the sentence in parentheses (unless it is a proper noun or proper adjective) or put a period after it.

- Are parentheses (they seem so useless) really necessary?

If the expression enclosed in parentheses forms a question or exclamation, put a question mark or an exclamation point inside the final parenthesis.

- Parentheses (will I ever master them?) may be the death of me.

If a sentence in parentheses stands alone, i.e., is not part of another sentence, capitalize the first word and put end punctuation inside the final parenthesis.

- Don't use too many parentheses. (Parentheses break the smooth flow of the material.)

If you want to connect a sentence in parentheses (Sentence B) to the preceding sentence not in parentheses (Sentence A), put end punctuation *after* the final parenthesis of Sentence B.

- Don't use too many parentheses (parentheses break the smooth flow of the material).
- CORRECT BUT TOO MUCH END PUNCTUATION: Parentheses may be the death of me (will I ever master them?).
- INSTEAD: Parentheses may be the death of me. (Will I ever master them?)

If parentheses within parentheses are needed, use brackets for the inner set. See the next section for brackets.

Brackets

If you don't have brackets on your keyboard, leave spaces and draw them in. This is neater than trying to use the slash and the underline to make brackets.

1. Use brackets when **explanatory material** needs to be added to a quoted passage, often when taking the passage out of context has left something missing or not clear.

- The politician's voice rose as he almost shouted, "On this next holiday [Martin Luther King Day] we will pay tribute to the greatest statesman the world ever knew." The brackets indicate that these words were not in his speech.
- "Only two years ago his college [Princeton] made him an honorary Ph.D."
- "[Jonas Salk's] work resulted in a victory over the crippling disease poliomyelitis." "His work. . . " was the exact quote, but the reader does not know whose work without the preceding sentence, which was omitted here—hence the bracketed clarification.

2. Use brackets around *sic* to indicate that an error appeared in the material you are quoting and that you copied it exactly, mistake and all. *Sic* in Latin means *so* or *thus*.

- "At a lovely four o'clock wedding, the bridge [sic] was beautiful in white satin trimmed with lace."

3. Use brackets to show that the writer has made a slight **change in quoted material** so that it will make sense the way he or she is using it.

- If you wanted to change this statement, "More lives are being lost in this war than in any previous war," from present to past, you would write it "More lives [were] lost in this war than in any previous war."

4. Use brackets instead of parentheses when you need **parentheses within parentheses.**

- The book you refer to (*How to Use Parentheses* by English Major [New York: Golden Rules, 1968]) is completely outmoded.

5. Use either brackets or parentheses to enclose **stage directions** in a play script. Be consistent—use one or the other. (See the previous section for parentheses.)

- GERALD [looking ardently into her eyes, kneeling in front of her]: Geraldine, I love you. Will you marry me?
- GERALDINE [smiling, stroking his receding hairline]: I thought you'd never ask. Of course I'll marry you.

6. Use proper **spacing** and **capitalization.** Follow the rules for parentheses.

Ellipsis Points

Ellipsis points are three spaced periods that show the omission of quoted material or hesitation or the "trailing off" of a sentence. Many students whose keyboard repeats the period when that key is held down use two or three dozen unspaced periods for an ellipsis. Remember the words *three* and *spaced*.

1. Use ellipsis points to show **omission,** usually of quoted material. Unlike the caret (see page 358), which indicates accidental omission, ellipsis points show deliberate omission. Be sure the words you omit do not change the meaning of the material.

Use ellipsis points to show omission at the end of a quoted sentence. Place the three spaced dots after the period (or question mark or exclamation point) at the end of the quoted sentence. You may end up with four dots, but only three are the ellipsis; one is the period at the end of the sentence.

- THE ORIGINAL QUOTATION: "Why is it that television stations turn up the volume during their advertising? It is offensive to the listener. It is a disgrace. Of course we have to have advertisements. Otherwise, the cost of watching television, the nation's favorite pastime, would be prohibitive."

- YOUR SHORTENED VERSION: "Why is it that television stations turn up the volume during their advertising? It is offensive to the listener. . . . Of course we have to have advertisements. Otherwise, the cost of watching television, the nation's favorite pastime, would be prohibitive."

Use ellipsis points to show omission within a quoted sentence.

- ANOTHER SHORTENED VERSION OF THE ABOVE QUOTATION: "Why is it that television stations turn up the volume during their advertising? It is offensive to the listener. It is a disgrace. Of course we have to have advertisements. Otherwise, the cost of watching television . . . would be prohibitive." Omit the comma after *television.*

Use a whole line of ellipsis points to show omission of a complete line or more of quoted poetry.

- Little Miss Muffet
  Sat on a tuffet

  . . . .

  Along came a spider
  And sat down beside her
  And frightened Miss Muffet away.

2. Use ellipsis points to show **hesitation or** the "**trailing off**" of a sentence.

- HESITATION: If I were a television program director, I'd . . . well, I'd certainly tone down the commercials.
- TRAILING OFF: If only I could be in charge for a day. Oh, well . . .

3. Use proper **spacing.** Leave one space before and one space after each of the three ellipsis points that show omission within a sentence. BUT quotation marks are placed right up against the ellipsis points. Omit internal punctuation before and after the ellipsis unless it is needed for clarity. Ellipsis points can either end or begin a line but cannot be hyphenated.

- He was convinced he was far better off ". . . to have loved and lost . . ." than he would have been if he had never met the beautiful Greek dancer.
- ORIGINAL VERSION WITH INTERNAL PUNCTUATION: If you find television commercials stupid, an insult to the intelligence, write to the station and to the sponsors of the offensive commercials.
- INTERNAL PUNCTUATION OMITTED: If you find television commercials stupid . . . write to the station and to the sponsors of offensive commercials.

Slashes

Slashes (also called slants, diagonals, or virgules) have very specialized uses.

1. Use slashes to express **options or dual functions.**

- He decided to take English 101 and/or Biology 101.
- The college had just instituted a pass/fail grading system.
- The instructor/department head advised him to take only one course.

2. Use slashes to separate lines of **poetry** in **short quotations.** Three or fewer lines of quoted poetry are written within the paragraph rather than set off by indenting (see page 335).

- From Tennyson's *In Memoriam* come the famous lines, "'Tis better to have loved and lost / Than never to have loved at all."

3. Use slashes in certain **shortened forms.**

- Send it to me c/o (in care of) Dean Carl Wischmeyer, Humanities Department.
- Light travels at a speed of more than 186,000 miles/second (miles per second).

4. Use slashes to form any **fractions** that are not on the keyboard.

- How far would light travel in 1/15 of a second?
- A yard is 3/5280 of a mile. In fractions, omit the comma after the first digit of a four-digit number if the larger number can be easily read.

5. Use proper **spacing.** Leave no space before or after the slash unless it separates lines of poetry, in which case leave one space before and one after.

Carets

Use the caret, an upside-down *v* placed under the line, to show that something has been **accidentally omitted.** Unlike ellipsis points, which indicate a deliberate omission, the caret is used to correct a mistake.

The caret is properly placed below the line with the point of the upside-down *v* touching the bottom of the line at the place where something has been accidentally omitted. The omitted material is then written neatly above the line where the omission occurred.

- In almost all classes except typing, where the name ˄*of* the game is perfection, instructors will permit you to make neat corrections, including using the caret to fill in accidental omissions.

QUIZ YOURSELF ON STEP THREE   Fill in the blanks.

    1. On a keyboard that does not have a dash, make a dash by typing _____ with no space before, after, or in between.

_____ **2.** The main use of parentheses is   (a) to enclose direct quotations.   (b) to enclose indirect quotations.   (c) to enclose explanatory material.

_____ **3.** (a) Brackets   (b) Semicolons   (c) Commas   are used to show that the writer has made a slight change in quoted material so that it will make sense in its present use.

_____ **4.** T or F. To make ellipsis points, type a whole bunch of periods with no spaces in between them.

    5. What mark of punctuation is handy when you want to shorten expressions like *in care of* or *miles per second?*

_____ **6.** A caret is like the letter *v*. It is placed   (a) above the line pointing down   (b) below the line pointing up   (c) sideways above the line to indicate that something has been accidentally omitted.

Answers on page 367.

QUIZ YOURSELF ON FIRST HALF OF CHAPTER 5 Fill in the blanks with the best answer. Use at least one of each of the following: period, question mark, exclamation point, semicolon, comma, and apostrophe. If no punctuation is needed, place a zero in the blank.

1. The literary genre___Gothic fiction___first appeared in 1764___when English author___Horace Walpole___wrote *The Castle of Otranto, a Gothic Story*___

2. A genre is a fancy___French name for a kind or type of literature or other art work___

3. Poetry is one genre of literature___watercolor is one genre of painting___

4. Walpole___s Gothic story was filled with more ghastly___ghostly___ happenings than a modern___Halloween___haunted house___Have you ever visited one___

5. Walpole___s story contained murky___underground___passages___a bleeding statue___a portrait that stepped out of it___s frame___and doors that slammed___for no apparent reason___

6. Violence___and supernatural___occurrences___all in very___spooky___ settings___fill the pages of Gothic literature___it___s not the kind of thing to read late at night___

7. Lacking Europe___s haunted castles for settings___American Gothic writers of the 19th century___had to settle for decaying mansions___like the House of Usher in Edgar Allan Poe___s___1839 short story___"The Fall of the House of Usher___ ___

8. In Poe___s work___as an unnatural___eerie fog moves in___the writer commands Roderick Usher___"You must not—you shall not behold this___ ___

9. The term___Gothic___is now sometimes used to describe stories that are short on haunted houses___but long on violence___and insanity___and sinister atmosphere___

10. If we want to go Gothic today___we do___n___t have to go any farther___than the nearest TV___"on" switch___

Answers on page 367.

QUIZ YOURSELF ON SECOND HALF OF CHAPTER 5 Fill in the blanks with the best answer. Use at least one of each of the following: double quotation marks, single quotation marks, italics (underline the words that should be in italics), colon, hyphen, dash, parentheses, brackets, ellipsis points, caret, and slash. Do not use any semicolons. If no punctuation is needed, place a zero in the blank.

1. Once there were 17 English students___in a computer lab trying to get an idea for an English composition___a few of them hadn___t taken a class in several years___

2. Leatrice opened the book___ Composing With Confidence___and found a chapter called ___Can You Plan?___ She said, "Do I know how to plan ___ ___ Did she say, "I know how to plan___ ___ Or did she say, "Do I know how to plan___ ___

3. She asked Mrs. Murphy___her instructor___ ___May I write about one of the subjects suggested in the chapter___ ___Can You Plan___ ___ ___

4. ___Yes___you may___ ___said Mrs. Murphy. ___However___I have a list of topics___ too___abortion___ AIDS___a college education___rock music___ and violence on TV___ ___

5. Kate wanted to write about the N.S.P.C.A.___National Society for the Prevention of Cruelty to Animals___because she had just acquired a honey___colored boxer___retriever from the animal shelter___

6. She told Mrs. Murphy___ ___ I plan to start my composition with this quote from ___Animal Encyclopedia___ ___ ___Animals all around the world owe a vote of thanks to Henry Bergh___founder of the N.S.P.C.A.___ ___ ___

7. This article said___ ___He___Bergh___organized the N.S.P.C.A. in New York City after traveling in Europe and seeing the cruel way animals were treated there___ ___

8. The encyclopedia account contained this serious mistake___ ___Bergh also founded the Society for the Promotion___*sic*___ of Cruelty to Children___ ___

9. Roberto said___ ___I think I'll write about ___ ___ ___ No___I guess I___d better not do that___ ___

10. Peter had decided that Einstein___s theories would be too hard *to* write about___

11. He decided that getting the punctuation right would be hard enough without worrying about the speed of light___he would just write about TV commercials___

Answers on page 368.

Answers to Exercises

Answers to Exercise 5.1, page 308

1. Kate, who is from Boston, Mass •, has decided she wants to be a nurse • .

2. After her first week of classes, she exclaimed, "Wow • ○ Are all my classes going to be this hard ? ○ "

3. Peter, who is from Poland, wrote his father that he was excited about becoming a journalist •

4. Peter's father told him to study hard and to learn everything he could •

5. Peter's secret goal is to get a job as a television newscaster like Mr • Peter Jennings or Ms • Barbara Walters •

6. Roberto is from Toluca, Mexico, isn't he ? ○ He helps students, doesn't he, with their Spanish homework ? ○

7. "This is great ‼ " exclaimed Roberto. "I got the job in the computer lab, and now I'm pretty sure I will have enough money to go on and get my bachelor's degree ●

8. Leatrice, who is starting college in her hometown, wants to go away to school the last two years, doesn't she ?

9. For tomorrow, will you please study the section on semicolons ●

Answers to Exercise 5.2, page 312

It would probably be better to use a semicolon in the following: (1) The country of Mexico is divided into states, one of which is called Mexico; Toluca is the capital of the state of Mexico. (2) Toluca is an old city; it was founded in 1520. (3) It is located in an important farming and cattle region; grain growing and livestock raising are important.

Answers to Exercise 5.3, page 313

1. Five people went to the basketball game; Peter, a handsome fellow; Kate, a freckle-faced blonde; Roberto, a tall student; Leatrice, a slender girl; and Dr. Jefferson. **2.** Correct. **3.** April 1; her sign. **4.** habits; she. **5.** average; however, you. **6.** Award; because. **7.** teaching; and one thing.

Answers to Exercise 5.4, page 323

___2___ 1. Kate parked her car in the school parking lo**t, p**icked up her book**s, a**nd headed for class.

___4___ 2. Because she had a final exam in Englis**h, s**he was thinking more about her schoolwork than about what she was doing.

___5___ 3. After clas**s, a**nd she thought she had done well on the exa**m, s**he looked for her car keys.

___4___ 4. She could not find them anywhere; howeve**r, s**he thought she might have left them in the car (after conjunctive adverb *however*).

___5___ 5. The car was no**t, h**oweve**r, w**here she thought she had parked it (to set off parenthetical *however*).

___10___ 6. "Jo**e, I** can't find my car," she said to the security guard after she had looked everywhere.

___9___ 7. "Maybe you parked in one of the other lot**s," s**uggested Joe.

__4__ **8.** "N**o, I**'m sure it was this one."

__11__ **9.** Joe began writing his report: Missing from Parking Lot **A, C**uyahoga Community Colleg**e, E**astern Campu**s, 4**250 Richmond R**d., C**levelan**d, Ohio,** Monda**y, M**arch 2**6, a**t approximately 3 p.m.

__5__ **10.** Kat**e, w**orried about what her Aunt Betty would sa**y, s**tarted toward the phone.

Answers to Exercise 5.5, page 323

1. Before the missing car could be reported to the polic**e, C**alvin Careless called Kate's aunt to say he was in Cincinnat**i, w**here he had changed his mind about "borrowing" Kate's car.

2. Calvi**n, a** seemingly irresponsible studen**t, h**ad decided to start his spring break early and take a nice trip; after al**l, t**he keys were in the car.

3. A student who doesn't care about schoolwork sometimes doesn't bother to show up for final exams. Correct.

4. Calvi**n, w**ho apparently doesn't care about schoolwor**k, s**ometimes doesn't bother to show up for final exams.

5. His twin sister Carla was alarmed when Calvin didn't come home. Correct.

6. The Careless twin**s, w**ho are very clos**e, l**ook out for each other.

7. All students who are very close look out for each other. Correct.

8. Calvi**n, w**ho was feeling terrible about what he had don**e, s**tarted the drive back home.

Answers to Quiz Yourself on Step One, page 324

1. F. **2.** T. **3.** b. **4.** a. **5.** T. **6.** a. **7.** F. **8.** main clauses. **9.** F. **10.** T. **11.** F.

Answers to Exercise 5.6, page 331

1. Kat**e's** Aunt Betty was upset about Kat**e's** carelessness, but she realized i**t's** hard to remember keys when one is in a hurry.

2. Calvin explained that his parent**s' i**rresponsibility, including drug abuse, had left him and his sister in bad shape; the parent**s' w**alking out on their children, leaving the rent unpaid, forced the twins to get jobs and find a small apartment.

3. Calvin had found that i**t's** hard to make **C's** at school while working 40 hours a week as a maintenance perso**n's** assistan**t's** assistant, and Carl**a's** working every evening as a waitress had certainly interfered with her getting **A's**.

4. The apartmen**t's** furnishings left much to be desired, resulting in Calvi**n's** sleeping on a mattress on the floor.

5. Carl**a's** grades were average; Calv**in's** were poor.

6. T**V's** distraction was no problem, though, because they could**n't** afford one.

7. But they had looked into a B.**S.'s** (possessive, not plural) requirements and thought the**y'd** eventually be able to get bachelo**r's** degrees.

8. "When I saw the keys in Kat**e's** car, I was overwhelmed with the thought of a few day**s' v**acation," said Calvin.

9. "Was**n't** I stupid! **I'**ve even lost my job."

10. When Kate and her aunt and uncle learned of Calvin and Carl**a's** hardship, they did not press charges for Calv**in's** having made such a bad mistake.

11. "Calvin and Carl**a's** troubles are**n't** entirely their fault. Le**t's** try to help them," said Aunt Betty.

12. Kat**e's** uncle got Calvin a job running errands in his law firm, 30 hour**s' w**ork for more money than h**e'd** been making; Aunt Betty took Carla clothes shopping.

13. The two student**s' g**ratitude was genuine.

14. Calv**in's** goals now include law school, and Carl**a's** include a career in fashion design.

Answers to Exercise 5.7, page 337

1. "**E**xactly what is a shooting star**?"** you ask.

2. Let's pretend the tour guide at the Museum of Natural Science is answering this question. "**A** shooting star is a meteor, a metallic or stony piece of matter from space that falls to earth**,"** he says.

3. Did he say, "**I**t falls to earth from somewhere out in space"**?**

4. "**G**racious**!"** **you say.** "**W**hat if someone gets hit by it**?"**

5. Did you say, "**W**hat if someone gets hit by it**?"**

6. Did you hear the guide say that they become visible only when they enter the earth's atmosphere? Correct.

7. "**W**hen they enter the earth's atmosphere**,"** the guide says, "**f**riction heats them to about 4,000 degrees Fahrenheit, making them glow so that we can see them**."**

8. "**D**o very many hit the earth**?"** you ask.

9. "**N**o**,"** the guide replies. "**Y**ou might like to read this article explaining the process**."**

10. He hands you a copy of "**W**hy Falling Stars Are Not Really Stars Fallin**g"** from a recent news magazine.

11. There is an expression, "**a** meteoric rise to fame**,"** which refers to a new "**high"** in one's career.

12. Used in an opposite way in *King Richard II,* Shakespeare's expression was, "**I** see thy glory like a shooting star / Fall to the base earth from the firmament**."**

Answers to Exercise 5.8, page 339

1. The guide at the museum told us, **"T**his article, **'W**hy Falling Stars Are Not Really Stars Falling**,'** says, **'M**eteors which fall to earth without burning up are called meteorites**.'"**

2. A woman in the crowd said, **"M**y son asked, **'W**hat are meteorites made from**?'** Can you answer that**?"**

3. **"T**here are two kinds of meteorites**,"** replied the guide. **"S**o-called **'s**tony**'** meteorites are made up of stony materials resembling minerals from volcanoes. **'I**ro**n'** meteorites consist mainly of iron combined with nickel**."**

4. **"F**ortunately**,"** concluded the guide, **"m**ost meteors burn up completely before they hit **'S**paceship Earth**.'"**

Answers to Exercise 5.9, page 342

1. Books on the summer reading list include <u>David Copperfield</u> and <u>Tom Sawyer</u>.

2. The English literature instructor suggested that the class watch Shakespeare's <u>Macbeth</u> on television instead of <u>Murder She Wrote</u> or <u>L.A. Law.</u>

3. An article in <u>The New York Times</u> called "The Election Is Over" gives the reader an idea of what will happen next.

4. Robert Frost's "The Road Not Taken," which you can find in the book <u>Sound and Sense,</u> deals with the problem of making choices.

5. So many words rhyme with <u>June</u> that June seems to be a favorite month of poets.

6. Just as it is annoying to hear someone use too many <u>you knows</u> (don't italicize the *s*) in speaking, it is hard on the reader to come across a <u>basically</u> in every paragraph.

7. A riddle I knew as a child went like this: "Railroad crossing, look out for the cars; can you spell this without any <u>r</u>'s?" The answer, of course, was <u>t-h-i-s</u>.

8. The comic strip <u>Peanuts</u> shows Charlie Brown looking at the famous painting <u>Mona Lisa</u> and saying, "I think she knows something we don't know."

9. In the sinking of the <u>Titanic</u> in 1912, 1,517 passengers and crew members lost their lives even though the steamship <u>Carpathia</u> rescued 706 persons.

10. When the crooked politician preached "Honesty is the best policy," by <u>honesty</u> he evidently meant not getting caught.

11. He based his sermon on Job, a book from the Bible. Correct, no italics needed.

12. My favorite part of the album <u>Oklahoma</u> is the title song, "Oklahoma."

Answers to Exercise 5.10, page 346

1. Olympic contests took place as early as 776 B.C. in Western Greece, according to sport**s-l**oving historians.

2. But there may have been much earlier Olympi**c-l**ike games because athletics had long had religious significance for the ancient Greeks.

3. For many years the Olympics were completely mal**e-o**riented, not including female contestants or even permitting female spectators.

4. The Olympics were a onc**e-e**ver**y-f**ou**r-y**ears happening, and the only event in the first 13 Olympics was a 20**0-y**ard footrace.

5. Winning these races boosted the sel**f-e**steem of the runners.

6. Added to the the**n-r**enowned running competition in 708 B.C. was the pentathlon: discus throw, javelin throw, long jump, sprint, and wrestling.

7. The fou**r-h**orse chariot race was added in 680 B.C. and a nea**r-d**eadly boxin**g-**wrestling sport in 648 B.C.

8. After the Roman Empire invaded Greece in the mi**d-1**00s B.C., the games began to lose their dee**p-s**eated religious meaning.

9. By 394 A.D. the games were no longer rac**e-o**riented events, so they were discontinued, not to be held again for more than 1,500 years.

10. Moder**n-t**ype games began in Athens in 1896, with lon**g-e**xcluded women first competing in 1900 and winter games beginning in 1924.

Answers to Exercise 5.11, page 349

1. At the zoo you will find many animal**s: l**ions, tigers, elephants, bears, giraffes, and monkeys.

2. At the zoo you will find lions, tigers, elephants, bears, giraffes, and monkeys. Correct, but compare it to No. 1—in No. 2 there is no complete sentence before the list of animals.

3. There is one animal that is of special interest to childre**n: t**he kangaroo.

4. For some animals, cages are not necessar**y: g**rassy or wooded areas surrounded by deep ditches or moats allow them to behave more naturally.

5. The zoo is open from **9:3**0 a.m. to **5:3**0 p.m.

6. The first group of animals that might qualify as a zoo was in Paris, France, in 180**4: s**cientific study of the animals was the purpose.

7. Please not**e: C**ollections of wild animals have been kept by kings and very rich citizens since before the time of Christ.

8. Have you seen the book, *The Zo**o: A** Place of Fun for All?*

9. The dairy farm is second only to the zoo as a favorite place for second-grade field trips. Correct.

Answers to Quiz Yourself on Step Two, page 350

1. b. **2.** c. **3.** T. **4.** direct. **5.** F. **6.** b. **7.** a. **8.** c. **9.** a. **10.** T. **11.** b.

Answers to Exercise 5.12, page 352

1. Listen to the fish story of the yea**r—p**robably of the century.
2. Marty Huotari is the yar**n-s**pinning fisherman.
3. He was in his fishing shanty on Clam Lake in Northern Michigan, catching goo**d-s**ized perch through a **48-by-20-i**nch hole in the ice.
4. Suddenly something struck his wor**m-b**aited No. 12 hook tied to a si**x-p**oun**d-t**est monofilament line.
5. His yar**d-l**ong rod bent nearly double.
6. For one and on**e-h**alf hours**—a**lternately reeling in, then letting out lin**e—h**e struggled with the impossibl**e-to-c**atch fish.
7. When he finally got a look at it, he saw a gian**t-s**ized muskie, hooked in the jaw cartilage rather than in the shar**p-t**oothed mouth, where the line would have been quickly cut.
8. Huotari yelled for muc**h-n**eeded help, but no one was near enough to hear.
9. Finally he brought the head of the fish through the hole in the shanty floor, reached down as far as he could, wrapped his arms around the fis**h—i**t was tired to**o—a**nd rolled out the shanty door onto the ice with the fish in his arms.
10. It was a 5**0-i**nch, 3**6-p**ound muskie, which he believes is a worl**d-r**ecord catch on a si**x-p**oun**d-t**est line.

Answers to Quiz Yourself on Step Three, page 358

1. two hyphens. **2.** c. **3.** a. **4.** F. **5.** slash. **6.** b.

Answers to Quiz Yourself on First Half of Chapter 5, page 359

1. The literary genre ⌣ Gothic fiction ⌣ first appeared in 1764 ⌄ when English author ⌣ Horace Walpole ⌣ wrote *The Castle of Otranto, a Gothic Story* •

2. A genre is a fancy ⌣ French name for a kind or type of literature or other art work •

3. Poetry is one genre of literature ⸵ watercolor is one genre of painting •

4. Walpole ⸴ s Gothic story was filled with more ghastly ⌄ ghostly ⌣ happenings than a modern ⌣ Halloween ⌣ haunted house • Have you ever visited one ?

5. Walpole ⸴ s story contained murky ⌣ underground ⌣ passages ⌄ a bleeding statue ⌄ a portrait that stepped out of it ⌣ s frame ⌄ and doors that slammed ⌣ for no apparent reason •

6. Violence ⌒ and supernatural ⌒ occurrences ⌄ all in very ⌒ spooky ⌒ settings ⌄ fill the pages of Gothic literature ⌣ it ' s not the kind of thing to read late at night ⦁

7. Lacking Europe ' s haunted castles for settings ⌄ American Gothic writers of the 19th century ⌒ had to settle for decaying mansions ⌒ like the House of Usher in Edgar Allen Poe ' s ⌒ 1839 short story ⌄ " The Fall of the House of Usher ⦁ "

8. In Poe ' s work ⌄ as an unnatural ⌄ eerie fog moves in ⌄ the writer commands Roderick Usher ⌄ "You must not—you shall not behold this ! "

9. The term ⌒ Gothic ⌒ is now sometimes used to describe stories that are short on haunted houses ⌒ but long on violence ⌒ and insanity ⌒ and sinister atmosphere ⦁

10. If we want to go Gothic today ⌄ we do ⌒ n ' t have to go any farther ⌒ than the nearest TV ⌒ "on" switch ⦁

Answers to Quiz Yourself on Second Half of Chapter 5, page 360

1. Once there were 17 English students ⌒ in a computer lab trying to get an idea for an English composition ⸺ a few of them hadn ' t taken a class in several years ⦁

2. Leatrice opened the book ⌒ Composing With Confidence ⌒ and found a chapter called " Can You Plan ? " She said, "Do I know how to plan ? " Did she say, "I know how to plan " ? Or did she say, "Do I know how to plan ? "

3. She asked Mrs. Murphy ⌄ her instructor ⌄ " May I write about one of the subjects suggested in the chapter ⌒ ' Can You Plan ? ' "

4. " Yes ⌄ you may ⌄ " said Mrs. Murphy. " However ⌄ I have a list of topics ⌒ too ⸽ abortion ⌄ AIDS ⌄ a college education ⌄ rock music ⌄ and violence on TV ⦁ "

5. Kate wanted to write about the N.S.P.C.A. ⟨ National Society for the Prevention of Cruelty to Animals ⟩ because she had just acquired a honey ‐ colored boxer ⌃ retriever from the animal shelter ⊙

6. She told Mrs. Murphy ⁀ ❝ I plan to start my composition with this quote from ‿ <u>Animal Encyclopedia</u> ‿ : ⟨ Animals all around the world owe a vote of thanks to Henry Bergh ⁀ founder of the N.S.P.C.A. ‿ ' ❞

7. This article said ⁀ ❝ He [Bergh] organized the N.S.P.C.A. in New York City after traveling in Europe and seeing the cruel way animals were treated there ⊙ ❞

8. The encyclopedia account contained this serious mistake ∴ ❝ Bergh also founded the Society for the Promotion [sic] of Cruelty to Children ⊙ ❞

9. Roberto said ⁀ ❝ I think I'll write about ⊙ ⊙ ⊙ No ⁀ I guess I ' d better not do that ⊙ ❞

10. Peter had decided that Einstein ' s theories would be too hard ⌃to write about ⊙

11. He decided that getting the punctuation right would be hard enough without worrying about the speed of light ⁏ he would just write about TV commercials ⊙

6 Capitalization, Spelling, and Abbreviation

Capitalization: Step One

Ten Hints for Capitalization

Rules for the capitalization of words are not too illogical. Most of the words that need to be capitalized are proper nouns, or proper adjectives derived from proper nouns. Proper nouns and proper adjectives refer to *specific* persons, places, or things. If you are in doubt about capitalization, consult your dictionary. The following hints will help you master the rules of capitalization.

1. Capitalize the **first word** of every sentence or fragment punctuated as a sentence (No. Amazing!), usually the first word of every direct quotation, the first word of an independent question within a sentence (The question is, How can we change our policy?), the first word of every line of poetry (unless the poet uses a lowercase style), and, some grammarians say, the first word of a complete sentence following a colon (see page 348).

2. Capitalize the names of **specific persons** and real titles (including abbreviations) that precede the names: Alice, Mr. Betts, Mother (when used as her name, not when talking about my mother), Mayor White (BUT Michael White, mayor), President Lincoln (BUT Abraham Lincoln, president of the United States), Aunt Sue (BUT Sue Ford, my aunt), an African-American (BUT a black), a Caucasian (BUT a white), words derived from proper nouns (Christianity, Murphy's Law). Always capitalize the personal pronoun *I*.

Do *not* capitalize pseudo titles and occupational titles like the following, even if they precede a name: billionaire Howard Hughes, proud father Joseph Jones, former world heavyweight boxing champion Muhammad Ali, author James Michener, attorney James E. Spitz. The occupational exceptions are doctors, ministers (say "Rev. Myers," but write "the Rev. K. Dean Myers"), and office holders. A general rule is that a real title is one you would actually call the person: you would not say "Hello, Author Michener," but you would say "Hello, Prof. Stock and Sen. Glenn." Don't capitalize *ex* before a title or *elect* after a title, as in ex-Mayor Jane Doe or Congressman-elect Joseph Doakes. See page 346 for capitalization after hyphens.

3. Capitalize the names of **specific organizations** and institutions, acronyms, and initialisms: Ways and Means Committee, Rotary Club, Democratic Party, United States Air Force, Phi Beta Kappa, Cleveland Browns, Saks Fifth Avenue, MADD (Mothers Against Drunk Driving), IRS (Internal Revenue Service). Once you have used the specific name of an organization or an institution or a state, do not capitalize a later general reference to it: (Miami-Dade Community College, the college, the Buckeye State, the state of Ohio, Ohio is a state that has contributed many of our country's presidents). Inside a company, departments are usually capitalized: memo from the Marketing Department. Outsiders would not capitalize a reference to the marketing department of the Jones Co.

4. Capitalize the names of **specific places,** including abbreviations: Boston, Mass., the South (when referring to a section of the country, BUT I was driving south on I-271), Southwestern Alaska, State Route 422, the Middle East, the Persian Gulf, the Atlantic Ocean, the Arctic Circle, Remington Drive, 4250 Richmond Rd., Blossom Music Center, Greater Phoenix, the East Side (a section of town, BUT I live on the east side of Grant Avenue), Federal Building.

Also capitalize countries and continents and words derived from them, including the language and the people.

- The French might argue that you should go to France to learn to speak French.

In speaking of college courses, languages are capitalized; other subjects are not unless you are referring to specific courses by number.

- I didn't think I'd like Greek or economics, but I did well in both Greek 100 and Economics 101.

5. Capitalize **days, months,** and holidays, as well as historic events, periods (BUT don't capitalize 20th century), and documents: Monday, February, Jan. 13, Fourth of July, Mother's Day, Passover, National Pickle Week, World War II, the Battle of Hastings, the Middle Ages, the Constitution (of the United States), the Treaty of Versailles. Don't capitalize the seasons unless they are personified (given human characteristics, usually in poetry).

6. **Adjectives** derived **from proper nouns** are usually capitalized: American, Buddhist, Rotarian, our March meeting. Of course, there are exceptions: the U. S. Constitution, our constitutional rights; the Bible, biblical. The best advice, as always, is consult a dictionary. And there are proper adjectives *not* derived from proper nouns—for example the word *Blue* in the Blue Room.

7. Capitalize **religions, holy books,** and usually references to God: When I read the Bible, I get such comfort from the thought that God cares for His children of all faiths.

8. In **titles and subtitles** of publications (as well as films, songs, etc.) and student papers, capitalize all words with four or more letters. In titles and subtitles, you should also capitalize the following words, no matter how short they are:

- the first and last word
- the first word after a colon or a dash
- all nouns, pronouns, verbs, adjectives, adverbs, and interjections, including those that occur in hyphenated compound words

Do not capitalize the following in titles and subtitles unless they are the first or last word:

- the three articles *a, an,* and *the*
- the *to* of an infinitive
- conjunctions and prepositions of two or three letters, unless a short preposition is paired with a long one ("News In and Around Town")

NOTE: In *The New York Times, The* is part of the name of the paper.

BUT: I read it in the *Detroit Free Press; the* is not part of the name of the paper.

9. Capitalize the first word and all nouns in the **salutation** of a letter, but only the first word in the **complimentary close** of a letter. However, proper nouns and proper adjectives are capitalized.

- My dear Sir
- Sincerely yours, Your American friend

10. Capitalize **brand names** except those that have become "generic" through overuse and misuse (General Electric, Mr. Clean, BUT nylon, china, bandaid, xerox copy), specific awards (Pulitzer Prize), specific degrees (Master of Arts) and abbreviations of degrees (B.A., Ph.D.), BUT not general reference to a degree (a master's degree), and most nouns followed by numbers or letters (Room 123, Exhibit A, Chapter 10, BUT not smaller units like page 1, paragraph 3, question 6, line 23, size 34).

EXERCISE 6.1 Circle the letters that should be capitalized in the following sentences. It's okay to use the guidelines in your text and/or to look up words in your dictionary.

1. it must be hard for you college students today to imagine what life was like when i was a girl growing up in indiana during the great depression.

2. for starters, i'll bet you can't visualize life without television or kleenex or scotch tape.

3. we had radio and handkerchiefs and paste. we were able to hear, not see, h. v. kaltenborn and lowell thomas deliver the radio news; on mondays, particularly in winter, my mother boiled our handkerchiefs before she washed them to keep cold germs from spreading; and we always had handy a big jar of carter's paste for sticking things together.

4. i remember writing a story in fifth grade titled "why i would like to travel to jupiter." i was complimented for my far-out 21st-century imagination.

5. we had all sorts of dangerous fireworks on the fourth of july, and we said the pledge of allegiance, without the words "under god," every morning at weldele elementary school.

6. veterans day was armistice day then; it always came on nov. 11, and every class stood and silently faced east for a couple of minutes at 11 a.m. in honor of the soldiers who had died in world war I.

7. we had to memorize parts of the constitution of the united states; an apple was not a computer but was what we brought the teacher.

8. woolworth's sold wonderful things for a nickel or a dime; baby ruths and double-dip cones were a nickel, and when i learned to smoke, which was the "in" thing for college students back then, a package of lucky strikes cost 20 cents. you could buy a chevy two-door for $600, and two gallons at a standard oil station cost 22 cents.

9. our cars not only didn't have air bags or antilock brakes—they didn't even have turn signals or brake lights. the driver rolled down the window, stuck his or her left arm straight out to signal a left turn, straight up bent at the

elbow to signal a right turn, and straight down bent at the elbow and swinging in and out to signal a stop. my dad taught me to drive, and i got a license that summer in michigan on my 14th birthday—no driver's ed, no driver's test, but dad was a tough examiner.

10. i remember a trip on a thanksgiving when i was quite small—in our first car, which didn't even have roll-down windows. it was a nash, open on both sides unless we snapped on rain-proof "side curtains" with small transparent isinglass panels.

11. i went to college in my home town in the hoosier state two years, and then i went away to school at duke university in durham, n.c., a fine university. my parents allowed less than $2,000 a year for my college costs: tuition, books, half of a double room in pegram hall, food, transportation, and clothes.

12. we traveled to school, and home for christmas and spring vacations, by train, the norfolk and western railroad; and if you're curious, as one of my children once was, no, we did not have dinosaurs, but, yes, we did have toothbrushes when i was a girl.

Answers on page 394.

Spelling: Step One

The Wonderful English Language, or
Is It Any Wonder Johnny Can't Spell?

I take it you already know
Of *tough* and *bough* and *cough* and *dough?*
Others may stumble but surely not you
On *hiccough, thorough, slough,* and *through.*
Well done! And now you wish perhaps
To learn of less familiar traps?

Beware of *heard,* a dreadful word
That looks like *beard* and sounds like *bird.*
And *dead:* it's said like *bed,* not *bead;*
For goodness' sake don't call it *deed.*
Watch out for *meat* and *great* and *threat*
(They rhyme with *suite* and *straight* and *debt*).
A *moth* is not a moth in *mother,*
Nor *both* in *bother,* or *broth* in *brother.*
And *here* is not a match for *there,*

Nor *dear* and *fear* for *bear* and *pear*.
And then there's *dose* and *rose* and *lose*—
Just look them up—and *goose* and *choose*,
And *cork* and *work* and *card* and *ward*
And *font* and *front* and *word* and *sword*
and *do* and *go* and *thwart* and *cart*—
Come, come, I've barely made a start!
A dreadful language? Man alive!
I'd mastered it when I was five.

Author unknown

Many spelling errors occur when suffixes are added after the base word. Certain rules apply—usually—and certain other rules—sometimes. If you skim through this section looking at the various rules, you'll wonder how you ever learned to write at all: drop the *e*, retain the *e*, double the final consonant, do not double the final consonant. But you'll need to refer to these rules if you have spelling problems, as most of us do. And don't forget to keep your dictionary or word book (a "dictionary" without definitions or pronunciations) handy.

Seventeen Hints for Spelling

1. To make most nouns plural, **add s.** Add *es* to singular nouns ending in *s, x, z, ch,* or *sh*. See pages 381-385 for complete information on the spelling of plural words.

2. Usually **drop the final silent *e*** before adding a suffix beginning with a vowel.

- argue = arguable, arguing
- care = caring
- desire = desiring, desirous
- move = movable, moving
- propose = proposing, proposition
- scarce = scarcity
- EXCEPTIONS: acre = acreage, mile = mileage, see = seeing.

Usually **retain the *e*** before adding a suffix beginning with a consonant.

- care = careful
- move = movement
- scarce = scarcely

- use = useful
- EXCEPTIONS: acknowledge = acknowledgment (preferred spelling), argue = argument, awe = awful, nine = ninth, wise = wisdom.

3. Also usually **drop the final silent *e*** before adding the suffix *y.*

- ease = easy
- edge = edgy
- ice = icy
- EXCEPTIONS: cage = cagey, whole = wholly (drop the *e* but double the *l*).

4. Words ending in *ce* or *ge* usually **retain the *e*** before suffixes beginning with *a* or *o* (to retain the *s* sound of *ce* or the *j* sound of *ge*).

- enforce = enforceable
- notice = noticeable
- service = serviceable
- advantage = advantageous
- change = changeable
- knowledge = knowledgeable

Drop the *e* before suffixes beginning with *i:* enforcing, servicing, changing.

- EXCEPTION: *singeing* (burning), which would otherwise be indistinguishable from *singing.*

5. Words ending in *c* usually **add the letter *k*** before a suffix beginning with a vowel in order to keep the sound of the hard *c: picnic, picnicking.*

6. In one-syllable words ending in a single consonant preceded by a single vowel, **double the final consonant** before adding a suffix beginning with a vowel or before adding a *y.*

- bag = baggage, bagged, bagging, baggy
- plan = planned, planning
- skin = skinned, skinning, skinny
- glad = gladden
- ship = shipped, shipping
- star = starred, starring
- EXCEPTIONS: tax = taxed, taxation, vow = vowing

7. In one-syllable words ending in a single consonant preceded by a single vowel, **do not double the final consonant** when adding a suffix beginning with a consonant.

- glad = gladly, gladness
- ship = shipment
- star = stardom

8. In words of more than one syllable ending in a single consonant preceded by a single vowel, **double the final consonant** before adding a suffix beginning with a vowel—*if* the accent is on the last syllable.

- begin´ = beginning
- occur´ = occurred, occurrence, occurring
- regret´ = regrettable, regretted, regretting

However, if the accent is not on the last syllable, **do not double the final consonant.**

- ben´efit = benefited, benefiting
- can´cel = canceled, canceling (one *l* preferred), BUT cancellation
- EXCEPTIONS: for´matting, hand´icapped, kid´napped (two *p*s preferred).

9. If a word ends in a single consonant preceded by more than one vowel, **do not double the final consonant** when adding any suffix.

- cheer = cheery
- chief = chiefly
- equal = equaled
- deceit = deceitful

10. If a word ends with more than one consonant, **do not double the final consonant** before adding any suffix.

- blitz = blitzed, blitzing
- hand = handed, handing, handy
- mass = massed, massing, massive
- return = returned, returning
- self = selfish, selfless
- sing = singing

11. If a word ends in a *y* preceded by a consonant, usually **change the *y* to *i*** to add a suffix; BUT retain the *y* if the suffix begins with *i*.

- beauty = beautiful, beautify, beautified
- reply = replying

12. If a word ends in a *y* preceded by a vowel, usually **keep the *y*** when adding a suffix.

- buy = buying, buyout
- delay = delayed, delaying
- employ = employed, employing, employment
- play = played, playing

13. If a word ends in *ie*, **change the *ie* to *y*** before adding *ing*:

- die = dying

Peanuts   by Charles Schulz

14. Take the **most famous of all spelling rules** with a spoonful of salt: *I* before *e* except after *c,* or when sounded as *a* as in *neighbor* and *weigh*. It's true in a number of cases.

- *I* before *e:* believe, chief, fierce, friend, niece, variety, view
- Except after *c:* conceive, deceive, ceiling
- Or when sounded as *a* as in *neighbor* and *weigh:* aweigh, beige, eight, freight, inveigh, inveigle, reign, sleigh, vein, weight
- EXCEPTIONS to the "*i* before *e* except after *c*" rule: caffeine, counterfeit, either, foreign, forfeit, heifer, height, heir, leisure, neither, protein, seize, seizure, sheik, sleight, sovereign, stein, their, weir, weird
- OTHER EXCEPTIONS: words that *do* have *ie* after *c,* include the following: ancient, deficient, efficient, financier, proficient, science, society, species, sufficient, and, of course, words derived from these words (insufficient, sufficiency, sufficiently)

The Born Loser   by Art & Chip Sansom

15. There's no substitute for a **dictionary** or a **word book** in determining the following word endings:

- *able* (advisable, dependable) OR *ible* (compatible, visible)
- *ant* (assistant, defendant) OR *ent* (dependent, insistent)
- *ance* (assistance, maintenance) OR *ence* (insistence, occurrence)
- *ative* (affirmative, imperative) OR *itive* (definitive, inquisitive)
- *cede* (most common: concede, precede, etc.) OR *ceed* (three words: exceed, proceed, succeed) OR *sede* (one word: supersede)
- *er* (advertiser, adviser—preferred over advisor in two out of three dictionaries) OR *or* (sponsor, vendor)
- *ise* (advertise, surprise) or *ize* (apologize, criticize) OR *yze* (analyze, paralyze)

16. Some **foreign words** that have become so established in English (or American English) as to no longer need italicizing may still cling to their accent marks (résumé, née, à la mode, maître d'hôtel, jalapeño). A dictionary is your best friend, or have I already said that a time or two?

17. There are varying opinions on when to **spell out numbers** and when to use numerals: Some authorities say to spell out all numbers that can be written in one or two words, but it seems queer to write *198, 199, two hundred, 201.* If it doesn't defy your instructor's edicts or your boss' style, use journalism rules: spell out numbers *one* through *nine;* use numerals for *10* and above. Always spell out numbers, no matter what size, at the beginning of a sentence (because you can't capitalize numerals). If the spelled-out number is too cumbersome (Five thousand two hundred eighty feet are in a mile), rewrite the sentence (A mile is equal to 5,280 feet).

EXCEPTIONS: There are many exceptions to the spell-one-through-nine rule:

- Use numerals for days of the month (Feb. 2, use the cardinal number; *not* Feb. 2nd, the ordinal number) and house numbers (6 Ninth Ave.,

7 W. 45th St.) and times (6 a.m.) even if they are nine or below and ages if they follow the name (Jenny Jones, 3, died today).

- Also write in numerals No. 1, 3 p.m., Channel 5, Room 2, page 4, Chapter 6, numbers with a dollar sign ($3), some decimals (1.08 percent but usually one percent), fractions other than the simplest ones (one-half but 15/32), mixed numbers (3 17/64), and small numbers mixed with large numbers in a listing:

> 97 percent for
> 2 percent against
> 1 percent undecided

- Use numerals and words for large round numbers, (1 million, $4 billion, 1.25 billion).

Spelling: Step Two

Fourteen Rules for Forming Plural Nouns

Nouns can be either singular (one) or plural (more than one). Formation of the plural follows certain rules, but the exceptions to these rules cause English teachers to change professions. Fourteen rules follow, but the best rule of all is to consult a good dictionary; most dictionaries show irregular plurals after the nouns listed.

1. **Add *s*** to most singular nouns to make them plural.

- one boy = two boys, one egg = a dozen eggs, one day = sixty days

2. Words ending in *is* form the plural by changing the *is* **to es.**

- crisis = crises, thesis = theses, basis = bases

3. **Add *es*** to singular nouns ending in *s, x, z, ch,* or *sh.*

- boss = bosses, Jones = Joneses, box = boxes, Max = Maxes, quartz = quartzes, Fritz = Fritzes, church = churches, crash = crashes
- EXCEPTION: ox = oxen

Do not use apostrophes to make nouns plural; save apostrophes for making nouns possessive. Only in rare cases, for clarity, is an apostrophe used to form the plural. (See pages 330-331.) If you want to say your Christmas card is from the Perkinses, or if you want your mailbox to announce "The Rodriguezes live here," or if you say "Six girls share a room," don't use an apostrophe. You want to make the nouns plural, not possessive.

4. If a singular common noun ends in *y* preceded by a consonant, **drop the *y*** and **add *ies*** to make it plural.

- baby = babies, berry = berries

However, if it is a proper noun, just add *s*.

- two Tobys in the class, not two Tobies; Mr. and Mrs. Perry = the Perrys, not the Perries

If a singular noun ends in *y* preceded by a vowel, just add *s*.

- monkey = monkeys, display = displays

5. If a singular noun ends in *o* preceded by a vowel, **add *s*** to make the plural.

- radio = radios, tattoo = tattoos

6. But if a singular noun ends in *o* preceded by a consonant, **get out** your **dictionary.** Add only *s* to musical terms and instruments.

- pianos, sopranos, banjos, altos, cellos

Add only *s* to some other *o* words.

- pimentos, autos, hairdos, and memos

But add *es* to certain other *o* words.

- potatoes, tomatoes, vetoes, echoes, heroes

7. Add *s* to most singular nouns ending in *f* or *fe*.

- beliefs, tariffs, fifes
- EXCEPTIONS: calf, elf, half, knife, leaf, life, loaf, self, sheaf, shelf, thief, wife, and wolf, which drop the final *f* or *fe* and add *ves*: elves, selves, knives, wives

8. Some nouns borrowed from other languages, even though they have been completely absorbed into English, still form their plurals in their **native tongue.**

- alumnus = alumni, alumna = alumnae, datum (the correct singular form) = data (but data is commonly used for the singular too)

9. A few singular nouns **do not change** to form the plural.

- one sheep = two sheep; also deer, species, series, trout, moose, corps

10. A few nouns **look plural** but are **really singular:** *measles* and *mumps* look plural but take singular verbs. Who ever heard of having one measle? *Mathematics* and *physics* and *news* behave in the same manner.

11. Other nouns have **no singular form.**

- pliers, gymnastics, acoustics

12. Still others have **no plural form.**

- furniture, equipment, luggage, tackle (as in fishing tackle)

A dictionary is a girl's, and a boy's, best friend.

13. In **compound nouns** that are one solid word, make the final element plural.

- toothbrushes, grandchildren

In hyphenated or spaced compound nouns, make the most important word of the compound plural.

- mothers-in-law, editors in chief, lieutenant generals

B.C.   by Johnny Hart

If there is no noun in a hyphenated compound, make the final element plural

- grown-ups, hand-me-downs

Just add *s* to compounds ending in *ful.*

- cupfuls, handfuls

A few compound nouns offer a choice.

- court-martial = courts-martial or court-martials

In a very few, change both parts of the compound to the plural.

- manservant = menservants

14. Usually just **add *s*** to capital letters, numerals, acronyms, and initialisms. There is no need for apostrophes here; you are making these expressions plural, not possessive, and their meaning is clear without an apostrophe: I got two Cs, a poker hand with four 10s, the 1920s, the '20s, zips with nine digits, she earned two B.A.s, TVs. For plurals that need an apostrophe for clarity, see pages 330-331.

Highly Irregular Plurals

Too many singular nouns form the plural in a manner so outrageous—as in one mouse, two mice—that we may suspect our ancestral linguists lay awake nights thinking up ways to puzzle their descendents.

A poem, or at least a verse, in a grammar book, long lost, from my childhood, also long lost, shows the illogic of the highly irregular plurals. It is called "Singular Plurals" and is all I managed to save from that book. The author was unknown even back then.

Let's start out with *box,* and the plural is *boxes;*
But the plural of *ox* must be *oxen,* not *oxes.*
Then one fowl is *goose;* strangely, two are called *geese,*
Yet the plural of *moose* should be *moose,* never *meese.*
You'll find a lone *mouse* or a whole lot of *mice,*
But the plural of *house* is *houses,* not *hice.*
If the plural of *man* is always called *men,*
Why shouldn't the plural of one *pan* be *pen?*
If I speak of a *foot* and you show me your *feet,*

And I give you a *boot,* would a pair be called *beet?*
If one is a *tooth* and a whole set is *teeth,*
Why shouldn't the plural of *booth* be named *beeth?*
Since the single is *this* and the plural is *these,*
If I wanted three *kisses,* I'd ask for three *kese.*
Then one would be *that;* two or three would be *those,*
Yet *hat* in the plural would never be *hose,*
And *rat* in the plural is *rats,* never *rose.*
We speak of our *brother* and also our *brethren,*
But though we say *mother,* we never say *methren.*
The masculine pronouns are *he, his,* and *him;*
Imagine the feminine—*she, shis,* and *shim.*
So English, I think you can't help but agree,
Is the craziest language you ever did see!

EXERCISE 6.2 Circle the words that are spelled correctly. Don't hesitate to consult the previous paragraphs in your text or to look up the spelling of these words in your dictionary.

1. When we of the older generation were growing up, we were taught not to argue with our parents or teachers; *argueing/arguing* was considered disrespectful even if we had a good *arguement/argument* on our side.

2. If we did something wrong, we were treated with *icey/icy* silence.

3. Yet our parents reared us with great care; they were *truely/truly* *careing/caring* and always *careful/carful* to give us opportunities to learn.

4. They made rules that were *enforcable/enforceable.*

5. But along with their *insistance/insistence* on our following their rules, they gave us *assistance/assistence* any time we needed it.

6. At the *begining/beginning* of November, our parents ordered Christmas items from the Sears catalog. They waited patiently for the merchandise to be *shiped/shipped* and for the *shipment/shippment* to arrive.

7. It never *occured/occurred* to us children that the things we found under the tree Christmas Day might have been *received/recieved* from Sears and not from Santa.

8. We had sent our list to the *Clauses/Clause's/Clauses'* weeks before by writing a Christmas letter and burning it in the fireplace so that Santa's *elfs/elfes/elves* could load our wishes on the sleigh in plenty of time for the *reindeer/reindeers* to get them to us Christmas Eve.

9. At our house, breakfast always *preceded/preceeded* the fun part of Christmas; but after downing the quickest meal of the year, we *proceded/*

proceeded to the opening of the presents and always *succeded/succeeded* in finding gifts that *exceded/exceeded* our *glorious/gloryous* expectations.

10. I had measles at Christmas time when I was a sophomore in college. Measles *are/is* a serious disease in an adult.

11. Life in the *'30s/'30's/30's'/30s'* was different from but not better than life now.

Answers on page 395.

Abbreviation: Step One

Abbreviation is the shortening of a word or a group of words for the convenience of the writer or speaker. Usually a period is required after an abbreviation. Examples of common abbreviations are listed below.

Abbreviations Usually Written With Periods

- a.m. = between midnight and noon
- p.m. = between noon and midnight

NOTE: For a.m. and p.m., lowercase is preferred: 6 a.m. In printed matter, small capital letters may be used for 7 A.M. and 5 P.M. Midnight = 12 a.m.; noon = 12 p.m. To be clear, say *midnight* or *noon*.

- C.P.A. = certified public accountant
- No., Nos. = number(s) (No. 1, Nos. 3 to 5)
- C.O.D. = cash on delivery or collect on delivery
- p. = page, pp. = pages
- Inc. = incorporated
- Co. = company, abbreviated only when used with company name
- P.D.Q. = pretty damned quick (slang)
- l. = line, ll. = lines
- Jr. = junior
- G.B. = Great Britain
- R.N. = registered nurse
- lb. = pound

- R.S.V.P. = répondez, s'il vous plaît = please reply
- i.e. = that is
- e.g. = for example
- et al. = and others
- etc. = et cetera = and so forth, and other things:
- NOTE: Since *and* is already there, don't say *and etc.* (redundant)
- Jan. = January
- St. = street
- Mass. = Massachusetts
- B.A. = Bachelor of Arts degree
- Ph.D. = Doctor of Philosophy
- M.D. = Doctor of Medicine

Abbreviate the following personal titles only when used *before* the person's name:

- Mr. = man, no marital status given; Mrs. = married woman; Ms. = woman, no marital status given
- Dr., Drs. = doctor, doctors
- Pres. = president
- Gov. = governor
- Sen. = senator
- Prof. = professor
- Capt. = captain
- Rev. = reverend
- WRONG: Pablo Picasso's father was a prof. of art.
- RIGHT: Pablo Picasso's father was a professor of art.
- RIGHT: Prof. Picasso gave his son Pablo lessons in art.

Don't be redundant.

- WRONG: Dr. Mark J. LeVine, M.D. You have said *Doctor* twice.
- RIGHT: Dr. Mark J. LeVine OR Mark J. LeVine, M.D.

Your instructors or your boss may have a preferred style for abbreviations. Naturally, you follow the rules in your classes or at your job. But for the use of abbreviations in most college compositions and in general writing, the hints below, which embody the style used in journalism, are practical.

Seven Hints for Abbreviation

1. Abbreviate the name of a **state** only if the name of a city precedes the name of the state; otherwise, write out the state.

- RIGHT: I live in New York, N.Y.
- RIGHT: I live in the state of New York.
- WRONG: I live in the state of N.Y.

The following eight states are usually not abbreviated: Alaska, Hawaii, Idaho, Iowa, Maine, Ohio, Texas, and Utah.

2. Don't abbreviate the name of a **city.**

- RIGHT: I live in Cleveland Heights.
- WRONG: I live in Cleveland Hts.

3. Abbreviate the **month** only if the month is followed by the day of the month; otherwise, write out the month.

- RIGHT: I was born Aug. 5.
- RIGHT: I was born in August.
- WRONG: I was born in Aug.

Don't abbreviate the months with short names: March, April, May, June, and July.

4. Don't abbreviate **days of the week**

5. Abbreviate **street,** road, avenue, etc., only if the name of the street is preceded by the house number.

- RIGHT: I live at 203 Madison Blvd.
- RIGHT: I live on Madison Boulevard.
- WRONG: I live on Madison Blvd.

6. It is usually not acceptable to use **symbols,** such as the percent sign (%) and the ampersand (&) in your writing. Write *percent* and *and* (unless the *&* is part of the formal name of a company).

7. Use proper **spacing.** Usually leave one space after periods at the end of abbreviations.

- Mrs. Murphy has an M.A. in English.

Leave two spaces if the abbreviation ends a sentence.

- Mrs. Murphy has an M.A. She needed it to get a job teaching.

If an abbreviation with its period ends a sentence, use only one period.

- WRONG: Picasso's paintings were influenced by clowns, circuses, cubism, etc..
- RIGHT: Picasso's paintings were influenced by clowns, circuses, cubism, etc.

If an abbreviation with its period is followed by another mark of punctuation, leave no space.

- RIGHT: Why was Picasso interested in clowns, circuses, cubism, etc.?

Abbreviation: Step Two

Periods Increasingly Omitted

1. Common abbreviations, more and more, are being written without periods.

- mph = miles per hour, aka = also known as, VIP = very important person, ID = identification, fax = facsimile

Some shortened forms of words became words in their own right and never did use a period: laboratory = lab, telephone = phone.

2. Acronyms, pronounceable words formed from the first letters of a series of words, do not require periods.

- radar = radio detecting and ranging
- laser = light amplification by stimulated emission of radiation

Acronyms representing organizations usually are capitalized:

- NATO = North Atlantic Treaty Organization, UNESCO = United Nations Educational, Scientific, and Cultural Organization.

3. Initialisms, initials representing words but with each initial pronounced separately, usually do not have periods.

- FBI = Federal Bureau of Investigation
- TV = television
- ACLU = American Civil Liberties Union

But some initialisms—for example, U.S.A. or USA for United States of America—may go either way, with or without periods. The best thing to do is to pick one dictionary or style book (yes, dictionaries and style books vary) and stick with it. Consistency is important—you don't want to use an abbreviation one way in one part of a paper you are writing and another way in another part.

Unfamiliar Abbreviations Explained

The first time you use it, write the long form of any abbreviation, acronym, or initialism your reader might not know. Follow this immediately with the abbreviation, acronym, or initialism in parentheses—or vice versa, short form first followed immediately by the long form in parentheses. After the first use, with explanation, use the short form.

- RIGHT: If Picasso had lived in this country, he might have belonged to the American Academy of Arts and Letters (AAAL).
- ALSO RIGHT: If Picasso had lived in this country, he might have belonged to the AAAL (American Academy of Arts and Letters).
- RIGHT (after you have written out the complete name of the organization once): Many countries have organizations similar to the AAAL to promote the arts.

Abbreviation: Step Three

Zip-Code Abbreviations

Use zip-code abbreviations for states and territories in addresses if the name of the city and a zip-code number are also used. No period is used after zip-code abbreviations. Zip is an acronym for zone improvement plan.

According to the United States Post Office, the last line of an address should be written as follows: city, no comma but two spaces, zip-code abbreviation for the state, no period or comma but two spaces, nine-digit zip-code number hyphenated between the fifth and sixth digit. Capital letters for the entire address are preferred, with no punctuation anywhere except for the hyphen in the nine-digit zip-code number.

> DR DAVID C MITCHELL
> THE COMMUNITY COLLEGE OF ALLEGHENY COUNTY
> 808 RIDGE AVE
> PITTSBURGH PA 15212-6097

It is important *not* to use periods and commas in the entire address because, with automation, the optical code scanner, which applies a bar code on the envelope, might misread a large period or comma as a number one or number seven or some other number.

It is quite likely that zip-code abbreviations will gradually replace standard abbreviations; but until they do, use the standard abbreviations for states for all purposes except zip-code mailing addresses. Standard abbreviations require a period.

The box below lists the zip-code abbreviations, which do not require periods, along with standard abbreviations, which do require periods, for the states and territories whose names are commonly abbreviated. (The eight states for which standard abbreviations are not used are listed on page 388.)

AL	Alabama	Ala.	MO	Missouri	Mo.
AK	Alaska		MT	Montana	Mont.
AS	American Samoa		NE	Nebraska	Neb.
AZ	Arizona	Ariz.	NV	Nevada	Nev.
AR	Arkansas	Ark.	NH	New Hampshire	N.H.
CA	California	Calif.	NJ	New Jersey	N.J.
CZ	Canal Zone		NM	New Mexico	N.M.
CO	Colorado	Colo.	NY	New York	N.Y.
CT	Connecticut	Conn.	NC	North Carolina	N.C.
DE	Delaware	Del.	ND	North Dakota	N.D.
DC	District of Columbia	D.C.	OH	Ohio	
FL	Florida	Fla.	OK	Oklahoma	Okla.
GA	Georgia	Ga.	OR	Oregon	Ore.
GU	Guam		PA	Pennsylvania	Pa.
HI	Hawaii		PR	Puerto Rico	
ID	Idaho		RI	Rhode Island	R.I.
IL	Illinois	Ill.	SC	South Carolina	S.C.
IN	Indiana	Ind.	SD	South Dakota	S.D.
IA	Iowa		TN	Tennessee	Tenn.

KS	Kansas	Kan.	TX	Texas	
KY	Kentucky	Ky.	UT	Utah	
LA	Louisiana	La.	VT	Vermont	Vt.
ME	Maine		VA	Virginia	Va.
MD	Maryland	Md.	VI	Virgin Islands	
MA	Massachusetts	Mass.	WA	Washington	Wash.
MI	Michigan	Mich.	WV	West Virginia	W.Va.
MN	Minnesota	Minn.	WI	Wisconsin	Wis.
MS	Mississippi	Miss.	WY	Wyoming	Wyo.

EXERCISE 6.3 In the following sentences, abbreviate words that are commonly abbreviated and write numbers according to the style suggested in the preceding section. Write the corrections above the line. One sentence is correct.

1. Sound travels at a speed of 764 miles per hour and light at more than 186,000 feet per second.

2. Summer officially begins June twentieth, twenty-first, or twenty-second and ends September twenty-second, twenty-third, or twenty-fourth.

3. Usually July and August are the hottest months.

4. When it is twelve o'clock p.m. in New York, it is nine in the morning in California.

5. The White House was built in Washington on Pennsylvania Avenue in the 1790s. The president's address is now 1600 Pennsylvania Avenue, Washington, District of Columbia, 20500.

6. Washington, Pennsylvania, is not far from the border between Pennsylvania and West Virginia; Walla Walla, Washington, is close to the border between Washington and Oregon.

7. Many young people want to become a registered nurse or a medical doctor in order to serve humanity.

8. Others would prefer to serve in other professions, for example, the ministry, teaching, counseling, social work, et cetera.

Answers on page 395.

QUIZ YOURSELF ON CHAPTER 6 Proofread the following letter for mistakes in capitalization, spelling, and abbreviation, making corrections above the lines. The paragraphs are numbered. (Kate does not really make this many mistakes.)

My dear best friend Mary,

¶1   I surly miss you. Tell the Gang I miss All of them. I like liveing here with my Aunt betty and uncle Fred while I'm going to College. Write me at 1429 Shoreway Drive, Cleveland, Oh., 44124. Of course, I'll be home for a long vacation in Dec. December 25 is on Tues. this year. But I'll be home next Month for a couple of days because I have a mon. off.

¶2   College isn't like High School at all. I'm doing alright in my classes, but History is hard for me. I like english very much, and journalism 101 is fun, but i've decided I want to be a Nurse. It hadn't occured to me until I started volunteerring to work half a day a week at Mercy hospital under Doctor Cohen, a pediatrician. People volunteer there anywhere from 2 to twenty-four hours a week. I work 4 hours. I want to be an R.N. and get a b.s. degree and some day a Dr.'s degree. Mrs. Biley, our School nurse, is encourageing me.

¶3   I need to go to the store for aunt Betty now. She says I'm her favorite neice. Write me; I love to recieve letters. Bye-bye for the time beeing.

                    love to You and all our Friends,

                              Kate

Answers on page 395.

Answers to Exercises

Answers to Exercise 6.1, page 374

1. It must be hard for you college students today to imagine what life was like when I was a girl growing up in Indiana during the Great Depression.

2. For starters, I'll bet you can't visualize life without television or Kleenex or Scotch tape.

3. We had radio and handkerchiefs and paste. We were able to hear, not see, H. V. Kaltenborn and Lowell Thomas deliver the radio news; on Mondays, particularly in winter, my mother boiled our handkerchiefs before she washed them to keep cold germs from spreading; and we always had handy a big jar of Carter's paste for sticking things together.

4. I remember writing a story in fifth grade titled "Why I would like to travel to Jupiter." I was complimented for my far-out 21st-century imagination.

5. We had all sorts of dangerous fireworks on the Fourth of July, and we said the Pledge of Allegiance, without the words "under God," every morning at Weldele Elementary School.

6. Veterans Day was Armistice Day then; it always came on Nov. 11, and every class stood and silently faced east for a couple of minutes at 11 a.m. in honor of the soldiers who had died in World War I.

7. We had to memorize parts of the Constitution of the United States; an apple was not a computer but was what we brought the teacher.

8. Woolworth's sold wonderful things for a nickel or a dime; Baby Ruths and double-dip cones were a nickel, and when I learned to smoke, which was the "in" thing for college students back then, a package of Lucky Strikes cost 20 cents. You could buy a Chevy two-door for $600, and two gallons at a Standard Oil station cost 22 cents.

9. Our cars not only didn't have air bags or antilock brakes—they didn't even have turn signals or brake lights. The driver rolled down the window, stuck his or her left arm straight out to signal a left turn, straight up bent at the elbow to signal a right turn, and straight down bent at the elbow and swinging in and out to signal a stop. My dad taught me to drive, and I got a license that summer in Michigan on my 14th birthday—no driver's ed, no driver's test, but Dad was a tough examiner.

10. I remember a trip on a Thanksgiving when I was quite small—in our first car, which didn't even have roll-down windows. It was

a (n)ash, open on both sides unless we snapped on rain-proof
"side curtains" with small transparent isinglass panels.

11. (I)went to college in my hometown in the (h)oosier (S)tate two years,
and then (I)went away to school at (D)uke (U)niversity in (D)urham,
(N)orth (C)arolina, a fine university. (M)y parents allowed less than
$2,000 a year for my college costs: tuition, books, half of a
double room in (P)egram (H)all, food, transportation, and clothes.

12. (W)e traveled to school, and home for (C)hristmas and spring
vacations, by train, the (N)orfolk and (W)estern (R)ailroad; and if
you're curious, as one of my children once was, no, we did not
have dinosaurs, but, yes, we did have toothbrushes when (I)was
a girl.

Answers to Exercise 6.2, page 385

Circle the following words: **1.** arguing, argument. **2.** icy. **3.** truly, caring, careful. **4.** enforceable. **5.** insistence, assistance. **6.** beginning, shipped, shipment. **7.** occurred, received. **8.** Clauses, elves, reindeer. **9.** preceded, proceeded, succeeded, exceeded, glorious. **10.** is. **11.** '30s.

Answers to Exercise 6.3, page 392

1. Sound travels at a speed of 764 <u>mph</u> and light at more than 186,000 feet per second.

2. Summer (capitalized only because it begins a sentence) officially begins June <u>20</u>, <u>21</u>, or <u>22</u> and ends <u>Sept.</u> <u>22</u>, <u>23</u>, or <u>24</u>.

3. Usually July and August are the hottest months. <u>Correct.</u>

4. When it is <u>noon</u> in New York, it is <u>9 a.m.</u> in California.

5. The White House was built in Washington on Pennsylvania Avenue in the 1790s. The president's address is now 1600 Pennsylvania <u>Ave.</u>, Washingto<u>n DC 20500</u> (no comma after Washington or DC).

6. Washington, <u>Pa.</u>, is not far from the border between Pennsylvania and West Virginia; Walla Walla, <u>Wash.</u>, is close to the border between Washington and Oregon.

7. Many young people want to become a<u>n R.N.</u> or a<u>n M.D.</u> in order to serve humanity.

8. Others would prefer to serve in other professions, <u>e.g.</u>, the ministry, teaching, counseling, social work, <u>etc.</u>

Answers to Quiz Yourself on Chapter 6, page 393

Salutation: <u>F</u>riend. ¶**1.** sur<u>e</u>ly, gang, <u>a</u>ll, li<u>v</u>ing, <u>B</u>etty, <u>U</u>ncle, <u>c</u>ollege, <u>D</u>r., Clevelan<u>d</u> <u>OH</u> <u>44124</u>, <u>D</u>ecember, <u>D</u>ec. 25, <u>T</u>uesday, <u>m</u>onth, <u>M</u>onday. ¶**2.** high <u>s</u>chool, all<u> </u>right, <u>h</u>istory,

English, Journalism, I've, nurse, occurred, volunteering, Hospital, Dr. Cohen, two, 24, four, B.S., doctor's, school, enouraging. **¶3.** Aunt, niece, receive, being. Complimentary close: Love, you, friends.

7 Usage

From grading student papers and answering questions (or looking up the answers) for people who called the Grammar Hot Line at our community college, I have realized how much **we all need help in** matters of **language usage:** things we need to review, things we have forgotten completely, and things we never learned in the first place. But, whether it's fair or unfair, we all need to use standard American English if we are to appear well-educated in this fast-moving society.

In this chapter, you will meet, **alphabetically, 100+ of the top troublemakers.** Each is preceded by a number corresponding to Steps 1, 2, and 3 in the text. The most common usage mistakes, the most glaring ones, the ones that should be corrected first are marked with the numeral 1; 2 means these are also common; 3 means you won't run into these on every street corner, but you'll want to get them right when you do meet them.

① **a, an:** Most of us learned to use *a* before a consonant and *an* before a vowel. But this is not the whole story. Use *a* before a *consonant sound, an* before a *vowel sound.*

- The following are correct: a historian, an hour, a master's degree, an M.B.A., a xylophone, an x-ray. The *h* in *hour* is silent; the *M* in *M.B.A.* is sounded *em,* and the *x* in *x-ray* is sounded *ex.*

Somehow, *an* is frequently misused before *historian* or *historic*. I once interviewed Bruce Catton, the noted Civil War historian. He said, "Don't call me *an* historian. I am *a* historian. You wouldn't say 'an house' or 'an history book' or 'an whore.'" He said it; I didn't.

① **accept, except:** *Accept* means to receive; *except* as a verb means to exclude; *except* as a preposition means other than.

- "The sorority *accepted* (verb) everyone *except* (preposition) me; this sorority *excepted* (verb) me because of my race." (Be glad you didn't get into that sorority!)

① **affect, effect:** Both words can be either verb or noun; but 99.99 percent of the time *affect* is used as a verb, and 95 percent of the time *effect* is used as a noun—the percentages are figures, if not figments, of my imagination. But a 95 is an A in anyone's league, so learn to correctly use *affect* as a verb and *effect* as a noun.

The verb *affect* means to influence or to touch the emotions. It is a transitive verb. Someone or something must always affect *someone* (direct object) or *something* (direct object).

- Smoking adversely affects the heart.
- Cloudy weather affects the way I feel.
- His tears affected her deeply.

NOTE: A much rarer meaning of the verb *affect* is to pretend or assume.

- He *affected* an air of indifference but inwardly was far from calm.

The noun *effect* means a result.

- Drugs have a bad *effect* on pregnant women.
- The *effect* of the new program on sales was spectacular.
- Anything that *affects* (verb) the lungs as seriously as cigarette smoking does must also have a bad *effect* (noun) on the whole body.

For the two most common uses of these confusable words, *affect* as a verb and *effect* as a noun, just remember *a* before *e;* the thing that influences or *affects* something has to come before the result or *effect*. (With **mnemonic** or memory **devices** like this, one must take care that the memory clues aren't harder to remember than the things themselves.)

Affect as a noun is a psychological term meaning a feeling or emotion (this is the .01-percent use of the word).

Effect as a verb means to bring about or to accomplish (this is the five-percent use of the word): The medicine *effected* a miraculous cure.

③ **all of:** *Of* is unnecessary after *all* unless the word following *of* is a pronoun.

- *All* the students who ate in the cafeteria got sick.
- *All of* them went home.

almost: See *most.*

① **alot: Should be *a lot.*** There is no such word as *alot.* The two words *a lot* are an informal way of saying *a great many* or *a great deal.*

① **alright: Should be *all right.*** True, *alright* is in the dictionary, listed as a variant or disputed usage; but then there are a lot of (make that *a great many;* see *alot*) words in the dictionary that my mother wouldn't let me use. The proper spelling is *all right;* like *all wrong,* it is always two words.

although, while: See *while, although, but, whereas.*

② **among, between:** Use *among* for three or more things or people; use *between* for two things or people.

- The vote was evenly divided *between* the conservative candidate and the liberal candidate.
- The vote was evenly divided *among* the four candidates.

However, *between* is sometimes used for more than two things or people if they are considered individually in a non-pair relationship.

- *Between* job, volunteer work, golf, and family, my neighbor Jeanie has little spare time.

Often awkward wording can be avoided by rewriting.

- Job, volunteer work, golf, and family leave my neighbor Jeanie little spare time.

② **amount of, number of:** *Amount of* refers to a quantity that can't be counted; *number of* refers to a quantity that can be counted.

- It takes a large *number of* potatoes to make a large *amount of* mashed potatoes.

See also *fewer, less; number.*

an: See *a, an.*

② **anxious, eager:** Although authorities are divided on whether *anxious* can mean the same as *eager,* you'll be correct if you use *anxious* to mean worried, and *eager* to mean enthusiastic.

- He was *anxious* about his grades, but his honor-student sister was *eager* to get hers.

as, as if, as though: See *like*.

① **associate degree:** Right! Not *associate's* degree. Illogically, however, bachelor's degree and master's degree are correct.

assure: See *ensure, insure*.

③ **backwards: Should be *backward.*** *Backward* is correct as either an adjective or an adverb; *backwards* is acceptable but not preferred as an adverb. So why should we ever use *backwards?*

① **bad, badly:** Although usage is gradually changing, you can't go wrong if you use the adverb *badly* after most verbs (He did the job badly) but use the adjective *bad* after being verbs. The problem usually arises with the being verb *feel*.

- I feel *bad* (means I am sick or I am sorry).
- I feel *badly* (would mean that my sense of touch is not working well).
- The dog smells *bad* (means Rover has been rolling in the fertilizer).
- The dog smells *badly* (would mean Rover doesn't notice the odor even if you do).

because: See *because, since; reason is because*.

③ **because, since:** *Since* (properly meaning from that time) has become interchangeable with *because* in meaning for the reason that.

- *Since* you are going to the meeting, I won't need to.

behalf: See *in behalf of, on behalf of*.

between: See *among, between*.

① **between you and I: Should be *between you and me.*** *Between you and I* is always wrong. Always say between *you and me*.

- If the money is divided *between you and me,* what will my brother think?
- Just *between you and me,* I don't care what your brother thinks.

③ **bring, take:** More often than not, *take* refers to motion away from the speaker; *bring* indicates motion toward the speaker.

- I will *take* potato salad to the picnic at school if you will *bring* hot dogs to the party at my house.

② **can, may:** *May* has traditionally been used for permission and *can* for being able to. Even though some authorities now say the two words are becoming interchangeable, the traditional use is still preferred.

- Yes, Johnny, you *may* leave class early; I know you *can* pass the exam tomorrow.

May is also used to show possibility.

- I *may* get the job.

① **can't hardly: Should be *can hardly.*** *Hardly* has a negative connotation, and *can't hardly* becomes a double negative.

② **come and, come to: Should be *come to.***

- Please *come to* (not *and*) see our new house. (Please do one thing, *come to see,* not two things, both *come* and *see.*)

See also *sure and, sure to; try and, try to.*

③ **compare to, compare with:** *Compare to* is to state likenesses; *compare with* is to seek both likenesses and differences.

- As a painter, he likes to *compare* himself *to* Picasso.
- Before he registers, he should *compare* courses at the community college *with* courses offered at the university.

② **complement, compliment:** *Complement* refers to making complete; *compliment* refers to praising.

- The beautiful leather shoes and purse *complemented* (or were a *complement* to, completed) her outfit.
- Her employer often *complimented* her (or gave her many *compliments,* much praise) on the quality of her work.

① **consensus of opinion: Should be *consensus.*** Omit *of opinion.* *Consensus* means a majority opinion or a unanimous opinion.

- The *consensus* was that the president is doing an excellent job.

① **continual, continuous:** It may be a losing battle because the two words are more and more being used interchangeably, but it is better to use *continual* to mean intermittent or recurring at intervals and *continuous* to mean going on without interruption.

- She talked *continuously,* and she *continually* referred to her high social position.

① **could of, could have: Should be *could have.*** *Could of* is always wrong.

- I *could have* (not *could of*) been president if I had campaigned harder.

See also *have, of.*

① **different than: Should be *different from*.** This is another losing battle, I fear, because critics are accepting *different than* when *than* is followed by a clause.

- Teaching is *different than* I had expected (clause follows *different than*). But skunks are *different than* pussycats? This surely sounds wrong even to the most liberal ear. So why not use *different from* all the time?

- Teaching is so *different from* what I had expected.

- Skunks are *different from* pussycats—if you don't believe it, try to pick one up and pet it.

eager: See *anxious, eager.*

effect: See *affect, effect.*

③ **emigrate, immigrate:** *Emigrate* means to leave a country; *immigrate* means to come into a country. Thus one person on one trip can be both an *emigrant* from his old country and an *immigrant* into his new country.

② **ensure, insure:** *Insure* is the only acceptable method of guaranteeing against a loss, as in taking out an insurance policy. Some authorities insist that *ensure* (and not *insure*) means to make certain.

- Hard work will *ensure* good grades.

But the two words are becoming interchangeable in this last usage. To add to the confusion, *assure* has the connotation of promising or setting the mind at rest.

- He *assured* the teacher he would study harder.

No matter how you spell it, most of us have to work hard.

② **enthuse: Should be *show enthusiasm* OR *be enthusiastic.***

- I could *be enthusiastic* (not *enthuse*) over the plan if it didn't cost so much.

except: See *accept, except.*

① **farther, further:** *Farther* refers to physical distance.

- His house is two miles *farther* down the road.

Further means additional and is properly used in every case except physical distance.

- Let's give this matter *further* thought.

① **fewer, less:** Use *fewer* for things that can be counted and *less* for quantities that can't be counted in numbers.

- If you cook *fewer* potatoes, you will end up with *less* mashed potatoes. (That figures.)

For more information about potatoes, see also *amount of, number of.*

① **firstly, secondly: Should be *first, second,*** etc. Leave off the *ly*.

- There are two main reasons we should learn to speak and write correctly. *First,* fairly or unfairly, others judge us by the way we speak and write. *Second,* knowing that we can speak and write correctly gives us a good self-image.

③ **flammable, inflammable:** The words are interchangeable to mean burnable. But since they are confusing, use *flammable* all the time.

further: See *farther, further.*

① **go, goes: Should be *say* OR *says* OR *said.*** A fairly recent indignity inflicted upon the English language by young people, the use of *go* or *goes* for *say* or *says* or *said* is completely inappropriate.

- I hear my daughter on the phone: "And then I *go,* 'What'd you do last night?' and he *goes,* 'I went to the singles bar.'"

① **good, well:** *Good* is an adjective.

- He ran a *good* race. (Here *good* modifies the noun *race.*)

Don't use *good* as an adverb.

- WRONG: He ran *good.*
- RIGHT: He ran *well* (use the adverb *well* to modify the verb *ran.*)

Unlike *good,* which is an adjective, *well* can be either an adjective or an adverb. *Well* may be used as an adjective after the being verb *feel* in reference to health.

- I feel *well* (the adjective *well* is preferred over the adjective *good* if you mean you feel truly fit).

I feel *well* could have either the usual meaning that I am in good health (adjective) or the much rarer meaning that my fingertips are doing a good job of touching (adverb).

- HOWEVER: *Well* is usually an adverb. He dances *well.*

③ **graduated, was graduated:** The older form, *was graduated,* once decreed the only acceptable way to get someone out of college, has given way to simply *graduated,* now preferred. But if you tell the name of the college, you must use *from.*

- She *graduated from* Yale. NOT She *graduated* Yale.

① **had ought to, hadn't ought to: Should be *ought to, ought not to* or *should, should not.***

② **hanged, hung:** The verb *hang* has two meanings: to attach to something above or to put to death by means of suspending with a rope around the neck. *Hung* is the past tense and past participle of the first meaning; *hanged,* of the second meaning.

- The flower basket had been *hung* too high.
- The criminal was *hanged* at sunrise.

① **have, of:** Don't mistakenly use *of* for the auxiliary verb *have.* In everyday speech, it's hard to tell the difference between I could *of* danced all night and I could *have* danced all night. *Could of* is always wrong, as are *may of, might of, should of,* and *would of.* In each case, the *of* should be *have.*

- WRONG: I may *of* been wrong, but I might *of* done the job better if I could *of* been sure I would *of* been paid for it. I should *of* found out before I started.
- RIGHT: I may *have* been wrong, but I might *have* done the job better if I could *have* been sure I would *have* been paid for it. I should *have* found out before I started.

If you think *of* is a verb, just try to conjugate it: I *of,* you *of,* he *ofs,* she *ofs,* it *ofs,* we *of,* you *of,* they *of.*

① **healthful, healthy:** Here's another pair of words about to become interchangeable when, properly, *healthful* means conducive to health and *healthy* means possessing health.

- If a person eats a *healthful* diet, he is likely to stay *healthy.*

① **he or she, he/she, his or her, his/her:** I'm as liberated as the next person, maybe more so, and I certainly want the "shes" and the "herses" to get credit whenever and wherever possible. But it can be exceedingly awkward to say *he/she* or *his or her* or *himself or herself* if the wording needs to be repeated several times. So, some grammarians do not fault occasionally using the traditional *he* and *his* to mean anyone or anyone's without reference to sex. But often the situation can be avoided by using the plural or by rewording.

- AWKWARD: *Each student* should complete *his or her* essay and turn it in to *his or her* instructor by Monday.
- PLURAL: *All students* should hand in *their* essays by Monday.

- AWKWARD: When a student comes in, ask *him or her* for *his or her* ID.
- REWORDED: When a student comes in, ask for an ID. The *he/she* bit can become almost as ridiculous as insisting on *person*-hole covers instead of manhole covers or updating the old saying to *He or she* who hesitates is lost.

② **hopefully:** This word was supposed to mean *feeling hope* or *in a hopeful manner.*

- CORRECT: He waited *hopefully* for the doctor's verdict.

Since the 1930s, however, the word *hopefully* has come more and more to mean *It is hoped that.*

- BECOMING CORRECT THROUGH USAGE: *Hopefully,* I will pass this course.

Some dictionaries are now saying this second meaning is okay.

hung: See *hanged, hung.*

② **if, whether:** Although *if* is commonly used instead of *whether, if* you want to be completely proper, use *if* to introduce an adverb clause of condition and *whether* to introduce a noun clause.

- *If* you know, please tell me *whether* (not *if*) I passed.

immigrate: See *emigrate, immigrate.*

② **imply, infer:** *Imply* means to suggest or to hint at something without actually saying it, and the person who does the hinting is the one who *implies. Infer* means to draw a conclusion from certain evidence, and only the person listening or watching can *infer.*

- He *implied* that the job was getting to him and that he might quit soon.
- Although he didn't come right out and say so, from the way he was complaining I *inferred* that he was so dissatisfied he might quit his job.

③ **in, into, in to:** *Into* may suggest motion more than *in* does (there used to be this distinction), but the consensus is that *in* and *into* as prepositions are interchangeable. There are also cases in which *in* and *to* are used together but are separate words.

- I gave *in to* his wishes (the particle *in* is followed by the preposition *to,* the verb being *gave in*).
- He came *in to* see me (the adverb *in* is followed by *to* as part of the infinitive *to see*).

③ **in behalf of, on behalf of:** *In behalf of* means for the benefit of; *on behalf of* means as the agent of.

- *On behalf of* the entire company, the president will now present the scholarships which were raised *in behalf of* students who could not afford to pay this semester's tuition.

infer: See *imply, infer*.

inflammable: See *flammable, inflammable*.

① **in regards to, in regard to: Should be *in regard to*.** *In regards to* is always wrong.

- *In regard to* your concern about this month's sales, let me assure you that prospects for next month look a great deal better.

insure: See *ensure, insure*.

into, in to: See *in, into, in to*.

① **irregardless: Should be *regardless*.** *Irregardless* is always wrong.

- *Regardless* of your mother's opinion, I am going ahead with our plan.

is when, is where: See *when, where*.

① **its, it's:** *Its* is a possessive personal pronoun. Possessive pronouns were somehow created with possession built into the words themselves (*my, mine, your, yours, his, her, hers, its, our, ours, your, yours, their, theirs*); they do not require an apostrophe to make them possessive as other words do.

- The dog wagged *its* tail (no apostrophe even though the tail belongs to the dog).

It's <u>always means</u> *it is,* a contraction with the apostrophe standing for the *i* in *is* that is left out. *It's* (although it has an apostrophe) is <u>never</u> possessive.

- *It's* (always meaning *it is*) hard to teach an old dog new tricks. If you have trouble remembering which is which, substitute *it is*. If that works, the correct form is *it's:* The dog wagged *it is* tail? I think not. So use *its*.

② **kind, kind of, kind of a:** Say *kind of,* not *kind of a*.

- I like this *kind of* (not *kind of a*) book.

This or *that* should precede *kind* (singular), not *these* or *those*.

- Try *this* kind (not *these kind*).

These or *those* should precede *kinds* (plural).

- *This kind of* public official is the reason *these kinds of* problems exist.

- DON'T SAY: It was *kind of a* painful ordeal. SAY INSTEAD: It was *a rather* painful ordeal.

The word *sort* is treated the same way as *kind*.

① **lay, lie:** Trying to untangle *lay* and *lie* is the "losingest" battle in the English language, I am told by my friends who persist in telling their dogs to *lay* down. But isn't it worth a little trouble to sound literate, even if your dog doesn't know the difference?

The verb *lay* that causes all the trouble (we don't have a problem when hens *lay* eggs) means to put or to place. It is a transitive verb (always has a direct object); someone always has to *lay* something or someone.

- I *lay* the <u>book</u> on the desk. Now I *lay* <u>me</u> down to sleep.

The verb *lie* that causes the problem (we don't have trouble with the verb *lie* meaning to tell a falsehood) means to rest or to repose. It is an intransitive verb (does not have a direct object); whatever *lies* does it all by itself.

- After I *lay* (put) the book on the desk, it *lies* (rests) there.

It's not a matter of animate objects *lying* and inanimate objects *laying,* as some have been misled to believe.

- Dogs *lie* on the floor.
- People *lie* in bed.
- Clothes that aren't hung up *lie* on the chair.
- Keys *lie* wherever someone *lays* them.

To *lay* something is to cause it to *lie*.

	Lie (rest, repose) *Intransitive*	**Lay (put, place)** *Transitive*
Present tense	lie	lay
Past tense	lay	laid
Past participle	lain	laid
Present participle	lying	laying

Life with *lie* and *lay* would be simple if we could stay in the present tense. **The real confusion arises because the past tense of the verb *lie* is *lay*.**

- I *lie* in bed until noon every Sunday (present tense).
- I *lay* in bed until noon yesterday (**past tense of verb *lie***).
- I have *lain* in bed until noon almost every Sunday of my life (past participle, requires auxiliary verb like *have*).

- I was *lying* in bed when the phone rang (present participle, requires auxiliary verb like *was*).

If you are going to use *lay* when you mean to rest or to repose, it has to be past tense.

The verb *lay* meaning to put or to place doesn't cause quite so much trouble.

- I *lay* the newspaper on the table every day (present tense).
- I *laid* the newspaper on the table yesterday (past tense).
- I have *laid* the newspaper on the table almost every day of my life (past participle, requires auxiliary verb like *have*).
- I was *laying* the newspaper on the table when the phone rang (present participle, requires auxiliary verb like *was*).

If you get confused, substitute the word *put*. If it fits, the correct tense of the verb *lay* is proper; if it doesn't make sense, use the correct tense of the verb *lie*.

- She had been (*laying* or *lying*) (*putting?*—no) in the sun too long. Use *lying*.

My pure-bred mutt Snoopi and I had a whole freshman English class believing she knew the difference between *lay* and *lie*. I had told them I had a dog who would obey only commands in proper English. This class conned me into having a term's-end party at my house. One student remembered my boast and put poor old Snoop to the test.

"*Lay* down, Snoopi," he said, a trifle indecisively. She just looked at him.

"*Lie* down, Snoopi!" I said firmly, standing a little closer to her so she would realize her "master" meant business. She hit the deck. The class drank their punch in awe. Of course, Snoopi didn't know a verb from a vestibule, but it was a neat way to impress a class. You might remember it this way: I can not lie to you, Fido; I want you to *lie* down."

No matter what, don't be dumb to kind animals; tell your dog to *lie* down. Snoopi has gone to Dog Heaven, but I have enough faith to believe that God *laid* a soft blanket in a spot of sunshine on the floor and that Snoopi is *lying* there this very minute.

Maggie

I taught my good dog Maggie to
"Lay down" when I commanded.
I also taught her how to "Set"
Whenever I demanded.

"I'll teach her now to speak," I said.
She labored to comply.
And when she learned to speak, she said,
You twit, it's 'sit' and 'lie'!"

Wallace D. McRae

From *The Cowboy Curmudgeon* (Gibbs Smith)
with permission of Wallace D. McRae.

less: See *fewer, less*.

③ **liable, likely:** *Liable* means legally responsible; *likely* means probable.

* It is *likely* that the company is *liable* for her hospital expenses because she broke her leg at work.

lie: See *lay, lie*.

① **like, as, as if, as though:** If you want to be correct, do not use *like* as a conjunction. Use *as, as if,* or *as though*.

* NONSTANDARD: Do *like* I say. He looked *like* he might explode.
* STANDARD: Do *as* I say. He looked *as if* he might explode.

As if and *as though* are considered interchangeable by most authorities.

likely: See *liable, likely*.

② **majority is, majority are:** *Majority* is one of the collective nouns that may be either singular or plural depending on meaning (one unit or many individuals).

* A *majority is* needed for the issue to pass (a certain number, one unit).
* A *majority are* interested in art (many individuals).

As a "portion" word followed by *of, majority* may be either singular or plural depending on whether the object of the preposition *of* is singular or plural.

* A *majority* of the <u>homework</u> *is* done at home.
* A *majority* of the <u>things</u> that cause trouble in usage *are* easily overcome.

may: See *can, may*.

③ **may, might:** *Might* is the past tense of *may,* but both words are used to indicate possibility, with *may* showing a slightly greater degree of probability than *might*. *Might* also sometimes has a connotation of scolding.

- You *might* have the courtesy to remember that I am your mother.

① **may of, may have: Should be *may have.*** *May of* is always wrong.

- I *may have* (not *may of*) said that.

See also *have, of.*

③ **might could: Should be *might be able to.*** *Might could* is always wrong.

- I *might be able to* go if I had more money.

① **might of, might have: Should be *might have.*** *Might of* is always wrong.

- She *might have* (not *might of*) been willing to take the job if we had offered to help her.

See also *have, of.*

① **more importantly, most importantly: Should be *more important, most important.*** As commonly used, these expressions mean what is more (or most) important (no *ly*).

- *More important,* our organization must provide excellent service to the customer.

More importantly would be correct if you meant in a more important manner.

- The visiting shah was treated *more importantly* than the president.

③ **most, almost:** If you mean very nearly, say *almost.* If you mean the greatest quantity, say *most.*

- She was *almost* frozen because she had covered the *most* miles in the dogsled race.

① **myself, I, me:** With rare exceptions, use *myself* only when *I* is also in the sentence.

- WRONG: Jones and *myself* will be in Houston next week.
- RIGHT: Jones and *I* will be in Houston next week.
- RIGHT: *I will* make the trip to Houston *myself* (correct because *I* precedes *myself*).
- RIGHT: Send the report to George and *me* (not *myself*).
- EXCEPTION: Finding *myself* two miles from shore in the canoe was a terrifying experience.

② **nauseated, nauseous:** Something *nauseous* (the cause) makes one *nauseated* (the result).

- WRONG: I feel *nauseous* (you feel like making someone sick).
- RIGHT: You feel *nauseated* (especially if you have eaten a *nauseous* combination of jalapeño peppers, kippered herring, and pickled pigs' feet just before bedtime).

① **negotiate:** Often incorrectly pronounced (knee go' see ate) by broadcast media people. Say *knee go' she ate.*

② **nowhere near: Should be *not nearly:***

- WRONG: She was *nowhere near* finished.
- RIGHT: She was *not nearly* finished.
- RIGHT (if referring to a geographic location): They were hoping to reach Oregon State College in Corvallis by Thursday, but they found themselves in Idaho Falls, *nowhere near* Corvallis.

① **nuclear:** Often incorrectly pronounced (nuke' you lure), even by a president of the United States. Say *new' clee er.*

② **number, a number or the number:** Usually *a number* is plural and *the number* is singular.

- *A number* of inconsistencies in the English language *are* pitfalls for the foreign student.
- *The number* of inconsistencies *is* appalling.

See also *amount of, number of.*

number of: See *amount of, number of.*

① **of:** Don't make the mistake of using *of* as an auxiliary verb instead of *have.* See also *have, of.*

② **off, off of:** *Off* means *off of,* so leave off the *of.*

- He fell *off* the ladder.

③ **oftentimes:** Though poetic and quaint, *oftentimes* doesn't do the job any better than *often,* so keep it simple and use *often.*

③ **on, upon, up on:** *On* and *upon* as prepositions are interchangeable. There are also cases in which *up* and *on* are used together but are separate words.

- He told me to follow *up on* the telephone call (the particle *up* is followed by the preposition *on,* the verb being *follow up*).
- He was *up on* the roof when the phone rang (the adverb *up* is followed by the preposition *on*).

② **party, person:** Don't use *party* to refer to one person (that's legal jargon).

- He's the *person* (not the *party*) who keeps the keys.

③ **plus, and:** *Plus* is not a coordinating conjunction.

- WRONG: I disliked my boss, *plus* I hated the hours.
- RIGHT: I disliked my boss, *and* I hated the hours.

② **principal, principle:** *Principal* used as an adjective means chief or foremost. *Principal* used as a noun means the chief or foremost person.

- The school *principal* gave economy and safety as his *principal* reasons for the new rules; the *principal* is my p-a-l.

Principal as a noun also refers to a capital sum of money excluding interest or profit.

- She withdrew the interest, but the *principal* remained to draw more interest.

Principle is a noun meaning a rule of conduct.

- Constantly striving to improve the environment is a *principle* of mine; destruction of natural resources is against my *principles*.

② **raise, rise:** Both related to going up, the verbs *raise* (raised, raised) and *rise* (rose, risen) are like *lay* and *lie* and like *set* and *sit*. *Raise* is a transitive verb, must have a direct object. Someone (or something) must *raise* something (or someone). *Rise* is an intransitive verb, does not have a direct object. Something (or someone) seems to *rise* all by itself. To *raise* something is to cause it to *rise*.

- As he *raised* the flag, I saw the stars and stripes *rise* to the top of the pole.

① **real, really:** Use *real* as an adjective and *really* as an adverb.

- He was in *real* pain (adjective modifying the noun *pain*).
- She was *really* (not *real*) tall (adverb modifying the adjective *tall*).

See also *sure, surely*.

② **reason is because: Should be *reason is that*.** Reason means cause, so *reason is because* is redundant.

- The *reason* for his arrest *was that* (not *because*) his pockets were full of stolen jewelry.

See also *reason why*.

② **reason why: Should be *reason that.*** Like *reason is because,* this expression is redundant, with both *reason* and *why* meaning cause.

- The reason *that* (not *why*) I failed was lack of time to study.

See also *reason is because.*

regards: See *in regards to; with regards to.*

rise: See *raise, rise.*

say, says, said: See *go, goes.*

secondly: See *firstly, secondly.*

② **set, sit:** The verbs *set* (set, set) and *sit* (sat, sat) are like *lay* and *lie* and like *raise* and *rise. Set* (to place) is a transitive verb, must have a direct object. Someone (or something) must *set* something (or someone). *Sit* (to rest) is an intransitive verb, does not have a direct object. People and things do the *sitting* all by themselves. To *set* something is to cause it to *sit.*

- I get out my good china and *set* the vase on the table; then it *sits* there.
- EXCEPTIONS: The sun and Jello-O can *set* without direct objects.

② **shall, will:** Many of us were taught to use *shall* in first person and *will* in second and third persons for expressing simple future, and *will* in first person and *shall* in second and third persons for expressing determination. The consensus is that *will* is now acceptable in both uses for all persons and that *shall* is on its way out, being used mainly to indicate possibility or need in the interrogative.

- *Shall* we meet at the theater? *Shall* I turn on the oven?

she or he, she/he, her or his, her/his: See *he or she, he/she, his or her, his/her.*

② **should, would:** Like *shall* and *will, should* and *would* no longer have different meanings for first person and for second and third persons. Use *should* in all persons to express obligation.

- He *should* study harder.

In *if* clauses, use *should* to express a somewhat-unlikely condition.

- If you *should* fail the test, be prepared to take it again.

Would is used in all persons to express customary action.

- Every morning all summer we *would* pick fruit for breakfast.

Would is also used in *if* clauses, to express willing condition.

• If you *would* change your plans, I could go with you.

① **should of, should have: Should be *should have*.** *Should of* is always wrong.

• I *should have* (not *should of*) told you sooner.

See also *have, of*.

since: See *because, since*.

sit: See *set, sit*.

② **somewheres: Should be *somewhere*.** *Somewheres* is always wrong.

• I put my keys down *somewhere* (not *somewheres*).

sort, sort of, sort of a: See *kind, kind of, kind of a;* use *sort* in the same way as *kind*.

③ **stationary, stationery:** *Stationary* is an adjective that means immovable; *stationery* is a noun that means writing paper.

• Don't try to move that bench; it is *stationary*.

• I ordered new *stationery* with my name and address printed on it.

① **suppose to, supposed to: Should be *supposed to*.** *Suppose to* is always wrong.

• I was *supposed to* (not *suppose to*) bake a cake for the party.

See also *use to, used to*.

① **sure, surely:** Use *sure* as an adjective and *surely* as an adverb.

• She was *sure* he was the guilty one (adjective modifying the pronoun *She*).

• He is *surely* (not *sure*) strong (adverb modifying the adjective *strong*).

See also *real, really*.

② **sure and, sure to: Should be *sure to*.**

• Be *sure to* (not *and*) come to the lecture. (Do one thing, *be sure to come*, not two things, *be sure* and *come*.)

See also *come and, come to; try and, try to*.

take: See *bring.*

② **than, then:** The two words are sometimes confused.

- She was a brunette *then* (*then,* meaning at that time).
- *Then* it's settled—we'll go to the movie (*then,* meaning in that case).
- She is older *than* he is (*than,* a comparison).
- I would rather play *than* work (*than,* a choice).

that kind: See *kind, kind of, kind of a.*

① **that, which, who:** The rule is *which* refers to things, *who* to people, and *that* to either things or people. But why use *that* if you are referring to people?

- They are the girls *who* (not *that*) signed up for the sewing class.

Which (not *that*) is used to introduce nonessential clauses unless the clause refers to a person or people; then use *who.*

- Margaret Mitchell, *who* lived from 1900 to 1949, spent 10 years writing *Gone With the Wind, which* (not *that*) was her only book.

That has customarily been used to introduce essential clauses.

- The novel *that* (not *which*) won the Pulitzer Prize in 1937 was Margaret Mitchell's *Gone With the Wind.*

That is still preferred to introduce most essential clauses not referring to people, but *which* is becoming acceptable in more and more essential clauses.

- Before becoming successful, most authors write many works *which* (or *that*—either is okay) are rejected.

② **theater, theatre:** Use the preferred spelling, *theater,* unless the word is part of a proper noun (James *Theatre*).

① **their, there, they're:** The personal possessive pronoun *their* means belonging to them; the adverb *there* means at that place or not here; *they're* is a contraction meaning they are, the apostrophe standing for the *a* in *are* that is left out.

- *They're* going to have a big surprise for *their* mother when she gets *there.*

② **theirself, theirselves, themself: Should always be *themselves.***

- Children will hurt *themselves* if they play with knives.

then, than: See *than, then.*

these kind, these kinds: See *kind, kind of, kind of a.*

this kind: See *kind, kind of, kind of a.*

those kind, those kinds: See *kind, kind of, kind of a.*

② **thusly: Should be *thus.*** *Thusly* is always wrong.

- Our competition has announced price reductions; *thus,* they will be aiming at a younger market.

① **to, too, two:** *To* and *too* have more than one use. *To* means toward.

- I went *to* town.

To is also the first word of an infinitive.

- She wanted *to* go with me.

Too sometimes means also.

- I want to go *too.*

Then again *too* may mean to an excessive degree. In this meaning many people accidentally leave off the second *o.*

- WRONG: Don't stay out *to* late.
- RIGHT: Are they *too* lazy?

Nobody seems to have trouble with the number *two.*

- Wouldn't English be easy if there were only *two* rules to remember?

① **toward, towards: Should be *toward.*** Always use the preferred *toward.*

- I was walking *toward* (not *towards*) my house when I heard a scream.

② **try and, try to: Should be *try to.***

- I will *try to* (not *and*) be on time. (I will do one thing, *try to be,* not two things, both *try* and *be.*)

See also *come and, come to; sure and, sure to.*

upon, up on: See *on, upon, up on.*

① **used to could, used to be able to: Should be *used to be able to.*** *Used to could* is always wrong.

- I *used to be able to* (not *used to could*) stand on my head, but now it makes me dizzy.

① **use to, used to: Should be *used to.***

- I *used to* (not *use to*) write with my left hand.

See also *suppose to, supposed to*.

② **very, very much:** Don't use *very* very often! Omit this overworked word if it is not essential. Omit it for sure if it is used with a word that can't be made more so.

- WRONG: Her playing was *very* perfect.

② **ways:** Unacceptable for *way*.

- You've come a long *way* (not *ways*).

well, good: See *good, well*.

① **when, where:** Don't use *when* unless you are referring to time or *where* unless you are referring to place.

- WRONG: A symphony is *when* many instruments are played together.
- RIGHT: A symphony is a complex musical composition in which many instruments are played together.
- RIGHT: I am going to the concert *when* I can spare the money.
- WRONG: English is *where* we learn about usage.
- RIGHT: English is a study of usage.
- RIGHT: The classroom is *where* we discuss mistakes in grammar.

whether: See *if, whether*.

which, who, that: See *that, which, who*.

② **while, although, but, whereas:** The use of *while* for these other words, especially *although*, is common, but you should save *while* for denoting time.

- RIGHT: *Although* (not *while*) authorities disagree on many points of English usage, certain standards must be upheld.
- RIGHT: *While* (denoting time) the rain was soaking the whole compound, we stayed dry inside our tent.
- DOUBTFUL: We committed several errors in grammar *while* (try *although, but,* or *whereas*) we should have known better.
- RIGHT: We committed several errors in grammar *while* (denoting time) we were working on the first composition.

who, which, that: See *that, which, who*.

① **who, whom:** A helpful hint: If you can substitute *he,* use subjective case *who;* if you can substitute *him,* use objective case *whom.*

- WRONG: *Who* can you trust? Substitute *he:* Can you trust *he?* Wrong.
- RIGHT: *Whom* can you trust? Substitute *him:* Can you trust *him?* Right.
- RIGHT: He was the only one *who* could do it (*he* could do it).
- RIGHT: He is a man *whom* I know well (I know *him* well).

① **who's, whose:** *Who's* always means who is or who has, with the apostrophe standing for the *i* in *is* or the *ha* in *has* that is left out.

- *Who's* coming to dinner? *Who's* seen the movie?

Sounding the same and often confused with *who's, whose* means belonging to whom; it is one of the pronouns with possession built into the word, so no apostrophe is required to make it show ownership.

"I can never remember when to use *who* and when to use *whom.*"

- *Whose* book is this?

will: See *shall, will.*

① **with regards to, with regard to: Should be *with regard to*.** *With regards to* is always wrong.

- *With regard to* your vacation, please make your plans soon.

See also *in regards to, in regard to.*

would, should: See *should, would.*

① **would have:** Don't use *would have* for *had* in an *if* clause.

- If only I *had* (not *would have*) sold the stock last week, I'd be $500 richer.

① **would of, would have: Should be *would have*.** *Would of* is always wrong.

- She *would have* (not *would of*) made a good teacher.
- I wish I *had* (not *would of*) studied harder for the exam.

See also *have, of.*

① **your, you're:** *Your* means belonging to you; the possession is built into this personal possessive pronoun, eliminating the need for an apostrophe to show ownership. *You're* is a contraction meaning you are, the apostrophe standing for the *a* in *are* that is left out.

- RIGHT: *You're* out of *your* mind if you think anyone can remember all this. **(Right, for sure.)**

Authorities consulted in connection with changing usage were *The American Heritage Dictionary, The Random House Dictionary of the English Language, Webster's New World Dictionary, Merriam-Webster's Collegiate Dictionary,* John B. Bremner's *Words on Words,* Roy H. Copperud's *American Usage and Style: The Consensus,* and William A. Sabin's *The Gregg Reference Manual.*

EXERCISE 7.1 Fill in the blanks with the correct answers.

_____ **1.** James A. H. Murray was (a) a (b) an historical lexicographer, a lexicographer being a person who writes or compiles a dictionary; historical lexicographers are those who define words by their various usages through time.

_____ **2.** Not too many people would (a) accept (b) except a job as a lexi-cographer because it requires so much patience.

_____ **3.** Murray, a London schoolmaster, was the greatest of the editors of *The Oxford English Dictionary* (*O.E.D.*), a scholarly work which has had a lasting (a) affect (b) effect on language throughout the world.

_____ **4.** Work began on the *O.E.D.* in 1857; its original 13 volumes contained 500,000 words and a million and a half quotations showing how the words had been used over the centuries—that was (a) alot (b) a lot (c) allot of work.

_____ **5.** The project required the labor of such a large (a) amount of (b) number of editors and voluntary readers that the first volumes were out of date before the last one went to press in 1928, 71 years after the work began.

_____ **6.** Although he was (a) anxious (b) eager to finish the job, Murray died in 1915, while still working on the Ts.

_____ **7.** Murray felt (a) bad (b) badly when he found "ghost words"—misspelled, ill-defined, or nonexistent words—that had been included in previous dictionaries.

_____ **8.** Just between you and (a) I (b) me , I know a ghost word, *dord*. It appeared for years in dictionaries meaning "density, as in physics," having been mistakenly coined from "D or d."

_____ **9.** By 1957 the (a) consensus (b) consensus of opinion was that the *O.E.D.* should be updated to include new words and new meanings of old words.

_____ **10.** Robert Burchfield, editor-in-chief, thought he was undertaking a one-volume, seven-year project before returning to his teaching job at Oxford University; it turned out to be quite (a) different from (b) different than his expectations—four volumes (added to the original 13) and almost 30 years.

Answers on page 427

EXERCISE 7.2 Fill in the blanks with the correct answers.

_____ **1.** *The Oxford English Dictionary* (O.E.D.), more than a century in the making, has gone (a) farther (b) further than any other dictionary in establishing a historical record of words.

_____ **2.** It tries to show the first published use of a word and then, by check-ing usage in books and magazines, to trace the change in meaning over the years—at least one quotation each century, (a) often (b) oftentimes more, for each meaning of the word.

_____ **3.** The editors of the original *O.E.D.* worked deliberately, first reading extensively for 21 years and (a) second (b) secondly deciding they needed 1,300 volunteers to read another three years before publica-tion could be considered.

_____ **4.** In 1989 previous volumes and supplements were combined with additional new words to make a 20-volume set; (a) its (b) it's a bit heavy to carry to school.

_____ **5.** However, a two-volume 18-pound microprint edition was published in 1971; but it requires a magnifying glass to read, making it hardly suitable for reading as one (a) lays (b) lies in bed.

_____ **6.** Updating a dictionary is a (a) continual (b) continuous process.

_____ **7.** Full-time lexicographers regularly read several hundred publications; all the while (a) their (b) there (c) they're watching everything from billboards to food labels to cartoons for new words or new uses of old words.

_____ **8.** When a new word or a new use is found, it is recorded on a three-by-five card called a citation; before (a) to (b) too (c) two long, a new edition of the dictionary is justified.

_____ **9.** *Webster's New World Dictionary,* whose editorial offices are in Cleveland, Ohio, accumulates more than 50,000 citations a year; (a) your (b) you're aware, surely, that not all these new words and uses get into the next edition of the dictionary.

_____**10.** And, of course, some words that are no longer used are dropped by the editor, (a) who (b) whom dictionary users have great respect for.

Answers on page 428

QUIZ YOURSELF ON CHAPTER 7 Circle the words that make the sentences correct.

1. Isn't a snake a <u>kind of/kind of a</u> flexible tool that a plumber uses to unclog pipes?

2. What would you do if one night your three-year-old said she had to go the bathroom, you flicked on the light, and rising out of the toilet, with no plumber in sight, was a gigantic snake, a real live snake, looking <u>as if/like</u> it might want your child for a midnight snack?

3. You <u>might have/might of</u> panicked; <u>between you and I/between you and me</u>, I think most people <u>would have/would of</u>.

4. But if you could keep your cool, you'd probably do what Marc Morgenstern did: slam the door, stuff towels under it, in case the snake could flatten <u>its/it's</u> body enough to escape, call 911, and tell your daughter that her having to go to the bathroom was not your <u>principal/principle</u> concern just now.

5. The police lieutenant who was dispatched to the Morgenstern home that night first aimed a flashlight at the snake's eyes, the <u>affect/effect</u> being to blind the unwelcome visitor.

6. <u>Second/Secondly</u>, he grabbed it behind the head, and dropped it into an oversized shopping bag, the snake being a four-foot-long python.

7. This is a true story <u>all right/alright</u>; however, because the fashionable suburb in which the Morgensterns live was embarrassed by having pythons in its plumbing, we won't give away the location.

8. It was <u>a/an</u> historic time in the life of the Morgensterns; they received <u>allot/a lot/alot</u> of unwanted publicity, from being written up in nationally syndicated columns to being asked to appear on television; but they <u>accepted/excepted</u> all this good-naturedly.

9. Because Mrs. Morgenstern let slip the name of her husband's law firm when she was being quizzed on a radio show, his office phone was quite busy for a while with calls <u>different from/different than</u> the usual ones: often when the secretary answered, she would hear a snake-like hissing sound, then a hang-up click.

10. <u>In regards to/In regard to</u> that snake, it <u>could have/could of</u> been that it not only preferred modern plumbing facilities but also knew how to dial a telephone—pretty hard, though, with no fingers.

11. The python spent several days <u>lying/laying</u> in a large glass aquarium in the basement of the police department.

12. Although the python was eating <u>good/well</u>—several live mice a day—the police officers felt <u>bad/badly</u> that it had to be confined.

13. The <u>consensus/consensus of opinion</u> was that it belonged in a zoo.

14. So the police gave it to the zoo. The Morgensterns speculated that their visitor <u>might have/might of</u> escaped from someone who keeps unusual pets, but no one knows how it got into the sewer system.

15. It <u>must have/must of</u> traveled <u>farther/further</u> than a few hundred feet before it decided to enliven the Morgensterns' previously routine life.

Answers on page 428

QUIZ YOURSELF FOR THE LAST TIME First, read the following paragraphs and underline any mistakes you find. Then check your underlined mistakes with the answers immediately below. In the blanks that follow, write your corrections.

¶1   It was the week before finals. The day of Student Governments traditional "Last Blast", the biggest money making event of the year. Student senators had been selling tickets for 2 weeks, the $5 ticket entitlling the purchaser to a lunch of barbecued ribs, potato salad and corn on the cob, and the $2.50 extra ticket including a jam session in the gym with a well known local group.

¶2   Mrs. Murphy had paid the whole $7.50; but had no intention of setting foot in the gym. Noisy noise annoys an oyster, was all she could think of as she joined Mr. Perez, and Ms. Larue at one of the long, picnic tables set up outside the gym, well within hearing range of the jaming.

¶3   "Would you like to join us girls?" said Mrs. Murphy as Kate and Leatrice walked by the girl's plates piled with food.

¶4   The four were chatting, about the coming vacation when Peter and Roberto interrupted. "Mind if we join you"? And in a moment Peter beckoned to Dr. Jefferson who sat down at the end of the table. Kate spotted the Careless twins; and excused herself to take them back to the table.

¶5   As she returned to the table with the twins Kate said excitedly, "I have some news for you, I want you to meet Carla and Calvin *Perkins.* My uncle helped them find their grandmother, who their mother had deliberately lost touch with. Mrs Perkins was finally located in Dubuque, Ia. and was delighted to be in touch with her grandchildren after twelve years. And Carla and Calvin have legally changed their name from Careless to Perkins which is much better then a name that makes people think you care less.

¶6   "Grandma sent Carla and myself some money to help us out", said calvin.

¶7   "I'll be working less hours now," said Carla, "and well have a little money to spare. We even bought Calvin a bed. And were certainly going to try and do better in school. Everyone has been great to give us their support."

¶8   "Thing's have a way of working out, said Mrs. Murphy.

¶9   The students grinned at each other then chorused, "Mrs. Murphys law!"

Check your underlined mistakes with these below.

¶1   It was the week before final<u>s. T</u>he day of Student Governmen<u>ts</u> traditional "Last Blas<u>t",</u>the biggest mone<u>y m</u>aking event of the year. Student senators had been selling tickets for <u>2</u> weeks, the $5 ticket enti<u>tll</u>ing the purchaser to a lunch of barbecued ribs, potato sala<u>d an</u>d corn on the cob, and the $2.50 extra ticket including a jam session in the gym with a wel<u>l k</u>nown local group.

¶2   Mrs. Murphy had paid the whole $7.5<u>0; b</u>ut had no intention of setting foot in the <u>gym. N</u>oisy noise annoys an oyste<u>r, wa</u>s all she could think of as she joined Mr.

Perez, and Ms. Larue at one of the long, picnic tables set up outside the gym, well within hearing range of the jaming.

¶3   "Would you like to join us girls?" said Mrs. Murphy as Kate and Leatrice walked by the girl's plates piled with food.

¶4   The four were chatting, about the coming vacation when Peter and Roberto interrupted. "Mind if we join you"? And in a moment Peter beckoned to Dr. Jefferson who sat down at the end of the table. Kate spotted the Careless twins; and excused herself to take them back to the table.

¶5   As she returned to the table with the twins Kate said excitedly, "I have some news for you, I want you to meet Carla and Calvin *Perkins.* My uncle helped them find their grandmother, who their mother had deliberately lost touch with. Mrs_ Perkins was finally located in Dubuque, Ia. and was delighted to be in touch with her grandchildren after twelve years. And Carla and Calvin have legally changed their name from Careless to Perkins which is much better then a name that makes people think you care less.

¶6   "Grandma sent Carla and myself some money to help us out", said calvin.

¶7   "I'll be working less hours now," said Carla, "and well have a little money to spare. We even bought Calvin a bed. And were certainly going to try and do better in school. Everyone has been great to give us their support."

¶8   "Thing's have a way of working out, said Mrs. Murphy.

¶9   The students grinned at each other then chorused, "Mrs. Murphys law!"

Write your corrections in the blanks.

Paragraph One:

1. _____   5. _____

2. _____   6. _____

3. _____   7. _____

4. _____   8. _____

Paragraph Two:

9. _____   12. _____

10. _____   13. _____

11. _____   14. _____

Paragraph Three:

15. _____   17. _____

16. _____

Paragraph Four:

18. _____   21. _____

19. _____   22. _____

20. _____

Paragraph Five:

23. _____   28. _____

24 _____   29. _____

25 _____   30. _____

26. _____   31. _____

27. _____

Paragraph Six:

32. _____   34. _____

33. _____

Paragraph Seven:

35. _____   38. _____

36. _____   39. _____

37. _____

Paragraph Eight:

40. _____   41. _____

Paragraph Nine:

42. _____   44. _____

43. _____

Answers on page 428.

Answers to Exercises

Answers to Exercise 7.1, page 419

1. a. **2.** a. **3.** b. **4.** b. **5.** b. **6.** b. **7.** a. **8.** b. **9.** a. **10.** a.

Answers to Exercise 7.2, page 420

1. b. **2.** a. **3.** a. **4.** b. **5.** b. **6.** b. **7.** c. **8.** b. **9.** b. **10.** b.

Answers to Quiz Yourself on Chapter 7, page 421

1. kind of. **2.** as if. **3.** might have, between you and me, would have. **4.** its, principal. **5.** effect. **6.** Second. **7.** All right. **8.** a, a lot, accepted. **9.** different from. **10.** In regard to, could have. **11.** lying. **12.** well, bad. **13.** consensus. **14.** might have. **15.** must have, farther.

Answers to Quiz Yourself for the Last Time, page 423

1. finals, the **2.** Goverment's **3.** Blast," **4.** money-making **5.** two **6.** entitling **7.** salad, and **8.** well-known **9.** $7.50 but **10.** gym. "Noisy **11.** oyster," was **12.** Mr. Perez and **13.** long picnic **14.** jamming **15.** us, girls?" **16.** by, the **17.** girls' plates **18.** chatting about **19.** you?" **20.** Dr. Jefferson, who **21.** twins and **22.** bring **23.** twins, Kate **24.** you. I **25.** whom **26.** Mrs. **27.** Iowa, and **28.** 12 **29.** Perkins, which **30.** than **31.** 'care less.'" **32.** me **33.** out," **34.** Calvin **35.** fewer **36.** we'll **37.** we're **38.** try to **39.** his or her; better to say, "Everyone has been great to support us." **40.** "Things **41.** out," **42.** other, then, **43.** Murphy's **44.** Law!"

Index